WORDS WE CALL HOME
Celebrating Creative Writing at UBC

EDITED BY LINDA SVENDSEN

Words We Call Home is a commemorative anthology celebrating more than twenty-five years of achievement for the UBC Department of Creative Writing—the oldest writing program in Canada. The more than sixty poets, dramatists, and fiction writers included provide just a sample of the energy and vision the department has fostered over the years. From Earle Birney's pioneering efforts in 1946, to the birth of the department in 1965, to the present day, the program has created a place for aspiring, talented writers. That it has succeeded is shown by the numerous authors who have received Governor General's Awards, Commonwealth Poetry Prizes, CBC Prizes for Poetry, and other distinguished awards. *Words We Call Home* is a collection of work that will hold a special place in the hearts of those who have watched UBC grow and flourish over the years and of everyone who loves literature.

The following authors are represented in *Words We Call Home*: Leonard Angel, Christianne Balk, Carol Bolt, Roo Borson, George Bowering, Robert Bringhurst, Frank Davey, Don Dickinson, Glen Downie, Daryl Duke, Kenneth Dyba, David Evanier, Marya Fiamengo, Michael Finlay, Dennis Foon, Cathy Ford, Eric Forrer, Bill Gaston, Gary Geddes, Kico Gonzalez-Risso, Elizabeth Gourlay, Paul Green, Genni Gunn, Geoff Hancock, Hart Hanson, Robert Harlow, Ernest Hekkanen, Gladys Hindmarch, Jack Hodgins, Margaret Hollingsworth, Debbie Howlett, Ann Ireland, Sally Ireland, Surjeet Kalsey, Lionel Kearns, Norman Klenman, Charles Lillard, Cynthia MacDonald, Kenneth McGoogan, Florence McNeil, George McWhirter, Kim Maltman, Jill Mandrake, Daphne Marlatt, Seymour Mayne, Jennifer Mitton, Daniel David Moses, Erin Mouré, Jane Munro, Rona Murray, Morgan Nyberg, Morris Panych, George Payerle, E.G. Perrault, Karen Petersen, Maida Price, Linda Rogers, Lake Sagaris, Andreas Schroeder, Robert G. Sherrin, Heather Spears, Richard Stevenson, Dona Sturmanis, Fred Wah, Tom Wayman, Ian Weir, Jim Wong-Chu, Andrew Wreggitt, and Derk Wynand.

LINDA SVENDSEN is an assistant professor in the Department of Creative Writing at the University of British Columbia.

WORDS WE CALL HOME

CELEBRATING CREATIVE WRITING AT UBC

EDITED BY **LINDA SVENDSEN**

University of British Columbia Press
Vancouver

ISBN 0-7748-0367-3

Canadian Cataloguing in Publication Data
   Main entry under title:

   Words we call home

   ISBN 0-7748-0367-3

   1. Canadian literature (English)* I. Svendsen,
Linda. II. University of British Columbia. Dept. of
Creative Writing.
PS8233.W67 1990   C810.8   C90-091317-7
PR9194.4.W67 1990

This book has been published with the help of grants from the
University Development Fund, University of British Columbia,
and from the Canada Council.

Royalties from sales of this book will go to the Earle Birney Fund
for Creative Writing at UBC.

UBC Press
6344 Memorial Road
Vancouver, BC V6T 1W5

Design by Arifin Graham
Typeset by Pickwick

For Earle Birney

CONTENTS

CONTENTS

ACKNOWLEDGMENTS

Grateful acknowledgment is made to the following authors and publishers for permission to reprint copyrighted material included in *Words We Call Home: Celebrating Creative Writing at UBC*. All selections are reprinted with permission.

LEONARD ANGEL: "Jungle, copyright © 1986 Leonard Angel. All rights reserved

CHRISTIANNE BALK: "Elegy" and "How Stories Get Started" are reprinted with permission of Macmillan Publishing Company from *Bindweed* (1986) by Christianne Balk. Copyright © Christianne Balk

CAROL BOLT: Excerpt from *Red Emma: Queen of the Anarchists* (1974), copyright © Carol Bolt

ROO BORSON: "The Gift, for Robert Bringhurst" reprinted by permission of McClelland & Stewart from *Intent, or the Weight of the World* (1989). "Wild Horses and "The Transparence of November" reprinted by permission of the author

GEORGE BOWERING: "Endless Vees," copyright © 1989 George Bowering

ROBERT BRINGHURST: "Jacob Singing," copyright © 1977 Robert Bringhurst. Reprinted with permission of the author. First appeared in *Jacob Singing* (Kanchenjunga Press 1977)

FRANK DAVEY: "How and Why John Loves Mary," copyright © by Frank Davey

DON DICKINSON: "Hogarth's Arrangement," copyright © 1987 Don Dickinson

GLEN DOWNIE: "Night Light," copyright © 1990 Glen Downie, first published in *Matrix* (1990); "The Wish for a New Hand," copyright © Glen Downie, first published in *Ariel* (1989); "Worker Classification: Material Handler," copyright © Glen Downie and Polestar Press, first published in *Canadian Literature* (1984), also appears in *An X-Ray of Longing* (Polestar Press 1987)

DARYL DUKE: "A Battlefield of Dreams," copyright © 1987 Daryl Duke, first published in *If You Love This Country* edited by Laurier Lapierre. Reprinted by permission of The Canadian Publishers, McClelland & Stewart, Toronto

KENNETH DYBA: "The River," copyright © 1988 Kenneth Dyba, first published in *Grain* (1988)

DAVID EVANIER: "Rockefeller Center," copyright © 1989 David Evanier, first published in *Story Quarterly #13*

MARYA FIAMENGO: "White Linen Remembered," copyright © 1989 Marya Fiamengo

MICHAEL FINLAY: "Somewhere East," copyright © 1973 Michael Finlay, first published in *Quarry* (1973)

DENNIS FOON: "Children's Eyes," copyright © 1989 Dennis Foon

CATHY FORD: "moving again, jailed again," "trial, feet & hands chained," "the morning, may 30, 1431," all copyright © Cathy Ford and all first published in *Saffron, Rose & Flame: The Joan of Arc Poems* (Gynergy Books 1989)

ERIC FORRER: "The Sea Ice," "Chignik," "Going West, Regardless" all copyright © 1989 Eric Forrer and all first published in *From the Nets of a Fisherman* (Doubleday 1973)

BILL GASTON: "Carp," copyright © Oolichan Books 1989, first published in *Prism* (1986), also published in *Deep Cove Stories* (Oolichan Books 1989)

GARY GEDDES: "The Strap," "Jimmy's Place," "Names of Great Men" all reprinted with permission Gary Geddes and Coteau Books from *Changes of State* (Coteau Books 1986)

KICO GONZALEZ-RISSO: "Caution: Contents Under Pressure," copyright © 1979 Kico Gonzalez-Risso, all rights reserved

ELIZABETH GOURLAY: "The Excuse," copyright © 1971 Elizabeth Gourlay, first published in *Prism* (1971); "The Discipline," copyright © 1987 Elizabeth Gourlay, first published in *Event* (1987); "Snapshot by Stieglitz," copyright © 1989 Elizabeth Gourlay, first published in *Event* (1989)

PAUL GREEN: "The Age of Gold," copyright © 1989 Paul Green

GENNI GUNN: "On the Road," copyright © 1988 Genni Gunn, first published in *88: Best Canadian Stories*

GEOFF HANCOCK: "The Stainless Steel Streamliner," copyright © 1989 Geoff Hancock, first published in *The Dinosaur Review*; also appears in *Fast Travelling* (Porcupine's Quill)

HART HANSON: "Beautiful Boy Fades," copyright © 1987 Hart Hanson, first published in *The Malahat Review* (1989)

ROBERT HARLOW: Excerpt from *Felice: A Travelogue*, copyright © 1985 Robert Harlow, first published by Oolichan Books (1985)

ERNEST HEKKANEN: "The Kite," copyright © 1980 Ernest Hekkanen, first published in *Canadian Fiction Magazine* (1980)

GLADYS HINDMARCH: "Ucluelet," copyright © 1988 Douglas & McIntyre, first published in *Iron 5* (1969) and later included in *The Watery Part of the World* (Douglas & McIntyre 1988) and reprinted by permission of Douglas & McIntyre

JACK HODGINS: "Earthquake," copyright © Jack Hodgins, first published in *The Canadian Forum* (1986)

MARGARET HOLLINGSWORTH: "The House that Jack Built," copyright © Margaret Hollingsworth, first published in *Endangered Species* (Act One Press 1988)

DEBBIE HOWLETT: "The Broom Closet," copyright © 1990 Debbie Howlett

ANN IRELAND: "The Doppler Effect," copyright © 1985 Ann Ireland, first published in *Event* (1985)

SALLY IRELAND: "Lullaby," copyright © 1989 Sally Ireland

SURJEET KALSEY: "Siddhartha Does Penance Once Again," copyright © 1982 Surjeet Kalsey, first published in *Speaking to the Winds* (Third Eye Publications 1982)

LIONEL KEARNS: "Ritual," "Trophy," "Birney Land," copyright © 1986 Lionel

Kearns, all first published in *Ignoring the Bomb* (Oolichan Books 1986)

NORMAN KLENMAN: Excerpt from screenplay "Woodsmen of the West," New Canadian Library, copyright © Pacific Entertainment Ltd., screenplay copyright © Bridgevale Management Limited Canada 1989

CHARLES LILLARD: "Night Sailing," and "Coastal Sanctus," copyright © 1984, both first published in *A Coastal Range* (Sono Nis 1984)

CYNTHIA MACDONALD: "Hymn in a Bed of Amherst," copyright © Cynthia MacDonald. "Two Brothers in a Field of Absence," copyright © 1984, 1985 Cynthia Macdonald. "Hymn in a Bed of Amherst" first published in *Alternate Means of Transport* (Knopf 1985); "Two Brothers in a Field of Absence" first published in *The New Yorker* (1984), also appears in *Alternate Means of Transport*

KENNETH MCGOOGAN: "Gazette Boy," copyright © 1982 Kenneth McGoogan, first published in *Quarry* (1982)

FLORENCE MCNEIL: "Ghost Town" and "Alice on the Train," copyright © 1975 Florence McNeil, both first published in *Ghost Towns* (McClelland & Stewart 1975); "The Hours of the Duc de Berry," copyright © 1979 Florence McNeil, first published in *A Balancing Act* (McClelland & Stewart 1979)

KIM MALTMAN: "The Technology of the Persistence of Memory," "The Technology of Metal, Turning," "The Technology of the Metal at the Heart of the Sorrow," copyright © 1989 Kim Maltman. "The Technology of the Persistence of Memory" first published in *Dancing Visions*; "The Technology of Metal, Turning," first published in *The Malahat Review*; "The Technology of the Metal at the Heart of the Sorrow" first published in *The Lyric Paragraph*

JILL MANDRAKE: "Marilyn and the Lucky Penny," copyright © Jill Mandrake, first published in *Event* (1989)

DAPHNE MARLATT: "eating," copyright © 1984 Daphne Marlatt, first published in *Touch to My Tongue* (Longspoon Press 1984); "shrimping," copyright © 1988 Daphne Marlatt, first published in *Line* (1988); "Compliments (of the camera)," copyright © 1989 Daphne Marlatt, first published in *The Capilano Review* (1989)

SEYMOUR MAYNE: "Trouble" and "The Oranges of Sicily" copyright © Seymour Mayne; "Another Son," copyright © 1986 Seymour Mayne, first published in *Canadian Literature* (1986), also appears in *Children of Abel* (Mosaic 1986)

JENNIFER MITTON: "The Weepers," copyright © 1988 Jennifer Mitton, first published in *The Malahat Review* (1988)

DANIEL DAVID MOSES: "Some Grand River Blues," "Grandmother of the Glacier," "The Chain," copyright © 1989 Daniel David Moses. "Some Grand River Blues" first published in *Whetstone*; "Grandmother of the Glacier" first published in *First Person Plural*; "The Chain" first published in *Arc*

ERIN MOURÉ: "Margins," "Hazard of the Occupation," "Poem for Rudolph Hess on His 80th Birthday (1974)," all copyright © 1989 Erin Mouré, all first published in *Empire, York Street* (Anansi 1979)

JANE MUNRO: "Satori" and "Woman Clothed by the Sun" both copyright ©

1986 Jane Munro, both first published in *The Trees Just Moved into a Season of Other Shapes* (Quarry 1986)

RONA MURRAY: "Blackberries," "When," "The Foghorn" all copyright © 1981 Rona Murray, all first published in *Journey* (Sono Nis 1981)

MORGAN NYBERG: "To Margarita," translation copyright © 1988 Morgan Nyberg

MORRIS PANYCH: "Last Call! A Post-Nuclear Cabaret," copyright © 1983 Morris Panych, first published by Harbour Publishing (1983)

GEORGE PAYERLE: "Wolfbane Fane," copyright © 1990 George Payerle, first published in *Event* (1974)

E.G. PERRAULT: "The Cure," copyright © 1950 E.G. Perrault, first published in *The Raven* (1950), also appears in *Stories from Pacific and Arctic Canada* (Macmillan 1974)

KAREN PETERSEN: "Cranefly," "Satyr's Rat Soup," "PMS Rules OK," all copyright © 1990 Karen Petersen

MAIDA PRICE: "Looking for Mexico," copyright © 1989 Maida Price

LINDA ROGERS: "Woman at Mile Zero," "Something Brilliant for One Hand," "Converso," all copyright © 1989 Linda Rogers

LAKE SAGARIS: "Circus love," copyright © 1987 Lake Sagaris, first published in *Dinosaur Review* (1987): "Let our children," copyright © 1984 Lake Sagaris, first published in *Contemporary Verse II* (1984): "El trauco," copyright © 1989 Lake Sagaris

ANDREAS SCHROEDER: "One Tide Over," copyright © 1976 Andreas Schroeder, first published in *Best Canadian Stories* (Oberon 1976)

ROBERT G. SHERRIN: "North by North by North," copyright © 1979, 1989 Robert G. Sherrin, first published in *The Capilano Review* (1980)

HEATHER SPEARS: "Powell Street Bus, Vancouver" and "Robert Noyes," copyright © 1988 (Wolsak & Wynn 1988) and reprinted by permission of Wolsak & Wynn

RICHARD STEVENSON: "New Black Shoes," "Why Does It Cry So?" "Split-Leaf Philodendron," all copyright © 1990 Richard Stevenson. "New Black Shoes" first published in *Sanskrit* (1990), "Why Does It Cry So?" first published in *Nebula* (1990), "Split-Leaf Philodendron" first published in *Dandelion* (1990)

DONA STURMANIS: "Bag Lady," copyright © 1989 Dona Sturmanis, first published in *White Wall Review* (1989) and reprinted by permission; "When Two Funny Women Died in One Month," copyright © 1990 Dona Sturmanis, first published in *New Quarterly* (1990) and reprinted by permission

FRED WAH: "Author 13" and "Biotext Fragment #57," both copyright © 1990 Fred Wah; "I'd get into Ruth's death business but," copyright © 1988 Fred Wah, first published in *Secrets from the Orange Couch* (1988) and reprinted by permission

TOM WAYMAN: "My Old Master" and "Did I Miss Anything?" copyright © 1989 Tom Wayman. "Did I Miss Anything?" first published in *Poetry Northwest* (1990)

IAN WEIR: "C'est la Guerre," copyright © 1989 Ian Weir

JIM WONG-CHU: "equal opportunity," copyright © 1985 Jim Wong-Chu, first published in *Chinatown Ghosts* (Pulp Press 1986); "hippo luck," copyright © 1986 Jim Wong-Chu, first published in *Chinatown Ghosts*; "of christmas," copyright © 1989 Jim Wong-Chu, first published in *Prism* (1989)

ANDREW WREGGIT: "Burning My Father's Clothes" and "Tools" both copyright © 1989 Thistledown Press, both published in *Making Movies* (Thistledown Press 1989)

DERK WYNAND: "Snowscape," copyright © 1974 Derk Wynand, first published in *Snowscapes* (Sono Nis 1974); "Stall," copyright © 1984 Derk Wynand, first published in *Fetishistic* (Porcupine's Quill 1984); "Queluz Palace," copyright © 1988 Derk Wynand, first published in *Heat Waves* (Oolichan Books 1988)

PREFACE

Back in 1971 when I was in grade eleven, the student council sponsored a literary reading during lunch hour. I remember it was a gorgeous sunny day towards the end of the semester, and the sort of noon one would normally sit outside braiding a friend's hair, chainsmoking, and listening to Black Sabbath on the school lawn, but a hundred of us, in a kind of hushed wonder, filed into the dark auditorium. We didn't know what to expect. A *writer*? I suspect the only *live* writers we'd seen were the dapper gent on *Front Page Challenge* and perhaps we'd read Joan Baez's autobiography and seen her sing morosely on *The Smothers Brothers Comedy Hour*. As we unwrapped our sandwiches, odours of egg and tuna sitting in the air, the council vice-president offered an introduction in a shaky voice and then the poet walked out and stood before us. She was a woman. She seemed very pleasant. She looked like she could have been a friend of somebody's mother, or perhaps a mother herself, or a business person; I don't know what I'd expected. I was moved by her words and the soft, clear way she read them. Sometimes she talked about what had inspired the poem, or how she had revised it, or the influence of another writer. When she finished reading a selection, there was a silence as brief and perfect as the one before somebody makes an important wish and blows out the candles. At one point, she told us she'd studied at the Department of Creative Writing at UBC, and I felt a shiver. From where I sat, only twenty miles straight west, there was a place people learned to write.

I had been writing, in the way many children write, since grade two: Barbie and Ken go-on-a-picnic stories, a six-page sequel to *Tom Sawyer*, and more recently, due to the patience of a biology teacher and in lieu of lab reports, poems about spunky microscopic bugs swimming in pond-water. Not long before, and I'm still talking about grade eleven, I'd read a novel by a young writer who'd attended the Iowa Writers' Workshop. I'd kept turning to his picture on the inside back jacket—something I still do when I'm reading and I want to know more about who is behind these words, who is dreaming this up—a black and white photograph, shot outdoors, with the writer looking extremely serious, moody, un-approachable, and exciting. The librarian had helped me find the address and I'd written to Iowa for information on applying and had been disappointed when they'd sent back a booklet and was informed they required a bachelor's degree first. However, after I heard the poet read at my high school, I discovered I could apply for Creative Writing at UBC as soon as I arrived there.

I didn't. It took another year for me to work up my nerve and send material for the introductory workshop. Doug Bankson, then the Head, instructed that particular class and he was the second writer I ever met. There were twelve of us around that table—sullen, shy, and terrified, wearing dark granny glasses, long skirts, bellbottoms, and loud go-to-hell boots. He had us write fictional unsigned autobiographies and read them aloud at the next class. He also commented on them, and encouraged us to tactfully offer our own opinions. That was intense. My heart felt like it was going to bounce out of my body through my brain. That was one of the happiest moments in my life. From that workshop, there are four of us (that I know of) still writing, seriously and professionally, eating by our words; those other three—Morris Panych, Dona Sturmanis, and Andrew Wreggitt—are included in this anthology.

It would also be fair to say that some of the unhappiest moments of my life occurred in writing workshops, not only at UBC but at Columbia, Stanford, and at Knopf editor Gordon Lish's notorious gatherings—when the report from peers has been less than enthusiastic, when the play has been missing the through-line or the story's ending "seems not quite there yet, I'm afraid." But there has always been that buddy from the workshop—who else in the world understands what you're going through?—who says, "Put the story under your pillow for a week" (or month, or year), or listens to you mumble in a depressed fashion over the phone for an hour, sometimes long distance, and says sleepily, "But I *liked* the beginning."

I returned to Vancouver last summer after twelve years in the United States and I'm now teaching Creative Writing at UBC. I'm sitting in a different place at that long table and it's still intense and terrifying and wonderful. I remember my own years in the program as five years of a whispered *Yes*. The forerunner of the Nike ad: *Just Do It*. Certainly I received pages of critical queries and suggestions for revision, but always the writers leading the workshops found something worthwhile, whether it was one line, a point of view, or sometimes a word well-placed, by luck or instinct, in a poem. And I believe every work—from the first deeply felt poem by a forestry student to that dazzlingly polished first novel from the dedicated grad—shows a soul, and the writers teaching here respond respectfully to the work in that way. It's always the work of a fellow writer with something to say; we're all just there to *get it said better, truer*. The other strength of UBC Creative Writing must be the diverse nature of its genre offerings: one doesn't have to hike over to Theatre to study stageplays, or to Film to pen scripts, or to Education or night school to write works for children. At other graduate writing programs, writers may often only officially work in one area, but here all the genres are offered and the disciplines of each craft reinforce one other. I didn't become a fiction writer until I'd studied playwriting and poetry. Many of the writers in this anthology shine in two or more genres.

The idea for *Words We Call Home* was born in August 1989 during a faculty meeting. In 1990, the Department of Creative Writing would be twenty-five years young, and it would also be the occasion of UBC's seventy-fifth anniversary. After I'd researched the project, I realized that one couldn't simply gather the writers of the last twenty-five years since the official inception; legend travelled further back, as far as Earle Birney's first workshop in 1947. I consulted several writers intimate with Creative Writing when drawing up a list of contributors: Sue Ann Alderson, Doug Bankson, Hart Hanson, Robert Harlow, George McWhirter, Daphne Marlatt, Jerry Newman, George Payerle, Andreas Schroeder, Bryan Wade, and Jake Zilber. I also received advice and support from Don Bastian, Roo Borson, Susan Crean, Cathy Ford, Cynthia Good, Bob Hilderley, Angela McWhirter, Keith Maillard, Pat Nakamura, Julian Ross, Blair Rosser, Cherie Smith, and Pierre Stolte and the UBC 75th Anniversary Committee. When I'd finally narrowed the list to sixty-nine writers who'd participated in a single UBC Creative Writing workshop, or majored, or graduated with an MFA—and it was a difficult decision to stop *there*—the contributor was invited to select their own work for submission. Sometimes, if the writers worked in more than one genre, I asked them to consider the one with the lesser word count. All I asked was that they loved their selection and that it didn't exceed the length requirements. They also included their own short biographies and introductions. Patricia Gabin, a graduate student in the department, took time out from her own writing to work on this commemorative project, and her editorial assistance was absolutely invaluable. The result is in your hands.

It has been almost twenty years since I heard the "lady poet" read at lunch hour in a Coquitlam high school. But, in a way, it seems as if there was a direct line from that very moment to this one, and when I read Rona Murray's submitted poems one late Friday night last January—holding the pounds of this manuscript on my lap—I felt another shiver, a different sort this time. It had something to do with being far away from home for many years and coming back; it had something to do with the impact of a woman writer and her poems on a young girl; it had mostly to do with the love of a gift passed on, when you care enough to give the very best, the words that travel.

Linda Svendsen

INTRODUCTION:
A WILDCAT CREATIVITY

I often see creative writing at UBC as a set of rigs which rise, ridiculously numbered and initialed Cr.Wr. 202–549, somewhere west of Alberta and south of Fort St. John. A few chug away through the spring and the summer, then the whole sector starts up in September. The first hole was sunk in 1946 by a legendary wildcatter called Earle Birney. He hit a gusher of talent right off, and nineteen years later, by 1965, a complete field was christened and in operation; but for the purpose of this anthology, those named and numbered rigs don't count. If there had been nothing down there, the whole caboodle would have folded. The writers and their writing that passed through their own unique refinements have made the venture real.

Like most of us who have worked in the program or taught individual courses at UBC, the energy, the friendships, the face-offs, the stimulation among the writers in the workshops never ceases to give a mix of pure and applied pleasure. Earle Birney, the pioneer, came back to UBC's English Department in 1946 on condition that he be given one course for the creative writer, naked in academe. Jake Zilber, always in pursuit of true grit, displayed it in struggling alongside of Earle from 1963 to 1965 when a separate university unit was set up, which would run on writers' rules. Bob Harlow, the first Head, came in from directing CBC Vancouver with the wisdom to let the talent for writing flow and he organized the teachers to supply the forms it needed.

I remember being stunned by the visionary blink of J. Michael Yates' dark glasses one summer in 1967. From 1946 until 1965 when he retired, Earle Birney, "the bearded prophet," blew the fences down all around his students' horizons in the same way. During creative writing's English Department days, if Earle Birney was aided by Jake Zilber in the workshops and through the curricular bureaucracy, he was abetted by Warren Tallman, impresario of the then-dissident projective verse and later, the post-modern. Warren was as sensitive and solicitous as Jake Zilber was steady and concerned; aesthetically at odds with Earle and Jake, but representative of the tension and the span of differences that keep UBC writing wide, alive, and in place, able to take the buffets of change because the program thrives on them.

Among the teachers, the best UBC tradition has always been to encourage difference and daring among its student writers. Until their respective retirements, Robert Harlow took pride and care in cultivating a sense of the special among his alumni; Jake Zilber's mission was to have every writer find the holy grail of true and pure experience that belonged to them; when not working with students at making meticulous exchanges of foreign words for English in the international treasure house of translation, Michael Bullock kept open the storehouse of the subconscious—as surrealist as Jake Zilber or Bob Harlow were realist; Doug Bankson, who could delight in the experimental, absurdist, farcical, or straight and serious scripts—UBC writing's major-domo of drama, was surrounded by students seething with talent and bitter wisdom as they learned that work for production and performance, if only just as valuable artistically, was much, much more expensive to pay for than literature in print.

The gargantuan economics and impossibilities didn't deter Jake Zilber's introduction of writing for screen and TV; it didn't stop the young playwrights from joining with fledgling directors out of UBC Theatre in establishing a playhouse or two, or poets and prose writers from reacting and launching magazines where none existed for their brand of new work. Their reaching has always exceeded our grasp.

From 1957 to 1977 *Prism* was the place for some new work by UBC student writers to appear until student energy took over the magazine from the faculty, thus cutting out their own contributions from its pages. Earlier, in 1961, reacting to their perception of *Prism*'s (and other Canadian magazines') glossy academic and Brit-beat, a group of legendary UBCers (and friends) created the "newsletter," *Tish*, which would mimeo text and tidings of a new Canadian tradition. *Prism* itself changed, becoming *international*, and the co-editor/founder of *Contemporary Literature in Translation* pushed literary boundaries even wider before graduating and moving that magazine off-campus. Another group of faculty and students in Creative Writing, reacting to the realism of Canadian fiction, established the *Canadian Fiction Magazine*, which has lasted, and another group set up *Melmoth* (a surrealist journal), which has not. Yet another UBC creative writer founded *Event* to pick up good writing that was squeezed out of the way by warring experimental factions.

Differences and new directions continue with new faculty. Writers drawn to the Writing of Children's Literature courses operate on the principle that young people, whatever their age, are a real audience and deserve writing in all genres that they can read and respond to with wonder as they learn and grow through it. It has an in-house magazine, *Chameleon*. The non-fiction program, introduced by Robert Harlow in 1973, has been expanded through the Maclean Hunter Chair of Non-fiction & Business Writing. That genre awaits its journal.

In a heated exchange of letters with Robert Harlow in *Canadian Literature*, George Woodcock lamented that these university writers weren't closer to the downtown and working out of a café, but they have never been far from those, or the bars or apartments where exchanges go on into the night and continue over the years. Intramurally, oh yes, there is technical talk, the hushed tones about that sacred p.o.v. in fiction, voice in poetry, motivation and the blueprint of the script in plays, and these things get exercised and the control learned, then forgotten, turned back into instinct, but it is the shared anticipation of those items that defies expectation, a knowing that we are just watchers and waiters on something special that keeps us sitting up and reading through the tedium of the late hours, like those wise virgins with our lamps lit, knowing if not exactly now, then later this one or that one is going to be taken with the *duende*, when craft and artistry are used up and, like the soft bow over the taut string, the raw talent crossing the right text thrills us once again.

The current faculty who came from outside UBC's Creative Writing (Sue Ann Alderson, Keith Maillard, C.J. Newman, Bryan Wade) and the writers from other campuses or corners of creation, who inspired for a month or a year or more (George Amabile, Chris Bruyere, Peter Bryant, Susan Crean, Robert Creeley, Jacqueline d'Amboise, Robert Duncan, Anthony Friedson, Allen Ginsberg, William Gough, Joan Haggerty, Walter Havighurst, Moira Johnston, Philip Lamantia, Joseph Langland, Dorothy Livesay, Pat Lowther, Alice Munro, Walter Perrie, Barry Pritchard, Jane Rule, George Ryga, Carol Shields, Audrey Thomas, Phyllis Webb, Tennessee Williams, J. Michael Yates), have all added their necessary difference and drive to the students' lust to write and the lustre of their work.

For me it is always hard to get over the shock of hindsight, the whiplash of looking back and realizing that in one small poetry group of twelve or so, in 1977, there would turn out to be a Governor General's Award winner, two CBC prize-winners for Poetry, someone who would edit Isaac Bashevis Singer, a president of the League of Canadian Poets, a now well-known native Indian poet, a respected anthologist, poet, and translator of Punjabi, a future teacher of literature at Berkeley. I would come in to Jake Zilber and say, "My son is reading *Terror in Winnipeg* and he thinks it's terrific." Jacob Zilber would turn and say, "*That author* was in *that* creative writing class in *that* year." "*That author* too??!!" I would say.

That name is missing from the writers included in this commemorative anthology, but to put them all in would require a series of sequels or a volume several times larger than this one. Not all the award winners are included either, although among the writers present, it is possible for me to identify (at a glance) four Governor General's Awards for Poetry, two for Fiction, one for Children's Literature; one of the overall Commonwealth Poetry Prizes; a Commonwealth Poetry Prize for the North American area, another for Fiction—North American area; a Seal First

Novel award; a Chalmers' Award for playwriting; one British Play-wrights' Award; five CBC 1st prizes for Poetry; two (League of Canadian Poets') Pat Lowther Awards for poetry; a National Magazine Award for Poetry; one newly-named Dorothy Livesay Prize for Poetry and an Ethel Wilson for Fiction (BC Book Awards); one League of Canadian Poets' F.R. Scott Translation Award; one O. Henry prize-winner, not to mention the writers who have been included in the *Oxford Book of Canadian Verse* (thirteen) and *Short Stories* (two), the *Penguin Book of Canadian Verse* (nine), *The Atlantic's Best of the Decade* (one), or the names anthologized in *Best Canadian* and *Best American Short Stories*, or my omissions.

The roll-call of honours already becomes obscene, turns the writers' vitality into a waddling parade-past of veterans whose medals stain their bosoms like chocolate mousse-droppings after a high-cal banquet. It doesn't do justice to their sense of the now that has always tested their teachers and now challenges their audience. There's not one of them who doesn't consider themselves any better than the latest piece of writing they have on the go; always edgy until it works and proves their presence again where it counts on the printed page, or stage and screen.

This is the twenty-fifth anniversary (going on forty-fourth) of an opportunity, of Earle Birney's sanctuary for creative writers. We, at the gate of the stockade, follow the migrations of the creatures imagined into life outside; and it is best that I do as we always have—let the gate swing open to let the curiosity roam, so that you can see some of those that came down through the years to drink at UBC and then moved on. Each of us has our favourites; you will find yours.

An Earle Birney Fund has been set up so that the tradition of keeping a living space for aspiring, talented writers can endure. The generous Arnold and Nancy Cliff Writers'-in-Residence Program will add immediately to the room. The University's Deans of Arts and Presidents have supported the creative writing venture through thick and thin. It is the great paradox of a great conservative institution that it has accepted this wildcatting creativity as a legitimate pursuit. Thanks are due to those teachers in other departments whose roles in providing knowledge and material to write about are not forgotten. A special thanks to the newly-reconstituted UBC Press which has shared the courage in making this its second complete publication of original creative writing.

George McWhirter
March 1990

WORDS WE CALL HOME

CELEBRATING CREATIVE WRITING AT UBC

LEONARD ANGEL

Leonard Angel was born in Montreal in 1945. In 1966 he came to UBC to the then new Creative Writing program leading to the degree of Master of Arts in Playwriting. He was in the first graduating class, and has gone on to have over fourteen plays produced on stage, including *The Unveiling*, *Eleanor Marx*, and *3000 Years of Sexual Politics*. He is also the author of three books of philosophy, including the AI book *How to Build a Conscious Machine*.

Jungle was written as part of Dancing on the Head of a Pin with a Mouse in My Pocket, *a collection of short plays commissioned by Theatre Terrific, a Vancouver-based theatre company for the disabled.* Jungle *has been seen by audiences at Expo '86 at Kits House, and performed to success at the Vancouver Fringe '86 Festival. Direction of the first production was by Sue Lister.*

Jungle
A Play in One Act

CHARACTERS
Willa *In her forties*
Henry *Willa's husband, also in his forties*
Norm *In his thirties, with a disability*

The action takes place in a contemporary suburban backyard, with part of the adjacent backyard.

It is late afternoon. Summer.

WILLA What are you reading?
HENRY D.H. Lawrence, *Sons and Lovers*.
WILLA Did you notice if he's home?
HENRY Who?
WILLA The fellow next door.
HENRY No I didn't.
WILLA He is. His car's in back.
HENRY Ah.
WILLA Will you go over and speak to him? Please? It's embarrassing.

We're going to have guests over on the weekend, and his lawn is a jungle.

HENRY It's his lawn, not ours.

WILLA But it's our barbeque and it's our guests who'll see into his yard.

HENRY Right now?

WILLA You said you'd talk to him last weekend. I don't know what you're waiting for.

HENRY I'm waiting for him to cut the lawn without my having to say anything. I thought he'd do it over the weekend. Alright?

WILLA Fine. Did he cut it over the weekend? Did you check? *(Glances over.)*

HENRY Looks like he didn't.

WILLA Will you please?

HENRY *(Puts down book, gets up, then stops.)* You know what I was waiting for?

WILLA What were you waiting for?

HENRY I was procrastinating. I admit it. I confess. I was procrastinating.

WILLA I had a suspicion.

HENRY But at least you know why. You do know why?

WILLA Why?

HENRY He has a limp. It's not fair.

WILLA It's not fair that he has a limp?

HENRY It's not fair to go over to someone who's . . . got this limp, and tell him his lawn is an eyesore.
(Norm enters.)

WILLA Why? You think the fact he has a limp gives him an automatic exemption from having to mow his lawn? Sort of a ticket handed out at birth from God: "You've got a limp, son, but at least you won't have to mow your lawn."

HENRY Fine. I'll talk to him.
(She exits.)
Hi.

NORM Hi.

HENRY How's it going?

NORM Fine, how about yourself?

HENRY Oh, not bad. We're getting set for a barbeque, having some people over on the weekend. Just a few friends. Not too many. I hope that won't disturb you.

NORM Me? Disturb me? Why should it disturb me?

HENRY The noise.

NORM No.

HENRY If it disturbs you, if there's anything we do that disturbs you—if you find anything about us disturbing, please let us know. We'd

	fix it. We'd do what we could.
NORM	Oh. Can't think of anything.
HENRY	Good. Because we wouldn't want to do something that you find disturbing and not know about it. We'd want to know so we could be, what would you say, good neighbours.
NORM	That's okay by me.
HENRY	You'd feel the same way, wouldn't you?
NORM	Depends.
HENRY	Ah, cagey aren't you. Won't commit yourself in advance I see.
NORM	Why should I?
HENRY	It's about the lawn.
NORM	Ah.
HENRY	This has nothing to do with me, you see. Absolutely nothing to do with me. It's my wife. I was commandeered. What the heck do I care if your lawn looks like some kind of trendy pasta factory. I don't care. And I don't believe the people coming to our barbeque will care. But my wife? She cares. She cares deeply. So here I am. I hope you don't mind my being honest.
NORM	No.
HENRY	Good.
NORM	I like my lawn long.
HENRY	Fine with me . . . I understand.
NORM	Understand?
HENRY	Yes, I understand, I understand.
NORM	Understand what?
HENRY	You liking your lawn long. I understand.
NORM	Understand why I like my lawn long? Why do I like my lawn long?
HENRY	The thought of cutting it—for you—must be too much. You have so much extra to cope with, just getting around and so on, you like to relax when you come home, I suppose.
NORM	And that's why I like my lawn long? Because of my legs? Is that what you're saying? I don't want to bother cutting my lawn because it's hard for me to get around? Is that what you're saying!
HENRY	Well, I . . . It's not an accusation. I understand. That's what I'm saying.
NORM	You understand! You don't understand anything.
HENRY	If I've made a mistake I'm sorry. If there's some other reason . . . I—I didn't mean to offend you.
NORM	What the hell do you know about me! What the hell gives you the right to think you know the first thing about me.
HENRY	Sorry.
NORM	I'm observing the growing of the grass.

HENRY What's that?

NORM I'm watching the grass grow. That's why I'm not cutting it.

HENRY You're watching the grass grow.

NORM That's right.

HENRY You're—a biologist. No, you weren't a biologist were you?

NORM No, I'm a dentist.

HENRY That's right. A dentist. No. I didn't think you were a biologist. But you're watching the grass grow.

NORM If you don't cut it. If you don't cut it—ever—and you watch, very carefully, you can see the grass growing.

HENRY Really?

NORM Oh yeah, there it is now. There! Did you see it grow?

HENRY No.

NORM You missed it then.

HENRY It was just growing?

NORM Uh huh.

HENRY Visibly?

NORM Do you want to see it?

HENRY *(Putting him on.)* Sure.

NORM Alright. You have to concentrate though.

HENRY Alright. I'm going to concentrate with all my power.

NORM You concentrating?

HENRY I'm concentrating . . .
(The grass grows noticeably.)
I saw it! I saw it! You're right. It grows, you can see it grow.

NORM Interesting, huh?

HENRY Amazing!

NORM Now you know why I don't want to cut the grass. Right?

HENRY Right. You bet! That's amazing.

NORM Nothing to do with my legs, wouldn't you say?

HENRY No. Nothing to do with your legs. I was wrong. I was definitely wrong.

NORM What will you say to your wife?

HENRY I don't know. I hadn't thought.

NORM Tell her I'm a lazy son of a gun, and if she wants the grass cut she'll have to come and cut it herself. Okay?

HENRY Okay. That's what I'll tell her.

NORM Okay.

HENRY Okay, and thanks for letting me see the grass grow.

NORM Sure thing.
(Exit Henry. Raised voices off. Enter Willa.)

WILLA I hear you're letting the grass grow because you like to watch it grow.

NORM Is that what he told you?

WILLA   That's what he told me.

NORM   I thought he was going to tell you I'm a lazy son of a gun.

WILLA   He did. That's what he told me at first. I ferretted the rest out of him. I ferretted the whole story, starting with the concentration, continuing with the visible growing of the grass. I got the whole story.

NORM   Good for you.

WILLA   But I'm not going to ask to see your grass growing.

NORM   No?

WILLA   No. That would be beating around the bush wouldn't it?

NORM   I don't know.

WILLA   You see, we have guests coming for our barbeque on the weekend, and there's nothing dividing your backyard from ours and, to be frank, it's embarrassing. Now I poopooed when my husband said it all had to do with your legs. I told him that's ridiculous, I said. Having to use crutches is a problem, but if Rick Hansen can wheel across the Great Wall of China, you can bloody well cut your lawn. I mean, I sympathize with your plight. I donate to the Kinsmen. I use Easter Seals, but really what happened to the spirit of Terry Fox and Steve Fonyo? You see, I have guests coming over here this weekend, and they're going to take one look at the jungle over there that serves as your excuse for a lawn, and they're going to make comments. They're going to make comments on our neighborhood. So, you have a problem with your legs but that does not excuse you from having to cut your lawn. And please, don't give me the routine about the grass visibly growing. Don't tell me to concentrate so I'll see it grow. I want one thing and one thing only. I want you to cut the grass. You disabled people want to be treated like anyone else, you're going to be treated like anyone else.

NORM   You have very nice teeth.

WILLA   I beg your pardon.

NORM   You have very nice teeth. I'm speaking professionally. I'm a dentist.

WILLA   Oh yes, I—I noticed you in your office in the shopping mall the other day. I saw you through the window. There was a sign in gold painted on the window advertising your services in dentistry.

NORM   In fact you have some of the best teeth I have ever seen in my whole life.

WILLA   Thank you.

NORM   May I? May I admire your teeth? I'd like to. Please?

WILLA   Well, this isn't going to deter me from getting your lawn cut.

NORM   I realize.

WILLA   If anything, this'll only get the lawn cut quicker.
NORM   How do you figure that?
WILLA   You like my teeth, easier for me to persuade you to cut the lawn. I appeal to you.
NORM   Sharp incisors.
WILLA   Really!
NORM   The sharpest.
WILLA   I'm not going to forget about the lawn.
NORM   I know.
WILLA   That was the purpose of my coming here.
NORM   I know. The thing is, with incisors like that, you could cut the lawn with your teeth.
WILLA   Pardon me?
NORM   You could bend over and start chomping. I bet you would do better than a power mower.
WILLA   I'll bet.
NORM   Should I get out my power mower? We could have a contest.
WILLA   I wouldn't even begin to get into it.
NORM   You'd get further than my power mower. Shall I get it?
WILLA   Don't be silly! *(She bends over, provocatively, and begins chomping at the jungle grass. The grass does not get cut.)* Look . . . doesn't cut a bit.
NORM   Hmm . . . not a dent.
WILLA   There. I win.
NORM   Hmm. So you do. I suppose I'll have to give you a prize.
WILLA   What can you offer?
NORM   Do you want a sample?
WILLA   Alright. *(He kisses her.)* Oh . . . *(She loses a shoe.)* I'll claim the rest.
NORM   Good.
WILLA   Inside.
        (They go off.)
        (Henry comes out, looking for wife.)
HENRY   Honey . . . Yoo-hoo . . . ? *(Notices grass.)* . . . Hmm . . . I . . . *(Concentrates. Nothing happens.)* Hmmm . . . Okay: Come on. Come on . . . *(Again, nothing happens.)* One more time: *(He concentrates again. This time the grass shrinks.)* I'd better not try that again. What's this? *(He finds her shoe.)* I guess they must be having a heated exchange. She must really be letting him have it. *(She comes out, buttoning up some clothes.)*
WILLA   Hi.
HENRY   You . . . uh . . . you lost a shoe.
WILLA   Oh did I? Thanks. *(She puts it on.)*
HENRY   So . . . ?

WILLA   What?

HENRY   What was the outcome? You did go in to talk to him about the grass?

WILLA   Yes.

HENRY   Did you get him to agree?

WILLA   To cut the grass?

HENRY   Yes.

WILLA   No.

HENRY   You didn't?

WILLA   No.

HENRY   Well—what's going to happen then? Is he going to cut it? I mean, is it going to stay long like that? What's it going to look like, for the guests, at our barbeque? What are they going to think? You're not going to let him get away with this, are you?

WILLA   No. Yoo-hoo!
(Norm comes out. She waves and then contentedly goes back to the house.)

HENRY   And?—Honey, what's going to happen. *(She's gone.)*
(Norm snaps his fingers. The grass grows taller still, right down the property line.)

NORM   Now your guests aren't going to be able to see in at all, are they? It's a fence, just call it a fence, my friend, only accessible to special people. . . . Oh, by the way, if you need a good dentist just ask your wife where my office is, alright? Bye.
(He leaves.)

HENRY   Bye . . . Honey?
(Henry goes back to his house, puzzled, looking back at the wall of grass once or twice.)

CHRISTIANNE BALK

Christianne Balk lives in Seattle, Washington, with her husband and daughter. Her first book of poems, *Bindweed*, was chosen by Anthony Hecht for the 1985 Walt Whitman Award and was published by Macmillan in 1986. Her work has appeared in *Pequod*, *Crazyhorse*, *Harper's Magazine*, *The New Yorker*, *Country Journal*, *Minnesota Monthly*, *Alaska Today*, and other magazines.

My time at the University of British Columbia was powerful. I'll never forget the day I found myself stuck in a traffic jam on a road leading to the University. All the cars were travelling slowly and the drivers were leaning out their windows staring up. I looked up and saw three young eagles performing acrobatics in the air, folding their wings and spiralling down, catching themselves at the last moment.

Elegy

In Wainwright they say the plane went down in the Brooks Range,
    perhaps near Porcupine River, or perhaps in the Arctic Ocean;
It was spring, the rivers were breaking up, and the mist settled in
    for weeks.
The plane went down in March, when it rains one day and snows
    the next;
When the ice fields split into islands big enough to crush ships.
The plane went down in the early spring, when the snow still drifts
    in the wind, snow so fine it works into the tightest weave
    of a man's coat;
In the north, where the snow is hardened and serrated by winter
    winds, where metal sled runners wear out in days, and where
    men do not leave heel marks;
In the spring, when the winds begin to drop, when the snow turns
    soft and honeycombed, and cannot support a man's weight;
In the spring, when the winds leave, and the insects come, swarms
    of insects that can weaken a man until he cannot walk;
In the far north, where magnetic compasses are useless.
Snowshoe frames can be made of metal from plane keels, sleds
    built from wings, harnesses woven from shroud lines;
Cloudy streams of fresh water can be found; and salmon, tomcod,
    needlefish, and pike caught;

But the Brooks Range stretches from Cape Lisburne to
  Demarcation Point, and few of its mountains are mapped.
The plane went down in the north, where valley glaciers crack
  into crevasses above deep, granite beds;
In the spring, when rivers swell with melt water, when
  snowbridges are swept away, and debris dams up the streams;
In the north, where the overflow fills the flatland with shallow,
  swampy lakes.
Beaver, marmot, and ground squirrel can be trapped; and molting
  spruce grouse, arctic loon, and ptarmigan can be snared.
Bushes can be dug for the starchy roots; cup-fungus, bracken, and
  the inner white bark of willow, poplar, and birch can be eaten;
But the north is filled with rose-capped mushroom, water hemlock,
  baneberry, and amanita.
A plane crashed six years ago in the Bering Sea, in water so cold it
  paralyzed the pilot's hands, but he used his teeth to lash
  himself to a raft with ripcord.
A man went under for forty minutes in the Yukon River, but was
  pulled up breathing because the water had been just cold
  enough.
But masses of sea-ice crowd into the bays in the spring, colliding
  with each other and the coast, and the booming can be heard
  for miles.
A woman lifted an ice-wall in Kotzebue, fracturing her spine, but
  she held the ice up so her husband could crawl out.
A plane crashed near Eagle, and a woman dragged her husband
  from the fuselage, and she melted snow in her mouth, and
  brought it to him, until help came.
A Galena trapper was lost two years ago, but his wife waited, and
  pounded beef suet, berries, and bacon with a wooden mallet
  into pemmican, for his next trip out, and he was found;
But tundra streams wander aimlessly in the spring, and often lead
  to marshes filled with mosquitoes, midges, and blackflies.

How Stories Get Started

You come across tracks. Big, cloven, packed deep
in the snow. The tips of the willow branches
along the trail are nipped off, as if a polite
but famished guest walked by, eating your trees.
The upper twigs are glazed with frozen
moisture from his breath. They glisten in the light.
Clumps of snow are held in the bushes' limbs—
undisturbed nests. Close to your feet a trough
is scooped out where he lay down for the night.
It is as deep as the bathtub in your mother's mother's
house. You lie down in the bottom of the bowl.
You dream of riding something big, unbridled.
Your arms barely reach the sides of its neck.
When you get off and try to touch its face
it steps too close to you and its lips curl
and he smiles at you, like a man you once knew.
He's just a visitor now. Polite, but famished.
The trees aren't enough. He wants to ride
his one-wheel bike with you on his back
on a tightrope strung from tree to tree. You want
to ride but you see what he wants and you run.
Then you can't run. You are buried neck-deep
and your head sways on its stem. Snow trims the barbwire
fence like crocheted lace. Someone has carved
moats in the snow around the base of each willow
and hand-packed the snow against the birch trunks
to keep you from seeing the black parts
of the bark. The bush branches bend
beneath the weight of the snow they hold,
curving over in arches to form snow caves
to shelter you while you sleep at their feet.
You hear someone tall breathing over you.
You hear the scrape of his blade as he digs deep
with his knife to find you. He pulls you out
and yanks out your bones. One by one, he hollows
each bone out, whittling the longest one
into a flute. He presses his mouth against you.

CAROL BOLT

Carol Bolt has written more than twenty plays for the stage, including *Buffalo Jump, Gabe,* and *Red Emma.* Her award-winning thriller *One Night Stand* was made into a film directed by Allan King. She lives in Toronto with her husband, actor David Bolt, and their son Alexander.

Emma Goldman was twenty years old when she came to New York hoping to change the world. Red Emma, Queen of the Anarchists, *based loosely on her romantic autobiography* Living My Life, *follows the events leading up to a plot to assassinate the capitalist Henry Clay Frick.*

from *Red Emma*

Most exits. Emma sings.
If the world were fair and fine
I could be a heroine
I could fight the battles
I could win
It's second place in every race
With rules against the way I ran
But reading Russian novels,
Reading Russian novels
I find out I can
Be brave and noble, fine and sure
Self-sacrificing, pure.

Sonja
In *Crime and Punishment*
Became a prostitute
To help her family
Sonja
Agreed to pay that price
Could make that sacrifice
So why not me?
If the world were fair and fine
Lightning flashes in the sky
I would change the world
And I would fly
But flying with the wings of man

The victory is bittersweet
Reading Dostoevsky
Reading Dostoevsky
Going on the street
I know I have a heart of gold
I know I'm bought and sold.
Frick enters. Emma strikes a provocative pose.
She is endearingly naive.

EMMA Would you like a good time?

FRICK With you?

EMMA Well, yes, of course with me.

FRICK Would you like me to buy you a drink?

EMMA All right.

FRICK At Sach's? The anarchists' cafe?

EMMA Not there.

FRICK A young reactionary.

EMMA Somewhere else. We can walk . . .

FRICK You don't do this very often.

EMMA You haven't seen me.

FRICK I haven't seen you because you haven't been here.

EMMA I have a natural talent for it.

FRICK Perhaps.

EMMA How much I know shouldn't concern you. If I'm willing.

FRICK I do not give lessons.

EMMA I know what I'm doing. I know why I'm here. Try me.

FRICK You look very sweet, my dear. I'm sure you made your dress yourself.

EMMA And the price is right.

FRICK Of course it is.

EMMA If price is a consideration . . .

FRICK I don't believe you've done this before. You are a seamstress. Some kind of dressmaker. You found yourself short of money so you've gone on the street.

EMMA I am a courtesan.

FRICK This is your first night on the street . . .

EMMA Don't concern yourself with my experience. I'm very experienced.

FRICK How much money do you need?

EMMA Ten dollars.

FRICK Here. Take it.

EMMA *(A delaying tactic)* You don't want to argue? Over the price?

FRICK I don't want to discuss it at all.

EMMA Of course not.

FRICK   You're a professional.

EMMA   Of course.

FRICK   I want you to take the money and go home.

EMMA   Of course . . . go home?

FRICK   I will walk you to your door, young lady, to make sure you are not accosted in this neighbourhood.

EMMA   Thank you.

FRICK   Tell me, young lady, why do you need ten dollars?

EMMA   I have to buy a pistol.

FRICK   *(Urbane)* Oh? And why do you need a pistol?

They exit. Berkman enters to be met by Kreiderman and Parks, who enter from the opposite side.

BERKMAN   I want to see Henry Clay Frick

KREIDERMAN   Whom can I say is calling?

BERKMAN   What?

PARKS   Do you have a card?

BERKMAN   What? Oh, yes. I do.

PARKS   You sell insurance?

KREIDERMAN   That says employment. He's from an employment agency.

BERKMAN   I want to see Henry Clay Frick.

KREIDERMAN   We understand that Mr. . . . I can't read your name.

PARKS   It's Berkman.

KREIDERMAN   But does Mr. Frick want to see you?

BERKMAN   *(He draws his gun)* I want to see your hands up.

KREIDERMAN   Who are you?

BERKMAN   *(Very nervous)* I want to see your hands up . . . I want to see your hands flat on the table . . .

KREIDERMAN   *(Very nervous)* But you want to see Mr. Frick. One of us will have to get Mr. Frick.

BERKMAN   Don't move.

KREIDERMAN   Stay calm. Keep calm. Calm yourself.

Frick enters. He is the only one who seems calm.

FRICK   *(Behind Berkman)* Who are you?

BERKMAN   *(Wheeling to face him)* I want to see your hands up . . . I want your hands flat on the table.

FRICK   *(To Kreiderman and Parks who are moving in)* Get him out of here.

BERKMAN   *(Dodging wildly)* Get back. Get them out of here. Get your hands up. I'm going to shoot. I warned you.

KREIDERMAN   *(Frightened)* How far would you get, friend?

PARKS   Put the gun down, friend . . .

KREIDERMAN   This mill is under armed guard.

PARKS   You wouldn't get out of this office.

KREIDERMAN You'd never get away with it.
Frick is impatient. He moves towards Berkman. Berkman fires wildly. Frick falls.
PARKS *(Grabbing him)* Mr. Frick . . . You've shot Mr. Frick.
Parks tries to pull Berkman away. Berkman is trying to stab Frick's legs.
KREIDERMAN *(With Frick)* Are you all right, Mr. Frick?
Kreiderman helps Frick offstage. Parks pulls Berkman downstage.
BERKMAN You can let go of me, I am not a criminal. I will explain myself.
PARKS Not on your life, friend. You stay here till the guard gets back.
BERKMAN This was not a criminal act. This was a political assassination . . .
PARKS Sure it was. You might have killed the guy . . .
BERKMAN I've lost my glasses.
PARKS There's more than that coming to you.
BERKMAN Can you take my statement?
PARKS Jesus, statement!
BERKMAN Will you take this down, please. I want a record of my explanation.
PARKS You'll hear it in court, friend.
Emma and Fedya enter the courtroom.
EMMA Does it say in the newspapers they'll allow Sasha to have visitors?
FEDYA It says in the newspapers he is a mad dog. Visiting doesn't seem to be an issue.
EMMA They must let his family see him.
FEDYA If he had a family.
EMMA I can be his sister.
FEDYA Perhaps.
EMMA Like Louis Lingg's friend. When Lingg was confined, his friend visited him in prison. They embraced and with the kiss, Lingg received a capsule of nitro-glycerine. I could make a capsule and take it to Sasha. Sasha will want to commit suicide.
FEDYA Sasha?
EMMA I don't know why he hasn't killed himself already.
FEDYA Sasha?
EMMA He has tried to kill Frick and Frick is still alive. He has been captured by the forces of reaction. His protest is over.
FEDYA Maybe he's waiting till the newspapers publish his statement.
EMMA It could be a posthumous statement.
FEDYA I was joking, Emma.
EMMA You don't think he wants to live merely to see his statement in

the filthy capitalist press.

FEDYA I don't think he wants to commit suicide.

EMMA Why not?

FEDYA Would you?

EMMA Of course I would. And Sasha would. Any of us would die for what we believed in.

FEDYA If we had to.

BERKMAN I have a letter from Emma and Fedya. It is bitter. They say that because Frick did not die, the moral effect of the act will be less. There will not be so much propaganda value. They actually presume to reproach me with my failure to suicide. How am I to kill myself? By banging my head against the bars of my cell? By what right do they reproach me? By the right of revolutionary ethics, I suppose, and they are correct. Emma the girl. Fedya the twin. Emma and Fedya will have to forgive me. I did not think that I could live in prison, but I find I must.
Kreiderman enters, as Judge. Parks escorts Berkman to the podium/witness stand on the lower level.

KREIDERMAN Is it true that the prisoner wishes to conduct his own defence?

BERKMAN Yes sir.

KREIDERMAN *(To Parks)* He will need an interpreter.

PARKS Yes sir.

BERKMAN I . . .

PARKS I . . .

BERKMAN . . . address myself to the people.

PARKS . . . make a speech to all.

BERKMAN Some may wonder why I have declined a legal defence.

PARKS Some may think funny I say no to lawyer.

BERKMAN My reasons are twofold.

PARKS I say two things.

BERKMAN In the first place . . .

PARKS One thing.

BERKMAN I am an Anarchist.

PARKS I am an Anarchist.

BERKMAN I do not believe in man-made law designed to enslave and oppress humanity.

PARKS I say no lawyer can make up laws made up to tie up and sit down on men.

BERKMAN Secondly . . .

PARKS I say two things.

BERKMAN . . . an extraordinary phenomenon like an Attentat cannot be measured by the narrow standards of legality.

PARKS A funny thing like an Attentat is not like law.

BERKMAN It requires a view of the social background to be understood...

PARKS It depends where you come from. What you think.

BERKMAN The translation is inadequate.

KREIDERMAN We speak English in this court.

BERKMAN My English is very poor. But it's good enough to know he's not saying what I'm saying.

EMMA *(To Fedya)* I have to speak to Johann Most. He can help us.

KREIDERMAN Silence in the court.

FEDYA If he wanted to help he would be here.

KREIDERMAN There is a disruption in the court.

EMMA We have to ask him, Fedya. We have to try. Come on.
They exit.

BERKMAN I have a statement. It's impossible to understand my act against Frick unless you hear the statement.

PARKS We don't want to know why you did it. We want to see if you did it.

KREIDERMAN Whatever it is that he's saying, we've heard enough of it.

BERKMAN The removal of a tyrant is not merely justifiable, it is the highest duty of every true revolutionist. Human life is sacred and inviolate. But the killing of a tyrant, of an enemy of the people, is in no way to be considered the taking of a life. In truth, murder and Attentat are to me opposite terms. To remove a tyrant is an act of liberation, the giving of life and opportunity to an oppressed people.

KREIDERMAN Alexander Berkman. You have been found guilty of the attempted murder of Henry Clay Frick. And the attempted murder of Harry Parks. Of trespassing three times on the property of the Homestead Steel Mills and of trespassing in the office of Henry Clay Frick. I sentence you to twenty-one years in the Western Penitentiary at Pennsylvania.
They exit. Helen enters, followed by Emma and Fedya.

EMMA I must speak to Johann.

HELEN He isn't here.

EMMA I must ask him to help Sasha. They are railroading Sasha into prison.

HELEN Yes.

EMMA Have you heard about it, Helen? Sasha in prison. It's dreadful.

HELEN Go away, Emma.

EMMA Johann will help us.

HELEN Go and ask him then.

EMMA He was our teacher. Of course he'll help.

HELEN I suppose Sasha thinks that terrorism is part of Hannes' philosophy.

FEDYA Sasha made his bomb from Hannes' book.

HELEN You ignore him except when you need him. You make fun of him behind his back. Fedya calls him Johann Sausage, isn't that right?

FEDYA Sasha's bomb didn't go off. Either Sasha can't make bombs or Johann can't write books.

HELEN I don't care what you say any more. You can't hurt me, Fedya. Because I'm content.

FEDYA Because you're smug.

EMMA We are all anarchists together, are we not? We help each other.

HELEN I've told you Emma, Johann isn't here.

Most enters and begins to speak to a public meeting. Fedya and Emma become part of his audience. Helen joins him on the platform.

MOST The capitalist press cries out against the anarchist. They want our blood. Why? Because someone has made an attempt on the life of Henry Clay Frick. Alexander Berkman waves our banner and hides behind the name of anarchy but he is an inept, self-seeking bungler, with too much faith in a master plan that was ill-timed, ill-formed . . .

EMMA I demand proof of your insinuations against Alexander Berkman.

MOST This is a public meeting.

EMMA Proof.

MOST These people haven't come here to watch Emma Goldman in temperamental display.

EMMA They haven't come here to listen to lies.

MOST I am an anarchist. Alexander Berkman has attempted a murder. He claims that I inspired him . . .

EMMA Attentat!

MOST A fool calls me a murderer.

FEDYA I call you a sausage.

MOST Berkman was my student. You were all my students. Berkman doesn't learn very well. A young man with a toy pistol and more concern for himself than the worker's problems. Berkman has failed to do anything but find himself the centre of attention.

EMMA His intention was serious.

MOST He is a child.

EMMA It was not a toy gun.

MOST It was not the gun for the job.

EMMA It was a cheap revolver. He had no money. Did you give him money? Did you help him at all?

MOST Of course not.

EMMA Attentat!

MOST The Attentat is the act which captures the imagination of men and women everywhere. It makes everyone brave. It makes revolution possible. Has Berkman done this?

FEDYA   Have you?

MOST   Talk to the strikers at Homestead. Berkman tried to "save" those men but they do not understand him. They do not sympathize. They think Frick cheated him in business, perhaps. I have been in prison because of the things I believe in. Berkman makes my philosophy ludicrous.

FEDYA   Berkman is in prison now.

MOST   I denounce him as a self-seeking fool.

EMMA   I call you a coward and a traitor, Johann.

MOST   As you will.

EMMA   You taught me. You called for acts of violence. Sasha is the one of us who moved against the injustice of Homestead. Sasha acts and you deny everything. Every principle you hold important, you deny.

MOST   You are hysterical.

EMMA   When I met you, you asked me for an ardent friendship. Now you call it hysteria.

MOST   It is hysteria.

EMMA   You do not act. You are impotent.

MOST   I do not think of anarchy as some kind of springtime sexual rite.

FEDYA   Johann Wurst. Johann Sausage.

MOST   Berkman's mistress attacks me in the columns of my own newspaper. Because I talk about his stupidity. Because I tell the truth. Berkman was arrogant, opportunistic.

EMMA   Stop it, Johann!

MOST   Egotistical, pretentious.

EMMA   Stop it!

MOST   Self-indulgent.

Emma takes off her belt. She rushes at Most. The belt comes down on his back.

EMMA   Be bold. Be arrogant. I am sure you will be brave.

MOST   Emma!

EMMA   Who is not with me is against me!

MOST   Emma!

EMMA   I think for myself. I speak for myself, Johann!

Emma is exhausted. There is a long pause. Though it may not be possible to arrange exits, Emma and Fedya are alone.

FEDYA   Anarchy is a glorious political theory. We have proved it doesn't work.

EMMA   No.

FEDYA   We said an act against a tyrant would begin the revolution. We found we were wrong. We said that man was pure and fine . . .

EMMA   Man is pure and fine.

FEDYA   You are.

EMMA   I believe in freedom, the right to self-expression. Everyone's right to beautiful, radiant things.

FEDYA   You are pure and fine and gullible.

EMMA   *(Sings)*

I know I can show you wonders
I can paint the flags I fly

I know dreamers can build castles
I know castles can have banners
I know dreams are going to flash across the sky.

There are no countries
There are no kings
Only the people and all they can wish for
All of the beautiful radiant things.

I know I will do my living
In my future not your past
There are certain stirring speeches
There are drumbeats every morning
And the chance that things will start to move too fast.

There are no countries
There are no kings
Only the people and all they can wish for
All of the beautiful radiant things.

Blackout.

ROO BORSON

I attended UBC from 1975 to 1977, receiving an MFA in creative writing. My first book was published in 1977, and six others have followed, the last two being *The Transparence of November/Snow* with Kim Maltman, and *Intent, or the Weight of the World*. I currently live in Toronto.

I once ate two UBC cinnamon buns, entirely by myself, right before a class in Chinese literature. The cinnamon buns aren't the same anymore, and Buchanan isn't as homey as the old quarters, so what I miss most are the gardens: Nitobe, Rose, and the magnificent rhododendrons.

The Gift, for Robert Bringhurst

All day, lonely for my childhood, I've been picking up apples and tossing them down again. Rotten. The birches, the maples have lowered their red and yellow flags to half-mast, and now and then a bird rises up into the sky, the blackened silhouette of a hand-drawn angel.

Here is autumn. Though I know you've seen autumn for yourself, take it. I've wrapped it in a little of all that surrounds us, hoping you won't notice right away there can be nothing inside, nothing to claim or give.

Knowing you know this.

Now and then, like someone tuning a harp, the isolated sprinkle of rain against the cabin window.

The Transparence of November

The orchestra of the dark tangled field.
The moon holds the first note.

Silver-grey, the old barn leans a little,
just beginning to rise.

Since early autumn the poplars
have been racing one another
and are almost here.

Whatever small flowers
I may have mentioned in summer:
forget them.

Wild Horses

There are horses of sorrow that
never change their expressions,
their faces hang like shadows, as if
suspended from something bright,
bright horses whose shadows
these faces are, horses
that roamed like an ocean wave across the plains
and left them bare, and the sky tells nothing
of where they went, the sky is too bare.

The horses (the dark ones) stand now in a stable,
no one comes to release them,
each face framed in its stall
of beaten wood, wood marred by weather
and the flanks of these horses
that have been here too long, restless,
with nowhere to go.

Now and then riders come to ride them
over the plains, but their expressions do not change,
fixed in the fixed wind, though they are roving
over territory those others owned
when they lived here, they are saddled with riders
and their shadows, they are shadows.

GEORGE BOWERING

George Bowering was born in 1937 in Penticton, BC, and received his MA from UBC in 1963. He has received the Governor General's Award twice, in 1969 and 1980, for poetry and fiction respectively. He has written and edited over fifty books. His most recent novel was *Caprice* from Viking/Penguin 1987.

In 1986 Robert Kroetsch and I did a series of combined appearances at universities (Ottawa, Toronto, Geelong, etc.), speaking about the practice of writing. This little poem is, I hope, packed with clever suggestions about one of Kroetsch's most famous theoretical concerns. See his poem about a hockey goalie.

Endless Vees

Why, I said to Bob in Ottawa,
worry about origins?
We're here, aren't we?

Above the city this morning
endless vees of Canadas
pointing north. I guess it was north;
you can never tell in Ontario.

After we landed in Toronto
a brown rabbit scampered
over the grass, away from our 727.

I'm just on my way home.
Right now I'm flying over
the town where I was born.

The girl in the short skirt
with chubby legs is telling
seat 29F how much she loves
living in Ottawa at last.

ROBERT BRINGHURST

Robert Bringhurst published his first book of poems, *The Shipwright's Log*, in 1972, and his thirteenth, *Conversations with a Toad*, in 1987. He was an MFA student at UBC (never once attending a class) in 1973–5 and a visiting instructor of Creative Writing during 1975–7.

I was hired on one day's notice to take over Pat Lowther's teaching duties at UBC when she was murdered in 1975, and I stayed for two years. Towards the end of that period, I wrote Jacob Singing. *Its chief provocation was the impending birth, in a wrecked marriage, of my daughter Piper, but the dedication is to two of my students who taught me most during that time.*

Jacob Singing
For Roo Borson & Joseph Keller

What I am I have stolen.
I have climbed the mountain with nothing in my hand
except the mountain. I have spoken to the god
with nothing in my hand except my other hand.
One against the other, the smith against the wizard,
I have watched them. I have watched them
wrestle one another to the ground.
I have watched my body carry my head around
like a lamp, looking for light among the broken stones.

What I am I have stolen.
Even the ingrained web
in the outstretched palm of this body,
limping on oracle finger and thumb,
dragging a great weight, an arm or a tail
like the wake of a boat dragged over ground.
What I am I have stolen. Even my name.

My brother, I would touch you but these
are your hands. Yours, yours, though I call them
my own. My brother, I would hold your shoulders
but only the voice is mine. My brother,

the head is a hand that does not open
and the face is full of claws.

What I am I have stolen.
These mountains which were never mine
year after year have remade me.
I have seen the sky colored with laughter.
I have seen the rocks between the withered water
and the quaking light. I have climbed the mountain
with nothing in my hand except the handholds
as I came upon them, leaving my hands behind.

I have eaten the sun, it is my muscle,
eaten the moon, it is my bone.
I have listened to the wind, whipped
in the heart's cup, slap and whistle in the vein.

My father said:
the wood will crawl into the apple,
the root will crawl into the petal,
the limb will crawl into the sepal
and hide.
But the fruit has eaten the tree, has eaten the flower.
The body which is flower and fruit together
has swallowed its mother, root and stem.
The lungs are leaves and mine are golden.

I have seen the crow carry the moon
against the mountain.
I have seen the sky crawl under a stone.

I have seen my daughter
carried on the land's shoulder.
I have seen the wind change
color above her.
I have lain in silence, my mouth to the ground.

I have seen the light drop
like a wagon-sprag in the crisp stubble.
I have seen the moon's wheels
bounce through the frozen ruts
and chirp against the pebbles.
I have seen the metal angels
clatter up and down.

I have seen the flushed ewes
churn in the pen and the picked rams boil
against the hazel. I have seen them
strip the poplar, scrub the buckeye bare.
I have seen the mixed flocks
flow through the scented hills like braided oil.
I who never moved as they do.
I have climbed the mountain
one foot up and one hoof down.

The breath is a bone the flesh comes loose around.

Flower and fruit together.
But this other, this other
who is always in the body,
his lungs in the belly and
his head between the thighs.
O his arms go backward,
his legs go side to side.

My son, you have asked for a blessing. I give you
this blessing. I tell you,

the eye will flow out of the socket like water,
the ear will gore like a horn
and the tongue like another,
the sailor will stay in his house near the harbor,
the laborer, blinkered and fed, will stay at his labor,
the soldier will soldier,
the lawyer will smile like milk and swill liquor,
the judge will glide like a snake keeping pace with the
    horses,
the man with gay eyes will like chocolate,
the roebuck will wrestle the air and you will hear music,
the rancher will prosper,
the wolf will walk out of your hand and his teeth will
    be shining.

But this one, my grandson, the young one,
this one will steal the eye and the tooth
of the mountain. This one will ride with his dogs
through the galleries of vision. This one will move
among the rain-worn shapes of men
with faces in his hands and the fingers writhing.

This one will slide his spade through the sea
and come away carrying wheat and linen.
This one, the young one, will steal
the sun and the moon,
the eye and the tooth of the mountain.
This one, the young one, how tall,
shaking hands and trading armor
with his dark-eyed brother.

My son, you must do more
than listen to the angel; you must wrestle him.
And one thing further: he must be there.
The muscle in the air, the taut light
hinged in the milky gristle
and the swollen dark, the smell
like the smell of a cornered animal.

I have oiled these stones to sharpen the wind.
I have come or I have gone, I have forgotten.
I hold what I hold
in this chiasma of the hands.

I have set my ear against the stone
and heard it twirling.
I have set my teeth against the stone
and someone said he heard it singing.

FRANK DAVEY

Frank Davey studied at UBC from 1957 to 1963 and edited *Tish* from 1961 to 1963. The poetry manuscript he submitted as his MA thesis was published as *Bridge Force* by Contact Press in 1965. His most recent books are *The Abbotsford Guide to India* (Porcépic 1986) and *Reading Canadian Reading* (Turnstone 1988). He is Carl F. Klinck Professor of Canadian Literature at the University of Western Ontario.

"How and Why John Loves Mary" was written in an olive grove near Monte Carlo during a moment of profound nostalgia for Canada.

How and Why John Loves Mary: Thirty-Seven Variations on Half of a Theme by Margaret Atwood

1. After finally getting Mary to go to bed with him, John can't face having to talk up, ask out and make friends with another woman.

2. John thinks Mary looks partly like Samantha Fox. He wants to associate himself publicly with Samantha.

3. In the dentist's waiting room John had read that older sisters make the best wives and Mary, who lives next door, not only has 5 younger brothers & sisters, but is a widely-trusted babysitter.

4. John feels sorry for Mary, who is blonde and very kind. Men are always taking advantage of her.

5. John knows Mary is his destiny. She is the girl he knocked up after the highschool graduation dance.

6. John wants to be popular.

7. Mary is always cheerful, & says "not to worry" whenever John is arrested for passing bad cheques or ejaculates prematurely.

8. Mary used to be the mistress of John's talkative friend Peter.

9. One of John & Mary is coloured, & John's family is outspokenly racist.

10. Each time John tries to break up with Mary she threatens to kill herself.

11. John's parents yelled at each other a lot & split up when he was fifteen; Mary's parents still serve Sunday dinners & often tell Mary to invite John.

12. Mary is a high-strung but talented dancer & needs someone like John to shelter her from the demands of life.

13. John & Mary are half-brother & half-sister & live in a poor farm family & after milking the 3 cows & hoeing the bean patch are too tired to get out & meet people.

14. Mary is the only teenage girl at the Pentecostal church.

15. Mary plays semi-pro basketball, & is an exhausting & stupendous lay.

16. Mary has had six nervous breakdowns, & John has felt mature and responsible each time he has driven her to hospital.

17. Mary has published seven novels. John, an obscure poet, wants to publicly associate himself with circulating literature.

18. John's mother has arthritis & difficulty getting up in the mornings; Mary organizes the Student Council bake sales & is vice-president of the 4H Club.

19. Mary's father beats her.

20. Mary wears unusual clothes, drinks more than most women, has lived with a man who held up gas-bars; John feels his life to date has been unimportant.

21. John's father shovels clay at the brick plant; Mary's father owns a milk store.

22. Mary was born out of wedlock, has had two abortions, has been picked up for shoplifting & John feels he'd be a cad to reject her.

23. Mary's real name is Marie-Ange; John is from Alberta.

24. Mary has two little blonde girls whom John loves very much.

25. John sees himself as a rebel, & Mary is his cousin.

26. Mary never smiles. She has long dark hair, dresses in black & has no friends.

27. Mary is one of those girls John has heard about who look cute when they're angry. She keeps yelling at John that she loves him.

28. Mary is Chinese, Japanese or Philippino & no North American girl has ever smiled at John.

29. Mary was once the lover of John's younger sister.

30. John is very devout, & when he thinks of Mary thinks of a near-goddess holding a small male child.

31. John (or Mary) studies painting and does nude modelling at the art school, while Mary (or John) is in computer science.

32. John hadn't really noticed Mary before their being marooned together by war, avalanche, shipwreck and an otherwise bad script.

33. Mary has been to Europe.

34. Mary's grandfather was murdered after a notorious stock swindle. The murder was never solved.

35. Mary is an insurance agent, a school teacher, a waitress, a driving instructor, a bank teller, or a typesetter, & like many men in late-capitalist societies John finds service industries reassuring.

36. John collects antique razors.

37. John, typical of his class, age and gender, identifies with Mary's innumerable unique qualities.

DON DICKINSON

Don Dickinson was born in 1947 in Saskatchewan. After attending university there he travelled for seven years to various parts of the world, working mainly as a labourer. His first book of short stories was *Fighting the Upstream* (Oberon 1987). Other stories have been anthologized in Canada and overseas. He presently lives with his wife and three children in Lillooet, BC, where he is at work on a novel and another collection of stories.

From 1977 to 1979 I was enrolled in the graduate writing program at UBC. For an ex-jock, ex-labourer whose only contact with other writers had been those solitary hours spent in books, what a joy it was for me to meet and talk with people who shared my passion for our craft and art. To the writers I met at that time and to my instructors I owe a debt of gratitude. They welcomed me as one of their own.

Hogarth's Arrangement

Crushed by a divorce which left him rattling around an apartment festooned with hand-crayoned greeting cards sent by his estranged children, Hogarth for several weeks drank large amounts of scotch and toyed with the idea of suicide. His ex-wife, a banker, had been beautiful, intelligent, and unfaithful, and whenever he thought of her in the arms of her Swiss lover—the two of them whispering mutual funds and international exchange rates—he felt the urge either to suck his thumb or hammer the walls with a chair. In retrospect it seemed inevitable that his wife should've outgrown him, but that she should've taken his two daughters—to Europe, he'd last heard—opened up holes in him where none existed before. At the advertising agency where he worked, instead of writing his usual copy he scribbled long lists of items such as razor blades, ropes, revolvers, and various brands of cleaning fluids. When at last he was found on a window ledge seven stories above the street, his superiors referred him to a company psychologist, a bluff, belligerently unorthodox man named Burdock who pointed out that suicide was a waste of insurance premiums.

"They never pay off on a diver," Dr. Burdock advised him. Large and athletic, the psychologist sported a virile bald head and a handlebar moustache that gave him the air of a retired sergeant-major whose parade-ground voice was meant to inspire confidence. "Dive, and your equity dives with you," the psychologist said.

Dr. Burdock's office was crowded with potted rubber trees, so that on each visit Hogarth had to slash his way through them to the couch, as if he were on safari. The psychologist prescribed sedatives, and showed his patient videotapes of poverty and natural disasters, a technique he called 'guerrilla therapy.'

"Guerrilla therapy puts your petty problems into global perspective," he told Hogarth.

"I like the alliteration," Hogarth admitted, "but my petty problems look pretty big to me. Maybe I lack compassion."

"Look at me when you speak," the psychologist said. "And come out from behind that plant."

"If I could hug my kids once a week or so," Hogarth offered, "if I could be sure they were all right, I think things would start to fall into place for me."

"Hey," the doctor rubbed his bald head. "Let's be frank. The kids are a ploy, a red herring. The flaw resides in you, Hogarth. It's hiding in there, sniping at your natural feelings. Let's launch an assault on that flaw, Hogarth; let's blast that flaw the hell out of there."

"I'm not sure I want to do any blasting." Hogarth sipped from his hip flask and studied the rubber trees. He wished he were smaller, living under their leaves.

After two months of therapy, Hogarth found he was drinking more. "I'm up to a bottle a day," he confided. "These films about starving kids have got me worried. They make me wonder if my own kids are eating okay. And the storms in the South Pacific we looked at scare the hell out of me because I can't be sure my kids aren't on a cruise somewhere. I don't even dare think about orphans or nuclear war. No, no," he said. "I don't want to dive any more, but I don't want to do much of anything else, either. I appreciate what you've done, but these sessions are costing me a bundle. I'd like to send my kids some presents, but I've had to move out of my apartment and I'm down to macaroni and cheese four days a week and I can't seem to get the hang of this global perspective thing."

The psychologist pondered for several minutes. "All right," he said finally. "Okay. I've got a strategy for this, something different." He started to hum. Or at least Hogarth thought he started to hum. He couldn't be sure: lately he saw and heard things through a caramel-coloured haze. Right now, for instance, he watched Dr. Burdock turn the colour of peanut brittle, tug at his moustache, execute a somersault and swing among the rubber trees like a gymnast on the flying rings.

Hogarth could hear himself sweat.

Dr. Burdock cartwheeled into the chair behind his desk. "The company pays me a retainer," he panted, "but this'll cost you extra. Two hundred bucks a session."

Hogarth lifted his flask and swallowed big. "I can't afford that." He closed his eyes. When he opened them again, Burdock was standing on his head on the window sill.

"Look," the psychologist said. "I'm going out on a limb here. The association could have my ass for this, but what the hell. There are ethical considerations."

"Ethics are okay with me," Hogarth said. "It's money that's the problem."

Burdock flipped off the windowsill and landed lightly on his feet. "Okay. Fine. We'll work around that." He brushed off his hands. "We'll waive the usual—the couch sessions, the workshops, the testing. We'll even skip the two weeks' orientation program. Why go retail when we can cut the frills? For a flat eight hundred, I'll send you right to the warehouse."

"Eight hundred dollars?"

"Seven-fifty then—but I'm dying. Seven-fifty and you're killing me."

"Maybe I could squeeze that out of my bank card," Hogarth said. He had a hard time following Burdock, who appeared to be whipping off some sort of handspring over the furniture. "What else would I have to do?"

"Take this," Burdock ordered, one-handedly pulling a business card from his breast pocket. "This will get you into the warehouse. After that you're on your own."

"Warehouse?" The card carried an address, but no phone number. "But how will I . . ."

"Whoa," Burdock hollered, as he landed in the splits on the desk top. "The card's in your hand. Let the warehouse boys take a crack at this. Friday night, nine o'clock. Oh, and take your passport."

"Am I going somewhere?"

"We're all going somewhere," Burdock said cryptically.

Hogarth reeled and tried to focus on the card in his hand. "I'm—I'm not sure how you managed to do this."

"I'm a professional, son," Burdock wheezed. "Pay my receptionist on the way out."

The warehouse was a low cinderblock building on a desolate road near the airport, and after Hogarth paid the cab driver and knocked on a side door he was rushed inside by a sweating bearded man in greasy green coveralls. "You're late, so let's move," the bearded man said as he snatched Hogarth's card. "We're always up to our necks on Fridays." He turned and led Hogarth through the warehouse, a miniature city of boxes stacked on wooden pallets. Whirring electric forklifts hurtled between the aisles at rush-hour speed, and one of them actually nudged Hogarth and sent him sprawling to the concrete floor.

"I broke my bottle," he told the bearded man, who pulled him to his feet.

The bearded man tugged at Hogarth's arm. "I'm crying you a river," he said.

They hurried past several workers in green coveralls who frantically threw styrofoam packing into wooden crates, while others nailed the lids shut. Now and then a jet roared by overhead, and it seemed to Hogarth that the ceiling rattled. Around a corner the bearded man pushed him into a tiny office that was cluttered with order forms and invoices. A few dilapidated travel posters were stapled to the walls: a castle on the Rhine, a Mexican beach, a koala bear chewing eucalyptus leaves.

"Sit down," the bearded man said. He poked his head out the door. "Sonia!"

A skinny, curly-haired person in green coveralls walked in. She went to a computer terminal and started to type furiously.

"This the last one of Burdock's?"

"Yeah." The bearded man checked his clipboard. "Drinker, divorced, two kids in Europe."

Hogarth felt dizzy. "Isn't that privileged information?" he wondered. "Look—" he tried to stand up, but found he couldn't. "I feel dizzy, I must've bumped my head on something. Do you have any scotch?"

Sonia looked at the bearded man and they both laughed. "God I love these guys," Sonia said. "Call me crazy, but I love these seven hundred buck specials."

"I paid seventy-fifty."

"Oh ho," Sonia said, leaving the computer. "The late flight. Here, have a drink." She handed him a glass of something and Hogarth gulped it down.

"What late flight?" he said—or thought he did. There was no caramel-coloured haze this time, but he certainly felt dizzy. The bearded man seemed to be going through his pockets, and wasn't Sonia rolling up his sleeve? Wasn't that a hypodermic syringe she was poking into his arm?

"Is that a needle?" Hogarth asked.

"Questions, questions," Sonia said. "God, I love these guys."

Hogarth drifted in his chair. The room bobbed up and down, and when he looked at his arm he found it'd become an oar. He was in a liferaft at sea. "Holy cow," he said. "I sure hope none of those storms comes this way." Something—a wave perhaps—picked up his liferaft and pushed it gently forward. A piece of seaweed drifted by his face.

"I don't see why we check them through on Friday nights," the seaweed said. "We're always up to our necks on Fridays. We're stacked up on the runways on Fridays."

"It's all those specials," a second voice said.

"There's too many of them alright." The seaweed's voice was shot through with bubbles.

"Lift his feet," the other voice said faintly. "That's it. Don't you just love these guys?"

A thin wall of green water rose in front of Hogarth's eyes. It's like looking through leaves, he thought, before he felt himself being hoisted into the sky.

When the plane landed in London, the rain was falling like a beaded curtain, but Hogarth didn't notice. In fact, he couldn't remember disembarking or going through customs.

"But I guess I'm just wound up," he told the driver of the delivery van. "The last time I was in London was fourteen years ago with my wife, on our honeymoon. It's quite a coincidence to be back here after all these years. I don't know why, but I feel really rested, and being back in London brings back happy memories."

The van driver grunted and shoved some clothes at him. "We're running a bit behind, mate," he said, "You'll 'ave ter change in the back as we go along." The driver was squat-muscled and wore a cloth cap and a navy pea jacket which fitted him snugly in the shoulders. "And don't drop them little styrofoam fings all over the carpet," he said as he started the engine. "I don't know what it is wiv you specials, you're always leaving them little styrofoam fings layin' about."

The van sped through the red-roofed suburbs and into the city proper. Through the narrow window in the back, Hogarth saw the grey wet streets and the sluggish waters of the Thames. Hunched over the wheel, the driver careened through narrow streets of grim apartment blocks, where dustbins leaned sadly in the rain, above the graffiti-slashed stone walls. ANARCHY RULES, Hogarth read. The raincoat he put on was tattered and smelled of mildew and rubber-tree leaves.

"Another coincidence," he told the driver. "The rubber tree smell, I mean."

"Bit of a bump, 'ere," the driver said. "'ang on." He wrestled the van around a sharp turn and geared down for a hill. "Nigel will wonder where we've got to," he said. At the top of the hill he stopped, rushed to the rear of the van and flung open the doors. "Right mate, out, out. I 'aven't got all day. You're not my only delivery, you know. Bleedin late flights," he said.

Stumbling onto a cobbled square, Hogarth squinted into the rain. He recognized the low, stolid outline of the Tower of London, and the span of Tower Bridge beyond. In front of him, on the puddled cobblestones, a sharp-faced man with no legs sat on a tin trunk.

"This is Nigel," the driver said. "Nigel, this one's the special—the divorced drinker wiv the two kids."

"'E's late," Nigel said. His trousers had been shortened and stitched over the stumps of his legs. " 'Ow's he going to learn it proper? 'E don't know nuffing about it."

The driver jumped back into the van. "Come off it, Nigel—do your usual." To Hogarth he said: "You'll be alright wiv Nigel. Just don't say nuffing about 'is legs."

"Wait a minute," Hogarth said. "Is this part of the deal?" He pointed at Nigel. "He looks familiar. Didn't he used to have one leg, fourteen years ago?"

"I wouldn't know mate." The driver threw in the clutch and madly shifted gears. "I'll be along to collect you when it's over."

"When what's over?" Hogarth wanted to know. But the driver waved and roared off.

The legless man had scooted off the tin trunk. He rode a little platform on wheels, like a skateboard. "The buses stop 'ere," he said, "so we'd best get a move on before they come."

"Hey," Hogarth said. "I remember now. You used to have one leg, and you wrapped yourself up in a burlap bag and lots of rope, and you tried to escape from it. And there was another guy here—what did he do?—I remember now. He was a chain-swallower, that was it. A tall guy with a beard in a ratty old raincoat. Helen—that's my wife, well my ex-wife actually—gave you guys a ten-pound note. She cried that night, did you know that? She thought you guys must be terribly poor. Do you remember her? Slim, brunette, good legs and a smokey kind of look in her eyes—"

"You specials," Nigel said disgustedly. "I don't know why I bovver, really I don't." He was busy unpacking the trunk, carefully laying out a burlap bag, coils of rope, and twenty feet of steel-linked chain.

"Holy cow," Hogarth said. "This is great. The same act with the burlap bag and everything. God, this brings back a lot of memories." Memories flooded Hogarth's mind so quickly he had to rub his forehead. "For instance, after we watched you guys fourteen years ago, I took Helen to St. Paul's Cathedral and we whispered to each other around the dome. I mean the dome is so perfectly constructed you can hear someone whispering fifty yards away. God, I thought I'd forgotten this. Helen stood on one side of the dome and I on the other and we whispered how we loved each other and how we'd be true to each other even if we had only one leg and had to make a living escaping from burlap bags. And then on the way out Helen got her shoes wet so I carried her to the tube station, down the escalator and everything. And later that night we made love and—I can't be certain about this of course—but I think our eldest daughter was conceived in a bed-and-breakfast on Earl's Court Road."

Nigel skateboarded around Hogarth's feet, spreading out the burlap bag. "Let's get on wiv it, mate," he said. " 'And us that chain, will yer?"

"Yeah, sure." Hogarth wiped his face with his sleeve. "Everything sort of started here with your act," he went on. "Of course the chain-swallowing was the big finale. No offence, but that guy who did the chain-swallowing number really got the crowd going."

"I know all about it," Nigel said. "Tall bloke wiv a beard and a tattered mac—right?"

"That's right." Hogarth looked down at himself: the raincoat he wore was tattered. He rubbed his bristled chin. "Hey, I get it," he said slowly. He was really sweating now. "I get it. We're doing some sort of rerun here, aren't we? That's okay, I can go along with that. All I need is a drink, okay?" He felt thirsty all of a sudden. "Sure, maybe a double, and we'll jump right into this."

"You specials," Nigel said. "Always going on about your bottles or your needles or your pills. Well, I've got news for you, mate. If you want to see your two kids proper, you've got to see them just the way a bloke in a tattered mac would. And that means swallowing the bleedin chain. No drinks, no nuffing. Just the chain. That's the arrangement, see. Look at youself, mate. You're a stranger then, aren't you? You're just a bloke in a tattered mac, that's all. That's the arrangement. Now, now, don't start. We don't 'ave time for that sort of carry-on. All the blubbering in the world won't change fings, will it then? There, that's better."

Nigel picked up the chain and dangled it above his own mouth. "Now, the trick is to open your froat up and keep it that way. You want to control what we call your gag reflex. Ovverwise you'll frow up, and that puts your audience off. 'Ere, you give it a go. That's it, tip your 'ead back, and let it slide straight down, like spaghetti. That's the ticket. You'll do alright."

"Something's happening here," Hogarth said. "I can see you and hear you clearly enough but I feel kind of shaky." The chain he held rattled uncontrollably.

"That's just nerves, that is." Nigel lifted his sharp face and listened as the first growl of engines echoed along the sidestreets. "'Ere come the buses," he said.

To Hogarth his daughters looked exceptionally healthy and mature, poised as they were under their umbrellas, in the crowd of tourists that included a horde of noisy uniformed school children and a knot of Japanese businessmen, in surgical masks for the cold. No hunger had shrunken his daughters' cheeks, no tragedy had scarred their foreheads or twisted their limbs. From what he could see—as he lowered the chain link by link into his stomach—his daughters had adjusted to their new lives much better than he had. Charlene, his eldest, now wore eye make-up, and laughed delightedly when he shook himself to settle the chilly chain in his innards. Emily, the youngest, smiled shyly, her teeth a testament to several years of orthodontics.

"Of course, I'm just talking about superficialities here," Hogarth told

Dr. Burdock later. "I mean what've mascara and no cavities got to do with anything? You have to look inside, don't you? God, I can't believe how cliché that sounds, but you know what I mean. Kids are pretty resilient, aren't they? Holy cow, another cliché. Well, it doesn't matter. The point is I got the whole chain down, I mean all the way down, because that was the arrangement after all, wasn't it? And when I turned to bow to the crowd while Nigel scooted around with his hat to collect the money, guess what I saw? Well, you probably already know this, but I saw Helen and the Swiss guy sharing an umbrella. She still looked beautiful and everything, but they were sharing an umbrella and my two girls were standing close to them, all of them laughing and then Charlene and Emily pestered the Swiss guy—their father, I guess you'd call him, and he dug into his pocket for a ten-pound note to put in Nigel's hat. That's pretty significant, I guess, but that's not the point. The real point is the way they pestered him made me think they were the kind of family that would probably visit St. Paul's Cathedral and whisper to each other around the dome. That's the kind of family they looked like to me.

Hey, didn't you used to have a lot of rubber trees in here?"

GLEN DOWNIE

Glen Downie was born in Winnipeg and graduated from the UBC Master's program in Creative Writing in 1980. He also holds a UBC degree in Social Work and currently works with cancer patients and their families in Vancouver. As a member of the Vancouver Industrial Writers' Union, he contributed to the work writing anthology *Shop Talk* (Pulp Press 1985) and the audio tape *Split Shift* (VIWU/Fraser Union 1989). His other publications include *The Blessing* (Pierian Press 1986), *An X-Ray of Longing* (Polestar Press 1987), and *Heartland* (Mosaic Press 1990).

"Night Light" was written out of the same nocturnal impulse that yielded my photographic studies of the Empress Hotel and the Ace Tattoo Parlour. "The Wish for a New Hand" was inspired by a style of Japanese calligraphy called grass script; the quotations are from Walt Whitman's Leaves of Grass. *"Worker Classification: Material Handler" derives its title from the terminology once used in the government's employment centres to describe unskilled warehouse labourers.*

Night Light

This is in honour of tired places, the old city's
moonscape streets that hum
expectantly. Where nothing is,
something is

waiting through the thin
hours, burning bright
for thieves. And always in the window,
the earnest apology of small
business: SORRY WE'RE CLOSED.
They know in their hearts
desolation

is bait. Bus depot. All-night
laundromat. Every common surface
worn, the greasy feel of things
at once essential and despised. But don't grieve.
These run-down worlds

read history in their sleep. They shine
as stages, having seen how the news turns to litter
between events. Where else can the resurrection happen
but here among the dead? Look. Even now
he stumbles in, wrapped in a green shroud
of trash bags, having slept it off
in a dumpster but still dying
for a drink.

The Wish for a New Hand

. . . one that snakes down the page like threads of wet black hair
left behind in the bath. A free hand,
very delicate, alive. It might take

a lifetime not to master but to serve, so many
fixed notions must first uncramp in old fingers, there are
so many tiny bones in the hand you have now.
And the musculature of the arm, the barbed wire
network of nerves knotting up in the brain

must be loosened, become as tendrils
from the heart, unfurling into
green song. Listen

to the whisper of the grass, and accept
dictation from each of the sun's innumerable children.
This grass is very dark, as the wish for
a new hand is a dark wish
to have names for the nameless inklings, *dark to come*
from under the faint red roofs of mouths.

Worker Classification: Material Handler

We work in the world you and I handling
coal chandeliers razor blades hamburger
whatever they ask us to carry sort shovel
A box of glass eyes or tear gas cartridges
Mud silk marshmallows guns potatoes
One man handles diamonds another garbage
Chalk or cheese we come home stained
skinned stinking

I have wiped the asses of grown men
You've smashed up old batteries
the splashed acid eats at your jeans
Do we work because we're hungry
for substance Is it even lonelier
for mathematicians

Pat cuts off a cancerous breast
The day's work has begun How does it feel
when a severed breast slips off into your hand
Catherine dresses up stillborns in the morgue
so parents can say goodbye
The babies are cold and pale as congealed fat
I ask her How do you handle a dead baby

This is the way the world works: you are building a house
as I tear it down We need each other
Hands must be full of something
Who knows how we came to be here
We are groping like the newly blind
for anything familiar
for anything at all

DARYL DUKE

A graduate in 1950 of UBC and Earle Birney's Creative Writing course, Daryl Duke's Emmy Award-winning career spans a wide range of feature films and television productions. The director of *The Thorn Birds, Taipan, I Heard the Owl Call My Name, The Silent Partner, Payday,* and many other films, his work has taken him throughout Canada and the United States, as well as overseas to Europe, the Middle East, and Asia.

In 1986, I concluded a thirteen-month spell of working in China on the film Taipan. *China, perhaps more than any other country I have filmed in, made me think long and hard about Canada, the country I call home. On my return, with the free trade debate under way, Laurier LaPierre asked me to contribute a piece of personal reflections to the book he titled* If You Love This Country.

A Battlefield of Dreams

Late fall, near the mouth of the Pearl River in China. The engines of the boat we are on have suddenly been slowed, then stopped. There is a strange hush. No wind, no waves, no birds. And, incredibly for China, no other boats: no freight barges, no fishermen, no rowers ferrying river passengers with their bicycles from one shore to the next.

There is just heavy fog. Glassy river water. A world without motion.

We have been shooting for over a month. The heat, the humidity, the long hours, the constant script changes, the incredible and mounting problems of shooting in China have slowed each person. There is now no sightseeing on the daily river route to our location. Most sleep. One or two half-heartedly read yesterday's *Herald Tribune* or an old *Newsweek*. Some just stare, neither looking forward to the day ahead, nor dreading it. The day is just there. Another day to be got through on the long climb to finish the movie and go home.

I get up and climb the companionway to the pilot house. The five-man Chinese crew is gathered there. They are smoking and talking quietly, looking out at the dense fog. They laugh when they see me. They know no matter how the film company may rant, the gods who deliver fog upon the Pearl River have decreed our day's shooting will not begin on time.

I smile back at the crew. All of them think filmmakers are crazy. But they have got to know us. And now they are very paternal, even protective, about us and our strange needs and ways.

One crew member picks up a large thermos. I nod, then thank him in Chinese and take from him a cup of blisteringly strong tea.

I step outside the pilot house.

The boat sits alone in a grey dream. I hear the crew debate something behind me, their voices raised for a moment, then falling silent.

I look but see nothing through the fog. I know that the rice fields are but two or three hundred feet away. That there are water buffalo nudging around the gates of the irrigation ditches. That on the water nearby a family—women, children, uncles, grandfathers, husbands, nieces—all will be living in the incredibly cramped cabin of some small freight barge full of stone, or coal, or scrap metal, or mountains of bamboo poles.

I hear a crew member clear his throat. Loud, uninhibited. A tremendous hawking sound. And then a noisy spit over the side and our realm of grey is silent once more.

China. I am in China, all right.

Then suddenly, like a breeze hitting one's face, I think of Canada.

Fifteen hours back through time. In Vancouver it is still yesterday. Three in the afternoon. People are still shopping, banking, taking coffee breaks. On the Lions Gate Bridge, the rush hour hasn't begun.

In Toronto evening is coming on. Dinners are just being cooked. Knowlton Nash hasn't done his news yet. Yesterday. In Canada it is yesterday.

I think of Vancouver sitting at the end of time. The wet November air filling the cedars, the winter underbrush still and dying, molecule by molecule. I think of those endless inlets of the British Columbia coast, without people on their shores, or vessels upon their waters. I think of my mother up that coast when she was young, pinning magazine pictures of John Barrymore and Clark Gable on the walls of a rough wooden cabin by the sea. I think of the exiles, of the immigrants, and of the slow filling up of those empty forests.

I hear the noise of an engine. I am back in China. The fog is separating, opening above to blue sky, and astern to another one of the boats the film company has chartered. This one is larger than the one we are on. This one carries extras for today's crowd scenes. Dozens and dozens of members of the Chinese Army. All young men. Teenagers really. At the location they will be put in 1830s wardrobe. Now they hang out of every space laughing, smoking, calling out to one another. Their boat slowly glides up beside us.

The skipper of our boat comes out beside me. He shouts to the other crew. There is an excitable, rather heated discussion of which I understand not a word.

My thoughts of Canada are torn from my mind. Our engines start up again. I am back in the job. Back in the today of China. On the Pearl River. A long way from home....

They say the beginning of mental health is to know who you are and where you are. I wonder how far for any of us that knowledge has progressed? And how far with such knowledge has this country, Canada, progressed?

Gabriel García Márquez wrote in *The Solitude of Latin America*: "The interpretation of our reality through patterns not our own serves only to make us ever more unknown, ever less free, ever more solitary." I read these words and think of Canada, struggling still to be born. Struggling perhaps more than ever to breathe in an atmosphere perhaps more than ever not its own.

This I do know. Ownership is programming. If free trade changes the ownership of Canada then free trade will change how we speak to one another and what we know of ourselves. In the end the hand that holds the shares holds the pen, the camera, the printing press, and the TV station.

Today, before free trade, how few films are made about who and what we are. And how few get distributed and shown in theatres of our own. How few TV shows speak of anything of substance. The CBC gropes for a philosophy like a blind beggar with a tin cup. The NFB is voiceless across the land. And our private broadcasters, those balletomanes of the bottom line, have for a generation made their yearly buying trips to Los Angeles, filling their TV schedules to the very maximum with the outpourings of Columbia Pictures, Paramount, Lorimar, Screen Gems, Universal. And this before the carte blanche of free trade.

Ownership is programming. Behind the boardroom door, does anyone worry about "patterns not our own"?

I return each time to Canada sensing how fragile is the knowledge we have of ourselves. In how few hands that knowledge lies. How slender the opportunity to speak. Who are we? Will anyone ever know? In the end will there be anyone to care?

This notion of Canada. How would I set it down for my sons? Or leave it in a bottle flung in the sea? Or in a capsule tumbling through the darkness of space?

For each of us what an indistinct scenario. For my sons I could but piece together a few stories told to me as a child before the illness of relatives, divorce, and time itself scattered the family and I looked around to find all the elderly gone. But for a few fragments the book of dreams and struggle was closed.

Chance brought my first relatives, my great-grandparents, to Canada. They were Quakers and in the mid-nineteenth century they found it was more than time to get out of England. They landed on the docks of Montreal and immediately discovered all their luggage—their heirlooms, paintings, furniture, everything—had been stolen.

Later, it was chance as well which moved the family west from the farms of southern Ontario. A great uncle spurned in love as a young man took the new railroad to British Columbia. By the turn of the century all his brothers had joined him. As a family they were educated, interesting, passionate. And all nearly unemployable. Especially in Vancouver still pulling stumps and clearing land for houses. One was an amateur astronomer. He went to Hawaii, met Jack London and Queen Liliukalani. I think he could have happily spent the rest of his life in the tropics. Another wrote nature stories for children and spent his days collecting insects and endlessly detailing the flora and fauna of the coast.

So many stories. My mother yearning to become an actress. Succeeding and playing Desdemona and Ophelia. But seldom with a cent of income. And my uncle playing Othello and Richard II, having to write musical reviews in order to get free tickets to operas and plays touring through early Vancouver.

How to bring alive for my sons a Canada before the CBC, the National Film Board, the Canada Council, Telefilm? Before any support for the arts? A Canada more than simply a picture of the Queen on the post office wall? How to tell them we long ago opted for a Canada that was distinct and not for sale?

The modern Japanese poet Okamota Jun wrote:

And on the battlefield
Of quiet dreams,
Amid the swirling cannon smoke
A tiny gentleness,
A flower that does not wither.

For any of us in the arts it seems the battlefield has not changed. We work to protect the quiet dreams of those who went before us and today especially of those who shall come after.

KENNETH DYBA

Born in Nordegg, Alberta, Kenneth Dyba received a BA from UBC and has worked as a journalist, radio announcer, arts reviewer, and dramaturge. He has directed many stage productions across Canada. His novels include *Sister Roxy, Lucifer & Lucinda*, and *The Long (and Glorious) Weekend of Raymond (and Bingo) Oblongh*. His stage plays include *The Sun Runner, Teaser!*, and *Lilly, Alta*. He has also written a biography of well-known Canadian stage director Betty Mitchell. He lives in Toronto where he works as a radio archivist for the CBC.

"The River" is from my novel-in-progress Gabe. *This novel had its true genesis in Jake Zilber's Creative Writing class at UBC. Those quiet, gentle one-on-one sessions with Jake in his book-bombarded office on campus gave me my first shattering glimpses into the intricacies of writing. With him I began to track the phantom coiling in the white spaces between the lines. Now, years later, I am still trying to touch this phantom, this allusive heart.*

The River

When the geese fly south their cry fills the night. The people of the forest fear this cry. When the holy birds fly, filling the air with the rush of their passage, soon the giant of winter will step from the sky and the white silence will fall. The giant will bring long suffering and pain and death. Even now the river's face is frosting, the fish gone. The animals sleep or hide from the coming white giant.

The Leader dreamlike, at the tip of the long V. Undulating through the vast night sky. The cold air quivers, shifts around *Great Green Eyes* and his flying brothers. Violet, rose and emerald—the sky is not black to those that fly. Or to one who stays below. And darker then emerald, darker than the darkest green moss that covers the earth below, the flying Leader's ancient eyes. These eyes scan the familiar cluster of tarpaper shacks which dot the river's bank like withered blackberries.

Great Green Eyes surges higher, then dips low. This will be his last flight from the coming white silence. It has been told in stories and in forest dreams. Now his eyes find the one tarpaper shack, set apart from others. Great wings drumming, the bird's urgent honking echoes to earth.

Beside the frosted river, inside the small shack, the boy kneels before his father. The boy's eyes are closed. He hears the flying geese. He was born to their wild cry. He has lived with their cry. Soon, with *Great Green Eyes* and his brothers, he will follow the river to the south.

He has always thought the geese sound like the strange barking he has heard in dreams. The barking of the sun's guardian dogs of fire which his father has told him about many times. The people of the forest have always made fun of him because they say this strange barking noise of the geese has for all time been known by his name—the *gabriel ratchet*.

And his mother, when he would cry as a baby and not stop, she would both scold and comfort him and tell him he was her very own strange-flying goose and this is why, because of his crying, he was named Gabriel. Or, his father would laugh, saying maybe this boy was more like a flying sun-puppy, all the time *barking-barking* and nipping the sun's flaming heels.

Sometimes his father would suddenly stop laughing, would turn away and would whisper, "—or like the dogs who have lost their home and must now howl at the floor of the sky."

There is a shuffling sound in the shack. Very soft. Feet sliding across the worn linoleum. Gabriel opens his eyes; green as dark moss in spring rain. He sees his mother turning from the small wooden chest. She is scooping out a handful of colours. She passes them to his father. Brothers and sisters are ringed in the candlelight around his father, their dark eyes on Gabriel. Only his best-loved sister is not looking at him.

Thelma stares out the small front window. Gabriel knows she can see the flying geese. He can see them too, because he is still kneeling on the floor and can look out the window and up at the sky beaded with September's stars. Gabriel knows Thelma is hearing the geese, not as his other brothers and sisters hear them now, but as she heard them last night when the two of them, brother and sister, made their vow near the waterfall, in pillars of spray. Under the cedar and to the barking night music of the geese as their great wings darkened the eye of the moon and the face of the river.

Thelma turns from the window. She looks down at Gabriel and he hopes that some day he may capture her dark face and hold it forever in the wood he carves. Her face is like running water in the spring. It is never still, it is always flowing, sun and shadow, her long hair a stream of shining black, her eyes now silvered with wavering light from the candle. She is for him, always, a part of this place he will soon leave: the aroma of black earth, sweet pine, boughs of cedar. He has never been able to carve her face in wood as it is carved in his heart.

Thelma tries to smile at her brother. She has to look away, at their father.

Gabriel's father hears the wild geese too. He knows that in the morning his son will leave the forest, like the holy birds. He knows too it will be the last journey for *Great Green Eyes*. Until the time when it is meant for the great one to be born once more from the moon's ice and the sun's fire.

Gabriel's father opens his hand slowly and the string of colours his wife passed to him spills forth. He loops the colours over Gabriel's head and around his neck. He places his hands on his son's shoulders. Gabriel can feel the deep quiver in his father's fingers, like the tails of many hummingbirds.

"These beads are our people. The brown beads, these are our men. The red—our women. The children—yellow. The children to come are the spaces between. You Gabriel, are the green one, *here*. The blue thread is the river that runs beside our home and the sky above our heads and both the river and the sky are in our hearts. If you wear these beads, always, you will fly in the sky, back to us like the geese. You will come home to our river."

He pushes hard on Gabriel's shoulders. The hummingbirds deep within grow still. Gabriel feels the blue river swelling, swelling, beginning to rush, a ceaseless roar, rushing through his father's body, his limbs, breaking from his father's fingertips and pouring into the beads, bright now against his chest. He hears the baying of the geese, a cry that engulfs the distant thunder of the waterfall, that rolls to the far north hills, tangling over trees and shawling the earth.

Gabriel lifts his head, long neck arching up from the beads—brown— red—yellow—and the-spaces-between. A vein twitches under his right eye. The one bead, *here*, dark gleaming moss between brown and red, green as his eyes which are now misted, as if the river's spray has entered the house. His father's face is fading, the river rising to claim it. His mother's. His brothers' and sisters'. And Thelma's face. The river takes them all.

His father's fingers push even harder, deeper, into Gabriel's shoulders, aging fingers willing a gift within—Gabriel feeling the warming of his own blood, the trickling, the rippling—a river rushing—feathers deep within wakening, budding from beneath his skin, breaking from his shoulders—the great wings of legends blossoming—lifting him, his heart, flying him free.

The geese cry.

DAVID EVANIER

David Evanier received the Aga Khan Fiction Prize in 1975 and his work was included in *Best American Short Stories 1980*. He was a senior editor of *The Paris Review*. He taught at Douglas College in New Westminster from 1970 to 1973 and founded and edited the literary magazine, *Event*. He has been a Fellow at the MacDowell Colony, Yaddo, and the Wurlitzer Foundation. His books include *The Swinging Headhunter*, *The One-Star Jew*, and, forthcoming, *Red Love*, which will be published by Scribner's in the winter of 1990.

"Rockefeller Center" was, of course, written in panic, in crisis, in desperation. Up until a few years ago, I found this to be one of the most fruitful states of mind for writing. It is still one good way to write, but not the only way for me. The theme? The plight of the writer who can do nothing well in life but write.

Rockefeller Center

PART ONE

I

I'm sitting in Rockefeller Center with my passport and five bucks. Today I'm seeing the two people I respect most in the world: David Goldstein, a poet, and Danny O'Brien, a playwright. Since getting back to New York from Vancouver seven years ago, I've been working up to it. Recently I began to run into them around the city, and we set it up: David for lunch, Danny for a drink at 5 p.m. I try not to take any libriums, for they put the people I love at a distance.

Now that David has moved into the neighborhood where I live, I've been bumping into him frequently. Every goddam time, I've been holding an ice cream cone. The first time it happened, I casually let it drip into the ground and my clothes as if it didn't exist. I don't know what to say when I see him—one afternoon I began by shouting, "Good morning, David." Realizing it was 2:30 p.m., I tried again as if nothing had been said: "Hello—Mr. Man Who Has Everything!" Bad, very bad. My wife, Naomi, was carrying a copy of the magazine David edits. He winced at the sight of it.

(I visited my father in Brooklyn yesterday, and realized just how much David has influenced me over the years. My early library is at my father's house and there were David's first book, the books of poets and novelists he had talked to me about, his reviews—all threaded through my possessions.)

Then a few weeks ago, high on two libriums, I ran into Danny, the other old friend, fifteen years older than I. "I thought you were in Canada!" he said. I had written him desperate letters from Vancouver, and in his own tight situation he could not answer them. His guilt about it ended the friendship.

Now he was delighted with my ebullient manner, and started talking about his situation with his wife as if we had never fallen apart. "She thinks she has her rights, she wants to fuck all the time, what am I gonna do?" It is great to hear his Bronx twang again, to have him confiding in me, to see he has come through his own crisis. He is writing again. "But after forty it became hard to remember things," he says. That comment frightens me. I know Danny never feels like a writer when he isn't writing. He doesn't feel like he's anything at all.

I told him about the difficulty I was having getting my book published, and he asked me to send it to him. I asked him about David, who is Danny's boss at the magazine. Danny is a senior editor there. "You know, Michael, David just doesn't know how to wield power. He hates his job. After all these years he doesn't realize there are the fuckers and the fucked. The week before his vacation, these throbbing veins in his forehead were about to burst. I was afraid he wasn't going to make it."

Danny held up his hand: let's meet, have lunch, call me. His wife came up on her bicycle. In the autumn sunlight, I waved goodbye to my radiant old friend, who could, as they say, charm a rattlesnake.

When I got home, the libriums lost their hold. When I could concentrate, I read his new play. I saw he was still alive—had found his way again.

The doctor in Vancouver had prescribed librium for my despair. This was in 1970. It is really remarkable. Librium is my friend. It puts you in that state of mind where, if someone approaches you and says, "I'm going to chop your arm off," you say, even before he finishes the sentence, "Sure, that's okay, go ahead."

And you think: "Sure, that's okay; I only need one arm anyway."

II

I am sitting in Rockefeller Center amid the waving flags of all nations, clutching my passport and wanting to escape but I only have five dollars. I had a fight with Naomi last night that lasted until morning. I am tired and drained.

The old man beside me is tall and brittle, with a cane. He holds envelopes on his lap labeled "Will and Other Contracts," "Cemetery Plan," "Obituary Directory." He shuffles away with short steps when I peek over his shoulder.

All over the city, the old men, rich and poor, sit in restaurants or on benches, smoking cigars, and then they are gone. My father, holding on, reads in the Donnell Public Library. I glimpsed him there this morning, good Jew of the Book, his head down over what he read, killing time. From afar I watched him, for I was in a hurry and did not want him to see me. I darted behind the card catalogue when he stood up and walked slowly to the door.

III

Since returning to New York, I have managed to speak on the phone once a year to David Goldstein. David is a known poet, fifty-four years old, and he has a powerful job. He does not use the job to help himself get ahead. He does not really get ahead. He does not promote himself in any way.

He wears J. Press suits. He is sober, short and elegant. He has a passionate artist face of twenty. His appearance, his speech, have a leanness, a concision. When he speaks my name, I have no doubt that he remains my friend.

I often tell myself I must learn to understand jazz before it is too late. I listen to a saxophonist and think: He is going all the way, he is playing his guts out. But I'm not sure I'm getting all he is giving. I am moved by David's writing. I think it is singular. But I do not understand it completely, and am embarrassed to ask. So I do not speak to him more than once a year—and now I will be seeing him for lunch at last. This raises questions about how many times I will speak to him in his—and my—lifetime.

IV

Lunchtime arrives and I eat Chinese with David. He is President of the International Da Villa Foundation for the Arts and the editor of their important magazine. What enormous power David has! But his life is in his work as a poet. So, when he gestures around his gold-rimmed office with contempt, referring to "this shit," I can only shake my head in commiseration.

This luncheon is laden with intensity for me. I didn't want to take the librium, but ten minutes before lunch I took three of my wife's red tranquilizers. As a consequence, I see David through layers of Venetian blinds. I strive, despite this hassle, to keep my cool. David has chunks of armor so thick that he does not notice my discomfort; or perhaps he does.

V

I have had a beer with lunch and am flying when I leave David. I pop over to the sex emporium on Eighth Avenue and look at the girls in their cages. I enter a cage. I put in four quarters and the curtain ascends. A blonde naked girl faces me behind a plane of glass and gestures for me to pick up the phone. "What's your name?" "Chip," I craftily reply. "What's yours?"

"Sweet Susan."

She says, "Let's see what you got to show me."

"I want to see what you've got," I reply.

She bares her twat and wriggles around in a circle, shaking her ass at me. I avert my glance, which seems to be the only polite thing to do. The curtain descends.

VI

The porno film at the emporium features a lady who takes three pricks in her mouth at once.

VII

It is only 3 p.m. I have two hours until I see Danny. I pick up my mail. I have applied for two prestigious writing grants. I am happy to see that I have won the first, which gives me free space; a well-lit, furnished studio to work in for a year. I have been turned down by the second, which included a $45,000 prize. I read the accompanying letter in some, but not total, amazement. The chairman of the committee is furious that "someone like yourself" has even applied for the award. He writes: "Let me ask you just one question: Why were you born?"

I am crushed by this. I call Naomi to scream at her about it, and forget to mention the grant I have received.

VIII

I return to Rockefeller Center and read the *Times*. There is a story about a Bowery hotel charging ten cents more a day for guests not sent by the Shelter. While I sit on the bench reading the story, a man comes along and starts hosing down the benches adjoining mine. He doesn't seem to be averting the hose from me. "I'm a paying guest," I hear myself say to him.

IX

My hands are shaking. Well, it is time to take a librium. I do. Soon I feel I own the world. An actress from college days in Boston sees me at the bench and stops. The kind that never gets an acting role. She says, "The friends I run into who are hitting their late thirties are so burnt out now. But you're not. You look alive."

X

How long can Naomi go on supporting me? I walk to the corner and call Myron Mishagoss, the editor of a meat magazine, *Jewish Brisket*. I have held a string of Jewish jobs since getting back to New York, each more futile than the last. Myron has an opening for assistant editor. If he hires me I will kill myself. "Oh *God*," I say "would I appreciate the job, Myron. Thank you for considering me, Myron, and thank you for returning my call."

XI

My wife is an empathetic person. Once when we were jogging in Central Park, a man along the path ahead of us stumbled. I heard Naomi say, "Oops."

XII

In murder or horror films, a drowned victim's corpse rises to the top of the water, confounding the murderer.

Sometimes I see Naomi's first husband, Henri, in my dreams. His body rises to the water's surface.

Although he was not drowned, or murdered, this is my dream.

XIII

Another poet I admire (and who admired David Goldstein) is Charles Reznikoff. I kept wanting to take the poetry of Reznikoff and the plays of Shakespeare and read them aloud with Naomi on the Brooklyn Bridge.

This struck me as a sign of aging—something that my best high school teachers might have done—idealistic, good men and women who would always be only admirers of the work of others.

Naomi and I did try to read Reznikoff's work aloud to each other on the Brooklyn Bridge. But we could not hear each other through the shafts of wind.

XIV

Parasites my age plague me these days. As Naomi and I were walking from the bridge, we were talking of one: Glory Flowers, his falseness, his florid manner. My teeth were grinding in memory of him. I turned to my left and Glory was talking to us, holding the bicycle he had drifted up on. How long had he been there? "Oh, yes," he said, "there you are! Oh my, to think! To think! How are you doing, my dear friend?" Glory said to me, handing Naomi a petunia he plucked from the bicycle's arm. "Are you really well? It was just today I was—after some time of French art— thinking of writers and artists who have passed away this year. There have been so very many." Glory stopped, paused, lowered his head, and silently contemplated those who had passed away. He raised his head. "The ranks have thinned indeed. It has never been easy, but I see you are still here, still amongst us, grandly ploughing ahead, and so let us laugh ..." Glory laughed. "And let us have a grand time. I'm sure we will, but oh, I must trundle off for the concert. Goodbye, my dear friends."

PART TWO

I

3:30 at the bench. The winds flutter the flags. Bright faces of tourists, roller skating to organ music. I read "Mr. 1–2–5 Street" in the *Amsterdam News*:

> *Det. Frank Waldron* is looking for the killer of (*Littlebit*) *Carrie Davis*, 45, who was found nude and spread-eagle in the rear of 43–01 22nd St . . . *John Wooden*, 33 of Jamaica, was arrested by *Det. Ronnie Singleton* of the 103 Squad and charged with posing as a medical doctor who explored the organs of a score of women . . . *Red Randolph* had a special birthday party at his Quintessence night spot . . . *Det. John Copeland* is looking for the owner of a Brooklyn record shop who fled after killing two stickup men, *Errol King* and *Adrian Smith* . . . The first annual *Arthur Bramwell Mapp Scholarship Luncheon* will take place Nov. 2 at the Marriott's Essex House. . . . *Charlene Tripplett*, 42, was molested and thrown off the roof at *Showman's Cafe*. . . . *Steven McNair*, 17, ran into the arms of his brother *Marty*, after he was shot twice . . . *Carlos Bailey* will not forget the Sunday morning dance at a Brooklyn basement club Sunday morning but he will attend the funeral of the dancing partner, Louis Cuthgort . . . *William Hilliard* was reported suffering from a broken arm and thrown in a cell at the Federal prison. . . . Remember your mother, grandmother and aunt. . . . Dazzling *Bessie Dudley* creates the most exquisite hats in her 125th street store. . . . *Subway Jimmy* said the girl was not chasing him when that car crashed into *Nat's Bar* and shot it up . . . *Derek Adams* was arrested and charged with the fatal iron-pipe beating of *Isaac Gordon* on Blake Avenue. . . . *Birtie Pilgrim* will have a bangup birthday party at *Paris Blue* on Saturday. . . . *David Thomas*, an alleged pimp, is accused of mutilating *Rose Medina*, 24, and dumping her at a Bronx hospital. . . . *Earlene Glenn* was honored as the Mother of the Year by the Senior Citizens of Wilson Major Harris Center. . . . *Sister Glen* said her spiritual awakening will renew faith in every man and woman and put a halt to financing huge auditoriums which detract the worshipper's attention from God. Call 722–4900, if interested . . . *Kathleen Lewis* 23, was murdered in the rear of a vacant building and left with her clothing removed below the waist. . . . *Justice Maurice Grey* enjoys looking at New York in the evenings admiring its picturesque beauty. . . .

II

In Vancouver in 1971, I parked the car in the Emory College parking lot, and staggered out into the sun. One of my students, Roger Browning—

headband, ponytail, in his thirties with a wife, kids and hash on a farm—waved. He was my favorite (at night in the pub after class, he said, "Man, in the long run the headband just doesn't make that much difference, you know?"). Close enough in age almost to be rivals, we usually circled around each other. Now I walked toward him, standing at the back of his beat-up truck.

"Are you okay?" he said.

"No."

I paused. "Naomi's husband committed suicide last night."

He tilted his flask toward me. I drank. He took a swig.

We stood together. I drank one more, and he said, "Anything I can do. . . ." I walked toward the campus.

III

Naomi and I met in Vancouver. She trembled when I held her. She had a haunting, Mona Lisa beauty. She'd been raised on the Dick and Jane reader. I'd been raised on the Holocaust.

We sat in her parents' riverfront home and her mother intoned, "A faggot was once a little piece of wood for kindling . . . gay was such a beautiful word. They have taken them away from us. And intermarriage: it's just like linking a human being with some animal."

Naomi told me of the custom of sewing up the pajama legs of newlyweds. "We did that," she said. "They also put rocks in the hub cabs to make noise when we drove off."

"What are hub caps?"

She roared with laughter. "Did you teeter-totter as a child?"

"I didn't have a childhood," I answered.

IV

In the kitchen of the Lenny Bruce Memorial Church in Greenwich Village, where I lived in the church tower, Lizzie, black as coal, said to the not-so-young man, flower in his lapel:

"Don't you tarry, Nigger Charles, hear? You know, Nigger Charles, I do believe you are *gettin' through*. Hah hah," she snorted. "Yes, you are gettin' through, ain't you Nigger Charles?"

"Shut your mouth," said Nigger Charles. "I'm a librarian and you know it." He sipped his yogurt.

"Martin Luther King, he say we are all gettin' through—you, too, Nigger Charles. Flossie Lewis, she call me the other day and say, "Lizzie baby, I am gettin' through. My agent call me and says, 'Flossie, I finally got you a start in a tee-vee commercial. Even though you are a nigger. In a Doctor Pepper jingle! How do you like that?'"

"Well! Nigger Charles, you listening? Flossie's all excited and then I don't hear from her and one day I sees a TV commercial for Doctor Pepper.

And sure enough! Sure enough! Hah-hahhhhh. There's Flossie! Flossie made it. This nice coupla white kids grinnin' and clean and carryin' on and a nigger maid holdin' a bottle of Doctor Pepper. Yes sir! There's Flossie, gettin' through, really gettin' through. HAH HAH HAHHHHH."

Lizzie danced around the floor and clapped Nigger Charles on the back. "You is gettin' through and Flossie—Flossie is gettin' through and I—I—is—what am I doin', Nigger Charles?"

"Now really Lizzie—"

"HAH HAHHH. Baby, I is—really—gettin' through!"

V

Our psychiatrist, Casper Eichner, is a German string bean in his thirties: a child prodigy. Giggles, twines his legs around each other in delight. He told us the other day:

"Naomi, Michael didn't kill Henri. And neither did you."

Walking out into the night with this faint praise.

The Nazis didn't finish Henri off in the camp for Dutch nationals. Neither did the Soviets.

VI

Every day after work Naomi presses herself back against the glass waiting-station wall, waiting for the train to come by and nearly hit her. "A charge of adrenalin," she calls it. "For the minute of life, fear, whatever you want to call it."

VII

I had tossed myself across the continent in 1970. I sat in my boarding house in Vancouver eating cheese crackers and drinking rum while the reformed hooker upstairs tried on new stockings. "I can hear you pouring your liquor," she said to me. "A lonely sound."

Naomi sat in her house with her boring life, listening to the Beatles.

Before I met Naomi, I saw Henri's first wife, Susan, in the library where she worked. Black leather dress, a cold, beautiful blonde, looking for a new victim.

"I thought everything was over," Naomi said. "Now with you, every day is exciting, an adventure.

"You gave me back my life."

VIII

4:15 p.m. I walk toward the bar where I will meet Danny. A guy in a raincoat holds up his hands in dismay. "Do you see that couple? I've been following them for a half-hour." He points to a boy and girl walking half a block ahead of us. "They're together, but they haven't talked to each other or looked at each other once. Come on, join me. We'll walk together.

You'll see." Just as he says this, the couple turn to each other and say something.

I comment, "Look, they're talking now."

The guy in the raincoat is furious. He shakes his umbrella in the air. "Now they talk to each other. *Now!* I swear to you on my mother's grave they haven't said a word to each other in thirty minutes."

The couple turn around and look at him, frightened. "*Now* they talk, *now*." They start to walk quickly, then run down the street.

IX

I was working as a typist in 1965 at the Da Villa Foundation when I first met David and Danny. David found me reading Allen Ginsberg's *Kaddish* on my lunch break and lent me Delmore Schwartz's *Shenandoah* and *Vaudeville for a Princess*. In those days I pretended a world-weariness to impress David, staying up all night writing in my rented room on West 113th Street. I didn't know then how hard it really would be—not to write, but to survive as a writer. David, poet of the city streets, the harbor and the bridge, has done it. He first struck me with his attitude toward writing: just do it. Or get off the pot. Don't expect anything for it. Don't want anything. Get a job. Get a family. Do it. Before you die.

X

The stranger came up to us on a freezing night when we were waiting for the bus on a deserted street off Times Square. He told Naomi and me to persevere in the realms of art he was sure we were involved in. He was rotund and jolly, an actor in his fifties. "You know," he said, "when you are young and the center, you're filled with yourselves and your quest for art. As you get a little older, you find it harder and harder to hang on to the feeling that *you* matter, that the artist you are matters."

He waved, and disappeared around the block.

XI

There was a little lump on Naomi's breast. On the night before going into the hospital, she said, "My eye is twitching. My eye twitches. I lose my uterus. I lose my breast."

In bed, she said, "This is the last time I come to you with two breasts."

"It doesn't matter."

"But they are nice," she said.

Before she fell asleep, she opened her eyes and said, "I feel I've come home to you."

The little lump was benign, and Naomi came home intact.

XII

On my way to Danny, I see a limousine drive up to the curb and deposit two young children, a boy and a girl. "Hi Daddy! Hi Daddy!" they call and throw themselves into the arms of a bald, affluent, banker-type in his fifties—a type I detest without reason, foreknowledge or forethought.

I stop, and look.

Let the fucking tears fall.

They'd be a pain in the ass anyway, day by day.

XIII

"I cannot have children, Michael," she said from the start.

XIV

A black is entertaining the crowd with *bons mots*. He eyeballs me as I pass through the circle. "I'll bet you blow a mean sax," he says. The crowd roars.

XV

Henri was a pharmacist. He had been a medical student in Holland, nearing his M.D. The Nazis used him as a doctor in the camp. The Soviets didn't. But when he came to Canada, his credits weren't recognized. How many times do you start over? At 52, he worked in a drug store. (The town movie house had recently turned to porn, and was running a film called *The Fabulous Bastard from Chicago*.)

The Indian psychiatrist did something that he had promised Naomi he would not do. He told Henri that Naomi had moved out of the house because she was in love with another man.

A pharmacist has no problem. Henri swallowed the pills. He must have been very, very tired. But now it was over.

XVI

Danny O'Brien is drinking wine as he talks to me. He is tall and wiry, a freckled handsome Irish face. My old friend, with his Chaucer and Blake, his aphorisms, his bifocals when he reads, his fine plays. But Danny only writes every few years. "My little play," he refers to the Pulitzer winner, and nothing I can say will retrieve it from the dead for him. It is over. Completed two years ago. To acclaim. He now quotes to me verbatim the one hostile notice it received. And he is full of schemes, defending his turf at Da Villa, where he hates to waste his days.

"What would you do at home?" I ask.

"Drink." He laughs.

"Did it ever help you to write?"

"Never. Alcohol is shit, Mike."

Since I mailed him my book, which is about a pastrami-eating contest in Brooklyn, he has been trying to help me get it published. "You know I felt bad when I called you and told you that your book had been turned down," he said.

"Why?"

"Well . . ." he pauses. "You said 'Shit'."

I laugh. "What would you have said in the same situation? You're my friend. Who else can I say it to?"

"I know . . . !"

He tells me what my book is about. "Well really, you know, it's about fucking: those who fuck and those who get fucked."

We leave the restaurant and walk along the Minnesota Strip on Eighth Avenue to the subway. "Hey, look at that, Oh, you beautiful thing." He points across the street, where at a considerable distance a pudgy woman in her fifties, wearing a blonde wig, black slacks and boots, and a black shirt, is walking. Alongside her, tagging slightly behind, is a toothless old man wearing a baggy coat and overlarge shoes without heels. "Let's follow them. Do you want to?"

Danny zips across the street. I try to keep up with him. As we walk, he reshapes his face into a toothless grimace and says breathlessly, "Wait a little, honey. You're so beautiful. I'll be good to ya. Gimme a chance. I'm an old man."

Danny lopes along and we are almost directly behind them now. "She's wearing him out. He'll have a stroke before he gets to her room." He laughs. "He's falling behind. He can't keep up. 'Oh you beautiful adorable creature. Let me hold you'."

The woman turns and looks at us suspiciously. She slows up. Danny and I fall back. "Let's see where she takes him. Jesus, she's still walking. She's going to bury him on the street. 'Let me touch one of your lovely breasts. That's all I ask.'

" 'Faster. Walk faster, buster.'

" 'I just need a little warmth in my old age. I ain't got much time left, ya know. I'll do anything ya want'."

Danny is whooping, hanging on to them and not letting go. "I swear she's not going to leave anything of him before she gets through."

Danny reverts to the old man's toothless voice, blowing out his cheeks. "Ah honey, you do something crazy to me."

" 'Shut up and keep walking, you old fart.'

" 'Sure, sure, anything you say, you're a lady and that's the stuff I like. It's a privilege to be beside you, honey. I ain't got nobody in this whole wide world 'cept you, won't you make me a little bit happy? I'll pay you good, anything I got is yours, you drive me crazy with that red lipstick and that beautiful hair.'

The couple round the corner at 57th Street. Danny starts to follow them, looks at me. "Fuck it," he says, and laughs. "We'll get your book published, Mike."

We part at the subway. What can I do for Danny?

The day is over.

XVII

I am surrounded by sacred Jews: some of them Irish, or dead. I swear they are everywhere, imploring me, supporting, helping, pushing at me with their committed selves. There is Naomi. There is David. There is Danny. And there was my black friend, Smitty, who stood at the building door on West 40th Street as I ran from my studio after a night of writing. Down the street at 2 a.m. in the morning, Smitty watching under the bright moon or pelting rain until I safely reached the subway's entrance.

Smitty and Pete had worked as guards and porters in the building for twenty-five years. They framed an entrance. Their round bellies, they said, almost met each other across the two doors. It wasn't true.

I arrived there at night, after the office job. One day Smitty told me that his son had been shot in the head a year before and found dead on the East River Drive on the morning of the first day of his first job. Probably shot "by some cracker," Smitty said. And "before he had a chance to scuffle up the ladder." When the police came to his home, he said, they warned him he had better sit down. He said, "No, I'm a man." When they told him, his head hit the floor first.

He needed to talk. "If I don't see anyone for hours, I just get to trifling," he said. He saved things so that he could give them away, even a shoelace: "There's a time someone might need one—*bad*."

He described the way he would get his wife to go to a movie or show. If he would suggest it outright, she would turn him down, because of the expense. So he would say, "Hey, let's just take a little walk." Then they would pass by a theater and he would look at the marquee casually: "Say, what's that playing over there? Maybe we should have a closer look at that? What do you say?" He showed me the facial expression he used on his wife: eyes wide with innocence, surprise at the theater in front of him, discovery. "What do you think—maybe we should take a peek inside?" And he winked at me.

I was away from the studio over summer vacation. When I returned, I saw only Pete standing at the entrance to the building.

He said, "Didn't you know? Smitty died."

Pete was waiting for me when I left at midnight. "I got to talk to somebody about him, but who? That man worked himself to exhaustion for his family. On his day off I'd see him sneaking in here at two or three a.m. 'Smitty, go home,' I'd tell him. 'I promised the fellow I'd clean his office,' he'd say.

"He was so melancholic, I tried to cheer him up. Ever since his son died. Smitty never got over that. I wouldn't be able to find him. I would look everywhere, and then there he would be, a bottle beside him, sitting on the stairs, his head cradled in his hands, crying. The man could not pull himself together. 'Smitty,' I said, 'you got to go on.' He just sat there, bent over, his head in his arms, shaking his head." Pete paused. "At the funeral home, his stomach was shrunken to nothing."

XVIII

Rockefeller Center is like a cruise or an airplane flight. Where you can fuck endlessly as you have never fucked before, not knowing the beating of the heart of the woman under you or over you, not caring, not being cared for. And when you are finished, you are both discarded refuse. The sixties. Put it on a tee shirt.

I lie beside Naomi and listen to her beating heart and know nothing can replace that heart in my love. An earned love. Walking among the parched old couples in Brighton Beach where they dance together as if on stilts in the area of concrete surrounded by a wire fence, dancing to rinky-dink music, I know that this is my love: Durante, Cantor, Coney Island love. The old kind, which has been replaced by no other.

XIX

At 6 a.m. the next morning I rise and dump all the libriums out of the bottle into the toilet.

Good riddance.

By 9 a.m. I am on the roof, greeting the birds with a song in my heart, a martini at my lips.

MARYA FIAMENGO

Born in Vancouver in 1926. Received my MA from UBC in 1967. I am a nationalist and a feminist in that order. The country, given the present government, may not survive; women will. I have published six books of poetry, the most recent being *Patience after Compline* in 1989.

I remember Earle Birney as a man of great intellectual generosity as a poet, as a teacher, and as a friend. He nourished the imaginative spark in whichever unlikely place he found it. As a teacher he was remarkable for his tact, tolerance, and empathy with the work of students. As a poet there are few better. "White Linen Remembered" is an elegaic tribute to my parents and their native Yugoslavia, where my family supported Marshall Tito's Partisans.

White Linen Remembered
"Tamo daleko ..."

I

Codes to existence.

If all manner of things
are to be well,
are to be well remembered,
as flowers are codes, birds
alphabets to existence

Then childhood
is white linen. White linen
cross stitched with crimson. With
petals. Flowers abstracted.

Gardens are roses. Carnations
and chamomile. Rosemary.
The grass sprinkled with thyme.
Border fragrance. Lavender.
The scent fond. Remembering.

Soft speech. Strangers
framed in doorways.
The custom of courtesy.
Wine served. The Best.
In the Sunday glass.

My father present
in absence. Counterpoint
of names which nourish
the folklore of fishing,
fables of origin. Namu.
Mostar. River's Inlet
Vis. Seymour Narrows
Sarajevo. Hecate Strait.

Hecate. Goddess
of crossings. Shadows.
We left behind in an
abandoned convent. Haunted
by ghosts of misplaced nuns.

Friends come. In the early
grace of the day's time. Large
corded men. Civil with
laughter. Welcome the dower
white linen of olive dark
women.

Sunlight on stone. Leeside
we shelter. Catch at confidences.
The harbour at Hvar. Olive
and lemon grove. Tapestry
of shared affection. Komiža.
ancestral fig tree. Prophetic
Niš. Skull tower. Ohrid.
Angelic fresco.

II

The Lime Tree

I pause. Bemused by traffic.
On a prosperous thoroughfare. Stand
in a shop. Listen to the simmer

of shoppers. Shopkeeper's talk.

Hear the familiar. The language.
Dialect maternal
accent paternal
content inimical.

Unwilling the ear records
faction. Small mean
hate. Malice of region
erupts in the spittle of failed
fascists. Love of commerce
not kindred. The remaining
rancid rampart of the blessed:
The Croatian Bourgeoisie.

Hint of contempt
in the price of purchase
black grapes green olives.
Hommage to Dalmatia
not Uštashi madness.

Accidental as pleasure. A lime
tree planted. Grown for fidelity.
Love of the allusive. Fitful
years later. Learn it sacred.
Sacred in Serbia.

Expansive with summer
the leaves fill the garden
face the salt
of the sea. Acknowledge
Eastern approaches to history.
The hard red star. Resistance.

The silt of iron settles
in the mouth of the river.
Olive dark the women,
ceremony of stitches
finished. Wither.

My father vatic traverses
the straits of narrowed
passage. My mother

elemental dissolves
into sea mist. The red
star rides on the tide
elegaic.

MICHAEL FINLAY

Michael Finlay received his MA in creative writing in 1972. His poems, short stories, and translations have appeared in a variety of journals and in *The Harpo Scrolls* (Sono Nis Press 1970). He has worked as a newspaper reporter and editor and is currently a producer-correspondent for CBC Radio in Toronto.

"Somewhere East" was conceived while reading Albert Speer's memoirs on a bus in Quebec about a year after the War Measures Act had been imposed. In the intervening years, some things have changed, some have remained the same. But as Harpo Marx often said: ". . . . ."

Somewhere East

Somewhere east of Ste. Thérèse,
The bus warms like an animal
Chased across plains
Where only ice grows.
Eyes surround, glare
Like the memory
Of a muzzle flash
And the breath
Of every passenger
Heaves slowly,
Waves trying to scale
Something
When there is no beach.
One by one,
Pages of politics
Turn in my hands.
(Limousines roll
Through the streets
Of Sarajevo).

None can say who will cross
And when there is no crossing
There is the best frontier
Or none at all.
(A new chancellor
Is proclaimed).

Three soldiers
From the Van Doos,
Two nuns,
Acadians still moving,
They have reasons:
The nuns to shop
In Montréal;
The gunmen to work
In the backyards
Of ministers;
The Acadians to push on.
(Something moves
Across the Yalu).

The language makes me fear
I will be discovered.
Behind their eyes
Is the knowledge
Of this road,
That town
(Not Cairo, not Algiers
Not yet)
And behind the smile
Of that young boy
Is the voice,
The word fired
From the tip
Of one finger:
"Anglais!"

Somewhere off this highway,
The Laurentians grow stronger.
Somewhere beyond the rain,
Railways and junctions
That history books shall learn.
Somewhere west of Ste. Thérèse,
Another Reichstag burns in my hands.

DENNIS FOON

Dennis Foon received his MFA in Playwriting from UBC in 1975. He has written extensively for adults and children and his plays have been performed around the world, winning numerous awards, including the British Theatre Award for *Invisible Kids* and the Chalmers Award for *Skin*, a recent Governor General's Award nominee. His books for young people include *Am I the Only One?* and *The Short Tree and the Bird that Could Not Sing*, both published by Douglas and McIntyre. A new publication of *New Canadian Kid* and *Invisible Kids* was recently released by Pulp Press.

Children's Eyes was first commissioned and produced by The New Play Centre in 1983. A half hour radio version was produced by CBC Radio's Vanishing Point in 1985. I am currently working on a full-length stage play, The Fisher King, *drawing from the same material.*

Children's Eyes: A Monologue

When I grew up my father was partly deaf so he couldn't answer a lot of questions that pressed in on me. And cause he had so much trouble listening—I mean hearing—I was sort of left alone with a lot of stuff. Now that I'm older and have a kid of my own, I'm glad I'm not deaf so I can hear her.

I find it kind of funny that I can stand here and have you look at me without turning away. You see, I can't look at myself. At least not for very long. Because on the outside, I might look alright, I might look okay; but I don't see what you see.

My dad was a high school star. Number One at all the sports, in the late thirties (even today) not a bad place to be. Sure, he was a little hard of hearing and had some red splotches on his skin, but that's no big deal when you're at the top. He married a very cute teenaged prize. When I look at this picture of them I get dizzy. They're both so beautiful—I mean, they have such perfect, well put together bodies. They were eighteen in this shot. Stay of execution: his psoriasis didn't get bad till he was twenty-six . . . authentic case history material, most of his body covered in thick red scaling crust. Itched like crazy, and when he scratched, it bled.

By the time I was four years old he didn't have what you or I would call skin anymore. Just this kind of red, reptilian covering. He was always scratching. On doorways, on sides of chairs, he'd take a fork sometimes at supper—no, he never did that. He wasn't that bad—maybe he was, I don't remember. His scales were everywhere. If you walked on any rug in the house with black shoes on they turned white. "It's not the scales, it's the static electricity," my mom would say as she brushed them from our shoes before Sunday School. But I knew other kids had static electricity and no scales.

He always wanted me to play sports with him, basketball or swimming. I hated going because everyone would stare. I'd want to say, "I don't know him, he's just this weird guy, he's not really my dad." We'd fight all the time because I wouldn't play sports. "You've got to compete, son, that's how you practise standing up to the rest of them." "I just don't like it," I'd say—but the truth was I didn't like him. I mean I didn't like his body.

Funny thing about real life is that bad situations tend to get much, much worse. His psoraisis was just the start because it triggered a far more serious problem: arthritis. And true to form, his arthritis was as virulent and overwhelming as the skin condition.

Such a strange revenge the body can take on itself. His attacks were classic: shouting, screaming, crying from the pain. He'd lay in bed and groan for hours just because the swelling in his joints hurt that much. I'd sit in my room and close the door but I could still hear him. I knew he wasn't dying. But I didn't know if I would want to live if it was me. And one thought stood in front of me: 26 was the magic number. If I could make it past that year, the year he got bad, I'd be safe. I'd be free.

Every birthday I'd check my skin for little red blotches. And the slightest rash terrified me. I made it past twenty-six, though. Well past. I'm genetically clean as a whistle. Not a scab, not a scale, not a scar. At least not to the average eye.

The years have passed and there are some positive notes. The psoraisis that caused his arthritis has been licked by modern medicine. It's virtually gone now. He has skin again. And his arthritis is in check. That is, it can't get any worse. All his joints have been distorted as far as they can go, his disease has completely exhausted its resources. His toes and fingers are treebranch knotted. They bend and curve in crazy patterns that would almost be art if they weren't toes and fingers. His spine is joining into one solid piece of calcium. Soon he'll have a nice, permanent bend. He has to be careful where he's looking when they make that final knit. Ideally he hopes to be left with a forward view.

He still can walk, in a manner of speaking. A kind of shuffle based on forward momentum. It's not a great idea to be in his path when he comes barrelling through, he can't stop. An odd throw-back to his football days, I guess. If my sense of humour was any weirder, I'd say his fate is an odd kind of justice for all-around jocks.

He has so much courage to withstand the pain, the deformity. "I just keep going, I can't stop," he always says to me. He's a gentle, remarkable man who has tried as best as he can to be a provider, husband and father. He's been more successful at that than many people I know. And in return, I've been nothing. Because I can't stand to look at him. As if to look at him is to become him. If he reached out, I might have been there, but never completely. I always held back something for fear that he was contagious. If I touched him, if I really let him near me, I would get everything that happened to him. So I always, ultimately, looked away. And I guess my tactic worked. As you can see, I made the magic number. I grew up clean as a whistle . . . on the outside.

Inside I got so infected, so contaminated, that nothing known to today's visionary scientists can ever help me. I put on a very good front, I appear to be quite a healthy young man. But this body is just an illusion, a trick of the material plane of senses. I know what I really am: My scab sore skin bleeds when you touch it—so no one touches me. We cripples live on islands. I'm deaf, I don't listen. It's not that I don't want to, I just can't . . . I've shut out the world, I have no choice, that's my gift for shutting him out, for never really understanding, for being so disgusted and repulsed by my own father.

Whenever he cries or shouts I feel like I'm suffocating from his pain and my pain, the pain of not being able to accept his pain. And I pull more away from him. I can't face him. I just can't face him. And the further I pull away from him, the further I pull away from myself, and the mirror keeps breaking.

Pause

My daughter is so healthy and strong. She looks at everything with such fresh eyes. She doesn't feel what I feel, she feels for herself. Is that what they mean, you keep learning from the child? I can't look at anything, I don't want to see. But she wants to see everything. She wants to eat the world.

I took her to my parents' house. She was four. My dad was having another attack. I closed my eyes, fighting it, fighting it—and she said, "Why's Grandpa crying?"

I took a deep breath. I had to open my eyes. I looked at her and said, "He's sick. He has arthritis. He has pains. Now go to bed."

"I want to see."

I want to see? How could I show her that? How could I let her see what I couldn't look at?

"I want to see Grandpa!" she said, and bolted into his room. I followed, racing after her, "Stop, stop!"

"You gonna die, Grandpa?"

"No, no, just hurts, Honey."

"Why's Grandpa's feet like that?"

"Because he has arthritis."

"My feet not like that."

"Because you don't have arthritis."

"Your feet not like that."

"Because I don't have arthritis either."

"We gonna be like Grandpa?"

"No, Honey, because we're not sick."

She looked and looked until she saw every knotted bone and swollen joint and until Grandpa stopped groaning and fell asleep. And then she wanted to go to bed.

I tucked her in and she asked again: "We're not like Grandpa, are we?"

And I looked at her and her pure eyes—so open, so open—and said, "No, we're not sick. We don't have arthritis."

I still feel remorse and guilt and shame. I still feel the echoes of my father's howls. I still avoid mirrors like any self-respecting vampire. I still feel repulsed by my repulsions, disgusted at my selfishness. But I'm trying to stand straight. I'm trying to look at things. At myself. After all, if my four-year-old can open her eyes, I should be able to. I certainly am bigger than her. Sort of.

CATHY FORD

Born Lloydminster, Saskatchewan; alive on Mayne Island. BFA, MFA at
UBC. Member, League of Canadian Poets, Federation of BC Writers, Pres-
ident, League of Canadian Poets, 1985–6; founding member of Feminist
Caucus, LCP. Also member of West Coast Women & Words/les femmes
et les mots. Work as writer, editor, teacher, publisher, and book designer.
Published nine books of poetry to date. Works in progress: *grief, or the
book of letters* (poetry), *thinking they are dreaming* (fictions and fables),
Moon in My Belly (novel)

These poems are selected from Saffron, Rose & Flame—the joan of arc
poems, *a project which variously challenged, provoked, and obsessed its
writer for over ten years. As a poet and fictioniste involved in the feminist revisioning of the english language, am most interested in the long
poem or lyric suite. Earlier publications include* Stray Zale, Blood Utter-
ing, Tall Trees, the murdered dreams awake, the Womb Rattles its Pod
poems, Affaires of the Heart, By Violent Means, *and* The Desiring
Heart. *Now working on a novel, and long poems.*

moving again, jailed again

at last, witness, the plunging, breathing sea
an unending ocean away
these stifling white fields or towers

birds pecking the trodden wine
beaks purple

raven pausing midair ravenous
up off a body
beginning to fail

portent of death
death of a different kind
it snows

twelve bodies fall to every one alive

picking the scalp, the dead
for singular white plump maggots
lice that moan life
beg you for it

i don't carry anything clandestine
                         that you call untruth
or in weak imputation, crawling,
lies.

It is true however
there are some things

danced in what bare feet
carry the legs
in what woman's chest shields the heart
that metals the bone that helmets the thought

which will not be told

trial, feet & hands chained

have had visitors
without whom
           & these chains

i might fly away
refused counsel

but i will not
         it is only
when returned to this room
though it is cold it is quiet
then i hear
then i know

        Catherine, bride of Christ
        patron saint of virgins

        baths, all this blood
        all this red blood
                stuff
        of dreams
        it being ours & that's it
        & the foolish woe

        there is no war
        we rock, we smile
        dreaded female prophecy
        we begin to chant with a hum
        a low blood red hum
        there is no disguising such things

        & they cannot be obliterated with water,
        water or chains

the color of the suit is black
seance over, for today
bloodshot eyes the only veins of color, precious gems
& over & over say to them

"dress is of small things the least"

i never wanted anyone to touch
or kiss
my clothes

the morning, may 30, 1431

it is bright
sun stinging my eyes

body

to be dealt with
tenderly
death by fire

it is bright
though the sun cannot be seen

white dress, black shift
feet bare, kerchief
i don't know what i have on
being covered

those tiny imperfections damnation

a mole catherine found
my arm grows thinner, grows another
hide it,
        hide it
faggots piled high, women's clothes

never ask for more, for anything, soul monger

women's clothes, cart rolls on

into brightness
that cannot be seen through

Catherine, Margaret, Michael
sacred fire in the heart won't burn
Catherine and Margaret, women, you will know longing
that sexuality, that humanity earth-bound, saying that

i never wanted anyone, finally, except Michael
to come, archangelus, angel saint, humble me yet
touch my soul with your luminosity, tattered wing tips,
the shimmering dreams in which i could never keep you,

alone, heretic paper mitre over my eyes, blinded
there are words on the paper

discovery of the body
of the text, no sun

paper also burns
words also burn

ERIC FORRER

Primary and secondary education by correspondence. College at University of Alaska and UBC. First novel *From the Nets of a Salmon Fisherman* published by Doubleday in 1973. Career in boat-building, ocean freight, commercial fishing, and contracting. Appointed Board of Regents, University of Alaska, 1989.

"The Sea Ice" is an excerpt from From the Nets of a Salmon Fisherman. *The other two are adaptations from a book in progress. Chignik is a place that has inspired others before me, including Sydney Lawrence, whose painting* Castle Cape *is of the entrance to Chignik Bay. The geology of the Alaska Peninsula at Chignik just makes you stand agape, and it makes you do whatever it is you do, be it write, paint, or drink.*

The Sea Ice
from *From the Nets of a Salmon Fisherman*

An old man is walking on the sea ice, pushing a sled with no dogs. He has been walking for days and his head is bent, his eyes closed. He keeps his direction by the wind against his cheek. There is no point in looking up—the blowing snow seals him in a white room without shadows. The ice is flat, he does not bump into unseen pressure ridges. Were he to open his eyes, the old man would not be able to see his feet or the nose of his sled—such is the dark whiteness of the snow. He smells land and open water. It is warm, the wind, and the old man knows it is the first Spring storm and that it must come from the south. And so he walks eastward, pushing the sled over the sea ice.

Above the sighing of the snow the old man hears a growl that comes from an unseen horizon. The noise approaches, growing through the storm until with a roaring crack it passes under his feet and fades toward another horizon beyond the whiteout. Bending down and opening his eyes, the old man sees dark water welling between the lips of a crack in the sea ice. He knows that he is standing on a fathom of solid ice over the mud shoals of a shallow ocean. As the old man watches with squinting eyes, the endless crack begins slowly to widen.

And he cannot answer the question—from which side of the crack can I reach land?

Chignik

In that smokey light of dusk when the sharp hills, the razor backs, are flat washes and the clouds settle down like a hand on your neck. . .

Rocks column along the river edge. Snow fields and glaciers jut from the ranges and droop into swirls of current. . .

In that smokey light I skiff across the bay, and my thoughts fin around me; out of a fluid depth their dorsals startle above the surface . . .

These thoughts, these finners, swim up current with a splash and a flurry and a long series of side-slapping leaps above the surface and then a rush just above the muddy bottom. . .

But eelgrass and shallows confuse the clarity, foul the blades as I move across the bay and this distraction keeps me sane under the weight of the hand that is like clouds. . .

Going West, Regardless

Black with the grease of machinery, I feel for a tool underneath the bilge.

Loading at Kodiak. The deck hand was half aloft and ugly as a hairlipped squirrel. Damn near dropped a drum of fuel on him.

Moved to the gravel hole underneath a bigger crane. Loaded gear twenty-six hours and when the tide went down the hull tilted and folded the wing house right over on the deck.

Into Shelikof. Thirty knots bow quarter. Ran over the load tightening.

Midnight wheel watch. Full moon and big glassy swell. Islands scattered all around. Crabber way out west on the radio. "I lost control of her OK.

Backed into the wind, ninety knots. Down to about sixty now."
ooming down the Peninsula, gale warnings.
Port main engine out.
Generator arched a wire and burned up.
Main fuse blew twice.
Iron mike out for two hours. Boat going in circles.
Lost center main. Back to Cold Bay.

Engine room full of water right to the flywheels. God damn deckhands won't check the engines when I'm asleep. Spent the day pumping. Nobody will come near me. The rat of my depression backs into a corner, flashing long yellow teeth.

Over the bar beyond False Pass. Surf all over the place. One engine down. Sparks out the stack scattering on the canvased load. Gas fumes in the engine room from broken bilge piping.

Two days in the ice. Sitting on an easy chair behind the wheelhouse watching whales spout in the sun.

Up all night pushing ice. Japanese freezer ship in the ice.
Hard aground. All afternoon eating an apple in the easy chair. Floated off on the tide. Radar out. Iron Mike out. Fuses popping. Centre main quit. Ice bent starboard shaft and vibration makes the compass card spin. Glassy morning. Drifting. Too much ice. Sea mammals all over.

Cabled a big growler to the bow and used it to push ice. Entire ice field blood red in the all-night sunset.

Broke out of the ice. Led the freezer ship out. Anchored up at Togiak.

BILL GASTON

Bill Gaston attended UBC in the seventies and taught briefly in both the English and Creative Writing departments. He spent his youth in Deep Cove, BC, out of which came the critically acclaimed *Deep Cove Stories*. Other books include a novel, *Tall Lives* (Macmillan) and the poetry collection *Inviting Blindness*. He is currently Writer-in-Residence at the University of New Brunswick.

This anthology being dedicated to Earle Birney, I thought "Carp" appropriate. I understand Birney knew Malcolm Lowry—a minor character in "Carp"—and visited him in Deep Cove. But more importantly, this story treats in both theme and setting the death of the fifties, an era of flux and Beat and cultural seedings, not the least of which was the birth of Creative Writing at UBC.

Carp

"Jhana," Max Betts said to his daughter, "I just quit smoking. My head's a mess. I've had too many beers today jus' like your mother said. But my life is going to change. Now it's going to be Japanese. Clean damn Japanese."

Clean Japanese. Even when drunk, perhaps especially when drunk, Max Betts had a way with words that made a ten-year-old girl sit up and take notice, if not quite understand. He sat sprawled in his shredding chair, his dirty T-shirt riding up his paunch, his head twisting and nodding radically as he spoke. Because his daughter was blind, he didn't have to care about how he looked. In this regard at least, Jhana's mother—his estranged wife—couldn't berate him for setting a bad example.

"Know what I mean, Jhana?" he said, got no answer, then let his head loll back. He spoke to the ceiling. "I need some clean lines, some clean black and white lines. Porcelain, some cold porcelain. Some fish in clear water. You remember seeing any Japanese art, Jhana? Straight lines. My head's a mess, darling. Your father's head's a mess tonight." He paused for a moment, staring now at his daughter. "Can your mother bring you over again next week, dear?"

"I don't know, Dad. She didn't say."

Jhana's tone of voice wasn't lost on Max, drunk as he was. For the voice betrayed a secrecy, and an allegiance that had been shifting for two years now. Losing a wife had been quick, clean, violent, a gash that healed;

losing a daughter was the hard part, the knife torturously slow in its work.

Jhana's mother appeared from the kitchen, her face red and her hands swollen.

"Okay, Jhana," she said. Putting on her coat, not looking at her husband, she added, "I should congratulate you Max. The kitchen, again, was unbelievable. Anyway, two hours worth. My roof shakes have been delivered. When can you come? Before it rains, I hope."

Their arrangement was such that, during visits with a shared daughter, she would clean his house and he would fix hers.

Mother and daughter left and Max was sad, as usual. But glad too, as usual, for now he could break out a bottle. He drank greedily. He had new purpose. In the hour of half-clarity left to him, he decided where in the room the Japanese prints would go, and where he would put the aquarium.

It was New Year's Eve. Tomorrow would be 1960.

The growing dissatisfaction had been gradual, but by 1959 Max discovered that he profoundly hated his life. He had just turned thirty-five. The past few years had seen his daughter go blind, his marriage break up. He had been fired for drunkenness on the job. He had been rehired, but even that seemed like more bad luck. Longshoremen's work was usually easy, but the men pretended it was always hard, if only to have an excuse to go nightly to the bar.

But the marriage, Jhana, the job—those were the obvious horrors. They felt like symptoms of a life's disintegration in general. What Max abhorred most was the quality of his plodding days, the shit-awful hangovers, the packs of numbing cigarettes, the coming home from work filthy with ship rust and sawdust, home to find rooms filthier than he was. So easy, so necessary, to drink; so easy and necessary to shower and meet his friends at the bar where he could eat hot dogs and peanuts for dinner and drink such a life away. But 1959 was becoming 1960. New years were times to resolve; new decades that much better.

He had been leafing through a magazine in a gas station bathroom, an arty magazine from New York. There was a pictorial on Beatniks, a cultural oddity that had begun to make quaint sense to the rich and idle in the east. Max was stricken by the pictures. He'd seen nothing like them. One showed an artist's studio, the high walls of which were bright white and unornamented. There were skylights. The only furnishings were two black cushions on the floor and an aquarium, holding two fish. The wood floor gleamed. Max, on the toilet, was dreadfully hungover.

The article spoke of the recent influx of Japanese art and style, spawned largely by these Beatniks. There were pictures of Japanese prints: stark clean suns over simple geometric landscapes. A simple twig on which rested a severe black bird. A huge bare canvas of white with but two black slashes, representing leaves, in its upper right corner. Max was surprised by these pictures, by the mode of thought they advertised. He felt suddenly energetic, as if the bathroom stall had received a blast of oxygen.

There were no Beatniks in Deep Cove, and none that he knew of in Vancouver. Max searched out the art shops and galleries, found little of interest, little that hinted at oxygen, but through these shops he placed orders to Toronto and to New York City itself.

It was February of a new decade, and Max had some friends over after the bar closed. They were stumbling drunk and wild, the kind of Monday night they hadn't seen much of since Malc had gone back to England; Malc, the mad Brit who claimed to write though no one cared, who in any case had no job to go to in the morning and so was the instigator of many impromptu parties. One summer Max and Malc had decided to bury three years' worth of bottles in the backyard—the quantity of bottles hadn't been great, really, but because they'd stolen a backhoe to do the digging, the bottle burial story took on mythic proportions.

So it was a Monday night of old. Max was acting strangely. Though very drunk himself he seemed wary of a stack of boxes in the room's corner. He guided reeling friends away from them if they strayed too close. There's an aquarium in there, he said. And at one point in the party he ripped open a box, withdrew from it two black cushions, and suggested they take turns sitting on them. Just try it, he yelled, and no one could tell if he was making a joke, or slipping off into one of his occasional but lately more frequent bouts of weirdness. In the wee hours the party was on the verge of winding down but Max wound it down for good when he donned a long, navy blue kimono, stood facing a wall, held his head tight with his hands, and moaned loudly to himself.

The carp were beautiful. A rare and expensive breed, midnight black, about five inches long, and they graced the confines of their three-foot home by hanging perfectly motionless. At times, to Max's delight, they would dart this way and that for no apparent reason; surprising bursts, he liked to think, of glee. He did not name them.

He set the aquarium against the front room's largest wall, in the centre. The wall he'd painted bright white, but he'd run out of paint and the remaining three walls remained beige. In a fit of spontaneity Max took up a small brush and on the wall painted a black ring, eight feet in diameter, to frame the fish. At first he'd tried a small ceramic pagoda in the aquarium's right back corner. Its edges were too rounded, cartoonish; it looked tacky. In its place he plated a lone vermilion weed.

He fed the carp leftovers. The man at the fish importer's (he'd been Japanese!) had said, "They'll eat anything, they're like goats." Max had felt vague disappointment at hearing this. Sometimes he fed them bits of steak, other times nightcrawlers he bought at the gas station where he'd found the magazine.

While Max's wife was off somewhere scrubbing, Jhana was made to sit stiffly erect on a cushion across from her father. She didn't seem to mind. Max went to great lengths describing the carp to her. Jhana seemed pleased. She told Max she'd gotten "A" in braille.

"Well that's just great dear," Max said. "Now I'll brag too. You notice how clean it is in here. The air I mean?"

"Yes. You've quit smoking. I'm glad, Dad."

Jhana's mother came in from her hour of work. She'd managed to finish only the kitchen. Removing rubber gloves, she surveyed the front room. All its furniture had been removed and stored in Jhana's old bedroom. In its bareness the room seemed huge. Max hoped his wife was noticing how much the room, shot with diagonal sunbeams that were filled with radiant floating dust, looked like one of Emily Carr's cedar forests.

"Well this is a switch," Jhana's mother said. "It looks like you're taking care of one room at least."

"It's a start," he said. "It's a style for the mind."

Max picked a piece of lint from the shoulder of his kimono. He felt content. In fact he found himself fighting smugness. His wife was eyeing him oddly. No doubt she thought he had a new woman, and this was her work. That was fine, he'd let her think that.

"My life's changing," he said to them at the door, after kissing his daughter. He smiled at his wife and then shrugged, as if in humility, as if to say that the change was now out of his hands.

Max was going to the bar less. As a consequence he ate more at home, something he'd done rarely since the separation. In order to keep the front room perfect he'd moved the eating table to the kitchen where he'd been taking his meals until he decided it was ridiculously cramped. So the table came back to the front room. A minor flaw, he told himself. He tried hard to remember to always clear his dirty dishes off the table, and though he often forgot to do so he decided that he'd use dirty dishes as a sign that his life was, or was not, progressing as it should.

Another flaw in perfection arose. The carp ate a lot, and so shit a lot. That was fine, Max thought. That was life, that was order. But the water, though he sometimes did manage to change it on schedule, grew quickly murky. When he phoned the fish importer, he was told to purchase a *placaustamus*, a filtering fish (a "shit-eater," as the Japanese man put it, which made Max no longer like him). That day at a local pet shop he pronounced the name of the fish carefully, and was shown to a tank of dull brown, lethargic creatures clinging to the rocks and glass walls with obscene sucker-like mouths. Fat, soulless and stupid. Max knew he could never allow such a shit-eater in with his carp. He bought the best electric filter the shop had in stock.

Once home, though, the filter proved noisy. He tried muffling the tinny whine with wads of cotton and electrician's tape, which only succeeded in changing the tone, not the volume. And the filter looked so awful with its dials, tubes and wires clinging to the glass wall of art like technology's metallic turd. He threw it out. He'd let the water take its course, going brown as the carp made it so. Then clean again, when he changed it. One into the other, a cycle like the tides, like day and night, perfectly natural.

Max had ordered a book on Japanese philosophy and when it arrived he read some of it, closing it only when he saw there was indeed much to ponder. It spoke of the new style, the new way of thinking. He closed the book and gazed through the murk at his carp. Sleek, they hung like streaks of blackest ink. They mouthed the water so calmly, a slow rhythm of O's. Sometimes a tiniest bubble would appear on a lip, and the next closing of mouth would trip the bubble on its tiny way to the surface. So sharp, and yet so calm. Max decided they were mouthing the word OM.

He woke sweating and shocked by the horrible dream. He got up to survey his front room and aquarium to ease himself before he tried to sleep again. The dream had been this: He was at his table, drunk and eating a steak dinner. He became angry at something, and tossed all his dishes and silverware into the air. Then he went to the bar, but none of his friends knew him. Later, it was days later, he saw that one of the carp was half dead, with ribbons of flesh and guts trailing from its body. Before he could do anything, the other carp was eating the wounded one, greedily, stupidly, like a goat. He quickly began to change the water. By the time he got it drained only a skeleton remained of the first carp. It flipped pathetically on the sand. The other carp lay on the sand too—it was bloated fat and white and filled the entire aquarium. In the back corner, wedged in against the ceramic pagoda, Max's steak knife stood point-up; it was against this the dead carp had first impaled itself.

When he woke in the morning, Max moved the eating table back to the kitchen, cleaning the front room of his nightmare and making it perfect again.

The catalogue from which he'd ordered two striking, oxygen-emitting prints also had a section on Japanese erotic art. Max had seen nothing wrong in sending for a selection of those prints as well. They arrived individually wrapped in tissue and were oddly beautiful. The contorted positions, the grossly enlarged genitalia replete with crimson membranes, blue veins, and delicately etched hairs might be taken for pornography by some, but Max understood that it depended on the artistic eye of the beholder. Sex could be simple and clean; it was a question of purity of mind. In fact, Max had deemed it necessary to introduce sex into his new lifestyle. It wasn't natural that he'd been without a woman for months. The book had said nothing about celibacy being part of the stark Japanese way, and these pictures were a colourful hint that sex was indeed to be included.

So one night Max brought a woman home from the bar. He had controlled himself, wasn't too drunk, and he wished she'd done the same. She was blonde and giddy-loud, and had small eyes and a big germanic chin. He came out of the bathroom naked under his kimono. You're fast, she said, and giggled. He led her over to the aquarium. She couldn't see the carp for the murk, so Max brought a flashlight. In the beam they looked too grey and large, and they huddled in the back.

"Tell me what they're saying," Max said.

She giggled and said he was crazy. But Max insisted. He was drinking whiskey now.

"I know," she said at last, pleased with herself, "it's 'Oops'."

Max spread a blanket. She asked why not the bedroom, and Max told her it had to be here. He brought out the pictures of Japanese erotic art and showed them to her. You're filthy, she said, but she giggled, shy now and excited.

It was April, and Max had friends over. All were drunk, and Max especially so. He'd quit smoking again; it had gone a week this time, and tonight he'd thought it only right that since he denied himself tobacco he would let himself drink as much as he wanted. He'd become quickly drunk and by midnight was halfway through a pack of borrowed cigarettes. At first he felt guilty, and then not.

For he wore his kimono, and stayed properly silent. Let his friends act like fools, he thought, let them yell and laugh like so many barfing dogs. He would keep his thoughts orderly and clean, and speak only when necessary. His friends were having a good time; he wouldn't stop them. Several women had followed them from the bar, and Max had moved the stereo back into the front room for dancing. He brought two chairs out to stand in front of the aquarium so no one would bump it. He hoped the fish wouldn't be scared by the music and laughter. As Max squeezed half the contents of a beef and bean burrito into the water for the fish to eat, he slopped some sauce down his kimono front.

He was proud that he decided to clean the stain immediately. Dabbing at himself with a soapy cloth over the kitchen sink, Max saw how dirty he'd let the garment get. He said to himself: I'm slipping. But tomorrow meant a fresh start. Tomorrow he would buy some white paint and do the rest of the front room. He would polish the floor and hang the prints on the wall opposite the aquarium. But first of all he would change the water, which of late was so murky he would see the carp only rarely, when they came forward out of the miasma, gliding black ghosts, to nose the glass.

Having decided all this, and feeling better, Max again decided that tonight he would drink and smoke as much as he wanted.

Ben Klaus had followed him into the kitchen. Ben seemed on a kind of mission, for on the edge of his thoughts Max had heard others in the front room urging Ben on. Go on, Ben, do it, he'd heard.

"Hey Max boy," said Ben now, not smiling. Their shop steward at work, Ben was plump and red, and though he wasn't bright he was courageous in the bar, in fights, with women, and on the job. Ben paused now, turned redder, smiled, then asked loudly and quickly:

"Hey. Boy, you're actin' sort of goof-off lately. So what the hell's the deal? Eh Maxie?"

Max regarded him coolly, said nothing. Ben began to fidget, and his smile went stiff and quivered.

"Prob'ly wife and kid stuff, eh? Well that's tough, that really is. Prob'ly no one's business but your own, and that's for sure. But, hey, Max, you got some friends here. . . ."

Max stared at him. In truth he didn't know what to say, or how to say it. Things were wrong, but always had been. But now they were getting better. Was it his fault the man couldn't see that? So he just stared. Silence is the mind's cleanliness, he'd read, and believed. He took a large gulp from his whiskey bottle, winced, and now ignored Ben Klaus altogether.

"Right then." Ben turned and left the kitchen, red now with quick anger.

Max scanned the empty beer bottles on his counter, heard the thudding music. He thought of running and apologizing to Ben, to all of his friends, but decided not to. For he saw that, like dirt, his words would cloud the front room with cheap sentiment. He recalled with fondness his old pal Malc, himself a master of silence. Though Malc wrote page upon page by day, by night he knew how to drink and leave things perfectly unsaid.

Growing suddenly drunker, Max watched the party disperse at Ben's urging. Curious murmurs. Angry murmurs. Twenty minutes later the last were out the door, one the blonde German woman with her bra in her hand.

Max reeled to the door, opened it, and supported himself against the frame. Cars idled out on the dark street, and friends whispered about him from window to window. Overhead, stars swirled, hissed.

Max screamed at all of it: "I'm inscrutable, like a chink!"

In the morning Max was badly hungover. But he felt good about starting a day afresh. He snuffed out his cigarette, realizing he hadn't been aware of lighting one. He stood in front of the aquarium now. On a whim and smiling, he bowed to it. He began the job of changing the water, which was opaque, almost black. It had been weeks and weeks. Max was shocked to see how much the carp had grown.

GARY GEDDES

Gary Geddes was born in Vancouver in 1940 and, except for a four-year sojourn in Saskatchewan, spent his childhood and youth on the coast. After working at Woodward's, CP Express warehouse, and the BC Sugar Refinery, he studied English and Philosophy at UBC and taught briefly on Texada Island. He studied Education at Reading University in England, then did his MA and PH.D. in English at the University of Toronto. He has taught at the post-secondary level at the University of Victoria, the British Columbia Institute of Technology, and the universities of Toronto, Trent, Carleton, Ryerson, and Concordia. He has also been writer-in-residence at the University of Alberta. In addition to several anthologies used widely in Canadian schools and universities, including *20th-Century Poetry & Poetics* and *15 Canadian Poets Times 2*, he has published more than twenty books of poetry, fiction, drama, non-fiction, and translation. His awards include the E.J. Pratt Medal & Prize for *Letter of the Master of Horse*, the National Poetry Prize from the Canadian Authors' Association for *The Acid Test*, the America's Best Book Award in the 1985 Commonwealth Poetry Competition for *The Terracotta Army*, the National Magazine Gold Award and the Writer's Choice Award for *Hong Kong*. He now lives in eastern Ontario and teaches at Concordia University.

After graduating from UBC, I taught at a small school in Vananda, on Texada Island, where I had the good fortune to meet left-wing activists and some remarkable individuals who were to leave their mark on my relatively unformed mind. One of these was Jack Leslie, known as the hermit of Clam Bay. Jack was one of those Englishmen who came to Canada to escape the class system and could not tolerate the privilege and injustice he found here. He spent much of his life organizing unions in the logging industry and trying to avoid the police, the draft, and the state in all its manifestations. When I met Jack, he lived in a shack on the shore, which he'd built himself from driftwood; his diet of clams, salmon, and simple fare was washed down with the most amazing home-brewed dandelion wine. Jack was an avid reader and a natural story-teller. I spent as much time with him as I could, imbibing his narratives and his wine. Once I told John Creighton in the English Department about Jack and he recommended that I try to write about him. To this day, I have not written Jack's story, but it has remained with me and been there as an inspiration for the many other poems and stories, many of them tales of hearsay, that I have written. "The Strap," "Jimmy's Place," and "Names of Great Men" are three poems that grew directly out of my Texada experience.

The Strap

No other sound was heard throughout the school
as Jimmy Bunn surrendered to the strap.
He stood before me in the counsellor's office
eye to eye, while the desk drawer gaped,
his farmer's hands stretched out in turn,
expectant as beggars. My heart was touched.
I gave them more than they had bargained for:
six on each. The welts, like coins,
inflated as we watched. Nothing he'd done
deserved such largesse, disrupting my sermon
on the Bay of Pigs invasion and how Americans
are hooked on violence, etcetera, etcetera.
They say there's a kinship in aggression
that knits the torturer and his victim;
we came to be the best of friends.
But each excuse and subterfuge exploded
in my brain as he dropped his puffed pink hams
and fought back tears. I put the leather tongue
into the gaping drawer and pushed it shut.

Jimmy's Place

We found the cow in a grove below the road,
leaning against an alder for support,
her udders swollen, her breath ragged and grating
as a rasp. I could have drowned
in the liquid eye she turned to me.
Her calf, though dead, was perfectly positioned,
forelegs and head protruding from the flaming ring
of vulva. Too large, perhaps, or hind legs
broken through the sac, dispersing fluids.
Much as we tried we couldn't pry it loose
and the flesh around the legs began to give
from pressure on the rope. The cow
had no more strength and staggered back
each time we pulled. Tie her to the tree,
I said, being the schoolmaster and thinking
myself obliged to have an answer, even here
on the High Road, five miles south of town
where the island bunched in the jumble
of its origins. It was coming, by God,
I swear it, this scrub roan with her shadow self
extending out behind, going in both directions
like a '52 Studebaker, coming by inches
and our feet slipping in the mud and shit
and wet grass. She raised her head and tried
to see what madness we'd concocted in her wake,
emitted a tearing gunny-sack groan,
and her liquid eye ebbed back to perfect white.

Names of Great Men

Paton's hands were made to grasp an engine,
not an era. History was a list
of paint jobs, previous owners,
not one a Father of Confederation.

He could fine-tune a carburetor
and gap a spark-plug
to the nearest thousandth of an inch
without a gauge. So he took leave of us,
dropped out, and started working
at the iron mine in Gillies Bay,
where brown ore rose in buckets
from below the level of the sea.

I saw him twice before he died.
Once in the soft drinks section
at Vananda, a crescent wrench
protruding from the pocket
of his striped overalls;
then in the dusty parking-lot at school
leaning against a candy-apple pickup,
the one hand raised above his head to wave
pausing to smooth a wayward curl.
His girl was in detention
and he'd come to help her with her homework,
so he said, bone up a little
for the test.

Stuck doors on the vertical mine shaft,
that was his last assignment.
On a slope high above the bay, where
a blunt-nosed freighter, loaded for Japan,
had slipped its moorings for the journey
home, this dancing escapee
performed his pirouette and disappeared.
The brief tattoo his workboots beat
upon the metal surface of the doors
rang unheard. He learned decline and fall
and memorized the path of his descent.

The names descended with him as he went.

KICO GONZALEZ-RISSO

An MFA graduate in Creative Writing in 1980, Kico founded and became Artistic Director of the Kitsilano Theatre Company, which has, since its inception in 1979, produced Canadian premières of internationally acclaimed plays. Kico's professional directing credits include classics by Calderón, Goldoni, Musset, Lope de Vega and Shakespeare, as well as contemporary plays by Vaclav Havel, Egon Wolff, Pavel Kohout, and Eduardo Manet. He also produced and directed premières of two plays by former Creative Writing Department Head, Douglas Bankson. Kico's writing credits include *Witchcraft* and *Voodoo* (produced in 1989); *Inspector Sly's Second-to-Last Case*, *Wonderville*, and *Art Attack* (premièred in 1988, 1989, and 1990 respectively at White Rock Theatre Festival); the book and lyrics for *Captive!*, a musical commissioned for Vancouver's Centennial; and various scripts for high schools. In 1988 he won an award in the CBC Literary Competition for his radio drama, *Phoning It In*. Kico has taught playwriting courses for UBC and the New Play Centre, and is Guest Associate Professor and Director at Western Washington University.

Caution: Contents Under Pressure *was awarded the Grant Redford Memorial Prize (at* UBC) *when it was written in 1976. That year it was produced at Le Festival du Théâtre de Trois-Pistoles, Quebec, and the following year at l'Université de Pau, France. In 1978 the play was translated into Spanish and performed in Salamanca, Spain. Finally, in 1979, the play was produced in Vancouver, as part of the inaugural season of our newly-formed Kitsilano Theatre Company.* Caution *recalls a favourite period in my life—a time when I was a graduate student with still enough time on my hands (I felt) to see the world. It is the play that followed me to Europe and then, before I knew it, led me into a theatre career. In 1989, in a reunion of sorts, I had the pleasure of directing it for Kitsilano Theatre as the closing production of our tenth anniversary season.*

Caution: Contents Under Pressure
A One-act Play

CHARACTERS
Amos Byrd *A young law student.*
Tanya Tripp *His fiancée.*
Tyrone Tripp *A judge. Tanya's father.*
Toni Tripp *Tanya's mother.*

TIME
The present.

SETTING
A cabin on an island. The action takes place in a large room. There's a desk, a hangman's scaffold, an old couch and a very large trunk. A door or exit leads to a kitchen offstage. There is also an entrance door.

(The stage is in darkness. The front door opens and Amos and Tanya enter struggling with the luggage. Sounds of bad weather outside can be heard. The door closes.)

TANYA   Well, we made it, darling. We're finally here.

AMOS   Madness! That's the word I want. It was madness to come at this time of night—and in this weather! That little boat very nearly capsized. Huh! That old fool must have a screw loose to make trips in this weather.

TANYA   *(Draws him close)* You wanted to meet my parents, didn't you? I told them we'd be over tonight and here we are. Now relax, dear Amos. You're shivering.

AMOS   Heat. Doesn't this cabin have any heat? Jumpin' Jupiter it's cold in here. And where's the light? I've work to do, you know, Tanya. I'm up to my neck in work. Essays, exams, research . . . .

TANYA   Ssh . . . .

AMOS   It was madness to come this weekend. I'll never be able to finish my thesis here. I won't make it. I know I won't. They'll kick me out of law school if I don't get this work done.

TANYA   Mother Toni! Daddy! We're here! Please relax, Amos darling. It's good that you came up. It really is. You'll be able to unwind.

AMOS   Not in the dark I won't.
        (The lights go on to reveal Toni standing by the light switch.)

TANYA   *(Rushes to hug her)* Mother Toni! *(They embrace.)* Have you been here all along?

TONI   It was mischievous, wasn't it? But I was dying to find out what you two would say if you thought you were alone. I'm sorry.

TANYA Mother Toni, you haven't met Amos, have you? This is the wonderful man I told you about in my letter.

AMOS Pleased to meet you, Mrs. Tripp. *(He offers his hand but Toni doesn't accept.)*

TONI Aimless? Where on earth did you get such a funny name?

TANYA Amos, Mother Toni. Aay-mmm-osss.

TONI Oh. Well I much prefer Aimless. Do you mind? Now, would either of you like a cup of tea?

AMOS That would be very nice, Mrs. Tripp. A hot cup of tea would warm us both up.

TONI You want it hot, do you?

AMOS Well, yes. *(Toni nods and goes to prepare the tea.)* What did she mean by that, Tanya? Do I want it hot? Jumpin' Jupiter, I certainly don't want iced-tea.

TANYA You can put your sleeping bag wherever you want, Amos. Just make sure it's next to mine. We'll have the stove going, it'll be warm . . . . What's the matter?

AMOS *(Pointing to the scaffold)* Over there. What is that?

TANYA That? Why . . . we use it to hang our coats on. Here, it's about time you took yours off.
(She tries to remove his coat but he pulls away.)

AMOS A scaffold! I don't believe it. Your father, a judge—and with his own scaffold! Eerie. That's the word I want. I'm not sure I like this.

TANYA Don't be silly, Amos. It's just for fun. Here, hang your coat on it. *(She helps Amos take off his coat and hangs it on a peg on the scaffold.)*

AMOS I won't be able to study with this thing in the room. It's a negative influence.

TONI *(Comes over and puts a flower in a vase.)* What's a negative influence?

TANYA Amos was just expressing an opinion, Mother Toni. He finds daddy's scaffold very realistic.

TONI He built it himself you know, Aimless. He's always wanted his own scaffold for some reason. Like a child wanting a toy. Look—*(She pulls down the noose.)* see how strong the rope is? Six ninety-five it cost me. I bought it for his birthday.

AMOS Where is the judge? I trust he's up here. I've always wanted to meet your husband, Mrs. Tripp. I've heard some wonderful things about him from my professors.

TANYA He's probably meditating.

TONI Yes. He still has a few minutes left. Why don't we all have a cup of mint tea while we wait?

AMOS   I'd like that, yes. *(Amos and Tanya sit.)*

TANYA   Why don't you make the announcement, dear?

AMOS   *(Takes her hand)* Not now, Tanya. It would be more proper if both your parents were present.

TONI   Tanya mentioned something in her letter about you two already looking for an apartment. I'm not a stupid woman, you know, Aimless. I can see what you're driving at. I know your intentions.

AMOS   *(Jumping up)* Oh, I didn't mean to imply anything, Mrs. Tripp. I imagine a lot of people know how close Tanya and I are. I just wanted to make an official announcement. Ceremony. That's the word I want. I sometimes like a bit of ceremony.

TONI   Yes, well don't get the idea that because you're my dear daughter's fiancé you can burst in here expecting the ceremonial treatment. I don't know how it is at your house, Aimless, but in our family we like a little respect now and then.

TANYA   Mother Toni! What's wrong with you? Amos hasn't done or said anything wrong. You've embarrassed me in front of him.

TONI   Have I? Oh dear, how stupid of me. Aimless, please forgive my mindless outburst.

AMOS   No, no, no, Mrs. Tripp. I probably let something rude slip out. I often do, you know. Rattling on, saying whatever comes to mind without stopping once to think about it. *(Chuckles)* That's probably why I'm so interested in being a lawyer.

TONI   You must think me a terrible hostess. I'm sorry. It's just that I'm not used to having guests up here. At home I'm entertaining all the time—I give the loveliest parties, you know. People talk about them for days. Up here though, I find it's a bit different. You're the first guest we've ever had, I believe, Aimless. You'll have to be a bit patient.

AMOS   I'd hate to be a bother, Mrs. Tripp. If even for one second.

TANYA   Never mind, Amos. Mother Toni, shall I make the tea?

TONI   I was just about to offer you some. Aimless?

AMOS   Yes, that would be very nice. *(A buzzer goes off.)*

TONI   Oh. His time's up.

AMOS   Pardon me?

(Toni pulls out a key and goes to the trunk. She takes the tablecloth off it and opens it. Tyrone gets out. He is wearing a ceremonial judge's robe complete with powdered wig.)

AMOS   Jumpin' Jupiter!

TANYA   Daddy!

TYRONE   Tanny! *(They hug.)*

TANYA   Daddy, come meet Amos.

TYRONE   Welcome to the enchanted castle, m'boy! *(He chuckles.)*

AMOS   Yes. . . . I'm honoured, Judge Tripp. We've read many of your astute articles in our advanced law classes. You certainly have made your mark in the legal profession, sir. I . . . I can't begin to tell you how excited I am . . . .

TYRONE Is something wrong, m'boy? You seem to be nervous.

AMOS   I'm sorry if I appear so, sir. I was a little surprised.

TANYA He didn't realize you were in the trunk, daddy.

TYRONE Is that so? Didn't you show him the trunk, Toni?

TONI   And disturb you? No, no, Tyrone. I know what a grumpy old man you become when disturbed. Make life miserable for everyone—threaten to hang the lot of us. I wasn't about to go near the trunk—not till my time came.

TANYA Mother Toni, could I have a word with you? *(She takes Toni aside.)*

TYRONE Come here, m'boy. I'll show you. *(He brings Amos over and opens the trunk.)* Beautiful, isn't it? Built it myself, you know.

AMOS   You seem to have a knack for carpentry, sir.

TYRONE Old-fashioned lock, you know. I like things simple up here. You can lock this trunk from the inside or the outside. If you ever come up here alone, m'boy, you can take the key in with you.

TANYA It's really comfortable inside.

AMOS   Excuse me. I'm finding it difficult to follow this. Am I to understand that one is locked inside this box? Literally locked in?

TYRONE Security precautions. You won't want anyone tampering with the lid once you're in.

TONI   My husband would be in there all day if he could. That's why I keep the key.

AMOS   May I be so bold as to enquire why you'd want to stay inside a trunk?

TONI   That's getting rather personal, isn't it, Aimless? We don't really know you well enough yet to answer.

TYRONE Nonsense! The boy's our guest, Toni. He's entitled to use the trunk whenever he wants. That's the rule up here m'boy. Enjoy yourself. Do anything you want. There's food in the cupboard if you're hungry, the floor's at your disposal if you want to lie down, you can make all the noise you want, you can jump on the couch, there's an outhouse about half a mile down the trail if you feel like taking a shit . . .

AMOS   Half a mile!

TONI   He's exaggerating. He often does.

TYRONE And if you just feel like hanging about . . . . *(He points to the scaffold.)*

TONI   My husband isn't a great wit as you can see. Don't feel you have to laugh, Aimless.

TYRONE Tell you what, m'boy. Why don't you pop into the trunk? Go on, get the feel of it.

AMOS Er . . . a little later perhaps, sir.

TONI Huh! Throw our hospitality in our face—is that your game? A little later, he says. Well yes, sir. Certainly, sir. Just ring the bell when a little later comes, sir. Huh!

AMOS I'm sorry. I didn't mean to sound impertinent , Mrs. Tripp.

TANYA If he doesn't want to try the trunk, he doesn't have to, Mother Toni.

AMOS No, it's all right Tanya. I am curious to see what it's like. Really.

TYRONE Roomy, eh? Plush velvet interior, headrest . . . . Like the colour?

AMOS Lovely. I . . . I've always been fond of black.

TANYA *(Kisses Amos)* Hey mister—did I tell you you're wonderful? Most men wouldn't understand the need for a trunk. They wouldn't even want to try it.

TYRONE She's right, m'boy. They'd ask all sorts of stupid questions.

AMOS You think so?

TYRONE Ha! No doubt about it. They wouldn't know what to do with one. You and I though, we're going to get along. We're alike in many ways, we are. I can tell.

TONI He's a law student, you know, Tyrone.

TYRONE Well there you are!

TONI Just like you were, so many years ago. This cabin may be his one day. Judge Aimless Byrd. That's what you want isn't it, Aimless? To be a judge? Like this man here?

AMOS Well that's a long way in the future, Mrs. Tripp. But I won't be anything if I don't get some work done.
(He tries to climb out but Tyrone stops him.)

TYRONE Work! Where do you think you are? In a concentration camp? You're not here to work, you're here to enjoy yourself. Let yourself go.

TANYA He really is busy, daddy. He's in the middle of a huge thesis.

TYRONE He is, is he? Let's have a look.

TONI Would anyone care for some jasmine tea. Aimless?

AMOS Er . . . love some, thank you.
(Toni goes to make tea and Tyrone goes to Amos' bags and starts looking through them. Amos steps out of the trunk and pulls Tanya close.)

AMOS Jumpin' Jupiter, Tanya. What is it with your parents? Why's your father dressed like a clown?

TANYA I meant to tell you, he's a little old-fashioned. Please, Amos, let him have his fun.

TYRONE *(Pulls out a folder)* Is this it? This is your essay?

AMOS   Yes, sir. I was hoping you'd give me some advice on it.

TYRONE *(Reads)* "A Legal Interpretation of the Existentialist Philosophy when Applied to the Criminal Code in Oriental Society." Hmph! Sounds like a lot of bullshit to me.

AMOS   Well, it was approved as a law thesis.

TANYA   Amos' professor said that Amos could become one of the great legal minds of today—just like you, daddy.

TYRONE He did, did he? Well, I'm not surprised. We live in strange times.

TONI   *(Comes over and puts a flower in a vase.)* My husband is so right, Aimless. You find the strangest people blundering their way through life today.

TYRONE And they all seem to wind up at your parties, my dear.

TONI   Well, I can't deny it. I try to keep the guest list down to my husband's closest friends, colleagues, business associates, or what have you. But it's like an infection. The list just spreads and next thing you know, there I am trying to entertain a hundred or so fruity socialites who do nothing but chatter, howl and slurp. The home becomes a regular madhouse.

AMOS   Yes, it must feel good to get away from it now and then.

TYRONE Now now, Toni, it's not all that bad. You seem to enjoy yourself. At least you don't have to work every day. Don't mind my wife, young man. She's always finding something to complain about. But that's all right. As long as she enjoys herself.

TANYA   Daddy, Mother Toni—since we're all here . . . Amos would like to make a very important announcement. Go ahead, darling.

AMOS   I don't think this is the proper time, darling. Occasion. That's the word I want. We should make it a special occasion.

TANYA   That's not what he meant, Mother Toni.

TONI   Just because he's a guest, he thinks we'll all run to do his bidding. Champagne? Yes, sir. Hors d'oeuvres? Only the best, sir. And where are the belly dancers? Coming right up, sir.

AMOS   Please, Mrs. Tripp. . . .
        (Toni takes off her blouse and starts belly dancing and humming Turkish music.)

TANYA   It's all right, Amos. Belly dancing is excellent for her nerves. It helps her loosen up.

TYRONE *(Clapping)* Just like my birthday party, eh Tanny? We had a little over two hundred guests for that occasion, m'boy. And in the middle of dinner I got up and announced that my wife would perform her famous belly dance.

TANYA   It was very unfair of you, daddy.

TYRONE Ho! They loved it! Laughing and cheering they were. She refused to do it at first. Said she was embarrassed.

AMOS That's understandable.

TYRONE We finally made her do it though. I threatened to reveal her age if she didn't. And here's the slammer—when it was all over, I got up and said, "There you have it, ladies and gentlemen—not bad for a fifty-three-year-old mother, eh?" She got an ovation.

AMOS Mrs. Tripp—please! You don't have to belly dance for me.

TYRONE Let her go, boy. Let her go. She wouldn't do it if she didn't want to.

TANYA *(Stops Toni)* Please, Mother Toni, you've danced enough. Please.

TONI *(Puts her blouse back on, puffing.)* Perhaps . . . perhaps you'd all care for some tea now. Aimless?

AMOS Please! *(Toni exits.)* Judge Tripp, do you think you'll have time to look over my thesis? There's less than thirty pages so far.

TANYA He'll be glad to do it, won't you, daddy?

TYRONE It's against my rules—but yes, I'll look it over. Only because I like you, m'boy.

AMOS I appreciate this very much.

TYRONE *(Opens the lid)* Bring me the flashlight, will you, Tanny. *(She goes to get it.)*

AMOS In there, sir? You're going to read it inside the trunk?

TYRONE Peace and quiet in there, m'boy. Believe it. You go ahead and enjoy yourself. My scaffold—you can play with my scaffold. Do you like it?

AMOS I found it very realistic, sir.

TYRONE That it is. Built it myself, you know. They wouldn't let me have one in the courtroom, believe it or not. So I built my own.

AMOS We read an essay of yours dealing with scaffolds and guillotines in the courtroom—how they were necessary.

TYRONE It's preposterous! A judge without a scaffold? Why not a doctor without his medicine? A pilot without his plane? A fisherman without his net? A whore without her—

TANYA Daddy! Here's the flashlight.

AMOS We all thought you intended your essay as satire, sir.

TYRONE Yes. I daresay a lot of people did. *(He disappears into the trunk and Toni rushes over with another flower.)*

TONI What's he doing? He can't have it twice in a row like that. It was my turn.

TANYA He'll only be a short while, Mother Toni. He just borrowed the trunk to read Amos' essay. You don't even have to lock it.

TONI So, you've put my poor husband to work, have you? You're not satisfied with having just me serving you—oh no. My husband is under your command as well.

TANYA Daddy wanted to read it, Mother Toni.

TONI   First me, then Tyrone, then . . . well you know who's next, don't you, Tanya? I can see he's already got you wrapped around his little legal finger.

AMOS   I love your daughter, Mrs. Tripp. And despite what you may think, I do not have her wrapped around my finger!

TONI   Oh! There's no need to drag sex into this!

TANYA   For God's sake, Mother Toni. Amos never mentioned a word about sex!

TONI   Yes. Well that doesn't surprise me.

AMOS   Mrs. Tripp, I don't know what you have against me. I can see something is really bothering you.

TONI   Hm! Now we get to the callous remarks.

AMOS   I'd like you to sit down, Mrs. Tripp. I want to talk with you. If you'll just sit down, *I* will go and prepare the tea.

TANYA   There. Did you hear that, Mother Toni? Amos has offered to make the tea. Let's both sit down and talk.

TONI   I can't believe what I'm hearing! You want me to sit down while a guest prepares the tea? Is that what I heard?

TANYA   Try not to think of him as a guest, Mother Toni. He's going to be your son-in-law. Think of him as part of the family. Please.

TONI   Dear Tanya, you're so young. Sit down, Aimless. You're our guest and I know how to make guests happy. With a piping hot cup of English Breakfast tea. *(She exits.)*

TANYA   Let's do sit down, Amos. We could both use a rest. *(She leads him to a couch.)*

AMOS   Absurd! That's the word I want. This whole thing is absurd. If I didn't know your father so well—that man in the trunk *is* your father, is he not?

TANYA   Yes, the Honourable Judge Tyrone Tripp.

AMOS   I've read six of his books and countless essays. If I didn't know him so well academically, I'd swear he was insane.

TANYA   Please understand, darling. My father's been under a lot of pressure at work.

AMOS   Well sure. I know what it's like. Look at me—don't you think I'm under pressure? Did you see my thesis? Do you know how far behind I am?

TANYA   Yes, yes, Amos. That's why I'm glad you came up. You can relax and finish it here.

AMOS   I've never been so far behind in my work. Talk of pressure! And yet you don't see *me* jumping into old home-made trunks.

TANYA   He's much older than you are, darling. Obviously you can handle the pressure better.

AMOS   And those clothes! What does he think this is? Hallowe'en?

TANYA   He's fond of the old ways. They'd laugh at him if he wore that costume in court today. At least up here he gets a chance to wear it.

AMOS   I suppose you're going to tell me your mother's under pressure too? I could understand why your father built the trunk if only to lock your mother inside. She dislikes me, Tanya. She really does.

TANYA   Please Amos, give her a chance. She's not used to meeting new people. She feels strange around you, but she'll get over it.

AMOS   Jumpin' Jupiter! She belly dances for a crowd of two hundred in the middle of her husband's birthday party and she feels strange around *me*?

TANYA   She's not used to meeting people individually. She does like you though, I know. She'll calm down after a stay in the trunk.

AMOS   If she offers me tea once more . . .

TANYA   Then I'll go make it. *(She kisses him.)* I love you, Amos. You know that, don't you?
(A pause)

AMOS   Tanya, tell me something. Have . . . have you ever been inside there? Inside the trunk?
(A pause)

TANYA   Before I met you, Amos . . . before we fell in love . . . I used to come up here once a week. I'd come with my parents. It was the only time I really got to see them. They're both so busy all the time. *(Pause)* Yes, I've spent time inside the trunk. I had to, you understand.

AMOS   Amazing. That's the word I want. I'm amazed that you would do such a thing. You're such a sane, rational girl. You're intelligent!

TANYA   And so are my parents, Amos. You've read my father's books.

AMOS   Oh Tanya, why didn't you tell me your family was like this?

TANYA   Would you have come if I *had* told you?

AMOS   Of course not! And I wouldn't have let you come either.
(Tyrone pops out of the trunk.)

TYRONE   It's a fine way to bugger up your eyes—reading this sort of bullshit, m'boy.

TANYA   Daddy!

TONI   *(Returns with a flower which she puts in a vase.)* You decided to come out did you? I don't have to tell you how rude it is to disappear like that when we have company.

AMOS   It's all right, Mrs. Tripp. I asked him to read my thesis.

TONI   Yes. Well, if you'll just step out, Tyrone, and let me get in there. *(Toni moves towards the trunk but Tyrone blocks her.)*

TYRONE Now, now, Toni. Don't you want to hear my final ruling on this?

TONI No thank you! I didn't come up here to listen to your rulings, Tyrone. Lord knows I have to put up with enough of them at home.

TYRONE Nonsense! *(He slams down the trunk lid.)* You're all going to hear the final judgment, and by golly you're all going to enjoy it! That's why we're all here—to enjoy ourselves! Now sit down! *(He goes to the desk and bangs on it with a gavel.)*

TYRONE This court is now in session.
(Tanya gently pulls Amos and Toni down so that the three are sitting on the trunk facing Tyrone.)

TYRONE The defendant will please rise and state his name.

AMOS This is ridiculous.

TANYA Go on, Amos—play along.

AMOS *(After a pause he shakes his head and gets up.)* Amos Byrd. Not Aimless, not m'boy, but Amos.

TYRONE Amos Byrd, the judgment of this court is that your thesis topic is bullshit.

AMOS I've heard that enough, thank you! *(He turns away.)*

TYRONE But . . . *(Amos stops and looks back at Tyrone.)* your logic is tight, your reasoning sound, and yes, you do have a fine legal mind. *(Bangs)* Case dismissed!

TANYA *(Jumps up and hugs Amos)* Oh, darling, you made it! You're fantastic!

TONI I must offer my congratulations, Aimless. They are in order.

AMOS Thank you, Mrs. Tripp. And thank you so much, Judge Tripp. Coming from you, that's a compliment I'll treasure.

TANYA Make the announcement now, darling.

AMOS Yes. Why not? Judge Tripp, Mrs. Tripp, I'm happy to announce that your daughter, the lovely Tanya, and I are officially engaged to be married. We ask for your blessings. *(He puts a ring on her finger.)*

TONI Did you hear that, everyone? Tanya and Aimless are going to be married! This *is* an occasion. An occasion that calls for the finest cup of Earl Grey tea! *(She starts to exit but Tanya stops her.)*

TANYA Please, Mother Toni, stay with Amos. I'll go make the tea. *(Tanya goes to the kitchen.)*

AMOS Yes, Mrs. Tripp, you've done too much already. Tanya can whip up some tea in a second.

TONI Did you hear that, Tyrone? It's already starting. Not even married yet and she's jumping to his command.

TYRONE She wouldn't do anything she didn't want to, dear. That's the rule here—she's enjoying herself.

TONI   It's too much for a mother to bear. Here, Tyrone, take the key and set my time. *(She opens the trunk and steps in.)*

TYRONE It's high time Amos here learned some family responsibility. Here m'boy. I'm going to let you hold the key. You'll be responsible for her stay in the trunk. Get used to it. *(He gives Amos the key.)*

TONI   No, Tyrone! Don't do this to me! He'll want to keep me locked up forever—I know his type!

AMOS   Look, why don't we leave the trunk unlocked?

TYRONE It's your own time, Toni. Do as you wish. *(Toni disappears into the trunk, slamming the lid closed.)* Amos, m'boy, come over here. I'll show you how my scaffold works—in case you ever want to hang the prosecution.

AMOS   Well, actually sir, I should continue working on my thesis now. I feel very encouraged after what you've told me.

TYRONE You don't seem to understand, m'boy. I didn't build this cabin for people to work in—it's here for you to relax in. It's for you to enjoy yourself. If you feel you have to do something constructive, then build yourself a scaffold. There's plenty of wood out back. You'll be wanting to build one sooner or later anyway—and not because you have to, but because you'll enjoy it.

AMOS   Judge Tripp, I don't know what your schedule's like these days. Myself, I'm under enormous pressure to finish my thesis. I don't mind fun and games when there's time, but just now I've got to face reality. I do have a lot of work.

TYRONE It's not something that you enjoy, is it m'boy?

AMOS   Well no, sir. I'd much rather have some free time to play around with. There's a scarcity of that these days.

TYRONE Not in the enchanted castle, there isn't! I know just how to solve your problem! *(He starts tearing up Amos' thesis.)*

AMOS   What are you doing! *(He rushes to grab what remains of his thesis.)*1 You're a bloody madman! A lunatic! Look at this mess! *(He starts picking up scraps of paper.)*

TANYA *(Enters)* What on earth . . . ?

TYRONE Make all the noise you want, m'boy! Enjoy yourself!

AMOS   If he weren't your father, I'd hang him, Tanya! He's destroyed all I've done!

TANYA Oh daddy, how could you do such a thing?

TYRONE He didn't want to work on that essay, Tanny. It was a lot of bullshit anyway.

AMOS   Well this does it! *(He stuffs his torn thesis into his briefcase and grabs his coat.)*

TANYA Amos! No! What are you doing?

AMOS   Good-bye, Tanya. Come with me if you want. I'm not staying here another minute.

TONI   *(Opens lid of trunk)* You're not leaving, are you, Aimless?

AMOS   Yes, yes, Mrs. Tripp. I can't impose on your hospitality any longer.

TANYA   You can't do this to me, Amos. If you leave ... I ... I'll hang myself! *(She goes and puts the noose around her neck.)*

AMOS   Tanya! Get away from that thing!

TONI   *(Steps out of the trunk and goes over to Tanya)* Yes, dear, let him go. He's showing his true colours—he doesn't care for you at all.

AMOS   Mrs. Tripp, don't you ever shut up!

TANYA   I love you too much, darling. I couldn't bear to have you leave me. I'll hang myself. Believe me, I will. If you try and stop me now, I'll do it after you leave.

TONI   Not even married yet and already he's put a noose around her neck.

TYRONE As long as he enjoys himself, Toni.

AMOS   Jumpin' Jupiter! Why don't you just come with me, Tanya? Leave these crazy parents of yours. They're not even concerned— they're a negative influence on you!

TANYA   I can't leave them, Amos. They *are* my family.

AMOS   Terrifying! That's the word I want. I'm terrified to think what you might have inherited from them.

TANYA   Please stay, darling. We'll all learn to love each other soon. I don't want to die and never see you again.

AMOS   I ... I really don't know what to do. My thesis ...

TYRONE Surely a thesis can't be more important to you than the life of a human being, m'boy!

TONI   Look who's talking.

TYRONE Cold-blooded murder! That's what it boils down to. Be careful, m'boy. Do you really want to face me in a court of law? Will you be able to look me in the eye when I'm giving the verdict? *(He draws a finger across his throat.)*

AMOS   Please come home with me, Tanya. If you do anything foolish, it'll be on my conscience. My head ... it's going to burst!

TONI   Can I get you something, Aimless? *(She goes to the kitchen and just then Tanya, reaching out to stop her mother, slips, causing Amos to jump in terror. Amos rushes over to Tanya and removes the noose.)*

TYRONE A wise ruling, m'boy. She was too innocent to hang.

(A pause as Amos looks from Tanya to Tyrone. Finally he throws his coat on the floor in defeat, grabs the flashlight, climbs into

*the trunk with his thesis, sighs 'Jumpin' Jupiter' and slams the
lid. Toni brings the tea over on a tray. They all sit on the trunk
with their tea.)*

TANYA   He didn't leave me. He loves me.
        (A pause)

TYRONE *(Sips)* He's a clever rascal, he is—that boy of yours. Did you
        notice? He kept the key. He'll be in there the rest of the week-
        end. He's got the trunk all to himself.

TANYA   He didn't leave me.

TONI   Not even married and already he shuts himself off from you,
        Tanya. *(Looks at Tyrone)* I've seen his type before, you know.

TANYA   My darling Amos decided to stay after all.

TYRONE *(Sips)* He's got a fine head on his shoulders, he has. He'll be a
        good son-in-law. *(Pause)* He and I, we're alike in many ways, we
        are. Fine legal minds.
        (A pause)

TONI   Poor Tanya, why do you smile? I can see you now—belly-danc-
        ing at his birthday party at the tender age of fifty-three.

TANYA   He loves me.
        (Blackout)

ELIZABETH GOURLAY

Born in Toronto, grew up in St. Stephen, New Brunswick, have lived in Montreal, Toronto, Halifax, in Vancouver since 1950. Married with two children, and now four young grandchildren. Also a painter, and a furious gardener, particularly enamoured of cultivating roses, species, hybrid teas, climbers, and miniatures.

Was in 1965, or 1966, that Earle Birney accepted a poem of mine for Prism *and suggested I might be interested in taking the newly initiated Creative Writing course at UBC. Shortly after, Earle Birney went back east, but I did study with Dorothy Livesay, Michael Yates, and Douglas Bankson; my horizons were immeasurably enlarged as a result, and I have been writing ever since, not only poems, but plays and short stories as well.*

The Excuse

After the Trojan war is over,
Ulysses, due to the enmity of Zeus,
is forced to travel far and wide,—

All the while Menelaus prospers
and his lady Helen lies in her long robe
along by her husband's side,—

I have to snicker
when I listen to
this sister of Clytemnestra,
sitting in the frescoed hall
explaining to Ulysses' son,
how it was Aphrodite blinded her,
who lured her away from her daughter
her bridal chamber
and her husband noted for his wit and his handsome
red hair.—

I think Helen smiles over at Menelaus when she says this.

Well, we all know Aphrodite. Her deceitful character.

No matter if she does ride in a white wagon drawn by doves.
She is lewd, lascivious, vengeful, a liar and a cheat.
But beautiful. And not to be resisted.

Aphrodite. Whom men often call by her other name.

Of Love.

The Discipline

This driver, wearing his visor cap, his thick gloves,
steps down from the bus, into the blowing fog:
tries to attach the trolley head into the wire up above.

In the beginning, a contact: there is a crackle, a whir.
flashes of blue fire, then the head, like a live thing,
breaks loose, sways back and forth, back and forth,
like a goose beak, or recalcitrant snake.

Four, fives times, the failure repeats itself,
but the driver is infinitely patient.
The power is up there, waiting,
he knows eventually the head will lock in the spot where
it is destined.

Snapshot by Stieglitz

Of course
the photographer has concentrated
on the artist's image, rather than the flower.
I am still trying to distinguish what the flower is:
a wild mandrake will hang its head like this,
beneath a whorl of leaves, single in its shape.
As children, we would search them in the springtime woods:
by late July, we sucked the gold round sickish fruit,
love apples, we called them.

Apparent
from the snapshot
Georgia's in a haste to catch the essence of the flower,
has brought to this place, no chair, no easel,
but holding to her brush, she crouches
beside her box of water colours, in front of the latticed porch.
Looks up, startled, with the camera's click.

Young then.
luxuriant dark hair, eyes smooth, skin petal soft.
Same porch where she and Stieglitz used to sit,
side by side, in separate rocking chairs, hands locked.
Sometimes, laughing, they would release their grasp,
regardless of observers, rush up the cottage stairs.
Georgia, meanwhile, unbuttoning her blouse.

History says
Stieglitz refused to let her have a child.
She did not argue, plead.
The erotic iris, lilies, roses disappeared.
The viewer is removed to other landscapes,
here are these desert mounds of sand,
in shape so like a body,
cow's skull, so many
delicate white bones.

PAUL A. GREEN

Born in London, UK, 1945. MA (Creative Writing) UBC 1970. Hyperactive CBC freelancer in early seventies (R&B DJ, *Ideas*, etc). Returned to UK 1973, to various "teaching" jobs. Poetry includes *The Slow Ceremony Bk1*, *Basement Mix*, and work in 1986 Chatto anthology *Angels of Fire*. Plays include *The Dream Laboratory* (CBC Radio); *Ritual of the Stifling Air* (BBC Radio 3); *Power/Play* (Capital Radio). Recent projects: with artist Jeremy Welsh: *The Slow Learning*, a "video poem," for the National Review of Live Art, Glasgow 1989, and a novel-in-progress.

The Slow Ceremony *is a sequence of "domestic" poems, written for my wife Cathy. Earlier sections appeared in* Prism 19/3.

13 Infinite Room Space
From The Slow Ceremony

oxygen   nitrogen   impurity
disturbed
by nerve electrics

opposite: altarpiece of mirror
a watering place
for optics

mirrored drapes fold
wrinkling by solemn expectation
in high erotics

the two wardrobes
trickle open
sleeping tactics

33 The Slow Process

The slow process

is another helix
of spiralling leaves

the time of years
misty with sparks and apples

and her careful placing of colours
constructs the whole house

to include small and defiant creatures
whose habitat is a sniff of dreaming

and sweet breathing

34 The Drift

To dart along red runnels
earth clogged quite sweetly
in nails/hard cracks

she needed wider breathing
pads of harebells
various worn stones

between blue flowers existing there/not here
and free-based tranquillity dreams

falls the shadow of many smiles
and the drift of some poppies

35 Field Effect: The River Wye

The sun went down, brown. Sheep were on hold. In their droll referendum position. The skein of silence can, be sure of it, be a great soother of waters. Stippled water can affect the listening, listing of continuity on the flat mud ooze. You are disappearing down a smooth beach cleft.

I was left behind. Everything was going down so slowly. The drifting dead are all present. All content. I would be. Quite so. The dream lines: *The wren has built its bushes and temples in our sleep*. The silence of the eel equals the science of a completed tower of dancing glass.

Here we go into a soft wish. The Holy of Days. To slip into the bank, its heaped blood-earth, a subsiding sun. That rabbit is virtually a rabbit to the play of a naked eye.

We went to walk right up into the pig-strewn field. Sheep grazing against the draft of higher air.

The united composition is divided by a jump-jet along the dark jots of horizon, hear this, demon vibrations fantasticated, cockpit death terror, a scythe of smoke, beyond belief.

Grey lion, grey bear, grey mole. Stand near the stones, please.

GENNI GUNN

Genni Gunn was born in Trieste, Italy, and came to Canada when she was ten. She received an MFA from UBC in 1984 and has published prose, poetry, and translations in magazines and anthologies, including *Best Canadian Stories 1988*. Her published works are a novel, *Thrice Upon a Time* (Quarry 1990), a book of poetry translations, *Devour Me Too* (Guernica 1987), and a short story collection, which will appear in the spring of 1991 from Oberon Press.

"On the Road" is one of a group of stories set in the music business— fictionalized accounts of the life of a female musician. My own experiences as a professional musician (vocals, bass guitar, and piano) since 1973 act as a backdrop to the exploration of the identity of the performer versus the myth/performer created by the audience.

On the Road

I'm going on the road, I said to Fletch (meaning, this is a good time for a separation).

I'll write regularly, I said.

You can fly out to see me, I said.

I won't be long, I said (packing enough things for two months).

I'll miss you, Fletch said (but he held me as if he knew it was the last time).

On the road. The layman (non-musician) calls this "touring." We are no more touring than if we were a pack of rats infesting a village in China. Touring implies tall, air-conditioned busses with smoked windows and portable toilets; impeccable sheets and starched pillowcases; hotel rooms with a view of the sea, or the mountains, or whatever; visits to museums, art galleries, and a famous/infamous dead person's home—all restored, of course, with period furniture.

We are on the road. From this vantage point, what we see is the hard grey asphalt, the vast slow movement of an orchestral forest and the frenzied rhythm of puppets in semi-darkness, whose strings we control from the stage. Or try to.

Five of us are squeezed into the van (I am the only woman) among guitars and suitcases, somebody's stereo and the front wheel of a bicycle. We're hauling a twelve-foot trailer which threatens to jack-knife at every corner. While travelling, we revert to two basic sounds: shouting or silence. I don't know which is worse. I take 222's before getting in. I've become the night driver. It is the best time—night. In the darkness, the road mingles with the forest; lines soften and I can almost forget the dreary grey of it all, dull as day-to-day existence.

I have devised a method to cope with the irrationalities to which is attached the nomenclature, "reality." I compose imaginary letters which say all the things which escape me in those times when I most need the right words. Language is plastic, therefore not bio-degradable. Thoughts are safe. I compose these letters most often during the silent night drives.

Chris keeps shifting in the front passenger seat. He always sits there at night. We've already settled into a routine. Like an old married couple. Chris is a drummer. He can't keep still—too many rhythms inside. We should be in Calgary by dawn.

Dear Fletch,

I was a gypsy travelling the taut edge of my nerves, singing to fill the caverns. You were a dark minstrel whose anguish scribbled your face. We linked arms and declared war. Our house had bunkers, sandbags all around. We were one against the world, our strengths and weaknesses carefully balanced in each other. A true illusion/delusion of equality. No one existed outside those barriers which forced us into close scrutiny. Now I see we are mutations

too intimate

two strangers discovered.

Our love was the leaf of a coastal winter. It took two summers to wither.

Was, Fletch, *was*. Time to move on.

If he could hear these words,
he'd say, why? (no, he'd shout it);
he'd say, WHAT'S WRONG?
he'd say, WHAT HAVE I DONE?
This is how Fletch is. Self-centred. What have *I* done, he'd say.

Dear Fletch,

It's not something you've done at all. It is *me*. I have realized:
I'm not your mother;
I'm not your slave;
I'm not your possession;
I am.

Chris says, you want one of these? He's popping a couple. Sure. Something to keep me awake (I'm not justifying here), no appetite, and my head buzzing as if a swarm of hornets are nesting in my brain.

Fletch, do you remember the nest I knocked down from the eaves above the balcony door? Sliced it open and found a perfect brain, or a condominium complex—all those nooks and crannies and floors and windows and doors. No honey, though.

It was the morning after the night you were so angry because you were late for work and couldn't get a taxi, and it was snowing outside (like it rarely does in Vancouver), and the car had no snow tires, and you didn't know, and

it's all your fault, you said;

why didn't you tell me, you said;

you must have *known* this would happen, you said (as if I'd planned it)

and then you smashed your fist into one of the nine small squares of the window in the balcony door. And a hornet flew in and bit you on the arm.

I should have laughed (I wanted to);

I should have said, you're absurd (I thought it);

I should have shouted, serves you right (and patted the hornet on the head);

but you were so *serious*. Knuckles bleeding, a welt on the upper arm, all held out to me for sympathy. And I led you like a child to the bathroom, dabbed on the alcohol (blow, blow, there, there), stuck on Band-aids that lifted when you straightened your hand, and avoided looking into your eyes for fear I would collapse and laugh until I cried. Later I did (laugh) after the taxi drove you away.

I'm wired, Chris says. How much longer?

I shrug. My teeth are clenched so tight I have to speak around them. A couple of hours. Maybe three.

He pulls out a pair of sticks from behind the seat and starts drumming on his knee.

You wanna do the States? he asks.

You got paper and pen? I say.

Yeah. Sure. Alphabetical or random?

Whatever.

It's one of our pastimes. Trying to name all the u.s. states. We always manage to miss a couple, like Oklahoma or Wyoming or Connecticut or New Hampshire. Never Hawaii or Alaska.

When we get to Calgary, we have to unload all the equipment, set it up, do a soundcheck. We're operating through sheer chemical force. Nothing natural about being up twenty-five hours. We all did a few lines before coming down from the hotel rooms. We're on fast-forward mode, gums desensitized, front teeth frozen, and the thoughts are racing so quickly we

can only verbalize one in seven:
    Would you move that. . . .
    Turn it into the. . . .
    When we get to the second set. . . .
    And the intro. . . .
    Forty-five min. . . .
    What do you mean three. . . .
    And when they said there was. . . .
    We're finished by 1 p.m. I need a drink, Chris says. I gotta come down a bit.
    Starting time is nine tonight. I go to my room, buzzing. Unpack. Iron all my clothes. Brush where my teeth must be. Undress. Shower. Pull on a nightgown. Lie down. Mattress lumpy and soft. I have to sleep. So tired. Unclench. Unclench.

The nighttime parts, the playing—hardly worth thinking about. After a few road trips, when all the newness rubs off (not unlike a love affair) you are forever desensitized. People cease to be individuals; towns cease to have names; dates cease to exist. You are only aware of Mondays (when you set up) and Saturday nights (when you tear down and drive all night, all day, sometimes all night again). So it all comes down to first and last night (which is exactly all you ever remember of a love affair too). At least in this business, there is a paycheque on that last night. Well. Perhaps it's only the currency that differs.

Dear Fletch,
    Thanks For The Memories. Hummmmm. Hummmmm. I don't know the tune. Only the title. (And besides, I can't hum in my head). Old songs, old clichés, old lovers—who can remember them all?

Dear Fletch,
    I do love you (which is not the same as being in love). Too many implications in that one word "in": in-sincere, in-secure, in-sensitive (notice all the esses, the feminine sounds). Snakes. Snakes. Hiss. Hiss. Emosssssions are feminine. Soft, supple, subtle, silly, stupid, sickly—all feminine descriptions, or effeminate ones. And now, Fletch, if you could hear this:
    Stop with that feminist crap, you'd say.
    You're making me a monster, you'd say (using all the male M-sounds).
    You're pampered and privileged, you'd say, that's the problem (male P-sounds).
    Too much time on your hands to think these thoughts, you'd say (male T-sounds).
    Trouble-maker-posing-problems-that-don't-exist, you'd say (using all

your maleness at once).

Well. Tough. Shut your ears if you want to. And your eyes. And your whole face. If it makes you feel better. You can't invalidate me. Not any more. Because I'm not playing.

Chris is starting to fall in love with me. God. It's only been two weeks. It usually takes a little longer. One of four men always does. This is
because we're on the road;
because he's too comfortable with me;
because I'm not his wife;
because I buy my own food;
because I don't expect anything from him;
because I'm independent;
because I listen to him without commenting; and
because he hasn't gotten me into bed.

Well. I know that once this happens, he'll expect to change all of the above, which will suddenly become threatening.
Women shouldn't travel alone, he'll say.
You shouldn't be so . . . friendly with men, he'll say.
They'll get the wrong idea.
How could you go off like that, all afternoon, he'll say, and not tell me?
Naturally, I assumed we'd have dinner together, he'll say, especially after. . . .
Why don't we share a room at the next place? he'll say. Everyone knows anyway.

And there would end all independence and I'd be back to where I was before I went on the road.

I can't even pretend to be falling in love with Chris. This sensation is too predictable. I used to deny the voice inside me and listen instead to a Mother's words telling:
Good girls only have sex with a man they love.
He won't respect you if you do.
Play the game.
Use it to get what you want.
Sex is your best weapon. Weapon. Weep. On.

Well. Weep is something I won't do. Weeping belongs to tragic heroines or victims or silly brainless twits. If I have the need to, I cry. It has a harder, more real sound. Plastic pellets falling on corrugated iron. It's only salt and water. The worst thing for wounds.

I've only declared "I love you" twice. Once, so long ago I don't remember, and the second time to Fletch in our early days, before I knew him.

I begin to avoid Chris, to spare him all the anxiety; treat him like one of my brothers, and all that happens is he falls in love even more.

We drive at night. Saskatoon, this time. (What routing.) He wants to play States.
  I'm sick of it, I say.
  Oklahoma, Wyoming, Connecticut & New Hampshire, I say.
  It's boring, I say.

Dear Chris,
  Why the hell don't you take a downer for a change, shut your eyes and quit giving me that hurt look.
  What else is there to do on the road, he says.
  Life is a bore, he says.
  I need adventure, he says.
  I don't love my wife, he says.
  You are beautiful, he says.
  You are desirable, he says.
  What's wrong with me? he says.

Back to that. I stare straight ahead and dig through my brain for the right phrases. The ones Mothers teach their daughters to go along with the TRUTH: Men have fragile egos.
  I'm already involved with someone, I lie.
  I think you're very attractive (half-lie).
  If there were going to be someone, it would be you (another lie).

Smile. (Fake.) There, in the dark. One side of my face cracks open. Christ, I can't feel my teeth. Everything's going to fall out all at once.
  Smile, you goddamn fool. It'll pass.
  I can't.
  Smile. Wider. Wider. Wider.
Christ. Every lie I ever told is falling out of the corners. Plastic.

I look at Chris. He smiles. Embarrassed but pleased. Well. Another lie gone direct to the muscles. He's sitting up straighter. I let him keep his hand on my thigh for a full thirty seconds before I say, get the pencil, we'll do the States. Every goddamn one of them (just to keep his fingers off my skin and his ego on the passenger side).

Dear Fletch,

I have always drifted alone in the fragile stalks of prairie wheat, lulled by the moans of farmers mourning losses. I'm settling into the knobby surface of a chenille bedspread, on an Alberta night, as stars mount hoodoos sculpted in sandstone—a Stonehenge transient as the wind's moods—windows open, enticing a shift in destiny. Above, the moon mimicks the earth. I have been treading the liquid warmth of friends, the undulating wave of lovers, the inevitable epiphany of self-preservation.

If only we could go on being lovers and never live together.

A Mother's voice says:
You don't mean that.
You need a man.
Sex is a tool, a weapon, a gun, an upper, a downer, a need, a want, a whimsical, fantastical sensation.
You need protection.
You need affection.
You need LOVE.

Well. Ok. It sounds nice (the last one, I mean). But. When I look inside the pictures of love, I see spent itineraries and women/marionettes bobbing at odd angles, mouths gaped wide as frames trying to utter sound.

And now I will tell truly the truth about what happens at night and why it is not worth thinking about.

There is a stage with a carpet black & red, black & blue, black & —.

There are five of us in our stage clothes (shiny, satin, silky—all those s-sounds) to go with the lights and the illusions (like women).

There are microphones, guitars, basses, drums, sticks, organs—all the male genitalia reproduced in wood and metal—a constant erection. (The females are only passive receptacles in the walls which the males plug into).

There is a room full of people who:
like music, and/or
are lonely, and/or
need a drink, and/or
are trying to forget themselves.

Dancing is foreplay. Watch two people dance. Hear their bodies speak. Feel the tension in the space between them, drawing them closer.

We are voyeurs and conductors; lavish orchestrators of fancies. Each set is carefully designed to bring this foreplay to a climax. Leave them breathless and pounding for an encore. Magic. Illusion.

In the daytime, we roam the streets, ordinary people. Unnoticed, unwanted, unimportant.

But what do you want to do for a living? they ask.

What an exciting life, they say.

You are so lucky, so talented, so free, so everything that we want, they say.

Well. So much for illusion.

On the road. Five, six weeks. My hormones are mutating. Malfunction. The asphalt grey, straight and narrow, bridges a hypnotic gulf back ten years, back to eighteen. My feet accelerate on the plank to the altar where a tall young groom awaits. My father transfers me man-to-man and I, versed in dependence, repeat the words, "honour and obey." At the motel, I shiver in a strange bed, listening to a Mother's eyes. This man can only possess the flesh; he cannot read inside my head the tablets inscribed with the betrayal of women.

There, in the pretence of that movement, the first seed sprouted when his foreign body claimed sovereignty.

Dear Fletch,

We have travelled the road together on the wings of a phoenix.

Remember the Oregon coast, rough and turbulent as the hardening jigsaw of my convictions, clouds heavy with the sweat of industry and the cold breath of atrophied women?

Remember a Nevada desert, arid faces eroded with desolation and the incessant sanding of the spirit?

Remember the concrete slabs, Arizona monuments; you erecting cardboard castles tall enough to ensure death in a fall, and I masoned into the four walls, observing the world through a sliver of lemon light.

Remember the lush green of New Mexico, communes, a social distribution. Serene faces, my emotions tie-dyed into the flowers of my skirt or around the neck.

Remember a Colorado park of red stone, blood caked dry.

I found myself suddenly alone.

I want to be in love, I think.

I want to make love, my body says.

I want LOVE, a Mother's voice shouts.

My heart's valves tighten. Function/malfunction. I spit out excess blood into Saskatchewan swamps when no one is looking, and wear lipstick to conceal the drained smile, my pupils glazed with the opulence of marble no man can scratch.

In my room, I lie in bed and listen to the whispers below my window; to the laughter next door; to the unoiled springs of a bed in the room above—those lonely, empty sounds of lovers battered one against the other, trying to find themselves still bleeding.

On the road. Where that cold hard surface permeates me; where I become the road, cracked but able to withstand the weight of many travellers.

When I return home, I haven't written Fletch a single letter, and all his things are gone. There is only the lingering of romantic memories, light as the whisper of air through the shattered pane of the window above the balcony door.

GEOFF HANCOCK

Geoff Hancock, BFA 1973, MFA 1975 (Creative Writing), is editor in chief of *Canadian Fiction Magazine*. He has published several anthologies of innovative Canadian short fiction. His recent books include *Canadian Writers at Work: Interviews* (Oxford University Press), *Published in Canada: The Small Presses* (Black Moss), and *Fast Travelling: Essays* (Porcupine's Quill).

"The Stainless Steel Streamliner" began in Jacob Zilber's introductory Creative Writing class, and in various forms and guises has become a central motif of my life, my modes of perception, my initiation, and my travels.

The Stainless Steel Streamliner

The past that is always in the present crashes like an aluminum tray in a steel sink. Boxcars slam like heavy artillery. I'm sliding back, with the twenty herz screech of wheels curving and sparking on a track. I'm on a heroic journey through memory and history. The great Canadian landscape that has no centre, and no history that can be written down, streams past the window of "The Canadian," CPR's stainless steel streamliner. Not any train, but Cosmic Train, the world's longest Dome Car Ride, a single force that keeps reviving a nostalgia for my discovery of literary Canada.

The Canadian Pacific Railway is Canada's most elemental construction joining idea to writer to reader. Robert Kroetsch, Eli Mandel, Andrew Suknaski, and Michael Ondaatje would call this the form we all share: the Canadian long poem. The poem is as big as a continent. This was the train of my youth. I moved into the world on the horizontal level. Not the corporate monster engaged in legal actions, not the official history with heroes so nobly portrayed by Pierre Berton; but the train of my ideals, the train that goes on and on.

This isn't real history, but memory acting as history. One of my past selves worked here as a dining car waiter for five summers and a couple of winters while I was a student of Creative Writing at the University of British Columbia. I am still connected by obscure lines to that distant place and distant time. A memory arises. I'm reading some Canadian fiction, some Canadian poetry. The stories, paragraphs, stanzas, lines, phrases, words link and unlink, a continual process of discontinuity. I remember trains, when I worked the Vancouver to Winnipeg run, on my feet the whole time, walking halfway across Canada.

I've been on many trains. The BC Rail to Prince George; dreadful trains in Turkey; a train stuck in a sandstorm in Iran; on a third class train in India, next to holy men with honey and dung in their hair. I've been to 16,000 feet in the Peruvian Andes, about to faint until the goatskin bag with oxygen was brought around. One summer, I took the Algoma Central to Hearst, Ontario,.moose capital of Canada.

Years of atmosphere and adventure reduced to narrative seconds. Every place I go is an extension of the stainless steel streamliner. The train taught me to be literary in Canada; to remember, to dream, to mythmake. On the stainless steel streamliner, a new self came out of my travelling self. A voice calls to me from those days. This essay is a form of memory; I try to write myself back into the past; the dilemma: how to do it. E.J. Pratt was right. The transcontinental railroad combines communication, history, and myth. In exile, I hunt my truth. The psychic wound is deep.

On the train, I learned about that rare species of Canadian—the railwayman. Conductors as regal as High Chancellors to brakemen swinging their red lanterns. I saw trackmen in the Rockies, their faces so sooty they turned into sasquatches. As a writer, I had to learn to speak for these men who had spent a lifetime working on the railways. Without people like me, their experience would not exist.

Elegance, romanticism, and utilitarianism; that curious combination of the CPR. This wasn't Via Rail with its practical pickles and hamburgers in a hurry, casual food casually prepared and indifferently served. Until the mediocrity of Via Rail, the CPR operated its 341 sleeping, parlour, and dining cars with tyrannical efficiency. This was to lead me to my moderate affection for post-modernism. I resisted the tyranny of efficiency as I resisted the tyranny of beginning, middle, and end in fiction.

"How do you like your job?" you might have asked me as a tourist.

"Chance to travel, meet people, not waiting in the rain for a bus, clean sheets every night, and ham and eggs on the job."

You expected a heroic tale. But all I can give you is what I remember. Or create.

What I needed to know was secret, even from myself. The geography unwound for me, a land as wide as hope. The sweetest corn in Canada pressed against the tracks at Medicine Hat; Winnipeg goldeye swam out of the lake; some Indians sold me illicit salmon in North Bend, BC. This was my small part in the drama of Canada. This essay, then, is a story. It's about why I am a nationalist, not a regionalist. Somewhere under the language of Canadian writing is a structure that links all the parts and maintains the tension that holds us together. It's fiction of a kind.

The CPR liked formal structures. The dining car was an ordered experience, the point of reference. Out there, chaos. The CPR had a specific view of how we fit into all this country. Based on etiquette and protocol, deadlines, schedules, timetables, committees: the Canadian way. Look around that dreamy dining room. Two rows of twelve tables. 48 seats. The pure beauty of rose bowls. White linen. Tinkling silverware, rubbing, as Ray Bradbury said, their little metal shoulders together. Napkins folded into elegant cones. Careful glaziers had etched frozen chickadees and magpies into glass partitions at each end of the room with as much care as medieval guildsmen. Yet children smudged the feathers with gravy covered fingers, as if to block out the landscape beyond. Out there: the pinto ponies of the Stoney Indian band raced over fertile Alberta, galloping with their mystery.

We were caught between order and disorder. As George Orwell remarked, if democracy is in the dining room, anarchy is in the kitchen. Or as we said, there are two ways of doing things, the right way, and the CPR way.

The kitchen was a short-term residence in hell. A stifling pinched space. Jostling men, bad tempers, the savage glare of fat chefs. As Dickens remarked, men with a great deal of train oil in their systems; men without the stamina and emotional muscle would quit in a hour. Off the train at the first stop. But a trip through hell can be an enlightening experience. I'm an Aries, fire is my nature. I like volcanic experiences. With eruptions come change. This is how I became a writer. Describing what I saw in front of me. Whether it was there or not.

The CPR needed trainmen, porters, and waiters during Expo '67. The railroad added extra cars, about 1924 vintage, which were later sold to Mexico. I had some carhop experience from a few months working at a Vancouver White Spot. With a urine test, and a haircut, I had a job on the train. Elsewhere in Canada, small presses were starting up: House of Anansi, Talonbooks, Oberon Press, Coach House Press, Very Stone House. But I had to discover Canada in a more pragmatic way.

The CPR preserved old values. Since the CPR lived in the past, it was appropriate I begin my career in a dead man's clothes. I needed a uniform. A sad-eyed Greek cook, sipping whiskey from his mickey, said someone died last week. I could wear his uniform. The uniform linked me, with a hitched waistband and large safety pins, to other lives in the solitary spaces of Canada. Ideas I would put to use when I began a different search for a Canada too large to know, when I explored surrealism, magic realism, and the various kinds of stories I would publish in my own literary magazine.

A Ukrainian waiter, one gold tooth, primed me with a repertoire of quips, puns, boffos, and oneliners. This is how we got tips. "Waiter, what's for dinner." I'd point to my apron stains: "Tomato soup, chicken curry, cherry pie. . . . "

My first steward, in his bowler hat and stiffbacked dignity, had 35 years of road experience. He no longer exists unless I write him down. That raises another problem about the stainless steel streamliner: how much surface do we need to describe a character? Can we explore a surface to the edge before it becomes a fragment?

The second steward I worked for said he had a frog farm. He raised frogs for French restaurants. Once they broke out of their breeding ponds and crossed the TransCanada Highway in such numbers they blocked traffic. So many wonders are revealed if only we say them. Trains can take us to many places, including some so odd we doubt they exist. The last spike was driven at Craigellachie, in the Rockies. Somebody stole the commemorative plaque. Looking out the window makes us aware of some kind of history. The CPR's west coast terminus was Port Moody, or New Westminster, no, it's Vancouver. Where does this train end? Which end is Mile Zero? Does this train go to Halifax? Is that the end? Or is it half an inch further east? Does this place at whichever end have a name or is it too bright to see? Sure, trains go to destinations. But not all places are on maps. What we remember, and what we hope, and what we do not see are also the destinations of trains. So is the literary theory. Consider: the CPR is a shared fiction—we are all characters in one chapter or another of it. What are the implications?

Crammed into the waiter's station were five men, whom we called "the boys." The pantryman was addressed as rudely as possible. "Hey, Pants!" They muttered creative oaths as filthy as any street punk, in Greek, Ukrainian, or good old Canadian foul mouth. These were the authentic European stories. Such multicultural diversity was more eloquently expressed when I published fiction from the unofficial languages of Canada. I realized one thing. Most railwaymen forged a significant identity, defined by their relationship to each other. As the ads in the *Globe & Mail* say, they were team players in a large system. The loner and the transient had no place here. Immigrants, the backbone of the railway working man. Though they keep moving around, they have nourishing roots.

The guys in the kitchen are expendable to railroads. Unlike hoggers, or engineers, with their shrewd eyes and strong unions, the CPR engaged and discharged employees as easily as shunting boxcars. Did you hear about the man who quit in a huff, changed his mind a day later, only to find he had lost 18 years' seniority?

Yeah, I heard it, a true story. The CPR was racist beyond belief. A black had no chance of employment beyond middle management. I hope that's changed now. The CPR was said to be built upon the bones of the Chinese. Many of the men I worked with were serious drinkers. I've seen many a steward flat on his face, and a waiter knock back a mickey and serve breakfast without losing his tray, his cookies, or his smile. I was learning about the Al Purdy school of writing. So I sat on his face; how do you like Canadian poetry, I asked.

I never went to the kitchen without a feeling of furtiveness, or incredible danger. From scalding, sharp knives, a chef's wrath. Temperatures over 100°. A job of sheer drudgery, like filling out a Canada Council grant application form. The fourth chef scraped and steamcleaned plates. Bad work; detergent stripped skin off hands, rubber gloves split in minutes. Third chef peeled potatoes, carrots. Second chef did all the work; apple and cherry pies, chicken salads, sliced ham. The head chef, with his attaché case of personal knives, pressed steaks with his thumb for tenderness. When I first joined the CPR, junior employees could not address the head chef or steward. We had to wait on the chefs, many of them foul tempered from a lifetime of cutting beef and steaming chicken on the CPR. The French-Canadian chefs were rumoured to piss in the apple juice.

Crammed inside the ten paces of a railway car kitchen, over 500 meals a day were prepared. The secret forces of nature were harnessed, reshaped according to the rules of the CPR and every steward had a thick memo book, with long-lost recipes for venison, bison, duck, trout.

The kitchen crew looked like fugitives from a chain gang, or promising writers at their first impromptu conference. Loose fitting white jackets, striped baggy pants, white hats and neck scarves to soak up perspiration. They drank quarts of apple juice, sucked on ice cubes, munched oranges. They operated in a closed world of chicken salad, Denver sandwiches, roast beef, asparagus soup, ham omelettes mixed in a five gallon steel bucket with a yard long whisk. They might go to the vestibule or the side door. Out there, the land was growing in size, away from all this mediocrity. Out there, Canadian gods and goddesses, and rites and rituals, the entire history and geography of our psyche. As Eli Mandel might write, it's *out of place, in another time*. Even then I asked that this place be guarded from my writing until I could express it.

"The Canadian" was made of stainless steel by the Budd Car Company of Philadelphia. The sculptured lines of the train seemed a testimonial to firmness, bluntness, stiffness. The jaunty beaver perched on the head end, before the new logo, was like an icon or pictograph. Like Yeats' mask, it cojoined and linked cultures. The train, rich with the fertile smell of grease, was the key that unlocked Canada. It seemed impervious to change.

But train time, like styles in fiction, had to change. First came the small delays. Freight trains before passenger. The slow erosion of service. Employee layoffs. Shutdown of branch lines, closing the whistle stop stations. The CPR had a new logo, a triangle within a circle. I read in the employee newsletter this symbolized progress within the transportation world. But like a pictograph whose story is lost, it also meant the end of the great days of dining car service as surely as Ben Jonson's *Volpone* meant the end of Elizabethan drama. And so these memories, a train trip filled with ghosts. The CPR was travelling in the wrong direction. Filled with an illusion of itself, it travelled the shortest distance between nowhere and nowhere. We should have gone in the other direction, back to the state before the railroad, before history was distorted by our version of it.

A sign: for hygienic reasons, wash your hands after going to the bathroom. Beneath this, a scratched warning: come the revolution, aint gonna be no more dining cars. 1967. Psychedelic music. Mother Tucker's Yellow Duck, the Addled Cromish Light Show. Countercultural forces were at work. Canadian literature and Canadian history were changing. Owsley Blue, the best LSD in the world, could be found in Calgary as well as San Francisco. We must change the world. These signs were scratches in the monolithic puritanism of the CPR.

Railroads are administered by men with military minds. They wanted memos, rules, regulations: the railroad was marked off in sections. A corporation needs systems, grids, mileage markers, schedules, large clocks. All the way stations of the CPR looked the same, and were built with standard plans. The CPR was not on the side of revolution, personality, anger, or outrage. The boys on the crew identified with Agatha Christie's *Murder on the Orient Express*. If a CPR inspector had been bumped off, we all would have done the crime. We cheered when the Stainless Steel Streamliner, on loan to an American movie company, smashed Toronto's Union Station to bits in the concluding scene of the Gene Wilder, Richard Pryor film, *The Silver Streak*.

"Getting a bit long back there," the steward would say, running a finger up the back of my neck. "Men have strangled on hairs in their soup. Women faint at hairs on their carrots." The CPR required reason, and brush cuts, to go along with its steel and lines of track. We called it Canadian Pathetic.

Attitudes banged and clashed like couplings on boxcars. The older crews were at odds with the summer help. Fast food the way of the future. The straight lines of railway thinking unable to channel the spiralling energies of our real natures. Hence this essay, a literary trick. What do I want to reveal of my real self then, and what of now? I face the magic double of myself in this recollection? So even this memory becomes a fiction as I meet myself as an identity of words, and those I quarrelled with in the kitchen.

My job then: an absolute maze of maddening details. Washing creamers, scooping out jam jars, fetching roast beef, topping up salt and pepper shakers, supplying cooks with ice water, filling sugar bowls, cleaning window ledges, taking crumbs out of the bread box, sectioning grapefruit, waiting on tables, sixteen people to a sitting. Any part of the job simple, but every detail must be perfect. And now: that job on the railroad a dress rehearsal for editing a literary magazine, with promotion, distribution, layout, design, correspondence, manuscript evaluation, editorials, proofreading, trips to the post office. An equally maddening maze of details. But I was ready.

The steward yelled: "You always use a stainless steel fish fork for salmon! Silver taints salmon! Taints!"

The head waiter yelled, "You don't trim celery root like that! Celery root is beautiful! You trim celery root like Michelangelo sculpted the chin of Moses! You care about your celery root."

The CPR built itself by overcoming such immense obstacles and impossibilities.

Each day was filled with such shouts. That was how we defined ourselves. We didn't have problems with finding our voices. But as George Bowering suggests, it was harder to hear what the language was saying. Each of us was the narrator of an unresolved fiction. How could we control this material? After all, the CPR sent telegrams across Canada: the first Canadian short fictions. Not enough information to make a proper long fiction. Small focussed perceptions. The CPR proceeds with linear understanding. Stop. But I had to return to the beginning to make the past. Begin.

The job (then and now) seemed impossible to do. Yet before long, I made it my true vocation. I was to serve. So I served horseradish as graciously as any aristocrat, changed a tablecloth in a split second, and replaced it with a full set of silver. In those days, the stainless steel streamliner had full silver service: tureens, creamers, coffeepots, underlining dishes, all silver. I appreciated standards before the decline. I could get a tip from a fat walleted diner as I explained how I could balance a full tray of dishes on a speeding train. Frank Lloyd Wright built his houses using the same cantilever principle. The job demanded the creation of imagination, order, and balance, in the midst of a welter of opposing forces. I even had a few seconds to appreciate a group of granaries full of wheat, sacks, and binder twine, or the sun hot as buffalo blood blazing off the windows of the rear cars as the train turned a corner out of Medicine Hat.

Four days of this mayhem, five days off, unless the train was late. I wish editing, freelance writing, and literary publishing was as rewarding. From sunrise to sunset, sixteen hours a day eastbound, eighteen hours westbound because of time zone changes. Lake Louise, which we called Lake Lousy because of the extra sitting of passengers, introduced me to the basic question of writing: which images should we choose? That was followed by the basic principle of modern art: the interchangeability of images. When I first wrote about magic realism, I mentioned Arthur Horsfall's work. Among his many magical paintings of Lake Louise is one with

Canada's most famous image as a series of life size postcards, with others visible beneath the upturned corner of the top one. The secrets of Canada are so obvious we miss them most of the time.

Some trips were pure Rabelaisian. We partied too much, passing the communal joint around the bunks in the baggage car. We had waterfights. We chased attractive passengers, wistfully dreaming of a sexy dalliance. The steward smirked, "let the train do the pushing." We told the new boys to look out at the Husky Tower in Calgary just as we passed the high pressure hoses of the scrubbing equipment. We ordered gourmet items or junk food not on the menu to annoy the cooks. They grabbed their nuts and said, "Here's some weiners and beans!" This was our ritual carnival, how we renewed ourselves against the CPR's extreme sense of order. We created new identities in our cook or waiter's costume; we did violence to our true identities to open up the several possibilities of ourselves.

Other trips became super-realist fiction. Mechanical and industrial reactions against romanticism. Even the solid order of a corporate railroad meets the unpredictable. Dramatic freight train derailments that spread potash over the prairies. Telephone poles snapped in half. Box cars twisted and ruined, solid wheels a quarter mile away. The train went through forest fires in the Fraser Canyon, rock slides in the Kootenays. Once, a four ton boulder slid 2,000 feet down a steep, wet slope, derailing the train, and nearly knocking it into a lake, ripping a day coach in half, and killing a young woman. For passengers, like readers, this is not a safe passage. Death and destruction are part of the world.

Language can save us when nature as critic makes a violent edit of our version of history. This isn't realistic fiction. This is remembered fiction. So it's better than it really was. The CPR as a vast cybernetic fiction, all technology and engineering, still couldn't turn us into machines. The CPR worked against me so I would be like them. With an active imagination, I worked against them.

Even at the worst moments, say a twelve hour delay, which sapped energy, strength, and imagination, led to a natural high. The work that nourished us became in Neruda's fine phrase "impure." We held knives sharp as razors; only the slightest hesitation kept us from killing each other. Then, the high. Trees took on outlines as sharp as any seen under the influence of good dope. In front of us, a new Canadian literature: trees about to reveal their secrets. Hell's Gate in the Fraser Canyon quenched our intellectual thirst as if we had drunk invisible water. As Neruda said, natural action is affected by deeper feelings that become translated into the reflective substance known as literature.

Usually, we weren't reflecting. We sang pornographic songs in the kitchen. Told dirty jokes. If some tourists tugged on apron strings to ask about the name of some mountain, we named it after ourselves. My own

Mt. Hancock. Our jokes held a messianic view of writing. Waiter, what's the name of that river? That's Hancock River ma'am. Or, that's the More River, ma'am. See, there's some more over there! To name is to liberate. To un-name, as Kroetsch says, even more so. Patrick Lane might add, he who names must kill with the grace called language. That's the irony: as writers we are killers, but we give life with language.

By making jokes of the original history, we reclaimed our right to name again. Those places where we are defined by the earth are not ruined by surveyor's nouns and verbs, or the whim of some lying politician. Why rename Castle Mountain as Mt. Eisenhower, for example? In our new names, we made a political statement as well.

The German poet Schiller would have appreciated a ride on the CPR. As he wrote in his *Philosophical Letters*: "Our vision covers too small a part of the universe; and the harmonious fusion of the vast multiplicity of discords cannot reach us." As a budding writer on the CPR, I descended upwards from things. I saw the power of objects as they are in this world. I depended on them even as they wore away and became something else.

For a few brief moments, I understood the various parts of Tiresias, in T.S. Eliot's *The Wasteland*. I was a witness to my own consciousness, and like Tiresias, I did not need a fixed point of view. While none of us on that train in the short hot summers became God figures—we were too over-heated, crowded, and trainweary for that—we wanted to experience that mythic life outside the window.

We were transformed; not so the passengers. Our future reading audience. Ripe with sleep in the day coaches, in abandoned postures, turning faces away from the windows. Those other passengers, cooped up in expensive roomettes. In the baggage car, a couple of corpses in coffins. For the living passengers, the dining car waiters were the big event of each day, at their breakfasts, lunches, dinners. The dining room on the Canadian was social centre, emotional centre, funhouse, and workhouse. While we were busy as the authors of their pleasures, we constantly misread the CPR. Our greatest fiction lacked the unity it was supposed to have created. How did you like your prunes, ma'am, we smirked.

We only earned $1.27 an hour. We needed as many tips as we could hustle, which we pooled in a silver coffeepot and split with the crew at the end of the trip. So many passengers, so little time. Solid stockbrokers with greying temples; oil company execs; vice-presidents of companies. Sometimes we had celebrities: Alfred Hitchcock, Sebastian Cabot, Gene Autry. Once I waited on famed explorer and CBS announcer Lowell Thomas out of Banff, but nobody on my crew knew who he was. We moved like pigeons in the park for those quarters and half dollars under saucers. Farm boys, despite their good natures, were of no interest to us. Nor were cadets going to Camp Borden Families with children: give them to the new waiters. Lonely people: sit them with someone incompatible, to get them out of the room quicker. We may be on earth to dream, we wanted standards, as bright as illuminated manuscripts. But they had better tip big!

Yet in spite of the jokes, the smutty stories, the railroad yarns, the fast hustles, the constant urging by stewards to keep our feet moving instead of our mouths, to make sure we had something in our hands at all times, Canada came to us, not in words, but through words. As an experience, Canada was created for me. By extending my personality, I found a country that was me.

The railroad days were ending. No future in passenger trains. The CPR wanted its investments in freight. The railroad had no nostalgia about its past. What counted was not the effort, but the achievement as measured on the bottom line. Rather than preserve the first locomotive in western Canada, the *Countess of Dufferin*, the CPR sold it to a finance company and let them pay for the restoration. The ideology of a corporation does not allow for the distant shapeless forms of myth and legend.

The corporation does not want us to know that distant locomotive leads us back to our past: unbelievable snow storms, the grave of the King of the Hoboes (just outside the western entrance of the five mile tunnel), Louis Riel, the spiral tunnel, the old timers with nine gold bars on their sleeves: 45 years service. Without those memories, nothing happened. That locomotive, rusting away outside Winnipeg's main station, gave us new possibilities. So did those other restored trains: the *Royal Hudson*, the Cranbrook train, the Wakefield excursion train. Nostalgia buffs have restored these trains for summer tourists.

If the CPR didn't care about its own old guys, what did the old guys think about us? They didn't read my kind of literary criticism, or books of culture, ideas, knowledge or interpretation, let alone the real stuff: poetry, fiction, drama. They had a different kind of compassion, a direct narration, a personal poetics. These men live on in a memory that would no longer exist except through how I choose to describe them. I have more to say. In my exile, the CPR gave me an initiation resilience that enabled me to shoulder anything as I entered the next phase: my literary life.

When the pressure was on, we didn't have time to ponder the bigger metaphors. As they say in the restaurant trade, we were in a real fog. We'd inhale like weight lifters, hoist a tray of dishes weighing fifty pounds or more, and push out into the dining room. I still say "hot and heavy" and "watch your back" in my own kitchen, twenty years later.

On a mountain, outside Field, BC, mountain goats were frolicking. We didn't have time to appreciate them. Our hands were blistered from scalding coffee. We sliced lemons, wrapped toast in napkins, poured syrup, served with a smirk, prunes. We learned the codes of the kitchen. Fried two is not the same as two fried; the first is one order of two eggs, the second two orders of two eggs. Its variant: fried three on two. Only a beginner asked for two boiled eggs, or worse, two orders of boiled eggs. It's two in the water, soft, or four in the water.

The Canadian highballed past the whistle stops—Elkhorn, Kirkella, Fleming, Moosomin, Red Jacket, Wapella, Burrows, Whitehead, Percival—those forgotten places where we find stories. Canada's hidden history glided by, a Canada beyond comprehension. We had only a vague idea how the parts were connected. We saw the tunnels where the hoboes were asphyxiated by diesel fumes. The sets for Robert Altman's film, *Buffalo Bill*; the section of track where the Ural Mountain sequence of *Dr. Zhivago* was filmed (opening sequence, part two), all those stories about someplace else. We saw the multimillion dollar wrecks of coal trains (the John Coal trains) that the CPR covered up from the press. In fact, the CPR covered up most of its wrecks—the news broadcasts usually featured CNR wrecks. Ghostly images, trains from the past, a track the only thread linking the bits.

The night rushed by, star streaked, illegible. I had a brief vision of the prairies, unfolding like a piece from Debussy, quite unlike the Requiem demanded of the Rockies. Canada: overflowing with meaning and expression. My dad, a postmodernist from Maple Creek, Saskatchewan: he would have distrusted the literary language of this essay. Where is the life in those words, he'd ask?

Canada had too much meaning and I did not have time to interpret. Too tense at night, I lay in my bunk in the semi-darkness. As Nabokov might describe it, the train creaked and crackled, things and bits of things, and shadows, and bits of shadows, began journeys to nowhere. Hours of thinking in the dark. This is how I learned about Canada.

For me, the tracks of the CPR do not run parallel. At some point they meet, as Eliot says in "Burnt Norton" at the "still point of a turning world." Or as Neruda says of Machu Pichu, at "the site." What endures is the collective performance of all I have traveled with, including my various selves. In the east-west trackage of the CPR, perhaps North is where it all comes together.

Sometimes, peeking through a small clear segment of the frosted glass by my bunk, I watched the red and green lights of the automatic signals, or the light of a farmhouse, or best of all, a heat lightning storm on the prairie horizon. The true beauty of it came later, when the railway was replaced by the long poem.

Finally, I had enough. I quit. The Stainless Steel Streamliner, with standards and ideals, full silver service, was replaced by Via Rail, the Plastic Train, with paper napkins, microwave ovens, and cutlery made from weird petroleum by-products.

Yet something endures. I remember my final trip. In Glacier National Park, near what the CPR calls mile 74 Mountain sub-division, is the photogenic Stoney Creek Bridge. The steep sides of a torrent fall through a gulch some 270 feet below track level. The contour of the land calls for a curve at the western end of a handsome delicate iron arched bridge. The official CPR photographs of the Stainless Steel Streamliner show the train crossing this bridge. Off in the distance, like a psyche that won't fit on a page, the panorama of the Rocky Mountains. We often tossed plates out the vestibule window when crossing Stoney Creek. They sailed for hundreds of yards before smashing on the rocks.

On that last trip, I took my waiter's tray, that four foot aluminum oblong which every waiter carries with him as a Spartan must carry his shield, and I threw it, as hard as I could, off Stoney Creek Bridge. It hung in the air, as intangible, as untouchable, as elusive as memory, the entire hand of the Rocky Mountains in soft focus behind it. Then it fell out of sight. The Stainless Steel Streamliner turned a corner. My days as a dining car waiter were over. This was an ideal moment, with its mysterious ringing. But the journey doesn't end at this still point. I was racing into the light of memory, faster than the shadow I left behind. It takes so long to forget. This essay is written for that lost train.

HART HANSON

Hart Hanson lives on Bowen Island in British Columbia. He works as a script editor and writer and teaches script writing at UBC. His short stories have appeared in *Antigonish Review* and *Malahat Review*.

This story arose from a lunch-time conversation in which one of my friends, a woman in her thirties, said of another of my friends, a man in his early twenties, "Isn't it sad when those beautiful boys begin to fade?" I thought his nose was too big to qualify for "beautiful"—of course since then he's become even uglier.

Beautiful Boy Fades

Beautiful Boy Fades like the countertenor's voice: inflating from the inside out, the edges blurred, growing fuller: beauty expulsed by potence.

His father never notices. His father is a sideways man, an unlovely man who never suffered pulchritude or grace. The beautiful boy's mother says, "Beauty comes from the *pia mater*, always, like a storytelling voice or musical talent."

The beautiful boy's mother makes these pronouncements despite her lack of comeliness. No one has thought her beautiful since her father died long before the beautiful boy was born. Her musical talent is restricted to an astringent voice singing nursery rhyme lyrics to warped recordings of Lizst and Grieg.

The beautiful boy's father slips bowlegged over the surface of life, staring down like a skater searching for fish below the ice. When asked an opinion, he is likely to reply, "Why would you ask me that? Ask me again later."

The beautiful boy's father is troubled by dreams of glaciers which scrape the armour off the world, fall into the oceans as icebergs; in melting, they pelt the ocean floors with boulders and shattered carapace.

The beautiful boy's mother likes to say that he was an easy birth: that he took his first breath while his feet were still kicking deep inside of her, his mouth gasping before his arms were free so that the doctor saw lips opening within lips opening and suffered a crisis of Faith, for in the darkness he thought he could discern evidence of the original replicating molecule, the basis of Life which denies Creationist teaching.

He told his priest, "It was like *God's* mouth, Father." The priest drew his thumbnail across the wound in Christ's side on the silver crucifix he was shining, flicked off the resulting detritus and said, "God is not man, that His mouth should bring forth falsehood."

The troubled doctor takes to the repetition of this when he delivers children or touches the perfect palpitations of an opened-up body or performs autopsies.

The beautiful boy believes his eyes are green but his mother says they are a supernatural blue, fleeting azure. His father will not even look, says no one knows their true eye colour until they suffer terrible loss, ask him again later.

At the age of eight, the beautiful boy is given a hobby horse by his mother's travelling brother, sent from Spain. It is five feet long with a carved mahogany head and a ceramic tail like that of a fish, spread wide and burnished, held four inches off the ground by a fist-sized ivory castor. The hobby horse has a fine mane—"made of maiden's hair," his mother says. "I would say she is a mare, wouldn't you?"

When the beautiful boy gallops with the horse, he holds its reins in one hand and lower lip in the other because above all things the beautiful boy craves control; even an imaginary horse is subject to shying and calamitous stampedes. The beautiful boy names the horse Le Chatelier, after something he has heard his mother and her friends say when they are dressed up to leave the house in their most excellent clothes, bedecked in pearls, smelling of perfume and powder, their voices pitched like whinnies in anticipation of Liszt, Ockeghem, in eager expectation of atonal, resonant talk.

When the beautiful boy is thirteen, the travelling uncle is asphyxiated by an accumulation of poisonous nitrile gases in a cavern in Kentucky and his father takes away Le Chatelier, saying that tragedy has transformed the toy into an expensive ornament meant to hang on the wall in the parlour where guests can admire the smooth wood and Castilian craftsmanship. His father takes to spinning the ivory castor as he stands talking to his tallest friends, denying things, shrugging.

The beautiful boy misses Le Chatelier, dreams too often of gripping her high up between his thighs. He sneaks down from his bedroom in the quietest times of the night, pauses at his mother's separate, silent chamber, stays longer at the doorway to his father's room, breathless, listening for a single word, a command, cool as marble, that might send him safe back to his bed. When it does not come, he slips his horse from her bonds and rides her through the park across the street where—according to the Polish man who takes care of all the machinery—naked women run crying all night, holding hands and entreating the moon to release them.

The beautiful boy clings to Le Chatelier's velvet lower lip as he canters in his pajamas, the key to the front door of the house thumping against his chest, creating a bruise his mother asks about nearly every night for two months when she comes to check on him in the porcelain bath. At the darkest and most still hour, when even trains do not run, when even night animals hunch and watch with eyes fully dilated out of moon's reach, the beautiful boy whispers to Le Chatelier, "You are a gift to me from far away, a gift from people who are tall and smooth and who terrify their neighbours, a people who love idols and sorcerers, where everyone in the population carries a sceptre. You obey no one but me, Le Chatelier, because God himself has ordered it so, and you read my thoughts and take me wherever I wish to go. . . ."

The beautiful boy drowses through school, dreaming that he is asleep, and his teachers can only watch, wondering if the other students notice the perfect pace of breaths through nostrils deep and fine, a face smooth because the boy dreams only of rest and so dreams undisturbed. One of these teachers, a young man inclined toward conscientious tutoring, within whom a quirky tendency toward ardent impulse tosses, leans forward and whispers into the beautiful boy's sleep-tilted ear, "*Motus animi continuus...motus animi continuus.*"

One night in the park, the beautiful boy leans against an oak tree, allows Le Chatelier a long drink at the stream. He lights a cigarette stolen from his mother, regards his own white fingers through the smoke and hears the sound of violence. The beautiful boy urges Le Chatelier up the path to see a group of older boys kicking a white-jacketed man, a waiter, who lies on the ground and screams. The screaming stops when one boy kicks him in the head behind the ear. The boys spit on the dead waiter, wipe the bottom of their heavy shoes on the cotton jacket, and leave—but the beautiful boy and Le Chatelier stay behind. The waiter lies on his side, his legs scissored, one hand grasped between his thighs, the other thrown up behind him as though he is still carrying a golden salver loaded with crystal and liquid. With his stolen matches, the beautiful boy looks at the fallen man's face until the policemen come and take him home.

The beautiful boy's father says nothing but takes Le Chatelier away forever, attaches the horse to the parlour wall with heavy duty wire driven through the whitewashed plaster into the thick dark joists behind. The beautiful boy would have to pull out part of the wall to get his horse.

He does not cry, he has already found another. He awakes one hot night with his new horse risen up from between his legs, ready to ride. The night air feels good on this new horse and the beautiful boy hangs onto the fine mane as he canters through the park. He tells this horse, "You are Swerve Scattered."

Fearing his father will take away this new horse too, perhaps bind it to the wall with heavy staples, twirl the castors with his cruel fingers while discussing the differences between saints and angels, the beautiful boy asks Swerve Scattered to be a hidden horse, a secret, something that appears only at night when they are alone.

On the fourteenth anniversary of his conception, he awakes and he is too tired to ride through the park but Swerve Scattered is adamant, stands stiffly, demanding his evening exercise. The beautiful boy is troubled by this loss of control and hangs on with two hands: the left clinging to the sparse mane against his belly, the right, also curled but more gently, firmly, against the soft muzzle, up short against the slight wetness of Swerve Scattered's fragile mouth.

And he rides, not gently, through the park. He gallops down the wide gravelled pathway where the waiter in the white coat was kicked to death by boys who called him names and disappeared, across a bridge and onto a long dark field with dew-soft grasses. Just ahead of him he sees the naked girls the old Polish man talks about, running along the top of the grass, and he turns Swerve Scattered to face them, urging the horse along until it begins to jerk of its own accord, faster, pulling him ahead. He holds the fine hairs of the mane in his left fist, tightens his grip farther up—but the horse is away, chasing the naked girls who now look back in fear as they run, their fingers parting the air in front of them, casting weak spells behind them, thin grasslike incantations which Swerve Scattered shatters into brittle, impotent mist. The beautiful boy feels the grasses on his thighs, hears his own sweet clamour as Swerve Scattered throws him high against the white mottled stars and the boy falls, hard, his right hand full of what is not blood.

He will not ride this horse again, not outside beneath the sky. Swerve Scattered is too impetuous, precipitous, and the beautiful resents the abdication of governance. Things are different now, he knows, rising as Swerve Scattered diminishes, and the naked girls disappear beyond the bounds of the park. His father is perhaps right. He is too old for hobby horses.

The beautiful boy learns soon enough that it is not important whether his eyes are green or blue. It is the question which matters: the fact that people will debate this, use it as an excuse to look into his face, sometimes, to touch his cheek. The beautiful boy begins to believe in the prevalence and immutability of his own beauty. He objects to the things about himself which are not perfect.

He learns to despise the lump in his otherwise sleek throat, the thin, light yellow down which occupies the space between his darker brown eyebrows, the way the hair on the right side of his head swirls up beneath his ear, the dark coarse snarl of black hair which grows where he used to be smooth and immaculate, the purple head of his penis when it becomes unsheathed.

He becomes aware of the other boys at school, sees all their blemishes and infirmities: asymmetrical faces, bulbous noses, eyes too close together and mud-coloured, erratic hairlines, coarse complexions, fingers which are thick and insensitive, dark nipples, oversized hairy asses, sloped shoulders, skinny necks, fat stomachs, bony splayed feet, crooked feet, pendulous genitals.

Because of his own secret uglinesses, the beautiful boy loves those who display the most imperfections best. He cannot understand the girls who are attracted to the strongest, toughest boys. He himself is only attracted to those girls who look like him, and when he beds one, in her lacy room, one Sunday afternoon in February, he is repulsed by the hairiness of her quim, by the stubble in her armpits, by the sweat that gathers in the hollow of her belly. He assumed that all girls looked like those who had run from him and Swerve Scattered that night in the park, looked like *he* had in the days before Le Chatelier nailed upright, the way he had, smoking mint-flavoured tobacco, watching while the waiter was murdered.

At night, when he walks around the city, hunched into a leather jacket his father hates, smoking cigarettes, older men smile at him in some neighbourhoods, and he can see the same want in their faces that could not be kicked off the waiter's face by a gang of mad boys. Though he loves these smiling men for their age and ugliness, he knows that in them his own secret faults are magnified a thousand times, beyond bearing, and he walks on, blowing a stream of smoke in their direction, looking down the way his father does.

The girls are better. They do not look so carefully, do not search out his ugliness so assiduously. They watch his face, mostly, or shut their eyes. Even when they use their mouths, they look elsewhere.

Some of them cry, afterwards, and one asks him, "What are you looking for?"

He says, "Nothing."

She says, "You don't need me for that."

He reads the story of Narcissus and himself falls in love with the boy who falls in love with the boy in the pond, but feels a brief agony when he realizes the boy will never fall in love with *him*. It is a strange feeling for the beautiful boy and he tries to recapture it, reading the story again and again, but the pain vanishes along with the love, killed by the same demands that have made him begin to hate his mother.

The first time his beauty begins to fade, it is like a guttering candle and those around him, afraid of the gathering gloom, feed the flame. Everyone wants to touch him and the beautiful boy decrees, "No, none shall touch me, especially not in worship." He decrees that he will be touched only in pain, in selfishness, in surprise, or by himself.

Someone's brother fights the beautiful boy and cuts him with a piece of green glass—and the scar adds an edge to his beauty and, for a time, he ceases to fade. The beautiful boy is emboldened and displays his ugliness to others: the redness, the coarse hair, the straining demand, and he is considered only more beautiful.

One night, walking along the broad gravel path where the waiter was kicked to death, the beautiful boy sees a fat man with a goiter praying, on his knees before the great oak tree that the beautiful boy used to lean against while Le Chatelier drank his fill.

"What miracle are you requesting?" the beautiful boy asks.

"A song." The fat man holds his hands, not at his chest or chin as the beautiful boy is accustomed to seeing, but up higher, as though he wishes to wriggle through some hole in the sky for an audience with God, or as though he is thwarting the hangman trying to put a noose around his goitered neck.

"It's a strange god would provide a song," the beautiful boy says. The man's eyes are shut tight. The beautiful boy thinks that perhaps this is to avoid having to contend with the ugliness of God.

"I wish you would ask on my behalf," the man says finally, putting his arms down. The hands are white, the blood having run out of them. "You look like someone who knows how to get action from prayers."

"You'd better ask my mother," the beautiful boy says. "She's the one who's had success in these matters."

But it is his first indication that any other sensibility exists, the first time it occurs to him that other people have needs and desires removed from his own. He is accustomed to seeing people desire *him* before anything else, or at least desire to be like him. Raising his foot, the beautiful boy pushes the fat man over on his face, hears him moan as the sharp rocks cut into the palms of his soft, white, supplicating hands.

The beautiful boy fades again, but does not know it. The candle gutters and flares but the edges are blurred, made indistinct, and, like the counter-tenor's voice, the beautiful boy thickens—his range is not diminished but there is a fulsomeness that registers in strong light.

The beautiful boy becomes ever more a creature of the night.

He feels like God. He ignores the pleas and orisons of those around him. He has control and power. He is alone.

All Hallow's Eve, he makes his solitary way through a carnival. He urinates in the dimness behind a tent, hears the *shush* of canvas against canvas and turns to see . . . a beautiful boy: a gymnast. He is dressed in a tumbler's costume, an acrobat's leotard. He is puzzled, because he has never been in the circus, never been a boy of skill and daring. The tumbler pulls off his leotard from the shoulder, down over his chest, down past his waist. The tumbler fumbles for Swerve Scattered and urinates, white in the refracted light from the ferris wheel.

The beautiful boy coughs and the tumbler turns and smiles. His stream diminishes slowly, withdraws. The tumbler leans over to the pile of clothing at his feet and straightens up, lighting a match. "Oh," he says, "it's you." The beautiful boy feels the flames wash over his face, caress the green bottle scar; he dies in the light.

The tumbler pulls his costume up. Covers himself. The beautiful boy has seen no ugliness to love, longs to look again.

"I've been searching for you," the beautiful boy says.

The tumbler smiles again. "Not for me."

"Yes, for *you*," the beautiful boy says. He reaches forward, offers himself for the first time. "What is your name?"

The tumbler steps away from the extended hand, his eyes a fleeting azure, a supernatural blue in the reflected light from the carnival tent. His face turns toward the expectant crowd and he leaves without hesitation.

The beautiful boy's name is Merrick. His eyes are a simple, muddy green. He thinks of Le Chatelier wired to the walls of his father's house. Inside the tent, he can hear the *thud-leap* of the tumbler, imagines that body twisting through the air in perfect annulets, surrounded by a sequined corona, landing still and serene on white feet, the people in the seats gasping as they watch, marvelling.

Merrick spits and laughs.

ROBERT HARLOW

Robert Harlow is a native British Columbian. He flew Lancasters and Halifaxes during the Second World War and afterward studied with Earle Birney. He then went to the Iowa's Writers' Workshop and came back to Canada in 1951 to work for the CBC until 1965 when he was appointed head of the newly formed Department of Creative Writing at UBC, a position he held until 1977. He has published seven novels and is now retired.

This excerpt from Felice: A Travelogue *(Oolichan Books 1985) chronicles a moment during Felice Gentry's unplanned visit to Auschwitz. She buys a guidebook at the gate and walks through reading it. This is the beginning of her conversion from Point Grey Housewife to hardrock citizen of a world that will forever contain Auschwitz.*

Excerpt from *Felice: A Travelogue*

We were beaten horribly. For hours we had to run, jump, crawl, turn around while kneeling in the gravel and sharp pebbles. Weaker prisoners collapsed. Older and stouter men fainted, blood rushed to the temples. Hearts burst due to excessive strain and exhaustion, particularly so as we had nothing to eat since we were arrested.

Felice moved on, feeling like a religious holding her breviary in careful hands before her, from one room full of evidence of prisoners' lives to another, and then out onto the street again.

"The SS apparatus," the book said, "was extended by means of the so-called prisoners' self-government, a body consisting at first almost exclusively of professional criminals."

Capos they were called, prisoners too, part of the system she didn't want to hear about. Without them the camp would have been very hard to run, and very expensive. But it was also true that without doctors, judges, businessmen, farmers, people from every part of society the place couldn't have operated. Even in Nazi Germany there had to be consent. The horror belonged to everyone.

She stood in the heavy yellow light of the sun, thinking. You are arrested, you have done nothing wrong and because you still believe in the rule of law, you are confused. There's been a mistake. Soon it will be corrected. But it isn't. It's like being born again fully conscious into a world with one secret aim, one unintelligible priority, one hidden direction known to everyone but you. Yes, they say, our world will be a better place when this policy we all agree with but do not reveal is fulfilled. And *you* are necessary to it. Here is the railway car where you must stand chest-to-back-to-sides with others of your kind; here is the camp with its odd promise that work will give you freedom (when death comes from work it does); here is the Rottenführer who has in hand a bludgeon; here is the future we have for you who are the enemy of the people. And we can give you this future because everyone agrees and everyone co-operates—even you.

And you do.

Because:

This is a mistake.

This is a nightmare.

You believe.

You hope.

Because:

Even what is happening to you is better than death.

You go to roll call. You can still walk, still stand at attention with your head uncovered no matter the weather. Thirty minutes is enough time for roll call, but today the Rapportfuhrer cannot achieve the perfection his whimsical German mind demands. You stand with all the others, at attention, from 7 p.m. and through the night until 2 p.m. the next day. Those who have dropped are taken away, shot. It is a temptation to run and die against the electric wire of the fence but you stand. Women who are weakened by fever or dysentery have been placed on stools or on the ground. Finally, the Rapportfuhrer has all the dying women brought from the barracks. They are laid in the mud on wet blankets. It is impossible not to look. They are like St. Elmo's fire on the ground beside you, and you don't have to look to see them. They are the real future.

"The water was not fit for gargling," Dr. Zunker will say at his trial after the war, which you will not live to see.

Doctors: you remember them, people who took a solemn oath to dedicate their lives to helping, saving, fighting. Once you gave your body to one, always a special one, in reverence, for cure. You connive and manage to get sent to the hospital. Surely it is safe here. But it is only another barrack, an anteroom to the crematorium. When it is overcrowded, doctors make a selection of patients as if it is the ramp where the trains stop and not to the hospital: you are killed with an injection.

And this is Block 10. Felice looked at it, beginning only to glance now, her emotions confused and confusing. This was where Dr. Clauberg, the elegantly trained gynecologist, experimented with women to find a sure and fast method of sterilization.

Dear Reichführer Himmler,

Should the investigations conducted by myself continue as expected—and I foresee no obstacles—then in the nearest future I hope to be able to say that a properly trained surgeon working in a suitably equipped surgery, with perhaps ten medical assistants, will most probably be in a position to sterilize several hundred or even 1000 persons in the course of one day. . . .

She dropped the book, let it go and watched it settle onto the dusty ground with its pages skewed. The horror in her was overcome, the core of cold gone. There were no more feelings she could allow through. The trains, the selections, the gassing, the work, the life, the tortures, starvation, deprivation meant now only that what the people here and in Germany had created was both as simple and as confusing as an explosion. She wanted to understand, and because she couldn't, she reassigned the blame. Yes: No German could escape it, living or dead. From Frederick the Great to the baby born this minute, to be German was to be refused forgiveness, ever.

There had been no adequate punishment. The lie that Auschwitz and a thousand other camps were an aberration was accepted. Their economy was rebuilt, their egos repaired, their fanaticism and devotion to orders and duty admired, their wish to forget supported.

A face was beside her. She looked into it. There was concern there. A question. Wonder. She told it, "I don't have to go through this. All this—*history*—I can't do anything about."

The man nodded and said nothing, but he looked distressed and walked away. She followed him, listening for words from him to build into reasons for leaving Auschwitz. He was tall, angular, his face creased with lines of concentration, and now he went through a gate into a courtyard between Block 10, where women were tortured, and Block 11 where the dungeons were. At the end of the yard was a wall.

"The wall of death," the man said, his accent heavy, Slavic. "Twenty thousand here."

The bodies piled up before her. Cordwood. Insane Germanic neatness. Row on row. Not Flanders' crosses but naked corpses of women and men unburied, with black holes in their heads. This whole yard filled, head to toe, twenty bodies high in a space big enough to parade a regiment. The wall was not a large one; it looked as if it might simply be a barrier in front of the brick wall that ran between Blocks 10 and 11, an impediment perhaps to young healthy men training to be commandos. A well-built wall, sturdy. Then, as she walked behind the man who had spoken to her, down the long gut of this gravelled space, the wall began to look like a backdrop to a service that could be religious. An altar might have once been there, with an image hung on the wall behind it to worship. She stood quiet before it, simply looking, trying to see.

"By gun," the man said.

He turned to see if she was still listening to him. "It was a small, quiet pistol they used." He looked down, away from her. "From the back of the head comes only a little trickle of blood. When Grabner was political section head here he himself shot ten, fifteen, twenty at a time. The whole political section could kill two hundred in an afternoon. Can you think about it?"

"No," Felice told him. She looked around. They had been joined by three men and a women. They were listening to this man who might be Russian.

"The condemned stood there." He pointed. "Stinking skeletons from being months sometimes in cells with no light or air. Behind them there were men with stretchers who were prisoners also, ready to take the bodies away. Then there were two more prisoners. One had a spade to turn over the sand here in front of the wall when blood got on it." He spoke slowly, always gesturing. "Another prisoner—a strong one specially chosen—runs the first condemned man to the wall. The Germans demand everything be done quickly, on the double. He holds the arms of the man with one hand and presses his face to the wall. Sometimes," the man said, and his voice fogged suddenly, became harsh and forced at its edges, "sometimes they could stand straight and shout Long Live Poland, or Death to Nazi Brutes. One last dignity. Then BLAM. Down with a groan. Grabner puts his foot on the head and peels back the eye. Life there yet. Another bullet in the temple. The prisoners with the stretchers run with the body. *Blam* a dozen more times. A hundred. Down there—" he turned—"is a pile of bodies by the gate." He looked around at his small audience. "Already you don't care. It is too much."

"Yes," Felice said.

"It is a game out of hand at school."

"Oh, I think not." The voice was British. Felice turned. The man was angry. His face was red. "If they'd been to school, none of this would've happened."

"Horst Shuman was a doctor," the Slavic man said. "There, in Block 10, he castrated men. He murdered a thousand by medical torture and killed ten thousand mental patients by carbon monoxide. Weber, Sauther, Kremer, Vetter, Clauberg, Thilo, Weibeck, Kitt, Entress, they were doctors with him too. Grawitz was a professor, Fischer and Bartsh were judges, Caesar a doctor of agronomy, Kromer a pharmacist. All here."

"Names," the Briton said loudly. "Exceptions."

"Men," the Slav said.

"A dozen out of thousands."

"Not many Germans were needed to run this camp. Just what you call a sample—top to bottom. The prisoners did the rest."

"You Russians know about camps," the Brit said.

"I'm from Krakow," the man said, and he smiled suddenly. "A professor, too."

"Who always makes points by exaggeration," the Englishman told him.

"School or not school, make up your mind," the professor said.

"I meant *school*, not mere studying." The Brit raised a hand in a vague gesture—he was speaking to a heathen—turned with his group away from the wall and made for the gate.

"Who was it?" she asked the man from Krakow.

"Who was what?"

"Shot here. By Grabner?"

"You are perceptive. Yes. My brother. Today in 1943. You have—what is it—caught me at my remembrances."

"We interrupted."

"No." He smiled again. "This has been a very good time, perhaps the best." He bowed. "Madam," he said, and walked away. His high narrow shoulders remained square as if by an effort.

For a moment she was by herself in front of the black wall. She looked down and saw that she was standing where prisoners fell. Did blood foam or simply pool? The prisoner with the shovel, more hungry, more exhausted than revolted, was the most important person there. The others were parts of a process, but the shoveller was not necessary to what was happening. Accessory only in the legal sense, he was an admission of guilt and an instrument of escape from it. "What blood? Do you see any blood?" It could not be left clotted like curdled red cream in the sand even for so long as it would take rain to come and wash it away. He waited with his spade for the body to be lifted away and then he ploughed under another red harvest.

Between shootings, what did the executioner do? Did he whistle? Walk in a tight small circle, head down as if to keep his concentration, like an athlete waiting for a referee's signal? Perhaps he fondled his gun. That was cinematic and sexual enough, a man's game, not far removed from the ritual of the duck blind.

Her innocent guide book was gone. The Brit and his friends could not listen. The professor knew what and where this was. She looked up at the wall. It *was* black. This was no schoolyard. Not something out of hand, but twenty thousand conscious acts.

She went close to the wall, saw the indelibly splintered, pocked surface and reached out to touch it with her hand. Still, there was a barrier in herself. Then, on her right, peripheral to her vision, she saw a piece of brown paper. It was wrapping paper. Someone had torn it into the shape of a heart no bigger than the palm of her hand and had pinned it with a miniature gold-coloured safety pin to the ripped-up wood. It fluttered in the small wind that eddied gently against the wall. She put her finger on it, held it steady and read: "John and Sally Luscombe, from Andover, England, were here."

The words were a shock. She had expected, hoped for, more: some guidance from a clearer mind. She didn't know whether she'd gone calm or empty; then she thought: They are right, there is no message, except that you've been, felt. Her tears surprised her. They arrived pressured by a grief she hadn't known was personally hers: a rag, a bone, a hank of hair. The Jewish woman in the cattlecar appeared—a portrait, nothing else, caught at that moment beyond knowledge where understanding begins. Her own tears were prismatic; they brought the cool precision of colour back to consciousness, along with a sense of herself weeping for something dead, uselessly lost. She couldn't remember, ever, not caring who saw her crying. There was freedom in that.

The Jewish woman with the neat brown hair, the green eyes, and the face of someone who was conscious that she was loved, stood once more in the stink of the cattlecar. That was not her Hell; her Hell was what she now understood: that she was to die when the door was opened, and that the moment of death would be hard. For her, time had slowed down, stretched out until it hurt. Every moment was a point of pain laid over the distant clatter of the wheels and her faded sense of the people crowded and crushed in around her. For them, for those others, time had speeded up as they murmured conscious excuses for the brutalities done to them, and, as they heaped hope like straw against a flood, they sent sweet simple reason out to say that the transport plan, their resettlement was good: some land for each of them, a place to rest; the Germans who had burned a hundred synagogues and thousands of Jewish businesses were not all bad. For these people time ran quick and evasive as a fox.

Felice was not alone now. A dozen others had come. A man among them wept, and through her own tears she could see others struggling with unexpected emotion. Why do we cry?

She tried not to speak out loud, but she did. "It's done." No one replied, or noticed. But she had given the sane answer: it was done. That is, it had been done. It was real. She could, with or without them near her, stoop and pick up the sand where the blood was hidden, she could touch the wall, see the buildings—the blind Block 10 with its windows boarded against the castrated seeing the skeletons being shot.

It was done. Damn it, it was done: the scapegoat Jew was sacrificed, the enemies of the Reich were murdered, fear and hate and revenge were sated, and the memories buried—this is what I know, all I know.

All I want to know.

I, she thought, I.

She wiped away her tears with her wrist—Phyllis again perhaps; herself very young. From her jeans pocket she took a paper handkerchief and blew her nose. Her eardrums cracked like the sound of stones knocked together under water, and she understood that until now she had been closed up, a deaf, blind, defensive fist. She could see, hear again: the dead bricks of Block 11 with its milky windows like eyes with cataracts and, beyond the wall, the highway gave back the horn of a truck that sounded like an imitation of the mosquito hawk she'd heard on still nights in her bed in her room in her parents' house near where the land ceased being town and abruptly became fields of grain. She looked up into the sky, blue at least from wall to fence, the sun high and warm but unable finally to light the sand and stones and blood-brick and weathered boards. The yard, longer and narrower than she'd first thought, gave back the impression of mummified skin, a husk, and the buildings were mausoleums.

Laughter simply happened to her, the kind that comes with wonder, disbelief: where am I? What am I doing here? What warp crippled the usual directions of life so that this place ceased being distant fact and became destination? Her mind flexed, stretched and held up for inspection the long journey from the camp gate—"Work Makes Freedom"—when time had slowed and her self had been ruptured, been violated, until now she was finished bending and was about to break against the substance of her own imagination.

ERNEST HEKKANEN

An author and artist, Ernest Hekkanen received an MFA in Creative Writing in 1981. He has published two books with Thistledown Press: *Medieval Hour in the Author's Mind* and *The Violent Lavender Beast*. In addition to being a self-employed contractor, he and Margrith Schraner operate a promotion agency known as Art-Lit Services.

Life is a dark dance with death, and it is the rhythm of this dance that I tried to capture in "The Rite."

The Rite

The house was silent except for the splutter of frying eggs and although Clem tried to make himself obscure by becoming more silent than the silence, he felt himself large and conspicuous, sticking out at every joint, an obstacle in the path of something inevitable. His father sat at the head of the table. He was a short man but thickly set, with a coarse, scowling face and crooked nose. His eyes were glossed. He directed them out the window at the dark, then at Ida moving in the kitchen. Clem looked down at his plate, examined the chip in the rim, recalled that he had eaten off the plate the previous night and that they had worked late burying the hens.

Ida took the frying pan from the cookstove and approached the table. There was a thin, weary look to her face this morning with her lips tucked into her cheeks and her skin pallid. She bent to scrape eggs and potatoes onto Clem's plate and her robe gave off a warm, musty scent that mingled and was lost in the breakfast smells. Clem took his fork but held it motionless as he watched her. When she was through filling the plates she took the pan back to the stove and, picking up a coffee cup from the counter, returned to the table. "Well," she said. "Have you decided what you're going to do?"

Clem looked at his plate. He messed the egg yolks and pushed the fried potatoes around in the yellow. Opening his mouth, he raised his head slightly to see down the table.

"I don't see we have much choice," Eino said. "They've got tracheitis. We have to get rid of them."

"Yes but what if they don't? There's always the chance."

Eino impaled his food, lifted it to his mouth. "Chances! My God, Ida. They've got tracheitis."

"Yes but what if they don't? What if it's something else?"

Eino shook his head. "It's not something else. It's tracheitis and they're going to die."

"Yes but there's always the possibility.."

"No, there isn't. They're going to die." His father reared from the table; the dishes jarred. "I'll be outside," he said, turning to Clem. "When you're finished you can come out to help me."

Clem heard the screen door slam and looked at this mother. Ida sucked at her coffee cup. She darted a glance over the rim at him and he looked down again, feeling the weight of her glance. He shoved a forkful of potatoes into his mouth and washed it down with milk. Though the chair to his left was empty, it seemed as if his father was still sitting there, only his father's presence was thinner now, like the stale, burnt smell that caught at his throat. "I'm going," he said.

His mother looked up. "Fine. Go."

The morning air was damp, chilly. He went to the washroom to get his boots and sat on the porch to tie them. Beyond the woods, a streak of grey lit the sky. He could make out the picket fence around the lawn and, farther off, the shabby row of outbuildings that included the tool- and woodsheds, a storage and the sauna. At the gate, the pickup truck sat with its hood raised while his father shone a flashlight at the engine and swore to himself in Finnish.

When Clem was through tying his boots he walked to the gate. His father snapped off the light and slammed the hood shut. "About time," he said.

"I ate as fast as I could."

They got into the cab. His father lit a cigarette as they waited for the engine to warm. The glow briefly waxed his face and faded. "Your mum doesn't understand," he said. "The hens have this disease. They're going to die. You can't save them."

The headlights came on. His father yanked the gearshift toward the seat and swung the truck back around the picket fence. He popped the lever into first and hit the gas. The truck bounced over the ruts and headed down the slope toward the chicken sheds.

"What we should do is burn them," his father said. "They're no good to us anyway."

Clem realized his father meant the sheds. It jolted him from his memory, where he had gone to isolate himself. "Burn . . . ?"

"Sure. What the hell good are they? We can't use them."

Clem braced himself for the sudden dip where the creek went under the road. They drove a bit farther and stopped. Clem ran over to the metal voltage box and threw the switch that brought on the lights in the sheds. His father backed the truck around to the door of the first shed, cut the engine and lights and climbed from the cab. He reached back inside for the cap hanging on the gun rack and tugged it on his head. "Sun will be up pretty soon. Looks like a hot day." He spat, turned to Clem. "Don't forget your gloves. You'll need them."

By noon, they had buried six loads of hens. Six loads of askew wings and wheezed-out, white bodies. Some of the birds were dead, others only dying, but Clem and Eino hurled them into the trench just the same, then sprinkled them with lime, then shovelled dirt over them. "Anyway they'll make good compost," Eino laughed. "That's one consolation."

They climbed into the cab and drove uphill to the house. After scraping the manure from their boots, they went inside and sat at the table. The heat fell against Clem's face: a close, damp heat. His mother set an enamel pot before them and ladled soup into their bowls. The ladle dug down and brought up steam that floated past her face. "How many died?" she said.

Eino gave the round slab of hardtack a sharp blow with his knife. He took a piece and buttered it.

"I asked you how many died?"

"Don't know." His father bit into the hardtack. "Twenty-five hundred. Three thousand. We didn't stop to count."

Clem took some hardtack, buttered it, added cheese. He felt independent of any will, floating, close to suffocation but breathing. The lime caked his nostrils and gave the bouillon an off-taste. He kept his head low between his shoulders and looked straight ahead at the checkered tablecloth, his automatic response to shield himself. They ate in silence. Now and then there was the sharp report of his father's spoon or the occasional word that erupted when something had to be passed. When they were nearly through his mother dug back into the pot and refilled the bowls. Clem became aware of the thickness in his throat but forced the soup past it. "Have you decided what you're going to do?" his mother said.

Clem looked up, realized his mother was speaking past him, lowered his head again, ate.

"Don't know," his father said. "Guess we could always sell."

"You mean the farm?"

"What else do we got to sell?"

"I don't know. But you can't sell the farm. My father practically gave it to us."

"Along with the rotting sheds and the bad plumbing. My God, I regret the day I ever let you talk me into it."

"You regret a lot of things, don't you?"

"Yes and I put up with a lot of things. Don't forget that." Eino pushed to his feet. Clem looked at him; he envisioned his father's face with a scar across the nose and cheek, an ugly pink ripple through coarse, brown skin. "I'll be at the woodshed," his father said. Clem understood: he would have to hurry.

Eino slammed the axe into the log-end, lifted the log and hurled it down so the log split on the upturned blade. He grunted, sucked air, raised the axe and slammed it into the chopping block. His face oozed sweat; a drop dangled from his nose, he wiped it away on his sleeve. "Fuck it," he said. "Get the jerry cans."

Clem got the jerry cans from the toolshed and handed them to his father in the back of the truck. There were six cans. The weight pulled at Clem's shoulder each time he lifted a can over the side. Then he and his father got into the cab. The truck roared from the yard and went clattering down the rutted driveway past the chicken sheds and turned onto the highway. His father rolled down the window and spat into the wind.

"Your mum doesn't understand." He shook a cigarette from the pack and let it hang at his lips. "You see, the hens have got this disease. Won't go away. Digs in." He lit the cigarette, blew smoke. "Let's say we put more chickens in the sheds. In two months, three months, same thing."

Clem looked straight ahead. The highway curved, the trees fell away on the left, cut clean by the perimeter of the sand and gravel pit. His father swerved the pickup in order to miss a dump truck nosing onto the highway. The jerry cans rattled in back.

"And besides, I hate chickens. Hated them ever since we took over the farm." His father braked the truck to make a curve and sped up again. "It's been one lousy fuck-up after another. I don't even know why I let her talk me into it. Stupid, I guess. Just like those damn chickens."

They hurled across the flatlands, the engine droned, wind came through the open windows and cooled Clem's face and neck. Other farms flitted by, houses set back from the highway, mountains swelling behind them, bluish smoke funnelling up from slash fires.

"She's got this notion," his father said. "Thinks everything will turn out fine. Everything will get well." He flicked his knuckles at a hornet that buzzed against the windshield, flattening it dead. "Well, this time things aren't gonna get well. There's no way they can."

They slowed to make the curve at the bridge. Railroad tracks flanked one side of the highway. The town sat on the other, comprising a general store, a truck stop, an open market and several gas stations. They stopped at the first station, filled the jerry cans and returned to the farm. The sheds burned quickly. Clem looked up through the flames and saw his mother on the hill, her hand held at her forehead to block the sun. And it seemed to him it would always be that way: his father and himself below setting the sheds on fire and his mother above, on the hill, watching the destruction.

Clem walked along the highway. He decided at the next bend to cut through the woods. Already it was dark. In the field he heard an owl engage its prey. He entered the path, walking quickly but not running. The path circled down around a swamp. He stepped over dead wood, through ferns as high as his shoulders. The swamp became still except for a warning croak here and there on the dark surface. The moon, a crescent, danced in the tops of the alders and once he found himself looking at it so hard he tripped on the undergrowth.

Climbing the hill opposite the swamp, he scared some crows perching in an old snag. The frantic beat of wings startled him. He crouched to the ground, his heart jumping in his chest, until he had fully comprehended the sound and knew it; then he rose to his feet and went on, down the hillside and past the gravel pit.

Back on the highway, he walked with his head down. The money made a weight in his pocket. He would give it to her, he thought. Just hand it over. He wouldn't even have to say anything. She would know.

He turned into the driveway and stopped, his nostrils pinching at the acrid smoke that engulfed him. The gutted chicken sheds gave off an orange glow in the dark and he remembered, earlier, watching them burn. He would give her the money, he thought. Just hand it over.

He crossed the creek and scaled the hill to the house. The lights were on and he found his mother in the front room, ironing clothes. She neither glanced at him, nor spoke. "Here," he said, and laid the money on the ironing board.

"What's that for?" she said.

"He told me to take in a movie. I didn't feel like it."

She gave a final swipe to the shirt she was ironing and snatched up the garment. "Where is he now?"

Clem stepped back. His mother turned to look at him. She threw the shirt on the pile in the chair. "I asked you where he was."

"In town."

"What's he doing there—drinking?"

Clem didn't answer, nor did he move.

"You'll find some stew on the stove," she said. "I think you better have some, then I think you better go to bed."

Late that night, he was awakened by the sound of the truck crashing into the picket fence. He heard his father curse and pound the door. The porch light winked on and he heard his mother telling his father she had locked him out. His father began to shout, a stream of words slurred by drink and rage. Clem scooted from bed and went to the window. Just as he got there the light went out and all he could see was the ill-defined shape of his father moving away in the dark. A little while later he heard something clang in the direction of the outbuildings, followed by the sound of breaking glass. Then it was quiet and although he tried to sleep he found himself unable to. He churned and tossed, stared at the dark shapes that dissolved as he stared at them.

When the alarm rang in the other room he got up as usual and went to get an armload of firewood. It was dark except for a thin haze beyond the trees. He pulled his jacket around him and threw up the collar. The truck sat askew in the yard, the grille nosed into the picket fence. He went through the gate and crossed the yard toward the woodshed. Passing the sauna, he noticed that the window was broken and knew his father would be inside. He moved by instinct more than sight. His left hand sought sticks and piled them on this right arm. When he returned to the house he found his mother at the cookstove, looking as pale as the faded robe hanging from her shoulders.

"Here, take this to your father," she said, handing him a cup of coffee. "Tell him it's time to get up."

He took the cup, stepped outside on the porch. He looked back through the window at his mother, went down the steps to the gate, closed the gate and crossed the yard. Pale light diluted the sky. He stopped at the sauna and inhaled slowly as he listened, the warm cup in his hand. Finally he pushed back the door. The thin light entered with him. He saw his father lying on the change-bench, turned toward the wall. He set the cup on the sill of the broken window and reached to shake the dark, breathing figure.

"You don't have to do that. I'm awake." His father's voice cut the silence. Clem pulled back, hesitated.

"I brought some coffee."

"Thanks. I can smell it."

Bits of broken glass grated beneath his boots. He stopped at the sound of it. His father neither moved nor spoke but lay, unmoved, breathing slowly and deliberately. The moment lasted, became longer. Outside some crows cawed in a nearby tree and Clem remembered last night, in the greater dark, crouching in sudden fright when he scared the crows in the old snag. He moved toward the door again. Stopped. The thin, pearl-like glow had increased, the window became a grey rectangle with shards of glass hanging from the sides. He knew the sun had topped the trees and that usually by now they would have been at the chicken sheds.

He would give her the money, he thought. Just hand it to her. She would know. But she didn't.

A groan erupted and his father, rolling over, sat up on the bench. Clem felt the urge to run but the sight of his father's face, cut and bruised from fighting, held him. "What's the matter?" his father laughed.

"Nothing." Clem looked at the window, thought better of it and looked at his father.

Eino pushed himself to his feet. "Why don't you build a fire while I go thank your mother for the coffee."

Clem wadded sheets of newspaper and then shoved the wrinkled balls into the firebox. He latticed kindling, struck a match and watched the bright flames pour up the stovepipe. He added larger sticks, finally some split logs. The fire rumbled. He threw a canful of water on the hot rocks;

steam gushed against the ceiling and came floating down around him in thick, opaque clouds. He threw more water, producing more steam; then he went outside.

The day had fully dawned now. He sat on the steps and looked through the branches of the birch tree at the house. Mist rose from the roof, a thin, grey vapour that vanished when the wind blew. The truck was still sitting with its grille in the picket fence. He looked down the driveway at the gutted sheds which gave off trickles of smoke, noticing that a neighbour's dog was poking through the charred mess.

I won't even have to explain, he thought. She'll know; but she hadn't. Suddenly there was a loud bang and Clem saw his father standing on the porch. He saw him and realized that his father was shirtless, wearing only trousers and boots. He watched him step from the porch and cross the yard. His father walked slowly, the boot-laces dragging in the dirt. There was a slight hunch to his body and he squinted from a swollen eye.

"Fire going?" His father unfolded a pocketknife and cut several birch switches. Clem nodded, transfixed by the cuts and bruises, the half-closed, swollen eye. There were three long scratches running down his father's neck into the hair of the chest: narrow scratches threaded with red.

"Where's Mum?"

"In the house." Eino cut another switch. Smiled. "She and I won't be speaking today, probably not for a good, long while."

His father shoved past him into the sauna. Clem followed, unbuckling his belt. His father threw canfuls of water on the rocks. Steam rose and billowed, getting so thick that it scalded.

"Here," his father said, thrusting the switches at him.

Clem lashed him until his arm ached; then he stopped, his arm numb and useless at his side.

"Why did you stop?" his father said. "Keep hitting me."

Clem raised the switches again. He brought them down, this time drawing blood.

GLADYS HINDMARCH

Gladys Hindmarch was born in Ladysmith, BC, teaches at Capilano College, and has published three books—*A Birth Account* (New Star 1976), *The Peter Stories* (Coach House 1976), and *The Watery Part of the World* (Douglas & McIntyre 1988). *Watery* is based on her experiences as a messgirl and cook aboard a Northland Navigation coastal freighter, the *Tahsis Prince*. *Peter* is a prose improvisation, five tales about Peter Pumpkineater and his two wives. *Birth*—short selections from which are in *Cradle and All* (Faber & Faber 1990)—details moments of two pregnancies and contains a prose re-enactment of labour.

When I read the first Peter story to Earle Birney's writing class, Earle told me he thought it was set in North Vancouver. Someone else said it had to be the Yukon, and another person said he saw Prince Rupert. When I said I had imagined Ladysmith in every sentence, we all laughed because we each were so absolutely certain about place. "Ucluelet" is a story where an actual place comes into being through language.

Ucluelet

Don't get lost, says Lefty as I step up onto the gangplank to get off at Ucluelet. I won't, I say. Are you sure, he says, we don't want you getting picked up by a fisherman. Sure, I'm sure, I say and keep going. Jan, bring us a back a couple of cold ones will you? says Beebo as I step off the gangplank. I'm not going to the pub, I answer. Make that one for me too, eh? shouts Ken, yummy-bodied Ken, who is standing, one jean ripped at the knee, just a few feet down the dock. You have to pass it, says Beebo, if you're going to go anywhere.

As Beebo talks, a load is swinging down from above and Hal is steering the empty towmotor over. I step out of the way of both. Hal jerks the machine, fast. It halts right next to me. For a second I'm startled but come to quickly, laughing slightly, and Hal catches my look, smiles; we're together a moment, and then I watch Ken and Beebo stretching up to touch the underside of the loaded flats. I can see all of Ken at first, his eyes dazed almost (like sometimes in bed) there but not there, his long chest and shoulder muscles pressing out from under a many-coloured T-shirt. He and Beebo grab the boards and slowly Ken's outstretched arms and face disappear behind the load, then his shoulders, his chest, a four-inch strip of tanned skin between his shirt bottom and belt, his hips; boxes of canned pears, sacks of potatoes, bales of wire come between us, and then suddenly, on top, I see his overgrown crewcut and blue eyes.

How about it? shouts Ken over the load. I don't feel like it, I answer as Hal shifts gears then centers the prongs and jerks them in, under, through the flats. C'mon Jan, says Beebo. I glance into his curliness, turn up to Hal who half-smiles. He backs the towmotor, fast, turns it, heads towards the edge of the wooden shed which is part of the dock and the green Ford truck there. Everyone will be too busy to notice, says Beebo as Ken wanders over to me. Why not? Ken asks. I'm afraid. Of what? he says, getting caught by the skipper? I don't look at him, feel my face tighten, look over to Beebo. Forget it, Beebo says, we were only teasing.

I walk towards the ramp feeling their eyes follow me, not just Ken's and Beebo's, but Hal's also, and the Second Mate's, Chuckles, and the three men's from town who are loading the Ford. I try to ignore it, notice my work shoes, feel the boards of the dock almost slap my feet 'cause they don't move like the *Nootka* does. Only a few yards more, but getting there, like walking through a corridor in high school, takes so long. And even if they're not looking, I feel the weight particularly of Hal's eyes, so centered, so certain, and Ken's, lighter, but knowing me in a way I don't like to be known. Because he has made love with me, he can make me feel awkward, not consciously, but he does it without thinking and in some ways that's worse, damn him.

I kick the damp dirt that covers the long, wooden ramp and glance up at the shining village: a curved slope which slants down; the crest, all covered in bush, is almost directly up from where I am; the buildings, their tops, some of the sides standing out through the green, are either over and down to the left or over and slightly down to the right; and the wet street, its blackness, runs at an angle from the ramp. I feel like I'd like to slide up over it, to fly through the cut it makes, to touch the fir tips, the unpainted fence, even the shaggy poles as I pass. Just as I start to run, a guy behind me on the dock shouts: watch out for the bears! The what? I say as I turn to the men beside the truck. The bears, says the Nordic one in an open green shirt, the woods are full of them. Okay, I shout back, I was going to stick to the road anyway.

I turn and again start to walk up the ramp. Bears, he's gotta be kidding, that's the type of thing my Uncle Andy used to say, only it was cougars. The village seems more distant now and, on a clearing high up to the right, the last of the sun makes a side window of a tin-roofed shack shine gold; but since it won't be dark for another half-hour or so, I've nothing to worry about, and besides that I've never been afraid of the dark or woods anyway.

I stop and lean on the railing for a moment, pick off a wet splinter, stick it in my mouth. I glance up at the gold window again and wonder about the people who live there, then turn to the water, the fishboats, a bobbing Coke tin. The boats, a few yards down the bank, are mostly white on top. Their poles form almost a forest as they sway, well over a hundred, above their bodies, the ships, the floats. The forest of white seems almost suspended there, the reflection, the extension of it, nonexistent because the land forest and the hill cuts off the light, creates a water/earth/tree darkness of its own. I pull the splinter out from between two back teeth but part of it sticks so I poke it with a piece of fingernail as I watch two men fixing an engine in one of the boats. Then, I make out five guys drinking/yakking/listening to a radio. One of them whistles up and they all look or shout or say something, but I can't hear what because of the distance and the *Nootka*'s noise, so I smile and start going again.

Ahead, on the right, there's a general store and old vine-covered house; then there's a curve in the land and everything else is the woods as far as I can see. I take a deep breath of salt-fish-boat-motor air and start to run. The first thing I notice when I step off the ramp onto the paved road or main street is how hard it seems; it feels as though the blacktop comes up to smack my feet rather than feet going down to meet it. I take four steps just to feel the hard surface then move off onto the dirt shoulder, past the library, which is new, just like any plaster building in Vancouver, but it has orange and yellow flowers growing haphazardly in its garden, and the grass hasn't been cut recently so in that way it's better even though the windows are aluminium framed and not nearly as attractive as the high criss-cross ones of the general store on my right. The store needs paint, but the light on what used to be is perfect; the store has a slow not-too-many-people-go-to-it-anymore look, but obviously, at one time, it was the main building in town. Maybe that's why the library garden looks okay—they didn't take it up and redo it all in rows—they must have just taken down a house and built the library on the land.

I pull out a piece of couch grass, suck the yellow-green tip, wonder what it was Hal said about rows. I guess he didn't, I just thought he did when he was talking about the guys not being able to keep a shore job, and I saw the city then all in straight lines and rectangles, the people moving evenly on the surface of its streets, no ragged indents, like here. Ahead, a little monument of some sort stands on my right, covered in salal and alder, and on my left, just ahead, the government liquor store, recessed back, not in line. It's closed, of course; it's past six. I step up onto the cement sidewalk, the Ucluelet Lodge, a two-storeyed ochre-coloured building, is flush against it.

French fries and coffee come into my nose as I pass the beauty parlour at the bottom end. White sheets cover the chairs. And next, the café, licensed; several men (the only woman in it is the waitress) are eating and drinking and two teenage boys, more dressed up than the others, are leaning on the juke box smoking cigarettes. They're not really dressed up; they both have on tight jeans, their shirts are ironed carefully, tucked in just so, and their hair has been combed towards the center with parts on both sides . . . like it didn't take just a minute to do it and definitely there was a mirror. I scurry past the windows of the empty lobby to the corner where the men's entrance to the pub is, look up at the hill, want to get out somehow, up there—the tips's only a block and a bushy half away—but don't for some reason. I turn, look down the angled road. I can't see the dock, just the edge of the ramp and the lights. I find myself going left, walking rapidly, not thinking about the men or the beer or Ken or anything at all.

Between the gravel there's a piece of coloured glass. I stoop, pick it up, roll the blueness in my palm. After a moment or so, I come out of the stoop and am right in front of a half-wooden, half-glass door. I step up to it, look through the thick-filmed glass; a big-bellied man is leaning over, doing something to someone who's sitting there; walls which aren't walls, I can't figure it out. I turn the brass knob. Open it slowly. Walk in. The men don't look up. The two of them, one a barber and the other an Indian, seem to hang there in a cubicle near the front on the right; while in the back, far to the left, pool balls bump each other. There's a closed Coke machine a few feet in front of me and stacks of empty pop cases and beer cartons form almost a wall to my immediate right. I watch the big-bellied barber, who I guess collects the empties to sell them later, slowly shave the old Indian with one of those long straight razors.

I step towards the pop cooler while looking at the two of them, and neither notices me. The barber dips his razor in an oval enamel bowl; he wipes it with a cloth, then holds the old man's head as he shaves. I glance to the counter on the left; behind it is a wall with one shelf covered in stuff: dice, cards, O'Henrys, Jersey Milks, Player's Tobacco, and three bags of stale popcorn stapled to a card which originally held twenty or more. To the sound of the balls, I open the pop machine and no one says anything—the barber keeps shaving and the men in the back move. Rather than see any of them, I look down into the metally water: Ginger Beer, 7-Up, Mandalay Punch, Coca-Cola, Ginger Ale, Orange Crush. I can't decide. Maybe I'm not supposed to be in here at all.

I look up at the beam in front of me. On a poster for a dance last month, there's a girl I recognize from high school who looks tougher now. I look down again, can't get over it, here, her, and one of the guys I used to play in a dance band with. I pick up the Ginger Ale—he must be no more than twenty-one and it's his band now—not Canada Dry but Nanaimo Bottling Works, much browner, the taste more full, I used to love it, but I hesitate, see that no one's watching, put it back, pick up the Orange, maybe this place *is* for men only, not Orange Crush but Mission, better than Crush; I place it on the metal opener but just before I open it, I stop, hold it, the cold wetness, don't know what the rule is if there is one about pool halls, see the Lime-Rickey, not the green stuff but the ouzo white which came out first. My god, they got every choice here, three I really want.

I look up at the barber. Maybe I'm taking too long. I assume he's the owner. He hasn't got on a white frock but a blue shirt with little red hairs coming through the splits where the buttons just hold over his belly. He's shaven the right side of the wrinkly brown face and is just beginning the left; probably doesn't even know I'm here yet, or, if he does, he's in no hurry. Well, the whole place is in no rush for that matter, kinda nice, so unlike the city. I can almost see the whole front section of the poolroom; after a man hits the ball, he picks up another stick, chalks it, and the other men (one Japanese, two white, one Indian) stand around while he takes another shot. I start to open the orange again, but don't, put it back, pull out the Lime-Rickey and open it. No one, not one person, has said one word.

I begin to go towards the barber but don't. Instead, I swallow sharp lemony-lime and delicate other tastes. I wander to the counter to the sound of bumping billiards and stand there, looking: Chuck-Wagon Stew, just two cans; handkerchiefs in dusty cellophane; rabbits' feet, four left on a faded card, a light brown. I drink my pop, look at the green metal light shade over the billiard table. The Indian kid is now shooting, is that what they call it, I don't know, anyway he has the stick and after he hits the balls with one ball the other men stand away while he gets ready for another shot. A skinny-legged spider skitters over nailclippers to one of the wooden crib-boards that lean upright from the shelf to the wall. I finish drinking and put the bottle down on the counter, wander over to the window, look at the dead flies on the sill, try to see out, there's nothing, turn slowly, and the barber smiles, comes over to me, belly jiggling, and I place silver in his wet hand which has a dab of foam on the index finger. He takes the money, puts it in this big-flied-pant pocket, and I say thank you and leave. The old man is still in the chair and still has not moved one bit. Mine were the only words spoken during this entire time.

I close the door softly and run in the darkness, where to, I don't know, along a dirt road, down a dirt lane. Bushes, grass, trees on the side. The *Nootka*'s engine and winch throb and whine louder and louder; wherever I am, I am getting closer to her, can hear her. The branches and leaves are shaking/trembling. Funny I feel no breeze, only the motion past my body, and ahead, through the darkness, there's a gulley, a clearing, maybe water moving. I come out of the bush the lane must have lead to and there *is* a small opening; that is, the trees stop and there's a trail ahead where they start again. I'm too far to the right, that's it, over there up the dip must be the library, but if I just keep going, surely this will lead me to it, the water, at least a moment ago I thought I saw it, and once I get there I can always get out, follow the shoreline that is. So I take the trail through the trees which again leads down, fast, it's sharp, I hold onto the salal, drop, catch my balance, lead more carefully this time with my right foot, get the feel of the rock first, then come down to it by clutching the wet roots and letting go once my foot knows where it is.

My left foot feels out through the dark wetness and again my hand clutches salal. I slide, land, and here I am surrounded by bush, and the ship's racket is loud, very close, but no light in this dense foliage. I grope out with my hands, touch wet prickly branches which drip on my skin, stoop, feel for an opening. And there is one, a thin slit, which I crawl through, not far, but scratchy. Stairs, there are stairs. I stand at the top of them for a moment just breathing as my hands do my long hair up. Then I start to walk down, to go towards the engine throb. No railings and my leg my skirt are caught in thorns, a blackberry branch. I try to lift it to disentangle, step closer. As my right hands hold the thick branch, my left pulls the skirt out thorn by thorn. I slowly move it with both hands, pass it, take two steps, let it fall back and suddenly, below me, I hear other branches and water.

The branches are getting louder. For a moment, I just stand there. The best thing to do, my dad always said, is stay put, don't move at all. I do, try to, my blood swoops to my center, and I try not to make noise as I gasp, gulp the air.

In a moment, I realize it is *someone* not *something* on the steps: thank god. Whoever it is, is coming up. I try to say, hi there. But I can't because nothing comes out. In a moment, there he is, a cowboy-belted young man just three steps away. Whatya doin' here? he asks. I just look down at him and he stops, waits for my answer: I, I, I'm trying to get over there. I point. Wanta have a drink? he says, I'll show ya. No, I say, can you, can you tell me how to get to the dock? I won't try anything, he says, I promise. I, I got lost, I say as I turn around then start to lift the blackberry vine again. Let me do that, he says as he brushes against my bum and back. I step down and he gets the branch while I still feel his touch and the motion through me. We don't have to be alone, he says as I come up to him, I'll get my buddies so we're not alone, you don't have to worry about that. No, I say as he lets me pass, you don't understand, it's nothing to do with you at all. I look at the step. I, I just have to get back. You sure got in the wrong place, he says as he lets the branch go. It makes a heavy crashing sound with light whips as the leaves cut through the air.

I know that, I think as I step off the last stair. Just go that way, he says as he comes up from behind me, it'll take you there. Uuh, thank you, I say as I turn and sorta smile but not really 'cause I'm scared and gotta get. Thank you, I say again and just leave him there standing on the stair as I head back. Sure you don't want me to come with you, he says. No, I say, I'm all right, I know where I am now, but thanks, I say as I step over a log, thanks a lot, I say to his outline, the face non-distinct, the body masked. And I turn/run along the narrow path, tall couch grass on its sides, no lights yet but the alder's getting thinner. The library, ahead I can see the library. I don't think (a light, a clouded light through the trees) I'd want to (it's at the end of the ramp) do that again. Suddenly, the trees stop and above the shed there's the *Nootka*'s light. I pause on the widening path, the *Nootka*, her light, my ship.

JACK HODGINS

Novelist and short story writer Jack Hodgins teaches creative writing at the University of Victoria. He grew up on Vancouver Island and attended UBC, where he took a degree in Education but enrolled in one writing workshop conducted by Earle Birney. His fiction has won the Governor General's Award, the Eaton's BC Book Award, and the Canada-Australia Prize. Titles include *The Invention of the World*, *Spit Delaney's Island*, *The Honorary Patron*, and *Innocent Cities*.

Back in 1959 Earle Birney taught us (among other things) to look for stories in our own back yards. This story began quite literally in my own back yard—or at least in my parents' back yard. The only thing I "made up" was the boat—then discovered later that in fact there was a boat on Comox Lake when the earthquake struck. I've decided there's no point in straining for invention; better things arrive all on their own.

Earthquake

Do you remember the earthquake of '46? Do you remember how the chimney fell through the roof of the elementary school and down through both storeys of classrooms and would have killed us all if this had not been a Sunday morning? (Would have killed Miss Gordon, too, lying out flat on her bench and fanning herself, in the midst of one of her spells.) Do you remember how the Post Office, which was the only brick building in the entire valley, collapsed in a heap of rubble where it had stood for twenty-three years, and how we were thrilled to think afterwards that it looked exactly as if it might have been bombed from the air? And how the bells on the little Anglican church went chiming, and the electric poles whipped back and forth like fly-fishermen's rods, and electric wires hopped low like skipping ropes and snapped tight and clearly *sang*, and how the earth came rolling up in waves and sent Cornelius Baxter's car out of control and up onto Millie Weston's porch?

Then you may also remember my uncle Neddie Desmond. Lived just down the road a ways from us in that little farm with the buttercup-yellow house. Well, my Uncle Neddie was the first one out in our part of the valley to install an electric fence. Power had come as far as Waterville just the year before and none of us had become accustomed to its magic yet, nor learned to trust it. Neddie went out that morning to pull the inaugural switch, and to prepare himself to have a good laugh at the first cow to find out what it would mean from now on to stick her nose into a field where she wasn't wanted. Neddie pulled his switch and immediately the air began to hum, the world began to heave and roll, the trees began to dance and flop about and try to fly. Two guernseys dropped directly to their knees and started to bawl; a third went staggering sideways down the sloping earth and slammed into the cedar-shake wall of his barn. Chickens exploded out of their pen in a flurry of squawking feathers as if the jolt of electricity had somehow jumped a connection and zapped them. Naturally he thought that he and his fence were to blame for this upheaval but he could not make it stop by turning off his switch. Poor old Neddie had never been so frightened; he started to curse and blubber, he hollered for Gracie to get out and give him a hand. Never much of a man for religion, he promised God at the top of his lungs that he would abandon his lifelong fascination with modern inventions immediately. But God took far too long to think this offer over; by the time the earth's convulsions had settled, all of his cattle had fallen and poor Ned had wrapped himself around a fence-post and begun to cry.

Now the scariest thing about quakes is that they change the way a fellow looks at the world. You may also remember my other uncle. Tobias Desmond. Owned the little sawmill up at Comox Lake. Uncle Toby drove down from his mill an hour after the quake had worn itself out and told us the entire lake had emptied in front of his eyes. Truly! Right to the muddy bottom, he said—he saw drowned trees and slime. Drained entirely down a crack which had opened up in the earth, and must have gone right out to the ocean somewhere, because it came back with tangled knots of golden-brown kelp and furious crabs and bouquets of brilliant purple anemones torn off the ocean floor and flung up on to the driftwood and shoreline trees and the sorting deck of Uncle Toby's mill.

He was uneasy about going back to his sawmill after that. Though the sound of the lake emptying all at once like water down a sucking drainpipe had been horrible enough to haunt him for the next two years, it would not have the effect upon him of those remembered moments when he stood and watched the water returning to the empty lake—leaking in at first, and then spreading, then racing outwards across the mud, and swelling, deepening, rising up the nearer slopes. *He* had no reason to believe it would know when to stop. By the time the first waves slapped against the pilings under his mill, he was in his truck with the motor running, yet later confessed that he knew he would not have the will to drive out of there even if that water had kept on climbing up the posts and started out over the land. He would just have to hang around to see what happened next.

Now my Uncle Toby was a truthful man. We believed him. You only had to walk along the lakeshore yourself to see things drying in the sunlight that shouldn't be there. The problem was that this incident would trouble him far too much, he couldn't stop telling people about it. And every time he told it there seemed to be something new he'd just remembered that he hadn't told before. A whole month had gone by when he turned away from the counter of the General Store one afternoon, watched a car speed past outside, and turned again to Em at the till: "My God, I just remembered! Why didn't I think of this before? There were two old men in a boat—I remember seeing them just before it started—two stiff gentlemen in coolie hats out on the lake in a punt." They weren't fishing or anything, he said. Just floating, talking, way out in the middle. When the waves started sloshing up they rocked and bobbed but didn't start rowing for shore. They turned and eventually slipped into the chute and corkscrewed down out of sight. "Now what do you think of that?" said Uncle Toby. "They didn't come back, they must've gone sailing out to sea." Of course no one believed this new addition to his tale. But he continued to tell his story to anyone who would listen, adding every time a few more details that would make it just a little more exciting and improbable than it had been before. He seldom went back to the mill, or sold much lumber. He spent his time on the streets of town, or in a coffee shop, talking the ear off anyone who came along. The earthquake had given him the excuse he'd been looking for to avoid what he'd always hated doing—an honest day's work.

So you see—that's the other thing. People will use an earthquake for their own purposes. My uncle's sawmill eventually collapsed from neglect, under a heavy fall of snow, but he hardly noticed. That's the worrying part. They're telling us now that we're just about overdue for another one. For an island situated smack on the Pacific rim of fire, as they like to call it, we've sat back far too long and smugly watched disasters strike other parts of the world. Apparently all those tremors we've wakened to in the night have not done anything but delay the inevitable; we will soon be facing the real thing all over again, with its aftermath of legend.

Myself, I was nearly eight at the time. My brother was five. My sister was less than a year, and still asleep in her crib in one corner of my parents' bedroom. My mother, who was kneading a batch of bread dough at the kitchen counter, encouraged the two of us boys to hurry and finish breakfast and get outside. It appeared to be the beginning of a warm June day. My father had gone out to milk Star the little jersey. He'd soon begin the task of sharpening the little triangular blades of his hay mower, which would be needed within the next few weeks for the field between the house and the wooden gate. Now, he had just started back towards the house with the pail of milk in order to run it through the verandah separator, when it seemed the air had begun to hum around his ears. Something smelled, an odour of unfamiliar gas. Off across the nearer pasture the line of firs began to sway, as though from a sudden burst of wind. The hayfield swelled up and moved towards him in a series of ripples. Suddenly he felt as if he were on a rocking ship, in need of sea-legs, with a whole ocean beneath him trying to upset his balance. He could not proceed. He stopped and braced his legs apart to keep from falling. The milk sloshed side to side in the pail, and slopped over the rim. Before him, our old two-storey house he was still in the process of renovating had begun to dance a jig. The chimney bent as if made of rubber bricks, then swivelled a half-turn and toppled. Red bricks spilled down the slope of the roof and dropped to the lean-to roof of the verandah, then spilled down that in a race to the eave where they could drop to the ground directly in front of the door I was throwing open at that precise moment in order to rush outside and join him. This was the end of the world he'd been warned about as a child himself; it was happening in exactly the way his own father had told him it would. In a moment a crack would open up somewhere and snake across his land to divide beneath his feet and swallow him, would swallow his house and his family and his farm and all his animals at once, but not until he'd been forced to stand helpless and unable to move on the bucking surface of earth while he watched his family bludgeoned to death by the spilling cascade of bricks.

My brother laughed, but wouldn't leave his chair at the kitchen table. The sight of a fried egg dancing on his plate was not an entertainment to walk away from. Cutlery chattered on the tablecloth. Milk tossed up bubbly sprays from his glass and splashed on his nose. His piece of toast hopped off his plate and landed in his lap. This was a matter for giggling. The world had decided to entertain him in a manner he'd always thought it capable of doing and this would make a difference to his life. From this day on, he would take it for granted that he might demand any sort of pleasant diversion he wished and need only wait for all laws of nature to be suspended for the purpose of making him laugh.

My mother screamed. Cupboard doors flew open and spewed dishes onto her counter. Drinking glasses and cups spilled onto the bread dough. Saucers crashed in the sink. Through the window she could see her husband swaying like a drunken man in the lane that led to the barn. When she turned—crying "The baby!"—she saw the drying rack above the stove sway back and forth over the heat. She snatched the clothing down and tossed it all in a heap on a chair. "You boys—get outside quick!" She went flying off through the french door and across the living room and into the bedroom. "I can't! I can't!" I heard her calling and ran to help. The crib had danced across the floor and was blocking the door. We pushed it open. She snatched up my sister and cried, "Grab your brother and follow." As it turned out, she was the one who would follow. The outside door off the living room was blocked by the china cabinet which had taken up the tune and gone dancing, its contents of silver and heirloom china clanging behind the glass. The baby cried at her hip. Between us we leaned against the cabinet but it would not move. "The other door!" she cried. But we had only got out as far as the verandah, saw my father hollering something at us we couldn't hear over a clatter on the roof above us, saw him waving his arms—he might have been signalling us to hurry and join him, he might have been telling us to stay where we were—when that fall of cascading bricks came crashing down off the roof just less than a running step before us. Beyond it, my father, rushing towards us, fell to one knee. We looked at one another, my father and I, with that thundering fall of red clay bricks between us. He might as well have been on the opposite side of an opening chasm, he might as well have been left behind on earth while we went sailing off into eternity. That's what he was thinking. Even trapped in a house that was shaking itself into collapse around our ears I could see what he was thinking in his eyes: What sort of a father could not put a halt to a tumbling wall of bricks? I was thinking the same myself.

Now how does it feel, to be an eight-year-old boy on a Sunday morning in June with the world deciding to throw itself into convulsions and scare everyone half to death? Why, how had I got to such an age, I'd like to know, still believing that earth would stay steady beneath your feet forever, fathers stay capable of heroic rescues forever, mothers stay calm in every sort of emergency forever, and houses you lived in stay solid and still and safe and true till the end of time?

When I was in my first year of school my father did not come home one day from work in the logging camp at the time he was supposed to. He did not come home that night at all; he came home the next morning from the hospital with his head wrapped up in great white bandages, nothing of him showing but two eyes, two nostrils, and a gaping hole for a mouth. He laughed. A falling limb had nearly taken off one ear, had opened up his nose. But he laughed. I could take him to school tomorrow for Show-and-tell, he said, and tell that teacher and all those other kids I'd dug him up in the yard where he'd been buried by the Egyptians five or six thousand years before. He would lie stiff, he said, until everyone was through with poking at him and smelling him and making notes for an assignment on the pleasures of archeology, and then he would let out a long groan and sit up and scare the teacher into immediate retirement. "This isn't funny," my mother said. "You might have been killed." But of course my father could laugh in the teeth of anything that would try to kill him in the world. The earth beneath our feet stayed firm.

Then this. What do you make of it? The bricks stopped falling. The house settled. Not a sound could be heard. It was as if the earth, worn out from its convulsion, had taken in a deep breath, and held it, while it gathered up its strength to buck and heave some more and go into another fit. Still we didn't move—my father down on one knee with his spilled milk bucket not far away in the grass, my mother holding my crying sister in her arms, my brother no longer giggling but looking as though he just might get scared at last. We held our positions as we if waited for someone's permission to move. Something foul-smelling had been released into the air. The light was wrong. Far off, if you listened hard, a rumbling could be heard going away beyond the trees.

Inside, one final piece of china crashed to the kitchen floor. This was a signal. Now, could you heave a sigh and laugh to show that it was all right? Nobody laughed. My brother, like the baby, started to cry. My father stood up and whipped off his cap to slap the dirt from his knees. He pick up the pail, and stood looking into it. Was he wondering where the milk had gone? It was splashed out all around him and already drying on the leaves of grass and on the gravel along the lane. My mother made a tentative move down onto the top step, and staggered a little. "What *was* that?" she said. "What *was* that? I thought for a moment the war might have started up again, an invasion or something."

"Quake," said my dad. He took a step towards my mother, found that he could keep his balance after all, and sort of threw himself into a lope in our direction.

"You wouldn't believe what went through my head!" my mother said. "I thought something might have happened in the barn. You and that cow—" She was almost laughing now, but almost crying as well. "Blowing yourselves to kingdom come and taking the rest of us with you!"

My father took the baby in one of his arms to hush her, and used his other arm to hold my mother against him. "You okay?" he said to me. I nodded. He didn't smile. Not yet. He would make a joke of it later but for the time being he solemnly held my gaze with his to acknowledge what we both now knew, what he must have known already himself but had kept secret from me too long. What was this thing we shared? That the world could no longer be trusted to stay steady beneath our feet? Perhaps, and that a father and son in such a world must expect to view each other across a space of falling debris.

Fifteen minutes later my Uncle Neddie and his housekeeper Grace were upon us in their pickup truck, to see how much damage had been done. By this time we had already heard on the battery radio that we'd been at the very centre of this quake, and that it had measured 7.3 on the Richter scale—the worst to hit the island since 1918. Grace drew fiercely on her cigarette, blew smoke down her nose, and viewed the world at a sideways glance to show she would never trust it again. She was not one to thrive on drama. Uncle Ned was white, and shaky. "My lord, I thought I'd caused it!'' he said. He wasn't laughing either. He looked as if he could still be convinced he'd been the one to blame.

"That sounds pretty normal," my father said. "I thought I'd caused it myself. I was just coming across from the barn and thinking how maybe we shouldn't've moved into this old house before I'd finished the renovations. Not with little kids—y'know? What a person ought to be able to do, I thought, was just pick up an old house like that and give it a shake and see what's left that's safe."

"I was making bread," my mother said. "You know how they make fun of the way I punch down the dough like I'm mad. This time I thought well *now* I've gone and done it, this dough's begun to fight back."

None of this was comfort to Uncle Ned, who was holding his hands together, then putting them into his pockets, then clenching them into fists that he pressed to his sides. "I mean I thought I'd *really* started it!" he said. "I pulled the switch on my electric fence and away she started to rip! I nearly peed my pants." So Uncle Ned told us what it was like: how he pulled the switch, and the earth heaved up, and the cows fell, and chickens exploded out of their pen, and the fence posts shook themselves free of the ground. Naturally we laughed. Naturally he had to laugh himself. Then he said, "I guess I had to come over and find out how far my damage had spread. But that don't mean I'm gonna get up on that roof and fix your chimney!"

Apparently it was all right to laugh. No one was hurt. The house was still standing. How important grownups must think they are! It had never occurred to me to think I was at fault. "Reminds me of that time that we was kids," said Uncle Ned to my father. "You remember that? You and me and Toby was sleepin' up over the garage and the Old Man he comes hollering out to wake us up? This was the time that fire got loose up behind Wolf Lake and started down across the valley towards us. The sky was red and boiling black, the whole world was lit up by its flames and you could hear the cattle bellowin' too, scared to death. Well you know what *he* was like, he got us up on the roof with gunny sacks slappin' at sparks that flew our way. Even when that fire'd nearly surrounded us he wouldn't let us high-tail it out of there." He was talking to my mother now. "Well it wasn't until the next day when the wind had turned it away that we found out he'd been broodin' about some little root-fire he'd started that he shouldn't have, and couldn't get it out of his head that he somehow might've sent up the spark that started that whole mountain burning—and sweeping down to give him his punishment. Hell, I bet every farmer in the valley had some reason for thinking the same! What's the matter with us that we can't believe things happen just because?"

My father looked at me for a moment before he said anything to that. "I d'know, Ned. Maybe we'd really *rather* be the cause of these things ourselves. On the other hand, maybe we're right. Who's to say it isn't a person's thoughts that do the damage?"

Uncle Ned shook his head. Of course he wasn't satisfied. He wouldn't be satisfied until he'd made some sense of this. He bent to pick up a brick from the front step, and then another, and stacked them up on the floor of the verandah. "I know this, I'll tell you for sure. I'm gonna dismantle that fence. Barbed wire is good enough for any cow, I'll just shoot the ones that don't pay attention to it. I know this too: I ain't never gonna flick a light switch on the wall of my house without flinchin' a bit while I do it, just in case. How's a fellow s'posed to know what to trust?"

My mother took the baby back inside. The rest of us started collecting the bricks, and stacking them on the verandah, and kept on picking up bricks until my Uncle Tobias' truck came roaring in through the gate and down the driveway. We stood up to watch him approach. Uncle Toby was out of that truck before it had even come to its usual stop against the walnut tree, and was running across the yard towards us holding his baseball cap on his head with one of his hands. "You feel that?" he shouted. "You feel that here?" I guess he was too excited to notice our stack of bricks.

"Feel what?" my father said. "What do you mean? We didn't feel anything here." He put one hand on my shoulder. "You see anything here that's *changed*?"

MARGARET HOLLINGSWORTH

Margaret Hollingsworth joined the UBC Creative Writing program in 1972 to complete work on a novel. She graduated in 1974 with an MFA in playwriting and theatre. Since then she has written over a dozen plays, some of which appear in two collections: *Willful Acts* (Coach House Press) and *Endangered Species* (Act One Press). All her work is available through the Playwrights Union of Canada. She has also written widely for radio, TV, and film and her first collection of short stories, *Smiling under Water*, was published in 1989 by Lazara Press.

The House that Jack Built *is one of a series of one-act plays collected under the title* Endangered Species. *Jack and Jenny are from a small northern Ontario town, and, as in other plays in this volume, they struggle to come to terms with the demands of the eighties urban environment.*

The House that Jack Built

SET
The porch of a house, two white rockers and a screen for slide projections. Under Jenny's chair is a capacious old-fashioned knitting bag and a book. Under Jack's chair, a catalogue, two bottles of beer, a pair of binoculars.

CHARACTERS
Jack *A young man about 24 years old, married to Jenny.*
Jenny *A young woman, 24 years old.*

This play is designed to be presented with It's Only Hot For Two Months in Kapuskasing.

Lights go down, the whirr of the slide projector is heard. A slide of a forest is projected, aerial view, acres of trees. Lights up.

JACK   We had it good as it comes. We was like a couple of love birds. Back then—

JENNY   Every year we'd go to the CNE—

JACK   Season tickets to the Blue Jays, not one, two, one for me, one for her—good seats, cost a fortune, smuggle in a six pack . . .

JENNY   The home exhibition, the horse show, the fall fair at Orangeville, and at Hallowe'en we'd go down to the front of our build-

	ing and hand out candy to the kids, in costume—me as a witch and him as a ghoul, every year—
JACK	Slow down. That was when we lived on Queen.
JENNY	Downtown.
JACK	Right. Living downtown's no good. No good for your lungs. Bad air. You live in a couple of rooms downtown, what do you ever know about spring? You open your window you hear street-cars and at night it's drunks and cop cars, drug busts. Women. Yes. That's why it's best to live out of the downtown. Don't feel too good to spend your whole married life with a poolroom sign flashin on and off in your window. And when you pull down the blinds the light splits through. I mean we was raised in Kap. Kapuskasing. We grew up where you just have to step outside the door to shoot a couple of ducks or a partridge. You got fish right down the street. All you need is the right gear.
JENNY	You never went fishin Jack.
JACK	I never had to look at no pool hall sign neither. Think of it that way. Think of it like that. "Think of it as the northern lights," she says.
JENNY	Think of it as the northern lights Jack.
JACK	I tried. But I never seen them. I never seen the fuckers. Not in Kap. Not on Queen . . . I never seen em. So I built her a house. I mean, what more can a man do for his wife? You meet a girl. It's too soon. High school, but what can you do when she's the right one. Chew on your nails? Jerk yourself off? No. You buy her a ring, right? You buy her a ring, and then you marry her. You do it right. You work for her, and you just have to hope she doesn't get herself pregnant before you've got her a house. That's the way it is. I mean you tell me different, don't matter who you are. There's no other way when you come right down to it.
JENNY	There's no other way.
JACK	First of all I bought the land. I got it cheap. It was on the edge of town. Ways out. Past the zoo. Near the 401 though. Near enough. Not so near the noise bothered you. No. You could hear it of course. In winter. Sound travels in winter eh? Off the snow. Sound travels because there's no leaves. So in the winter it was a whole different ballgame. I didn't know that. I bought the land in spring. There was turtles out there. One day I saw maybe thirty turtles on the other side of the swamp. Before it got drained. They took the turtles away. They didn't die or nothin. They didn't kill em. I know that. They loaded em up and took em away. To the zoo maybe. Someplace.

(Slide view of forest from the ground, burgeoning summer growth.)

JENNY   This is it?

JACK   What's wrong with it?

JENNY   It's wet.

JACK   Of course it's friggin wet what do you expect?

JENNY   It's a swamp.

JACK   Where else are you gonna find a 50 foot frontage?

JENNY   Frontage?

JACK   What do you mean "frontage"?

JENNY   I mean . . .

JACK   You mean you don't like it? Isn't it quiet enough for you?

JENNY   What's that noise?

JACK   It's frogs that's all. Just friggin frogs. And traffic.

JENNY   What about a basement?

JACK   You want a basement?

JENNY   It's too wet for a basement.

JACK   You want a basement you'll get a basement.

JENNY   Don't all houses have basements?

JACK   If that's what you want, you'll have one. All you gotta do is just say what you want.

JENNY   I wanna stay on Queen.

JACK   You just gotta say the word. Basement.

JENNY   All these trees.

JACK   Yes. They said this is the only red maple swamp in . . . I dunno . . . This is the only red maple swamp.

JENNY   All those trees!

JACK   You don't like trees?

JENNY   Reminds me of Kap.

JACK   We don't have red maples in Kap.

JENNY   They gonna cut them down?

JACK   Sure. Course they'll cut them down.

JENNY   I dunno.

JACK   So, you happy now?

JENNY   I guess.

JACK   *(Leans forward.)* Billy and me see, we got the foundations in in six weeks. 1750 square feet. Bill Danielson gave me a hand. He's in the trade. I got a good rate on the concrete and I never even had to rent the mixer. You'd'a thought she'd'a been happy right? Her own house that she picked out? I mean most women woulda died for it. *(Turning to Jenny.)* Why don't you come out there tomorrow? Take a look.

JENNY   What's to see?

JACK   A big mother of a hole that's what. You can take a picture if you like. For the record.

JENNY   Great.

JACK   What's the matter with you? *(Leans forward.)* You might just smile once in a while. I knew she wasn't into it. But what I also knew was that it was only a question of time. I mean it was just a hole in the ground right? Full of water. It takes imagination to see a house. But you gotta be ahead of it, right? From the beginning. A family room. One and a half baths. Tile floor, maybe, three beds, double garage, matching fixtures . . . she shoulda been happy.

JENNY   He went on this canoe trip once. Just after we got together. Up north. He brought me back this thermos full of ice. He came back covered in squito bites, cussin . . . with this thermos full of ice.

JACK   Building on a swamp in spring's no hell. The larvae was hatchin. The guys filled the swamp—there was a bit of water still standin that's all. That's all they need! I dressed up in white and wrote home for some McCurdy's. Stuff they make down here's fly piss. I drowned myself in it . . . woulda kept a grizzly away. Squitos kept biting through though.

JENNY   He said that ice was off an iceberg. 20,000 years old. And the oxygen in it was 20,000 years old. We put it in our beer and it fizzed! But how did he know there was icebergs here back then? 20,000 years ago? Jack!! *(Reaches out for Jack blindly.)*

JACK   Hey, hey babe.

JENNY   There was nothin to do weekends. He was up at six and out for seven Saturday morning. I'd go down the market for eight. All the vegetables looked like they been specially shined. When I'd looked around I had a couple of doughnuts and a coffee and I'd walk over to Queen West and watch all the punks on the sidewalk, sellin red suspenders and weird earrings and lace collars and such. Then I'd pick up a pizza and take it home, only it wasn't lunch time yet but what the hell I ate it anyways. Then I'd put this spoon down my throat.

JACK   She's always on about the past. About Kap. I'll tell you about the past—there's this I always remember. There was this cat got locked in her basement. She called me up. Said it'd been there three months. Her and her mom had it cornered behind the furnace. She wanted me to get it out. It was scraggy as all hell. No hair on its back. I went to grab it and it bit me. So I got it in her dad's landin net. Threw it in the back of the truck and took it to the lake. It was skeeterin about all over the floor but it couldn't do nothing in that net. She wouldn't come with me. I threw the whole shebang out as far as I could then I drove back to her place like a bat out of hell. By the time I got there she'd figured out that cat had rabies. So she went after me to get all these shots. No way. So she wouldn't have nothin to do with me. And her dad was mad as hell that he lost his net . . . And I just kept hearin that cat yowl. And now she wants a basement. Huh!

JENNY   Then I'd put the TV on and watch the cartoons and make myself a tub of popcorn. Then at two o'clock I'd go out and get my hair done, I'd go to HisanHers every week so they knew me, and every week I'd try to get the nerve up to ask for somethin, you know, outrageous or somethin. You know. After that I'd go home and get the photo albums out—he can't stand lookin at pictures so I do it when he's not there. I start off with the ones of me when I was a kid. There's me standin outside City Hall. They've got the road up. And me at the harness races that time my dad hoisted me up in the cart and the horse took off. I don't remember that. And there's me and my nana Morin on the porch of the Golden Years Home in Timmins. And there's my graduation picture with the dress. It looks real old-fashioned now but I can still get into it. And there's Jack in his pale blue sports jacket and a bow tie and pocket handkerchief made out of the same fabric to match. And our wedding album—and then there's Binnie's album. That was the worst having to leave Binnie in Kap, but you can't keep a dog in a downtown apartment can you? It wasn't anyone's fault that she got shot except maybe Jack's for pickin out a dog that was the same colour as a rabbit. He knows what they're like back home, shoot first ask questions later. That's why I'd rather live in a city. Then there's the album with all my friends' weddings. Some of them've stayed on in Kap. And I'm startin one for their kids. Then I cooked his supper. He always likes chicken on Saturday. Sometimes I fancy it up, but he'd rather have it plain roast with a can of corn and a baked potato. That's his favourite. I like it too. Sometimes of an evening we'd walk up to the Eaton Centre and look at the displays and maybe have an orange julius and sometimes we'd walk along Yonge and look in all the windows of the porn shops and go home by the park and watch the young girls on the job—some of them look younger'n I was when I first met him.

JACK   She was thirteen and a half the first time we done it. It wasn't my first time. I was fourteen.

JENNY   He always got sexy after that. I really liked livin on Queen.

JACK   *(Brings out the catalogue and hands it to Jenny.)* So what do you think?

JENNY   *(Flicking through.)* I like this one.

JACK   That one?

JENNY   Doesn't it remind you of a music box?

JACK	With all that fancy crap round the roof?
JENNY	Oh—
JACK	You choose.
JENNY	This one's nice.
JACK	Too much work.
JENNY	How about . . .
JACK	You want a sunken living room?
JENNY	Oh—oh yes, I see what you mean—

(Jack reaches for the catalogue and guards it on his lap. The slide changes; now there are fewer trees.)

JACK   Stage two. I was ready to build in June.

(Jenny rocks.)

All I wanted was for her to be happy. I never chased tail. I'm not that kinda guy. I just wanted her. And I wanted her happy. That's all.

(Jenny rocks.)

I took my two weeks vacation. Everything went great. I hired a coupla guys to help me for the first week. We got it all framed in. It wasn't hard. You just have to follow the instructions right? Any fool can do it.

JENNY   *(Picks up a cookbook from under her rocker. Reads.)* A cup of butter. *(Looks up.)* A cup of butter. *(Reads.)* Two cups of sugar. Two cups of sugar *(Reads.)* Cream together. *(Reads.)* Two cups of flour. Two cups of flour. Sift.

(Jenny looks up as if seeing the flour sift softly from above, sifting all around her and settling in a fine white dust. Jack is reading from his catalogue as she does this.)

JACK   Traditional methods for partitioning, sole plate, studding, sills, trimmers, headers and cripples where called for.

JENNY   *(Reads.)* Add baking powder to rise.

(Jenny and Jack rock.)

(Reads.) Two cups sun-dried raisins. Washed! Eggs. *(Picks an imaginary egg from the air and cradles it in her hands, then cracks it violently.)*

JACK   *(Without looking up.)* Smells good.

JENNY   Muffins.

JACK   Great.

(Jenny stares at her feet, where the imaginary egg is dripping slowly into the flour.)

Wanna beer?

JENNY   No thanks.

JACK   Oh, c'mon.

(Jack brings out two beers, opens them and hands Jenny one.)

You're a fuckin genius, you know that?

	(They rock.)
JENNY	So, you finished?
JACK	Pretty near.
JENNY	*(Neutral.)* That's great Jack.
	(They drink.)
JACK	She just started a new job about then so she didn't have no vacation comin. She went to work for Canadian Tire.
JENNY	I went to work at Canadian Tire. They give thirty percent discount to employees but you have to work Saturdays.
JACK	It paid good. Thing is it paid in Canadian Tire money! *(Laughs.)*
JENNY	I liked it—see me and the other girls—
JACK	She knew she'd have to give it up once we moved.
JENNY	We were always horsin around on the lunch break. Me and the other girls.
JACK	I went there once and watched her. She didn't see me. She was on the cash register her and this other girl. It was like watchin a stranger or somethin. I never let it bother me.
	(They rock and drink. The slide changes. Now there are two trees.)
	I didn't stop her from workin even though she knew she'd have to give it up once we moved. I work shifts and we just got the one truck and it's hard enough to keep up the payments on that. See there's no regular transport out where we are. Not yet. No mail service. No mail service no bills eh? No bills no hassles. *(Laughs.)* Billy bet me I couldn't get the roof on by mid-July.
JENNY	See I wanted—
JACK	I won, then I got the dry-wallin started.
JENNY	I wanted.
JACK	Plaster dust everywhere—I guess I shoulda had that under control right?
JENNY	I wanted—*(Drinks.)* I love him. It's not that, but I wanted . . . I want a house, it's not that.
JACK	I shoulda friggin had it under control right?
JENNY	It's okay.
JACK	Yeah, I know it's okay.
JENNY	I told you it's okay.
	(Jenny reaches under her chair for the knitting bag, opens it slowly and empties out an array of sponges, some natural, some synthetic, brightly coloured, shaped like hearts. They spill off her lap onto the floor.)
JACK	*(Ignoring them.)* You don't know dick.
	(Jenny squeezes a sponge.)
	You don't know what it takes out of you.

JENNY   I just like it where we were that's all. You work. I work. We had
        action.
JACK   You shoulda said so before.
JENNY   I like the city. It's been there a long time.
JACK   What about kids.
JENNY   Kids live in cities.
JACK   Yeah and they're all fucked up. I'm doin all this for you. You
        haven't as much as picked out a shower curtain. *(He kicks a
        sponge.)* Your mother doesn't *have* to make the drapes you
        know.
        (Jenny rocks and strokes her sponge.)
        So we moved. It was September. September the 28th.
JENNY   In spring yellow spotted salamanders migrate to the breeding
        ponds. At night. In spring. Yellow spotted salamanders migrate
        at night to the breeding ponds.
JACK   There was still a pile of work to do. But it was ours. It was ours
        and I wanted her out there.
        (Slide changes to a single tree in fall.)
JENNY   I was arrested for shoplifting from Shoppers Drug Mart. They
        asked me why I did it. I said I didn't know. We don't need that
        many sponges. They didn't charge me so I didn't have to tell
        him. I paid for them so now they're mine. This was alive once.
        (Tears the plastic wrap off one of the sponges with her teeth.)
JACK   You haven't taken the label off the friggin sink!
JENNY   Don't have any Ajax.
JACK   You can walk.
JENNY   It's alright. I'll get some.
JACK   I get you a double sink and you can't even be bothered to take
        the friggin label off, what are you doin all day?
JENNY   There's plenty to do.
JACK   Darn right. *(Rocks.)* She buys about two million dishmops and
        swabs and such and she never picks one of them up!
        (Slide changes to a single tree in winter.)
        There's a shopping plaza just down the street a couple of miles
        . . . a shopping plaza full of stores and signs on the windows
        askin for help.
        (They rock.)
        We'd been moved in three months . . . three months and we
        didn't even . . . not once. And we used to do it every night. I
        mean how are you supposed to start a family if you don't . . . ?
        Well you know! *(Pause.)* I bought a futon for the guest room so
        that if my mom or her mom and dad wanted to come down for
        Christmas . . . we never had the room for them on Queen. Some-
        one told me a futon's the thing to buy. So I bought it.

JENNY   It smells like earth. Like layin on old roots. I might as well be layin in the yard.

JACK   *(Hopefully.)* You don't have to sleep on it.

JENNY   I don't mind. *(She rocks.)* It was the first time I'd slept on my own in my whole life. The first time I ever slept in my own room. I bought a poster of Meryl Streep.

JACK   She bought this poster of Meryl Streep. I took it down and hung it in our room. If she wanted to sleep with Meryl Streep that was okay with me, but I didn't see why I should be left out of the action, right?

JENNY   *(Staring straight ahead.)* I love you.

JACK   I love you too.
         (Slide changes to a placard reading "Save the Frogs.")
         One thing about not having a sidewalk you don't have to shovel it in winter!

JENNY   You never shovelled it on Queen!

JACK   We had a ton of snow that year.
         (They rock.)

JENNY   They drained the swamp. Endangered species include two varieties of orchid under our driveway. Mud puppies right where the double sink is—they're dying out—they use them for research. A Canada Goose nest under the garage. Geese mate for life. Tree-frogs, Fowler's toads, lungless salamanders. Bullfrogs. We eat their legs. A frog. Does not. Drink up. The pond. In which he lives.

JACK   She found the first placard when it melted. Yeah. She musta been rooting around out there on the street. When I was at work. Yeah. When the snow melted. It was somethin to do with frogs.

JENNY   Save the frogs!

JACK   The frogs didn't come back that first spring.

JENNY   *(Yells, full voice.)* Save the frogs!

JACK   I guess they found some place else or they got sucked down the sluicepipe or somethin. The frogs didn't come back but the woman who started it did. She came knockin on our door. What do they want? It's done. Number 23 Pine Crescent. A whole friggin street. It's done. Thirty-two houses with double garages and porch lights—fire hydrants, water and sewage. It's done, right? If I didn't do it, someone else would. Right? *(Rocks.)*

JENNY   Save the swamps!

JACK   It gave her somethin to do. Didn't bring no money in, but I didn't say nothin. She was on the phone for hours to this one and that one. Then I'd come home and there'd be all these

women in rubber boots in our kitchen. I didn't say nothin.
(Jenny rocks.)
First she baked for them. Then she started organizin. She organized walks. She organized petitions—we had pamphlets up to
the ceiling in the living room. She got guest speakers in, wine
and cheese, she even got her name in the *Star*. Up to then she'd
never organized a friggin raffle and all of a sudden that's all
there was. Organizin. And I'd come home and there'd be all
these women leavin coffee rings on my oak finish.

JENNY   *(Dismissing him.)* Oh Jack!

JACK   The papers are full of protests. Nobody reads them. Who cares?
It's done. You gotta live with it. Don't you know that? It's done!

JENNY   Their ancestry can be traced back more than twenty-six million
years.

JACK   It's too late.

JENNY   If you stand in the bush and run your finger along the teeth of a
comb a frog will answer.
(Jack belches.)
When they're displaced they always return back to the place
where they lived. They keep returnin back for ten years.

JACK   She moved back into our room. Me and her and Meryl Streep.
Things improved. As long as we didn't hafta talk too much
things were more like they used to be. I never asked her what she
did with her day no more.

JENNY   *(Shrugs.)* I never go back to Queen. Even when I have to go
downtown I walk down other streets.

JACK   I mean how many guys would wanna come home from the shop
floor and talk about frogs right?

JENNY   They often lose part of their tail to escape an enemy but a new
one grows back.

JACK   Hey—what did the leper say to the prostitute? You can keep the
tip! You can keep . . .
(Jack laughs, looks at Jenny expectantly. No response.)
You see? I mean, I'm the one who wouldn't go huntin, she's the
one who used to tell me I was chicken. She was never interested
in nature. *(Suddenly, violently to Jenny.)* You coulda stopped
me!
(Jenny rocks, with her eyes closed.)
I put in a clothes-line and built the steps up to it to make it easy
for her. I brought in topsoil. Got a vegetable garden dug in out
the back. It was a bit wet. So what? I bought her a freezer so she
could freeze the fuckers. And all the time she was out there with
those women, goin on about the "Environmental Corridors"!

(Shuts his eyes tight.)
(Slide changes. A cross-section of a tree trunk, showing the rings.)
It was the next spring. The next spring they came back.
(Jenny suddenly becomes alert.)
They were in the basement. Just a few of them at first. Cute little green ones.

JENNY   Oh look Jack!

JACK   Then they moved into the kitchen.

JENNY   I told you they'd keep coming back!

JACK   The living room. They sat down to meals with us.
(Jenny draws her feet up, scared.)
(Opening his eyes, and getting into it.) She went up to Kap for a visit and when she came back I told her they were in all the cupboards, in the sink ... when you sat on the toilet ...

JENNY   Where? Where?

JACK   I told her they were in the bedroom. They were jumpin and crawlin all over Meryl Streep's face. They were in the friggin bed. *(Jumps to his feet.)* The whole friggin house is overrun! The whole street!
(Jenny screams.)
Like a slimey green rug, heavin under your feet—and when you walk on it you feel it squelch ... you feel it under your feet, and then you're up to your knees in it and then it's up to your chin. They're on your shoulders, in your ears ... they're takin over! It's frogs. Your friggin frogs!

JENNY   Do somethi-i-i-i-ng! I hate them! Kill them! Kill them! Kill them! Kill them! Kill them! Ki-i-i-i-ill!
(Jenny and Jack shrink back to either side of the stage and stand, transfixed.
Lights go out, leaving the slide. This also disappears, leaving the screen blank. Finally the screen is also dark. Lights come up to reveal Jack and Jenny back in their chairs. Jenny is very pregnant.)

JACK   I decided against a lawn. I put down gravel and cedar chips. The weeds got through so I kept a bunch of weedkiller in the garage. It's not hard to control them if you get the right stuff. *(Picks up the binoculars.)* You can't go on livin in the past. You gotta look forward. Right? *(Hands binoculars to Jenny.)* You ever look at the sky Jenny? You ever look at the stars? Really look I mean. Really look.

DEBBIE HOWLETT

Debbie Howlett was born in Montreal in 1964. Her short fiction has appeared in a number of Montreal-based journals, including *Passions & Poisons* published by Nu-Age Editions, and most recently in *The Malahat Review*. She is presently completing her MFA degree in Creative Writing.

"The Broom Closet" is a story I started writing shortly after my arrival in Vancouver. I'm not sure where the story came from. I think it might have been an early reaction to being 3,000 miles away from home for the first time and not at all in control of what was happening back there.

The Broom Closet

After my father's funeral, the entire family gets invited over to my grandmother's apartment to drink Chivas. It's a one-bedroom in the West End of the city she shares with another widow.

I go with my brother and Uncle Lenny in my father's old white Impala which still smells like cheap cigars. Frank gets to go along too because Lenny thinks he looks like an associate of my father's. "So, you're in the magic business too," says Uncle Lenny, sizing him up. Frank and Lenny are about the same age.

At Gram's place Frank sits in the same chair mostly, probably trying to stay as innocuous as possible, and nurses the drink my grandmother shoved into his hand when he first arrived. He looks worn out and wrinkled and he's still wearing the same grey suit he wore on the plane. I stand watching him from behind my old auntie's fox, but when he looks my way I pretend to be admiring it.

"Is this real, Auntie?" I say.

She cocks her head in my direction, which is good because it makes us look like we're really having a conversation together, and then shouts, "What?"

"Is this . . ." And then I stop because I can't really ask her if it's real because it wouldn't be very polite.

"What?" she shouts again, but this time I'm not saying anything.

I can feel the blood rushing up to my face, and across the room I can see Frank spying on me through the bottom of his Chivas glass. In the glass, his face is gross and distorted and his teeth appear closer together.

"Is this fox?" I say loudly because everyone's listening by now anyway.

My auntie says, "Yes," and tweaks the fox on its petrified nose as my mother brushes past me and barks, "Don't be dense, Paula. Of course it's goddamned fox!" I duck back behind my auntie and continue circulating the pigs-in-blanket because I don't want Frank to see my mother and the family resemblance. When I pass the table with the Chivas on it, I splash a little more into my glass.

My gram sidles up close to me, holding out her own glass. "Be a dear," she says. I hold out the Chivas bottle for her but as I look at the glass, I notice a hairline crack that starts on the edge and continues down the side of it. A trickle of blood slowly slides off my grandmother's lip.

"Gram." I reach out and wipe the corner of her mouth with a cocktail napkin that has MANY HAPPY RETURNS emblazoned across it.

I get her a new glass and fill it an inch high with liquid. She smiles at me, swirls the booze around in her glass and says, "That's a dear." She stays quietly beside me, sipping on her drink until I begin to move away. She yanks on the back of my dress and catches the hem in one of her rings. The dress tears a little, but not so anyone would notice.

"Yes, Gram?" I turn and look at her. Her spectacled eyes are fixed on something on the other side of the room. I carefully follow her gaze. They're fixed on Frank. I look away.

She points at him with a shaky finger and says, "That man is no friend of your father's." And then she begins making her way across the carpet, squeezing through the crowd of people assembled in her living room.

I'm not sure what to do, so I disappear into the kitchen to refill my tray. My mother is in there, whispering softly into the ear of a man I don't recognize.

"What exactly are you doing?" she says to me. The man doesn't look up from my mother's neck.

"I'm filling up." I gesture to the sterling tray commemorating twenty-five years of marriage between my grandmother and grandfather. I throw on a few cheese twists because I don't see the pigs-in-blanket, and because I suddenly feel as if I have to justify my being in my grandmother's kitchen there with them.

"I know what you've been up to," she says quietly and then she and the man I don't know file past me and into the living room.

I drag a chair across the linoleum floor, and sit down when it's next to a half-empty bottle of Chivas and a tray of sandwiches in the shape of little hearts.

Frank. I say this to myself because there's no one else in the room.

I met Frank on a wide-bodied 747 from Vancouver to Toronto. He had a nice face and even teeth. We said hello, ordered a few of those miniature airline drinks, and played a hand of gin rummy. We watched a bit of

Blame It on Rio until we couldn't stand it anymore, and then ordered a few more of those mini drinks on account of they were so mini. On our way to the baggage carousel we did it in a broom closet with DO NOT ENTER on the door. It was smelly and hot, but not totally without romance. And it was quiet; quieter than I remembered it in a long long time. After it was over, and Frank and I were still waiting for our luggage to come down, he asked me if everything was all right. I couldn't remember anyone ever asking me that before, so I said yes, it was okay.

We didn't see much of each other in Toronto, at least not like we saw each other in the broom closet at Pearson International, but we did bump into each other a few days later in the Kensington Market. I was coming back with Clare, who'd insisted on buying a live chicken for dinner and strangling it herself, when I spotted him. He was walking along the street with a woman my age.

"Shit," I said, "That's him."

"Who?" Clare said.

"The guy from the plane, the guy from the closet," I said, but I'm not sure why.

"Which guy?" But the expression on my face must have told her which guy because she simply smiled and said, "So."

Then she grabbed me and kissed me full on the mouth, hoping he'd sort of walk on by, without a second glance. I knew what she was doing because we'd done it before. So there we were, in the middle of Kensington, necking like crazy, when Frank said, "Hello again," like it was a line from a love song.

I grinned and tried wiping Clare's lipstick away.

"I'm sorry, we haven't met," Clare said, linking arms with me. "Are you a friend of Paula's *too*?" I wanted to kill her for the extra emphasis she put on the word *too* because nothing was going on and for some reason I wanted Frank to know that.

"A friend of Paula's," he repeated for whatever reasons.

"Frank, Clare. Clare, Frank." I waved my hand back and forth between the two of them, then gave up with the lipstick.

That's when I glanced at the woman beside Frank. She had the exact same niceness about her face and evenness about her teeth that Frank had.

"This is Leslie," he said. "My daughter," but he didn't have to.

He introduced me as an old friend from Vancouver, but neither of us bothered introducing Clare. He didn't even flinch at the thought of us standing there kissing, a chicken in a gunnysack pressed between us.

When we were just about to leave, Frank reached out and squeezed my hand. It was a warm and friendly squeeze that told me he remembered the broom closet. His daughter watched us wordlessly, and it occurred to me that she was probably a very good daughter. Then he said, "I'll call," and they were gone.

"So," Clare said again. Then we went back to her place and she strangled the chicken while I threw up.

In the kitchen, I sit there slurping Chivas and imagine my grandmother slipping stealthily through the crowd to where Frank's sitting. But Frank doesn't get up, he just keeps sitting there holding onto his drink while my grandmother's eyes pierce holes through him. Then this very bright light starts shining through the holes. And when he opens his mouth, I hear him saying, "Yes, Gram," and I don't know why *he's* calling *her* Gram. "I did it in the broom closet, and I did it in the funeral parlour, and I'll do it here." And then all the blood circulating in my grandmother's body starts to drain out of that damned cut in her lip and there's not enough cocktail napkins to clean it all up.

And while I'm sitting there, I also try to imagine the words *doing it* come out of Frank's mouth, but I can't. He wouldn't say something like that; I would. So I rest easy for a bit knowing that it's just my imagination, and maybe there's no Frank after all. No Frank, no fucking, no funeral. But then my auntie comes into the kitchen still wearing the fox around her neck and I know it's real. The fox's fur is matted and sticky and smells suspiciously like Chivas, but she doesn't seem to mind.

"Paula!" she says, holding onto the fox. Pieces of fur float in the air around her and stick to her hands. I know she wants me to talk to her, but I'm not sure I can. Besides, I suddenly feel reluctant to leave my spot by the sandwiches and the Chivas even for a moment. But then she starts shouting again and I begin whispering to her not to worry because everything is going to be all right after all.

I pull fox hair from her face and hands. It upsets my auntie quite a bit that the fox seems to be shedding. She opens and closes her mouth furiously.

"I knew that man wasn't a friend of your father's," my grandmother says, swinging into her kitchen. "I simply knew it." She says *knew* but it comes out sounding like *canoe*.

"Paula," my grandmother says softly, "Why didn't you tell me?"

When the phone call came, Clare and I were touring around the Canadian National Exhibit. We were making our hair stand on end in the Science Centre, eating pink cotton candy, and laughing and laughing and laughing. Frank and the broom closet were a million miles away. And Clare was trying to get my mind off it because that's why I went to Toronto in the first place.

And when we finally got back to Clare's, the little red light on her answering machine flashed hysterically at us. She pushed the play button, but she didn't have to. It was my brother's recorded voice saying, "Paula." And then he paused for a while. "I hate these fucking things." And then the line went dead and stayed dead for a very long time until the machine kicked in and turned itself off. Then I phoned Frank because I didn't know who else to call and I didn't feel like being alone in a strange city with Clare asleep in the next room.

ANN IRELAND

Ann Ireland was born in Toronto in 1953 and attended UBC from 1972 to 1976. In 1985 she won the Seal First Novel Award for *A Certain Mr. Takahashi* (McClelland & Stewart/Bantam). She has just finished a new novel and has gone to Mexico to start a play and another novel. She lives with Tim Deverell (a painter) and their son, Thomas (age 2).

I haven't written short fiction since I started working on novels. "The Doppler Effect" was written in 1981, soon after I returned from New York. I must have been remembering the night the Puerto Rican speakeasy across the street got raided. Such a commotion. Nothing like that happens in Toronto.

The Doppler Effect

"Are you sure you won't stay?" he asks, leaning against the door frame as Ellen picks up her giant carry-all with its collection of books and eyeglasses.

"No love, I can't. The cat needs feeding." She brushes hair out of her eyes and smiles at him.

"It was a fabulous dinner. I've never had fish done like that. What did you call it?"

"En croûte."

"That's right. It was wonderful."

He nods assent.

She pauses a moment before reaching out to him, bag swinging so it catches his hip. They hold each other in a bearhug which Cody, drunk, presses into.

She gives him a little squeeze and expects to be let go.

"Just a minute." He feels her ample flesh pushed into his yet she pulses a different heart rhythm, slower and more dignified. He lets go: she's gone unmistakably limp.

"I hope I didn't . . . " She pauses, one hand on the door knob.

"No—no." He waves her off.

Cody locks and latches the door then swings across the dead bolt. He watches her retreating shape through the eye of the peep hole. She crosses the tiled hall to the stairwell where she disappears and he listens to the clop clop of her heels, gently diminishing as she descends five storeys of the walkup. Back home to her building with the elevator and doorman.

Waiting until he hears the street door shut Cody crosses the room to the window which is open to let in whatever draft cuts through the smog of midsummer Manhattan. He leans out.

She waves up at him, laughing silently. He thinks she looks relieved.

"There's a cab!" He points to the intersection.

She's off, racing to flag the beat-up Plymouth. An unnecessary squeal of tires, which raises no interest from the group of Puerto Rican teenagers huddled in the stoop, and she is gone.

Cody realizes he is breathing heavily. Too much to eat and drink. Too little air. He unbuttons his white shirt and tosses it to the floor near the laundry basket, but not before noticing two holes, one below each arm. Fucker must have shrunk in the wash.

He lowers himself wearily on the bed, kicking off his sweaty sneakers. It's stinking hot. What else is new? And only mid-July.

The meal, he has to admit, was a triumph. Homemade Puff Pastry had turned out blissfully flaky, surrounding the moist fish like a satin jacket. Fiddleheads, imported from Canada, were carefully rinsed and steamed the barest, thinnest amount, and piled alongside like magic spirals unbending.

"Damn right it was fabulous," he says aloud.

She'd watched him poke around in the railway kitchen, worrying the salmon, talking to the browning pastry, "C'mon baby, c'mon," and getting progressively drunker from the bottle of cooking wine.

Cody's stomach wrenches.

Salmonella? Very funny. He grabs a handful of antacids from the bedside table.

His skin is dripping sweat, part nerves, part metabolic heat. He remembers a suggestion someone once made, and though it seems like a lot of effort, he swings out of bed and pads off towards the kitchen.

Every inch of counter is covered in dirty dishes and bits of leftover food. Quickly, he opens the freezer, pulls out an ice tray and knocks its contents into a bowl. He carries this back into the bedroom and places it in front of the decrepit fan. Then lays back and waits for an ice-cooled breeze to come his way.

At some point the evening took a false turn and never found its way back. She was so sure she had him figured. But why did he let it get to him? And—Cody jams two pillows under his neck—where does his delicate sensitivity find him but alone on this wretched night?

Before supper she'd posed on the edge of the chair smoking one cigarette after the other, her giant bag lounged alongside, like a guard dog. She wore a narrow, short skirt, something out of a sixties French film, and a loose blouse that she moved inside dramatically. He poured drinks and she talked compulsively of her family. She darted looks at his apartment, particularly the bookcase, as if she might find clues there. Of his safety, he thought.

"You been in this place long?"

"Ten years," he said. It looked it.

Then a funny thing happened. She leaned over and ran a finger along the bookcase shelf, gliding through a year's accumulation of dust. She realized what she was doing an instant before the next step, which would have been scrutiny of the dirty finger, and gave a snort of embarrassment.

"God Cody, please excuse me. How *rude*. I don't believe I could do such a tacky thing—I don't know—" Flustered, she dropped her hand to her side and five minutes later unobtrusively wiped it against her hemline.

At supper she'd asked him about his childhood in Saskatchewan. Moved by her interest he took the old Vanguard disc of Saskatchewan folksongs out of its sleeve and played,

When the Iceworms Nest Again.

She was charmed. He knew all the words, despite the fact he'd left the prairie for good when he was ten.

After eating she got up and came round to his side of the table so she could show him the scar where she'd jabbed herself with a Rapidograph pen. He'd felt the warmth of her for the first time. As he held the injured finger, examining the dark spot, her warmth and the warmth of all the food and drink he'd consumed flooded into his body. He suddenly saw how it would happen: he would carry her down to the floor in his arms, tipping the half-filled bottle of wine so it splashed over them and she would unfold, one limb after the other, wrapping herself around him like a starfish on a rock.

Instead he'd said, perhaps too urgently, "Stay with me tonight."

And though her smile said she'd expected it she nodded with a false sadness, as if it were a tragedy neither could escape, and said, "No Cody." Then, pretending it was in no way connected to the exchange she moved back to her seat across the table saying,

"I can't eat another bite."

She took her coffee into the other room and strolled with it, clicking spoon against china as she wandered first over to the window, a quick peep in the street, then nearly into his bedroom. She caught herself at the threshold.

"You must think I'm really nosy."

"Not at all, I like it," he said.

It was true. He liked seeing this woman walk through his apartment examining his things. Oddly, it made it more completely his. He liked to imagine what the arrangement of furniture, books and magazines might signal to her.

He watched her eyes skim the framed map of Newfoundland that hung just inside his bedroom door.

"Go on, take a look," he urged.

She took two tentative steps and stared at the big rabbit, which stared back at the Atlantic rim of Canada, chin-first.

He waited until she began to giggle.

"Listen to this Cody. There's a spot called 'Lushes Bight,' and 'Push-through,' and—" a hoot of laughter. 'Seldom.'

She turned to him, eyes wide. "What *is* this country?"

"Newfoundland." He pronounced it correctly, with the accent on the last syllable.

"New-found-land," she nodded and set one hand on her hip. The thin material of blouse stretched across her back and he could see her bra strap, a thin white line.

She peered a moment longer before asking, "Have you been there Cody?"

"Sure, and I'm going again next month if all goes well."

"Really? What do you do there?"

"DO? Fish. I fish."

She threw her head back and laughed easily. "I love it. I can just see you in hip waders. Cody, I demand that you take me to this place. See—" She pointed to a dot on the Avalon Peninsula. "'Heart's Delight.' I want to be there on August 21st, my birthday."

She jabbed the glass with her finger, smudging it.

"That can probably be arranged." He tried to mimic her tone. But his chest was seizing. She was tugging the end of a long rope that looped up inside touching his every nerve.

Then Ellen picked up the L.L. Bean catalogue and stated waltzing through the livingroom, flipping its pages with one hand while finishing off her coffee with the other.

"I'll need one of these—definitely!" she giggled. "A fisherman's hat with netting for foul weather—oh, and long underwear for those chilly nights. Cody, look at these darling slippers with the socks attached! And a string hammock—absolutely essential in the bush."

She looked towards Cody, her eyes bright.

"You think I'm joking, don't you?"

"Aren't you?"

"I'm not sure that I am."

She settled on the couch beside him.

"Can you imagine, a girl from the Bronx in Heart's Delight?" She rested one hand on his wrist. "Please take me there." Her look was doleful, full of mock yearning.

He slid his hand out. "I don't know; they're not used to women like you."

"They'd think I was from Mars!" she cried.

The catalogue slid off her lap onto the floor.

Useless to try and sleep. He's been lying there for hours, tossing and turning. Cody rolls off the bed and steps onto the floor. He blows his nose loudly to try and ease breathing. No use, there's no air left in New York this summer; it's all gone to Long Island, trapped in the lungs of the rich. He crosses the room to the record player, taking care to step lightly. He replaces the Saskatchewan record in its sleeve.

Something has gone wrong. Suddenly there is nothing to do. The apartment surrounds him like an itchy coat. Quickly he reaches for the dregs of the bottle Ellen brought—a thin-bodied Burgundy.

He presses his thumb against his eye socket. A headache's forming, sure and thick as a fog off Frenchman's Cove. Tomorrow is the subway ride to Brooklyn, to City University's most remote college housed in a converted train station. Gangs of punks lurk near subway exits, chuckling in anticipation of his arrival.

He will lecture on, "After Graduation: The Real Work."

"You don't need me. You're like some fifties American car, overbuilt for the road," a woman once told him.

"I *do* need you," Cody protested.

"You don't need *me*," she declared. "You need a *nurse*."

Bottle in hand Cody steps in front of the Newfoundland map. The Great Rabbit. With a corner of his t-shirt he rubs the smudge Ellen left there. Port-au-Port Bay. His heart quickens. On August 15, all going well, he'll drive off, far from this wreck of a city, in search of the Trout, and especially, the Salmon. He pictures himself in hip waders stepping into a bright stream and delicately casting off. And later, the strike followed by the delicious struggle, salmon running towards the other shore then twisting back, each time Cody tiring him a little, occasional flash of colour as it jumps the waterline, teasing, cackling fish laughter.

There is a woman, half a mile down the trail, reading in a hammock. She will prepare supper with the catch, adding to it freshly picked herbs, berries and green leafy things. She will have baked rough Arab bread in a hole dug in the ground, like the Bedouins. And she will not come looking for him.

This woman is not Ellen. Her name fluctuates, but tonight she is "Teresa," Cody decides. A prairie woman, broad-hipped and reserved who waits hours for him without irritation. She braids her long blonde hair and fastens it back with pieces of twine. She hardly speaks, unless it is for something important:

"Shall I pour the wine?"

She prefers to reserve her intensity for bed. The evenings are drawn out as long as possible in anticipation of that moment. They lick fish grease off each other's fingers and slowly fall to the sleeping bags, under the softly crooning Newfoundland moon.

Cody bends over the blue trunk in the cupboard. A giant waterbug lumbers away, annoyed at the disturbance. Cody pulls out several boxes and bags and a leather case containing the new rod. All winter he has pored over catalogues, sending away for nearly everything.

He sits on the floor, one leg curled, and surrounds himself with the gear. He unzips the leather sheath, touches the gleaming fibreglass rod as it lies, sectioned, surrounded by navy velvet. He pulls out each piece and fits it together and, still sitting, gives a tentative cast towards the cupboard door. Feels good. Resilient. He casts again, harder. This time he flips a yellowed calendar off the wall—1973—the year he arrived, and it flutters to the floor. He sets the rod carefully on the carpet and opens the fly case. He opens it the way a child opens a giant box of crayons, breathless in anticipation of future pleasure. Without touching the delicate objects, he gazes at them, and imagines the way they'll look catching the sun's light through water.

There is also a manila envelope which he shakes so the contents fall out. It's a telegram postmarked Stephenville, the nearest town to Rory, the young guide who lives with his family in an outport.

RECEIVED 100 DOLLARS STOP BE READY AUGUST 16

It's all the proof he needs. Already he feels a cooling breeze brush his forehead.

What did Ellen say?

"I want to be there, on my birthday."

A joke of course. She'd hate the black flies.

Cody squeezes his eyes shut and somewhere, he nearly has it, is the sound of white water. He is about to catch the biggest fucking Humpback in the province. But the sound of the stream dips, pitching low, like a subway leaving the platform just as he struggles down the stairs—late as always. Or like a cab spinning up Second Avenue merging into the white noise of traffic as he stands on the curb, still waving.

What's that called?

The Doppler Effect.

Cody's eyes pop open. He must have been dozing.

Sirens, which he is accustomed to hearing as backdrop to his thoughts, are getting louder and seem to be stopping under his window.

Reluctantly, he hoists himself to his feet and turns off the light so he can see better.

What a commotion. The street, usually empty at this hour but for a few junkies nodding in the doorway of the burned out building, is sprayed with blue police cars, their red beacons blinking. How many? Cody counts: One-two-three, they keep arriving—eight now, all screeching to a stop and fanning out. One cop springs out of his car and raises a bullhorn to his mouth. He roars something in Spanish at the house opposite Cody's. A dozen more blue suits get out of the building.

Cody hasn't seen anything like it since the last time they raided the nightclub, two months ago. The street crackles with excitement, radios and voices barking as the bullhorn makes another authoritative demand. Heads appear at the windows of neighbouring tenements. The club is on the third floor. God knows what they do in there.

Cody leans his head out and yells into the racket:

"GO HOME!"

Of course no one hears or listens. Forget sleep now. Despite himself he feels a rush of adrenalin, not unpleasant, like when he put the new rod in his hand and swung it back.

As he watches, an extra drama is being played out. On the west side of the building a window on the third floor pushes up and a brown head peeks out then darts back in again. A moment later a pair of legs negotiate the sill and then—it happens so fast—a slightly built man leaps to the ground. It's a good thirty-foot drop. As he lands on the pavement he seems to shrink into a little ball, like certain bugs when you touch them with the end of your shoe.

No one sees him—except Cody.

The young man slowly rises to his feet and begins to hop towards Delancey. Cody can see there's something wrong—his leg's all twisted in funny directions. Yet he makes his way, dragging the injured limb and darting frightened looks over his shoulder. He couldn't be more than sixteen.

"C'mon kid, come on," Cody chants. "Hurry up asshole. Don't look back!"

He squeezes his eyes shut just for a moment, trying to picture the young Rory picking his way down the cliff face to the water below.

But outside cars gun their motors, the bullhorn blares on and the other image sandwiches itself in: the dumb-assed Puerto Rican kid pitching out the third floor window and splaying on the pavement. About to be picked off by some trigger-happy cop.

He looks again. Where'd the kid go?

Gone. Disappeared. Then a car door slams, there's a flash of yellow and a Checker cab squeals off the corner of Delancey and Grand, the kid's face pressed to the window.

"Made it!" Cody yells gleefully into the fracas below. "Slipped right by you idiots!"

He whirls back into the room and slaps his naked belly with his hands. Where's that wretched record? He drops it onto the turntable and points the needle to its favourite spot. Then he cranks up the volume so it can be heard above the street din and, propped up against the windowledge, starts to sing,

"When the Iceworms Nest A—gain!"

SALLY IRELAND

Sally Ireland graduated from the MFA program in 1988. Since then she has worked as a freelance writer and course designer, while continuing to write long and short fiction, and poetry.

This story is based on scenes that came up during a counselling session. While the events depicted may not be actual, they are real.

Lullaby

Very high up a bird crossed the still centre of the sky, while all around the child trees whirled. She heard Ollie's barking turn into frantic yips. As trees and sky blurred together she dropped to the grass and began rolling down the bank toward the cottage where the ginger kitten lived. Then, in a moment of lovely confusion, the roll crossed the orbit of her dizziness, and suddenly the world was inside her tummy: the grass was there, and the trees, the sky and the bird; Mummy, Daddy and Malcolm were there, and so were Ollie and the ginger kitten.

She came to rest in the shade at the foot of the bank. Ollie's tongue licked her shoulder, and she answered him by running her hands through the perfectly white soft hair on his chest.

"Di-nah," a voice called down to her.

She lay still with her eyes closed. She didn't want anything to disturb her cool peace.

"Di-nah, come here this instant," Mummy's impatient voice said.

The child rose to her knees and hugged Ollie, then slowly she stood and walked up the bank with him beside her, his feathery tail batting her naked legs.

In the hallway Daddy, who had just come home from work, said, "There's my sweetheart," and swung the child up, level with his shoulders. Daddy loves me tonight, she thought. With her arms around his neck she sniffed at the sweet smell of his skin beneath the starchy collar, which scraped her cheek as she nuzzled him.

Malcolm clattered down the stairs from his room.

"What a sight you look, Dinah," Mummy said. "For heaven's sake, Malcolm, get her cleaned up. I've almost got dinner on the table."

"Come on, Puss," Malcolm said and took her into the washroom where he picked a bit of grass out of her hair as he handed her the soap.

"What have you been up to?" he asked. "Looks to me like you're getting ready to grow a lawn on your head and a potato patch under your fingernails."

"I was putting the world in my tummy," she explained to him.

"What a good idea," he said. "That way you can keep everything real handy for whenever you need it."

At dinner they had shepherd's pie, which the child loved; but there was too much, and as she took her last mouthful, Malcolm reached across the table for her plate. Glancing from side to side, first at Daddy then at Mummy like some mad starving beast, he started shovelling the remains of the meat and mashed potato into his mouth with a fork in one hand and his dessert spoon in the other.

The child giggled, but Mummy said, "Malcolm, stop it this instant. You're supposed to set an example for your little sister."

When they began dessert Daddy cleared his throat.

"I wonder what G.L. stands for," he said.

Malcolm looked down at his bowl of peaches.

"Can you tell me?" Daddy asked him.

"Some kind of a . . . ," Malcolm mumbled so that the child couldn't hear the rest of the sentence.

"What did you say?"

"For goodness sake, Malcolm, don't mutter," Mummy told him.

"Some kind of abbreviation, I guess," Malcolm said more clearly, but in a low voice.

"An abbreviation . . . ," Daddy said, examining his words, " . . . standing for what?"

There was a blind glitter in his eyes that hadn't been there when he first came home.

Malcolm shrugged.

"Standing for . . . ?"

"G.L.," Malcolm said, "Get Lost."

Mummy gasped.

The child wished someone would take away the nasty twisting feeling in her tummy.

"Mightn't G.L. be someone's initials?" Daddy continued.

"Yeah, I guess."

"And where might one find those initials?"

Malcolm cupped his hand around his lips and mouthed something at the child who didn't understand anything but the last word, which was *ass*.

"What did you say?" Mummy demanded. Then she turned to the child and asked, "What did he say to you?"

She hated the way her parents kept throwing up questions, unable to stop, just as if they had the flu.

"Mightn't they be engraved on the back of a watch?" Daddy asked. "A silver watch with an expansion bracelet? Which you stole from one of your classmates, a boy by the name of George Lesakis?"

The child saw Malcolm flinch.

"And what does all this make you?" Daddy demanded. He waited a moment, and when Malcolm didn't answer he said, "A thief—a Common Thief—C.T.," and laughed at the joke he'd made, his eyes glittering and his forefinger stiffly tapping the placemat.

Suddenly it was as if Malcolm had gone away from the table and left his body sitting on the chair, hunched over his bowl of peaches, his hand cutting the fruit into smaller and smaller segments with a spoon.

"Where is the watch?"

"I don't have it anymore," Malcolm said in a voice that came only from his mouth, but not his mind.

Daddy closed his eyelids, as if he were trying to keep the glitter from shattering his eyes.

After a long silence Malcolm said, "I hocked it for a knife."

"Hocked?" Mummy said, frowning. "Where did you get your language? I'm sure we never taught you to use words like that."

"Then where is the knife?" Daddy demanded, looking as if Mummy's interruption annoyed him. "By the time I get back from work tomorrow afternoon, you'd better have the knife ready to hand over to me."

Malcolm's eyes stared at the peaches he hadn't eaten.

"I will not tolerate a thief in my house. Is that understood?"

The next afternoon the child heard a baby crying up in Malcolm's room. As she climbed the steep chrome-edged stairs sharp pieces of grit, which were caught in the treads, nipped at her bare soles. At the top syrupy rays of light trickled through the window. The child stood in the sticky light, listening to the baby's cry. Just beyond Malcolm's room there was an opening in the knotty pine wall that she had never seen before, and beside the opening, leaning up against the wall, a door, or a lid, also made of knotty pine. The baby's cry sounded as if it came from inside.

The child crept over to the opening and looked in, but she couldn't see anything because the sunlight had dazzled her. The dark space was filled with the baby's crying and a heavy, sweetish smell. It was such an unhappy baby.

Suddenly, she saw a glimmer as something shiny and moving reflected back the light from the hallway.

"Malcolm?" she whispered.

There was a scuffing sound inside. Then Malcolm's face appeared, with the same dead glitter in his eyes that Daddy sometimes had.

"Curiosity killed the cat," he said, and pulled her into the dark. She felt a clammy hand around her wrist, but it didn't feel as if it belonged to her brother.

"What are you doing?" she demanded.

The hand let go of her arm.

She was beginning to get used to the darkness, and as Malcolm moved away, she saw that he had no pants on.

Over in the corner something moved as the baby started crying again.

Oh, baby, poor, poor baby, the child thought. Then a shadow, which was and wasn't Malcolm, passed in front of her and picked up a squirming, crying bundle of rags.

"Let me see the baby," she said.

Malcolm thrust the bundle at her. It was wet and sticky. But there was no baby. What she saw was the tufted ear of the ginger kitten from the cottage at the bottom of the grassy bank. It was the kitten that was crying.

Suddenly the child felt herself pushed back against the wall. In one hand Malcolm held the kitten; in the other, something that flashed—a knife. And he stabbed the kitten in the tummy.

The child felt her own tummy clench and twist.

He stabbed the kitten again.

"Stop," she cried. "Oh, stop. The poor, poor kitty." She kicked at her brother's bare legs. She hit his arm. But he was breathing like a crazy man with hard, noisy gasps and groans as he stabbed the kitten again and again.

"Christ," he called out, then he went limp and let the knife drop to the floor.

It was quiet in the small dark room. The child watched her brother in the doorway, where he sat slack-jawed, wiping away the spatters of blood from his legs with his shirt-tails while he held the blood-soaked front crumpled in his fist. He worked carefully, spitting on the shirt tails, rubbing at the blood, methodically working up his leg, from ankle to calf to knee to thigh. By the time he'd wiped the blade of the knife and folded it away he was Malcolm again. As he cleaned away some blood the child had got on her hand from touching the bundle, he began to weep noiselessly, the tears leaking from his eyes.

"They're gonna fuckin' kill me," he said.

The child answered, "I know." And to herself she thought, After they've finished with him, they're going to start on me.

At that moment she heard a noise on the stairs: the scrape of leather soles on the chrome-bordered treads.

"Malcolm. Dinah. Where are you?" Mummy's voice called.

The child ran out the doorway through the syrupy light to the top of the stairs.

"You can't come up here," she said in a voice that was very loud and strong as she looked down at Mummy, who was climbing the stairs in red shoes.

"And why not?" Mummy demanded in a tone that said to the child, Okay, I'll play Let's Pretend if you want, but only for a little while.

The child answered, "Because I've got a big dog up here, and she's very fierce, much fiercer than Ollie, and she'll tear you apart if you come any closer." If Mummy believed she was playing a game, then she'd play it.

The child dropped to her knees and did everything she'd ever learned from Ollie, but made it fiercer. She growled and barked and paced back and forth at the top of the stairs. When the red shoes came close she nipped at them. Mummy shoved her aside with her leg as if she really were a dog. And so the child became one. And bit Mummy on the ankle.

"How dare you," Mummy said. She hit the child, but the dog growled back at her.

"Malcolm," she called sharply.

To keep Mummy away from him, the dog ran growling and whining between her and the doorway that lead into the small dark space.

Suddenly Malcolm emerged blinking into the sunlight. He had pulled on his pants, and instead of the bloody shirt, he was wearing an old sweater with a hole at the elbow. Although the smell of blood seemed very strong to the child, Mummy didn't appear to notice it.

"What have you been doing in my storage cupboard?" she demanded.

"It was Dinah," Malcolm sighed. "She insisted on playing caveman, and so . . . . " He shrugged his shoulders and looked bored.

But the child saw a spot of blood on his wrist, so she started to growl at Mummy again and nip at her ankles.

"Dinah, that's quite enough," she said. "And look how filthy you are from grovelling about on the floor like that. For heaven's sake get yourselves cleaned up. Your father will be home any time now."

She turned away, and a moment later the child heard her red shoes clattering down the stairs.

"You were great," Malcolm whispered to the child. He was suddenly all energy and excitement. "Now help me get that thing out of here."

At the back of the storage cupboard they found a suitcase, and when they opened it up, a smell of mothballs filled the air and cut through the heavy, sweetish blood smell. At the bottom they discovered a white woollen shawl, which they wrapped around the bloody shirt and the dead kitten. The child held the bundle while Malcolm replaced the door to the small, dark space. Then, so Mummy wouldn't hear them, they ran barefoot down the stairs and out the back door.

The scrape of Malcolm's spade against a stone made the child shiver as she sat beneath a tree, eating the sour cherries he had picked for her. In one arm she held the bundle and rocked it while, between bites, she sang All Things Bright and Beautiful.

"Knock it off, will you," Malcolm said. "You're not even in tune."

"I'm singing my baby a lullaby," she told him.

A breeze blowing in the cherry branches shifted the leafy pattern of shade on the child's bare arms while a dark stain spread slowly through the crocheted woollen shawl.

"Poor baby can't hold the world in her tummy anymore," she whispered to herself and then she started singing again: "All things wise and wonderful . . . the Lord God. . . ."

Putting the spade down Malcolm said to her, "Okay, I've finished. Hand it over."

The child heard the sound of an engine and hesitated.

Malcolm snatched the bundle from her.

"No. Stop," she said. "Give me back my baby."

But Malcolm dropped the bundle into the hole he had dug, and as soon as he had shovelled the dirt over it, he threw down the spade, grabbed the child by the arm and pulled her to her feet.

"Don't you say a word," he told her. "I'll handle Dad."

Dragging the child after him, he walked so quickly that she stumbled as she tried to keep up. But as soon as Daddy came into view Malcolm slowed down and sauntered toward the driveway. Daddy stood watching him, his arms folded across his chest.

"Found her down there eating sour cherries," Malcolm said when he got to within a few feet of Daddy. "If she gets a belly ache, don't blame me."

The child hoped that Daddy would pick her up and call her his sweetheart. If he did, it meant that she was still safe.

"So . . . had a good day at the office?" Malcolm asked.

"Aren't you forgetting something?" Daddy said in a tight monotone.

Malcolm let go of the child who began to rub her arm where he had left finger marks. He reached into his pocket, took out the knife and handed it to Daddy.

"That must have been an expensive watch," Daddy remarked as he opened the blade. While he was examining it, the blind glitter came back to his eyes.

"I'll deal with you after dinner," he said. Then he closed the knife, dropped it into his pocket and walked away from them toward the house.

The child started to follow him, but Malcolm pulled her aside.

"It's our secret," he said to her. "You understand?"

The child nodded.

"If you say one word to him. . . ." He looked down at her and added, "There are plenty of knives where that came from, and don't you ever forget it, little Puss."

The child suddenly broke away from him.

"Where are you going?" he cried out.

Ignoring the panic in his voice she ran into the middle of the lawn where she turned round and round until the treetops whirled, and only the centre of the blue sky was still.

SURJEET KALSEY

Surjeet Kalsey was born in Punjab, India, worked as a news broadcaster on All-India Radio, and came to Canada sixteen years ago. She received her MFA in Creative Writing from UBC in 1978. She has published the poetry collections *Paunan Nal Guftagoo* (Raghbir Rachana Parkashan, India 1979), *Speaking to the Winds* (Third Eye, London, Ontario 1982), and *Footprints of Silence* (Third Eye 1988). She is also a scriptwriter and has edited and translated an anthology of Punjabi poetry forthcoming from the Punjabi Literary Academy in India. She lives with her husband Ajmer Rode and their two children in Richmond, BC.

I wrote this poem when I was a student in the Creative Writing Department doing my MFA under the supervision of Michael Bullock and George McWhirter from 1975 to 1978. This poem was actually written in the fall of 1976 and was first published in Contemporary Literature in Translation *(Spring 1977). Then the poem was included in my book* Speaking to the Winds. *The poem reflects a journey of an immigrant mind who tries to rationalize his/her migration to Canada, passing through the uprooting and the deep sense of displacement. The cause of his exile is very simple—economic necessity (the poem is about a young farmworker) who finally gets "enlightenment" (paycheque) under the Bo trees (North American System). This theme is an inversion of traditional theme (Buddha ran from wealth) but this time without respite.*

Siddhartha Does Penance Once Again

I

I'm leaving a seed
in your darkening cave
if you bear a son
it's not necessary
to name him "Rahula"
if you bear a daughter
do not feel sorry
call her a fortunate being

You know   I know
Our hearth was cold last night

we pretended to sleep
Now the moonlight
glows on your guileless face
I observe
         You're really asleep
         and I'm scared of my inner tumult
Kissing your brow I'm ready to go

I've thrust into the world—
                    "the home of miseries"
to search for contentment   happiness
in any of its corners
How long can we survive the erosion of self?

II

I   a Siddartha
nailing a journey to my feet
once again
         leaving the pregnant beauty asleep
         leaving my "sumptuous palaces"
         (mortgaging my inherited land and house)
         friends and kin
         familiar streets   my city   my country
I've begun to do penance
denying my emotions and feelings . . .
(my hungry body does not need, for the time being,
                    "spiritual enlightenment")
I've begun to search for
the other salvation this time

III

Wandering a long time
I've now reached a place
where "Maya" is a panacea for all miseries
I've met a few hermits: Contractors
who every day tell the secrets of "spiritual purification"
to me and several Siddharthas like me
Every day they pack us into closed wagons
to dump us unto the raspberry or blueberry fields
When the sun dives down the other side of the mountain
we are brought home shaken and tired
I throw myself in   the fourth corner of the common room

swallowing several bitter draughts of somrus

Every day I try to write to you with my aching fingers
so that I may tell you
I'll come home very soon
or I'll apply for your immigration very soon
so that with your own eyes
you can touch that "Holy Tree"
under which, doing penance,
I've found the path to salvation from hunger
Now I've transmigrated from Siddhartha to
                              "Enlightened Buddha"
(an artist within me has died
          I've become one of the dumbly driven cattle)

IV

Searching and wandering
wandering and searching
                    for spiritual enlightenment
the glow-worm I had found
with which I went on a mission to enlighten the world
was not able to offer satisfaction
                              to my hungry body
I had to bear the shame throughout the ages
Now I've done penance again
The "Maya" I once condemned
has lit the path to salvation
and I'm coming back home embracing it
but this time in the state of
"to be or not to be"
about going on the mission again.

LIONEL KEARNS

Lionel Kearns was born in 1937 in Nelson, BC. Between 1955 and 1964 he studied at UBC, where he took Creative Writing courses from Jake Zilber and Earle Birney. The author of nine books of poetry, Kearns lives with his family in Vancouver and works as a consultant in educational multimedia.

My poems often objectify significant moments of my life experience. The poem "Birney Land" celebrates one such occasion in the early seventies when my partner and I were visiting Earle Birney at his summer cottage on Galiano Island. "Trophy" and "Ritual" go even further back in memory for their imagery and feeling.

Ritual

On the day before Spring, the pale winter sun
melts the snow and directs a small boy
to launch his stick canoes in the gutter rapids
at the side of the road, the current swirling them
under the overhangs of dripping ice, past cliffs,
through canyons, on down toward the whirlpool
above the storm sewer culvert.

On the day before Spring, a man stands
in the pale warmth of the February sun, watching
a small boy racing his boats at the roadside.
Both of them are experienced hands in this kind
of navigation, with mud on their boots
for the first time in three months of snow
and suddenly the bare tree branches
are full of noisy birds.

This is the day before Spring, and a small boy
and a man are shooting the dangerous rapids
of an early run-off. The boy asks how long
it will take the water to reach the sea,
and the man, who knows the question, does not
know the answer: birds, slush, buds on the bushes,
a puck among the emerging debris, and in the air

the hint of rotting cabbage.

It is always the same on the day before Spring
and marbles and bicycles, as the warm wind
melts the old snow and slowly bares last Fall's
dead leaves to the thin pale sun. It is always
the same for this boy and this man
who present themselves each year, performing
the ritual without nostalgia or regret
with the ice dripping and the snow melting
and the stick boats racing toward the sea.

Trophy

There were no grouse that day, but because
we were hunting I had to shoot something,
so I shot a jay as blue as the autumn sky
as he sat on a branch above me in the yellow
glow of those leaves. I was eight years old,
and my father was teaching me how to shoot
grouse in the head so as not to spoil the meat.
But this killing was not for food. I wanted
a trophy. One feather I pulled from the bird's tail
as I held it warm and limp in my hand.
This feather I put in my hunting hat
and I glanced at my father and behind him
I glimpsed the jay's mate gliding, circling through
the darkening tree tops. "Better shoot that one too"
said my father, "You shouldn't leave her alone."
But I couldn't get a shot at her, and we left
with the knowledge that I was now
a small sure source of sorrow in this world,
and my father, who was teaching me, said nothing.

    Where is that father? Under the old earth.
    Where is that place? Under the new lake.
    Where is that boy? Inside an old man.
    Where is that feather? Inside the boy's mind.

Birney Land

Rising late the first morning after a good night's sleep,
we eat and go down to carry water up from the spring.
Slowly city poisons rinse from bodies and minds.
After lunch, walking back from the old cemetery,
Maya and I lose our way and end up high on the cliffs
overlooking the sea. Freighters and ferries
are dodging fish boats and sounding their horns
as they enter Active Pass. We undress
and salute the water, the islands, the sun, the sky,
and life itself that here beside us snaps
dried gorse seed pods, twitches the chattering chipmunk
on a twig, sends a little snake skittering into the leaves
along the trail. It's hot, so we make love in the shade,
and afterwards climb down to the rocks for a cold swim.
When we get back to the cabin, Earle is still typing.
Maya begins to make supper, and I go out on the porch
to catch poems as they come zinging in on the wind.
Later that evening we talk about Kootenay Lake
and the old stern-wheelers that Earle and I both knew
when we were boys. The moon comes up
and lays down a silvery path across the water
to our feet. It is all part of an old story
I had almost forgotten.

NORMAN KLENMAN

Norman Klenman was a member of Earle Birney's first writing groups at UBC. He is a screen and television writer, and until recently co-owner of a local television station. He lives on Salt Spring Island.

Woodsmen of the West, *a screenplay in progress, is based upon Allerdale Grainger's memoirs, published in 1908 and never since out of print. The motion picture film will be directed by Allan King, formerly of Vancouver, best known for his film of* Who Has Seen the Wind.

from *Woodsmen of the West*

(Hauling through calm waters from Knight Inlet toward the Vancouver mills their harvest of logs—one of the largest log booms ever assembled—Martin Grainger, Carter the logging boss, and Bill Allen the captain of the tug Sonora *are struck by a hurricanic storm. The boom is scattered like match wood, the tug sunk, the native woman Molly Wetsikan lost overboard. Grainger searches the black water for Molly. Carter and Allen cling to the waterlogged rowboat.)*

IN THE STRAIT. STORM
Fierce high wind and water thrash the rowboat. At last Grainger sees Molly. He puts his head down and strokes hard toward her. As he does, the sound of the storm ceases abruptly. We hear instead eerie bubbles, gurgles, in the foreground; and, faintly, the distant cries of Carter and Allen.

Now Grainger thrusts his head above water, staring through the driving rain searching for the girl. The sound of the boiling storm is heard again, the hoarse cry of Carter demanding his return to the boat. Grainger stares wildly about him, calling out to Molly. His voice is lost in the wind.

Once again the roar of wind and waves ceases, replaced by the eerie sound of bubbling underwater. Then the surface breaks beside Grainger. In arrested motion, to our eyes "stop frame," the body of Molly Wetsikan, deathly still, arms dead at her sides, face turned away, rises out of the water, sprung from the deep by an unknown force. Then the body sinks back into the water beside Grainger, limp. He gathers the body to him.

Together they bob up and down in the waves like a clump of sea-weed.
The sound of the storm returns, rolling thunder, intermittent with flashes of sheet lightning.

ABOARD THE ROWBOAT
Carter and Bill Allen wrestle Grainger, still clinging to Molly, into the rowboat. Carter stands precariously in the bow, facing upward into the driving rain, his wet face and glinting eyes illuminated by strobe-like lightning, shaking his fist at the black heavens.

CARTER You god damned filthy son of a bitch. You gave it all to us. You got us this *far.* Then you snatch it all away. But while I got life in me, you fucker, I'm goin' after whatever I want, any ways I can get it. I ain't stopping till you kill kill me first. So fuck you. Fuck you. Fuck you.

Carter sinks down into the rolling boat, clutching the gunwales. His head drops to a stoop. He shakes the rain from his face, from out of his eyes, in defiant despair.
Bill Allen kneels over the exhausted Grainger, still cradling Molly in his arms. Through the darkness, streaks of saffron sunset light the horizon.

FADE OUT

FADE IN. BEACH. DAWN
It is dark and wet, but no rain falls from the low cloud. The rowboat beaches itself. Carter stumbles from it, followed by Grainger. They lift the body out of the boat, Grainger holding it under the shoulders, Carter at the feet. Bill Allen drags himself after them. They set Molly down and huddle in a depressing tableau on the sand a few yards above the waterline.

VILLAGE OF THE KWAKIUTL
Molly's village, the place of her last meeting with her father. People stand near a longhouse. Drumming men beat their instruments not so much in rhythm as in a ritual used by Molly's family. Her father watches, with Grainger at his side.
Molly's friends bring their bundle from around the longhouse. It is Molly's body, tightly wrapped in woven fibre matting, tied by twine.
The drums quieten. There is some singing in the back of the

group as Molly's father leads the way into the forest.

PROMONTORY
*A rise of ground, a high mound of rock jutting out over the
beach a hundred feet below. Slanting rays of early sun peek
through the clouds. The cold light reveals the people of the Kwakiutl village bearing the bound fibre bundle.*

*Some of the boys climb the tree they have selected, a stout old
fir that had been severed twenty feet from the ground, possibly
by lightning years ago.*

The body is raised to its place and bound to the tree trunk.

MARTIN GRAINGER
*With Molly's father beside him, watches the boys finish their
work and clamber down.*

GRAINGER   I guess it's the custom here, but I don't figure it.
MOLLY'S FATHER   Some of the villages use different ways. We've always
done it this way.

FIBRE-MATTED CORPSE TIED TO THE FIR TREE
Lit by the warm rays of early morning sun.

GRAINGER   She was Catholic, wasn't she? Shouldn't there have been a
priest or something?
MOLLY'S FATHER   Maybe. There's no priest near us now, there used to
be. But this way is fine. Come back with me, we'll have a cup of
tea before you go.

*Molly's father puts his arm into Martin Grainger's for support;
the young man helps him as they disappear back along the path
into the woods.*

TOP THE BURIAL TREE
*View past the fibre-wrapped corpse in the foreground, up the
inlet. Sunshine brightens the scene: green water with diagonal
straightedges of whitecaps; encircled by mountains topped with
snow. Eagles whirl in the distance, swooping toward the sea.*

CUT TO:

BEACH. GREY BLOWY DAY
*A fire of driftwood. Bill Allen sits on a stump beside it, roasting
salmon on a split branch.*

CARTER
On his knees beside the overturned rowboat. In one hand he holds birchbark fashioned into a shallow pan full of hot pitch. With a short stick he is stuffing bits of dry vegetation dipped in pitch into a seam in the bow.
The sound of a voice in the distance attracts his attention. Bill Allen hurries over. They strain their eyes toward the ocean.

THEIR POV
A boat, made from a hollowed log, approaches.

WATER'S EDGE
As the boat pulls in. Two young native men leap out to beach it. Martin Grainger follows them to be greeted by Carter and Allen.

CARTER It's time you got back. How the hell long am I 'sposed to wait?

Grainger shrugs. He gives Bill Allen a friendly hand shake.

CARTER So okay, let's get movin'.

Bill Allen amused. The native boys are bored, sitting on their haunches waiting.

ALLEN   You know what this man thinks? Christ, he better tell you himself.
GRAINGER   I don't even need to guess.
CARTER You're damn right. Just remember what we all got up in Knight Inlet. We got a donkey engine waitin' to be fired up. A camp. A cookhouse, a bunkhouse, we got supplies. Look! *We got a million board feet of the finest first growth timber ever grown.* It's ours, see? We're goin' back for another boom bigger than the one we lost. Curse and fuck anyone tries to stop us.
ALLEN   And that I suppose includes God.

He grins at Grainger, winks and nudges the younger man.

CARTER You're damned right it does. You with me Grainger? Hell, it's your lease, it's your trees. And you're my partner, you get fifty percent of everything.

The native boys watch with interest.

ALLEN   You got away with that once, Carter. By the skin of your teeth.
Even you can't be a complete fool. Why, you don't even have no
tug no more. You can't be serious.

CARTER Oh man, you don't know me, Bill, even after all these years of
the Carter and Allen Company.

ALLEN   Well, count me out.
(To Grainger:)
You can't be crazy enough to go with him. If you are, you got
my share of the trees.

CARTER You worn out old camp chair. Where the hell ya gonna go? Vancouver? You think Meg'll take you into the roomin' house? To
do what? Haul buckets of piss for your board?

ALLEN   What'll you do better?

CARTER Go north. Right back an' get that wood. If you ain't comin'
with me, Grainger's comin'. An' if he ain't, I'm goin' alone.

GRAINGER   How the hell will you get there?

Carter grabs Grainger by the arm and drags him to the rowboat.

CARTER I made a sail. I caulked every god-damned seam with pitch.
Here, gimme a hand.

*With Grainger's help they turn the rowboat over. Under it are
the make-shift sail, the oars, and a food roll of leaves. Carter
leaps for it, unwraps it. Shows it proudly.*

CARTER See? Salmon. Smoked 'em myself. Enough to feed us to Knight
Inlet.

GRAINGER   *(Grinning, shaking his head in wonder)* You think you can
actually navigate this piece of driftwood to Knight Inlet?

CARTER *(With all his charm)* That I can, partner.

ALLEN   I leave you madmen to it.

Allen walks over to the native boys.

ALLEN   You fellows give a man a ride somewhere?

*One of the boys helps Allen into the boat, the other shoves off.
Grainger and Allen exchange farewell waves. Carter barely nods
and is back to business, loading the food, oars and sail into the
rowboat. As Grainger helps him push it into the surf:*

GRAINGER   You really think we can make it?

CARTER Would I lie to my partner in crime, my best sea-going pal, my greedy wild mad fellow-adventurer?

INTERIOR ROW BOAT
As Grainger rows with one oar over the side, Carter strives to fix the make-shift sail in place.

GRAINGER They buried Molly in a tree.
CARTER Sorry son. She was a clever one. Pretty too. It goes that way. Everything comes to you, and then it goes. What do you do? You keep right on goin'.

Grainger wryly addresses no one in particular.

GRAINGER Heading right back north. For another million logs, worth a million dollars in gold and diamonds. Another woodsmen's dream.

Carter, having gotten the sail in place, slaps Grainger heartily on the shoulder and laughs out loud.

DISSOLVE TO:

THE STRAIT IN BRILLIANT SUNSHINE. (ENDING SHOT)
Below, seen as through the eyes of a swooping eagle, which are our eyes now: Carter and Grainger in their vessel, its sail fully extended in the wind. They pass among the loose logs, the flotsam of their last dream. As the eagle's eyes watch, the vessel heads north.

SUPERIMPOSE:
Farewell to loggers and my youth,
Farewell to it all . . .

Dedicated to my creditors, affectionately,

M. Allerdale Grainger
July 1908

FADE OUT.

CHARLES LILLARD

Charles Lillard is the author/editor of some twenty-five or so books—
biography, poetry, history, anthologies, editions—and contributes to a
variety of papers and periodicals. He lives in Victoria.

Do Creative Writing departments today teach the one elemental truth:
writers write, whatever it may mean? In the sixties this was ignored at
UBC. "Writers die," we were told, the insinuation being they died of a
lack of fame; how wrong this was. Novelists die, sabbatical leave poets
die, while the rest learn to punch time clocks. Writers write. What else is
worth doing?

Night Sailing

This Pacific roll jitters with anchor lights.
The nearby and familiar fade
as I round the long south-hanging sweep:
Gordon Head, Ten Mile Point, and Smugglers' Cove
the very toe of that sloping land.

Before me the Sound's gleam is argillite.
The wind rises like the horn's call at Roncevaux
and under these faltering and shifting colours,
under this pattern of dawn-hawking gulls,
I am tired and so tired of knowing why.

Although I have kept few of my promises—
there are three books that bear my name,
but I have taught, lectured, and it is all a game.
The goal: proportion, order, and harmony, ignores
the landfalls, guts, and churning tides, uncoiling
astern of the shoal-horn's bleat, the coast pilot's caution.

That boy sailing into Alaska knew
the Night Raven's metallic falsetto as he tacked
chartless, his compass swinging west continually
into the moonveins of that marine country,
with his girl asleep in the horizons of their bow-cuddy.

Following their coastal whims
they turned into themselves, and discovered their roles
hiding in placid coves, on bleaching docks,
and heard again and again,
from men and women, their spots and dots,
"You must go back, this is no land for the young."
Warnings were cape-bells;
mill-town winters and gyppo-camp wages—
the waves that flung them
and each passage marked the hull,
but a southern beach broke their keel's oaken spine.

Tonight I am here with this longing,
standing on a deck braced
against black rollers and sucking troughs;
low-lying islands, that growling shore—
out westward's mouth;
and should I find that boy, should the girl be there
on the water, this time I will keep her,
I will keep everything.

Coastal Sanctus

It is raining in Sitka;
on Indian Town's slabbed streets
the pale drizzle's lustre is more like frost
than water on rutted timbers.
We sit here in this saloon, knee to knee,
artist and poet, sprung from this raincoast,
our imagination wrung from this looming weather.

She teaches art at the summer school,
while I teach words.
It is raining from Puget Sound north to Haines.
No one cares.
The bartender buys this round.
We watch salmon below a purling bow,
eat eulachon oil and spuds in Wade's village,
and the springs at the headwaters are still pulsing.

At Neltushkin people claim their ancestors
saw a thunderbird's great red wings
and each remembered the frozen dark—
even those whose songs belonged to Frog
saw that blind time, the caribou villages
and the one word for South,
the seventeen for Hunger.

In this blue air, under these amber lights,
our pleasures in that world we loved;
the eagle-beak of heaven,
those Ravens and Wolves quarrelling,
Norman tracking reverie to this Dark North,
the People greeting him in the off-shore mists.

Herring roe. Eulachon grease in carved faces.
Marius Barbeau testing the drumhead.
An ocean river shifts in the corners;
above the swan's-down a spark dances upward,
briefly, one more star in the constellations
young men studied
above those smokeholes of Koona.

Franz Boas and George Hunt belly up to the fire.
I hear a voice in my mouth speaking Kwakiutl.
Next to me, Charlie Edenshaw watches Elena's auburn hair,
his thoughtful eyes, gray as Michelangelo's.

Before the talking returns to its many directions,
Wade McKenzie steps out to gather our aimless watching.
"Now we shall go to Fort Far Out;
we'll dance with the murres and Winter People
and where heaven's mouth swallows light,
it's our turn to rule the western edge of the world."

The old images bear their own weight—
Wade's speaking high Tlingit with a Sitkan accent.
Klu-sa and Norman are the first to go,
then Edenshaw, such is their right,
steersmen each.

One by one we gather our tackle.
Songrise.
In one corner Muzon Woman sings fair winds.
We will drink saltwater, Southeast will die
and I roll the old ways on my tongue, tasting
magic sweet as soapberries,
then it is my turn to step through
that oval darkness between Eagle and Frog.

Outside it is Sunday.
The bells of St. Michael's call the faithful.
Above this pealing, above this blue-edged water,
a raven does a double wingover, calling, calling, calling
the Coastal Sanctus.

CYNTHIA MACDONALD

Cynthia Macdonald has published five books of poems. Her sixth, *Living Wills: New and Selected Poems*, will be out in January 1991 (Knopf). She teaches at the University of Houston in the Graduate Program in Creative Writing, which she founded in 1970, and is also a practising psychoanalyst. Among her honours and fellowships are three National Endowment for the Arts grants, a Rockefeller Fellowship, a Guggenheim Fellowship, and an award from the National Institute and Academy of Arts and Letters in recognition of her poetry.

I began writing poetry when I lived in Vancouver, BC, from 1960 to 1963. We—my husband, baby, four-year-old, and I—moved from New York City, my home town. I'd already embarked on a fledgling career as an opera singer (while in Vancouver I won both the San Francisco Opera auditions and was a finalist in the "Met" auditions), but I also started to write, probably because of the emotional pressures of young children, isolation, and Vancouver's beauty.

Earle Birney took me into his graduate workshop for my last three months in the city, just before we left for Japan. He was wonderfully kind and incisive, an ideal mentor; his voice and vision were a sustaining presence during the next years' much greater isolation.

Hymn in a Bed of Amherst

There is a certain chill so deep inside it will not yield
To layers of down or wires telegraphing warmth through wool—
Another quilt upon the mound—no comforts can amend it.
Passion's enactments—flaring, flaming—trumpet heat and melt
The flesh yet—like a stone-graved alphabet—the granite cold
Is there incised and sharp. Even anger's once sure fire
Burns with ice flamed dry. Long lines—extended like a wartime
Queue for meat—accrue no remedy; extension is
A form of prolongation—the poet's cure—but what will be
Prolonged cannot be willed. Nothing is impossible
To understand: one times nought is nought, which leaves one clear
Of lover's rubble. And warm as love conceived in logic's sphere.
When heat resists all stratagems, escape to greater cold,
The wrap of arctic circuses—go North to vault the Pole.

Two Brothers in a Field of Absence

Because as they cut it was that special green, they decided
To make a woman of the fresh hay. They wished to lie in green, to wrap
Themselves in it, light but not pale, silvered but not grey.
Green and ample, big enough so both of them could shelter together
In any of her crevices, the armpit, the join
Of hip and groin. They—who knew what there was to know, about baling
The modern way with hay so you rolled it up like a carpet,
Rather than those loose stacks—they packed the green body tight
So she wouldn't fray. Each day they moulted her to keep her
Green and soft. Only her hair was allowed to ripen into yellow tousle.

The next weeks whenever they stopped cutting they lay with her.
She was always there, waiting, reliable, their green woman.
She gathered them in, yes she did,
Into the folds of herself, like the mother they hadn't had.
Like the women they had had, only more pliant, more graceful,
Welcoming in a way you never just found.
They not only had the awe of taking her,
But the awe of having made her. They drank beer
Leaning against the pillow of her belly
And one would tell the other, "Like two Adams creating."
And they marveled as they placed
The cans at her ankles, at her neck, at her wrists so she
Glittered gold and silver. They adorned what they'd made.
After harrowing they'd come to her, drawing
The fountains of the Plains, the long line
Of irrigating spray and moisten her up.
And lean against her tight, green thighs to watch buzzards
Circle black against the pink stain of the sunset.

What time she began to smolder they never knew—
Sometime between night when they'd left her
And evening when they returned. Wet, green hay
Can go a long time smoldering before you notice. It has a way
Of catching itself, of asserting that
There is no dominion over it but the air. And it flares suddenly
Like a red head losing her temper, and allows its long bright hair
To tangle in the air, letting you know again
That what shelters you can turn incendiary in a flash.
And then there is only the space of what has been,
An absence in the field, memory in the shape of a woman.

KENNETH M^CGOOGAN

Kenneth McGoogan is a fiction writer and a literary journalist. Born and raised in Montreal, he has lived and worked in Greece, Tanzania, California, Quebec, Ontario, British Columbia, and Alberta, where he is currently literary editor at the *Calgary Herald*.

"Gazette Boy" *appeared originally in* Quarry Magazine *(Spring 1982).*
This revised version is part of a recently completed novel about growing up English in French Quebec.

Gazette Boy

"Look, Madame Francoeur!" I was pulling hundred dollar bills out of my pocket and flinging them into the air. "The rent money's nothing! How much do we owe you?"

"Daniel, it's time."

"No, no." The best was yet to come. Out of another pocket I pulled a thick wad of bills and started peeling off hundreds, counting aloud, one and two and three and . . .

"Ten past five, love."

. . . and it was just my mother, shaking me awake: "Time to do the *Gazettes.*"

"Okay, I'm awake."

My mother went out and left the curtain open so I wouldn't fall back to sleep. From the kitchen came the sound of the radio, the announcer saying it was thirty degrees below zero, forty below with the wind-chill factor. I listened while the man ran down the names of schools that had already closed because of the blizzard. Lake of Two Rivers High wasn't one of them.

I kicked off the covers and, still with my eyes closed, swung myself upright. The floor was freezing cold. I grabbed my socks from the box beside the bed and pulled them on, tucking in my pajama bottoms.

"Twenty past five, Daniel," my mother called from the kitchen. "Better get a move on."

"I'm up, I'm up." It was cold enough that I could see my breath.

My brother Eddie, in the top bunk, rolled over and mumbled, "Be quiet, will ya?"

I pulled my jeans over my pajamas and stood up, being careful not to bang my head on Eddie's bunk. I scooped up the rest of my clothes and, shivering, ran out into the kitchen to finish dressing by the oil stove.

My mother was hunched over the table in her old bathrobe making lunches. The *Gazette* bag was on the arm chair behind her, empty. I groaned. Before waking me, my mother always flung a coat on over her bathrobe, stepped out the door and retrieved the papers from the top of the stairs. I pulled on a third sweater. "No *Gazettes?*"

"Not by the steps. It's snowing pretty bad. I don't know whether the driver made it down the street."

"Jesus."

My mother looked up but said nothing. I pulled on my big grey duffle coat and did up the buttons. Then I buckled on my boots and moved the rug away from in front of the door. My mother handed me the flashlight. "You should quit this job," she said. "It's crazy, going out in a storm like this. You could earn enough money just doing odd jobs, working for Mr. Therrien."

I grunted. I let Dusty outside, then followed and jammed the two doors shut behind me. The steps were treacherous. Going down I hung onto the rickety wooden railing my father had erected. Enough light streamed through the window over the kitchen sink that I could see around the bottom of the stairs. The *Gazettes* weren't there.

I flicked on the flashlight and made my way down the side of the driveway, kicking at the drifted snow. Dusty looked at me, puzzled. I was so bundled up in sweaters and scarves that I didn't feel cold. But the wind was fierce and on the highway the blowing snow would sting—tiny flakes coming thick and fast, pinpricks on my face. Didn't look as if the truck driver had made it down the street. I'd have to get the wire cutters, pull my scarf up over my face and fight my way up Avenue des Oracles to check in front of the hotel. Maybe the truck driver had been able to get that far and no farther.

If the papers were there I'd begin delivering at Mrs. Johannson's and do the route backwards. If they weren't my mother would have to phone the circulation office and get them to send another batch. They wouldn't arrive until noon. If school was cancelled, no problem, I'd be home. If it wasn't my mother would have to bundle up and deliver the *Gazettes* herself, hauling Maureen along behind her on the sleigh.

I was about to abandon the search when, five or six feet from the end of the driveway, at the base of a fort Eddie had built, I spotted an odd pile of snow. Turned out to be the *Gazettes*. I picked them up and brushed them off. The truck driver had just flung the bundle out the door, pulled a U-turn and taken off. But at least I wouldn't have to go up the street empty-handed.

I left the dog outside—he wouldn't sneak off on a day like today—and brought the papers into the house, stood waiting on the rug while my mother cut the wire around them. "School cancelled?"

"Not yet." She was folding the papers in half, one by one, and stuffing them into the blue-and-white *Gazette* bag. "At least you don't have basketball practice."

I grunted. I was the only seventh grader to have made first string on the junior boys' interscholastic team. Practices were held Tuesday and Thursday starting at 8:00 a.m., one hour before classes began. On those days I'd deliver my *Gazettes* and then, instead of going back to bed for an hour, eat breakfast and hitchhike into Ste. Thérèse. But today was Wednesday and if school wasn't cancelled I'd catch the bus in front of the hotel with the other kids. Wouldn't have to worry about not getting a ride, like on the morning that kept coming back.

Usually I'd get a ride right away and be standing, flapping my arms, at the front door of the school when the janitor arrived. If I didn't get a ride within fifteen minutes I'd start walking, hitching as I went. That morning I'd had to walk all the way to school, just over two miles, and so arrived late for practice. I changed as quickly as I could and ran down the hall to the gym just in time for scrimmage. Not until first period, scripture, did I remember the rent money.

Now I slung the *Gazette* bag over my shoulder. "All here?"

"Ten." My mother opened the door for me. "I still think you should quit this job."

"Mother, please," I said. But as I descended the stairs for the second time that morning, I wondered. Some days I enjoyed delivering, even in winter. One morning the previous week the snow on the street had been hard-packed as ice and the sand truck hadn't yet been around. I'd laced on my skates and flown up and down pretending that I was Rocket Richard, cut normal delivery time in half.

But today I wasn't enjoying. The cold, the dark, the wind. Snow was slicing down in sheets. Already Dusty was covered. At the end of the driveway I turned right, glad that to begin I had the wind at my back.

All of my winter customers but one lived, as we did, on Avenue des Oracles. First I'd go down the street towards the lake—Arsenault, Callaghan, Boyd, Therrien, Old Pelletier. Then I'd head back up, past home, glimpsing my mother through the front window, hunched over the kitchen table making my father's breakfast. Belanger, Middleton, Laflamme, Talbot, then along the highway past the grocery store, Marche Champroux, and up along the train tracks to Mrs. Johannson's.

I looked to make sure Dusty was still with me, then moved to the middle of the street and closed my eyes. I'd open them only when the crunch of the snow beneath my feet told me I'd wandered. This way, I'd found, I could dream while I worked. Once or twice I'd woken up outside Mrs. Johannson's with a left-over *Gazette* in my bag, wondering if my mother had miscounted or if I'd missed somebody. And praying it wasn't Monsieur Laflamme.

Crunch, crunch, crunch—the snow was getting deeper. I opened one eye, checked for the dog, straightened myself out and closed it again. If I could just hang on a few more months, summer would be here. I'd have thirty, thirty-five customers, all within a mile of the house. I'd ride my old bicycle and see how fast I could deliver. The sun would come up while I worked. If I wasn't going to set a record, I'd stop a moment beside the lake and toss a couple of sticks into the water for Dusty to fetch. Barring a flat tire or trouble with the chain, I'd be done in three-quarters of an hour and back in bed by six-fifteen. With tips, I'd clear five or six dollars a week.

Callaghans' was dark. I went up the stairs, opened the outside door and banged on the inside one. Down the hall a light went on. I placed the paper between the doors and headed back onto the road. The summer people returned to Montreal as autumn arrived with Labour Day, and then my route shrunk to ten or eleven papers. Still, I'd clear three dollars a week—and it was steady. I could continue to ride my bicycle and the whole route took me only eighteen, twenty minutes.

The trouble with autumn was the rain. Once or twice a week my mother would bring in the papers and half of them would be soaked. We'd have to decide, then, who was going to get a wet *Gazette*. We tried to alternate victims but Monsieur Laflamme, for one, could never be given a wet newspaper because when Saturday rolled around, collection day, he'd refuse to pay for it. I'd have to make up the difference myself—and I thought again of the rent money.

That's what we called it, though really it was payments on the house. Once a month after school I had to deliver this rent money, trudging twenty minutes along the highway to Madame Francoeur's house in St. Eustache. I hated this chore. I didn't mind missing the school bus and having to hitchhike home. And Madame Francoeur I liked. She'd invite me inside, offer me milk and cookies. No, what I detested was being given a receipt for May's rent in October, or for last November's rent in July. And Madame Francoeur, honestly confused, flipping through her records, saying, "Can that be right?" And me having to say, "Yes. Yes, that's right."

So always I'd put the rent money out of my mind until I actually had to deliver it. Remembering it suddenly that morning, first period, I realized that in my rush to get to the gym for basketball practice I'd neglected to lock my locker. I decided to check my wallet, just to be sure. My home room teacher, Mrs. Podherny, was droning on about loaves and fishes.

Under my desk I opened my wallet—and couldn't believe what I saw. The rent money was gone. The room began to spin. I turned my wallet upside down and shook it, then stumbled to my feet and made for the door.

Mrs. Podherny, startled, jumped out of the way. "Daniel?"

"Got to see the principal!"

I ran out the door and down the hall, took the stairs two at a time, didn't stop running until I reached Mr. Herder's office.

But a car was coming. I opened one eye. Old Leroux's taxi, its diamond-shaped roof-top light glowing orange through the blowing snow, was fishtailing up the street towards me. Dusty was sniffing around up a driveway. I moved over and let the taxi pass, then stepped into one of the tracks it had made and closed my eyes. The track made walking easier.

In a couple of months, as spring cleared the roads of snow, I'd get out my bicycle. I'd be looking forward to a rash of new orders from summer people, and also to delivering in daylight. The only problem with spring was the lake, which crept through the town as the snow and ice melted all the way upriver to Ottawa. Usually the water came no farther than the crossroads, about one third of the way up Avenue des Oracles, and I could reach my hardest-hit customers simply by wearing rubber boots. Bad years the water came right past our house, turned the place into an island. We'd borrow a little flatboat from Mrs. Middleton on the understanding that if the flood reached her place, she got it back.

To deliver the *Gazettes* I'd climb into the flatboat with Dusty and my bicycle and pole my way up the street to water's edge, where the truck driver deposited the papers. I'd leave the flatboat there, deliver the top half of my route by bike, then return and do the rest by boat. One morning, I'd arrived at water's edge and found the flatboat gone. I had to stand there hollering like a fool, and with Dusty barking furiously, until my mother heard me.

Luckily, we had a second boat tied up out front that week, an old green rowboat that had to be bailed out every couple of hundred yards. My mother came out in it and picked me up. I dropped her at the house, along with Dusty and my bicycle, then rowed on down the street to finish delivering.

Everybody I met I asked about the flatboat. Finally Mrs. Boyd said she'd seen three men, summer people, pole by in it. She'd assumed they had permission. I finished delivering the *Gazettes*, then rowed along the street that fronted the beach, bailing when necessary. Near the bottom of Avenue des Archanges I spotted the flatboat tied up outside a flooded summer camp. Inside, three men were moving furniture around, splashing and cursing and swearing.

I sat a moment, thinking. The cabin was up on stilts and inside it the water was maybe six inches deep. That meant it was roughly four feet deep out here. A hike up the street would be cold and uncomfortable—but not impossible. Quietly I climbed into the flatboat and untied it. Then, towing the leaky rowboat, I poled madly for home.

"Mr. Herder, I've been robbed!"

"Are you trying to break down the door?" The principal looked down at me through thick glasses, his eyes huge and blue and watery. "Come in, then."

Mr. Herder closed the door and motioned me into a chair, then sat down behind his desk. "Now, Daniel, what's happened."

"I've been robbed. I—"

"You mean something is missing. Don't be too anxious to accuse." He leaned forward and made a steeple with his fingers. "Now, what's missing?"

"Forty dollars."

Mr. Herder's eyebrows went up.

"I had it in my wallet. Now it's gone. I want to talk to my mother."

"What were you doing, carrying around that much money?"

"It was rent money. I was supposed to deliver it."

"Where did you lose this rent money?"

"In the locker room." My voice quavered. "I went to basketball practice and . . . and I left it in my locker."

"Ahhhhh." Mr. Herder sat back in his chair. "Now we're getting to it. You forgot to lock your locker."

I didn't trust myself to speak. I looked at the floor and nodded.

"How many times do I have to tell you people? Never leave your lockers unlocked. Never, never, never."

"Mr. Herder, could I use your telephone please?"

"So now you've lost forty dollars."

"I want to call my mother."

"All right, Daniel, go ahead." Mr. Herder got up from his desk, went to the window and stood looking out, his hands clasped behind his back.

I turned into Mr. Therrien's. If his dog was out I'd have to leave the *Gazette* in the box at the fence. Dusty didn't bark, though, so I marched through the gate and up the path, climbed the back stairs. Mr. Therrien was bent over the stove, his back to the door. I knocked. His dog barked. Mr. Therrien shut him up, then opened the door a crack. I handed him the *Gazette*. "Want your driveway shovelled this afternoon?"

"Not today, thanks Daniel. I'm taking the day off. I'll do it myself."

I waved, went down the stairs and back out the gate, shutting it carefully so Mr. Therrien's dog wouldn't be able to get out. That was the trouble with odd jobs. I swung onto the road. You couldn't count on them.

"Mum? It's me, Daniel."

"Daniel? Is something wrong?"

"Mum, I've lost the rent money."

"The rent money?"

"I've lost it."

"What? All of it?"

"Yes, Mum." My voice broke. "I forgot to lock my locker. When I got back from practice the money was gone."

"Okay Daniel. Don't cry."

"Mum, what are we going to do?"

"Don't worry, Daniel. I'll think of something. We're always a little behind."

"I'll pay it back, Mum."

"Don't talk foolishness. And stop crying, now. Where are you calling from."

"The principal's office. Mum, I'll pay it back."

"Stop crying, Daniel, please. Go back to class now. Forget about the rent money."

"I'll pay it back, Mum. Out of my *Gazettes*. I'll pay it back."

I deposited Old Pelletier's paper on his back porch, checked for Dusty, then turned and paused automatically, stood staring out into the blackness that shrouded the frozen lake. Already I'd saved nine dollars, almost a quarter of what I'd lost. I pulled my scarf over my face and, leaning into the storm, started back up Avenue des Oracles. No way I could quit my *Gazette* route. Maybe after I paid back the rent money.

Except then it would be spring. I'd have a rash of new orders coming. I'd be able to ride my bike, and the sun would come up while I delivered.

FLORENCE M^CNEIL

I was born and raised in North Burnaby, on the fringes of Vancouver. I took both my BA and MA at UBC; my MA thesis was a book of poems which later became my first publication, *A Silent Green Sky*. I have published eight books of poetry, three children's novels, and a non-fiction book on poetry writing, have edited two anthologies of poetry, and had a play workshopped and produced. I'm working on a novel for adults, and have a new and selected book of poetry about to be published as well as an anthology of poems for children.

The following poems show my interest in the historical, especially its reflection through visual art.

Ghost Town

How did we obliterate you
in a hundred years
you in your torn undershirts and hip boots
arms akimbo
by your muscular diggings
you with stumps for haloes
whose obsessed eyes
glitter through wavering lines
you by your wheels and rockers
with legs of stone   mountainous
in your temples   the flumes
pouring endlessly like blood.

Here in the same mountains
there are new minted diggings
and tourists photographing themselves
in your rebuilt saloons
giggling at the barber shops   the gilded dance halls
and taking images of your plaster
replicas.

oh but you have outwitted them
crude as the nuggets you sweated for
your past is missing from this landscape
leaves no trace on their negatives   their coloured screens
won't hold your five minute pose
which stopped the hills   the flumes with motionless energy
a century ago
and now defying immortality
declines a present
too secular
to be haunted.

Alice on the Train

You are out of place with your prim head
that tidy curtsey
that great accusing face
a child from a nightmare
that disturbed Carroll and Tenniel
and told us their Victorian rest
was only temporary

who put you on a train

and wheeled you into our untidy times
(where wheels and gears and levers
mesh into discordant jolts
crack the porous glass   smash the
precise chessmen)

they should have given you a broom
relegated you to a frontispiece
a sampler in a dusty frame

but here you are passing through our lives
threatening us with your propriety

we who can understand the ferocity of cards
              and kings
or the madness of grinning apparitions
flinch at the gravity of
your quiet wave

Saunter through your own underworld
Alice
or jump across your sunny oxford brooks
and leave us to think there are no
machines that bind you to this age

give us permission to take you off the train

The Hours of the Duc de Berry

Crushed into one corner of the frame
                without perspective
they look happy enough
these medieval men at dinner
          there is a dog eating a unicorn
               on the floor
heads in flemish hats standing on one another
                    their tunics french blue
       there is a vermilion scramble to fit in at all
At the top of the picture there are
                    knights
                          looking for
    faces
        through jigsaw horses
       someone has lost a spur
Are they fighting and eating all at one time
or do all worlds come together
thrown sumptuously into a human frame
One thing seems clear
               through it all   the jocular eating
      the strange slow toppling of war
          with knights folding over like pieces of a fan
there are white hands   out of their gauntlets
             away from their meat
      serenely   lifted
    so that the eye of the beholder
      centuries later is forced
  to look up (as they did)
to a brilliance that is calm and superb
         and senseless
      to the rational eye.

GEORGE MᶜWHIRTER

George McWhirter was born 1939 and raised in Belfast's Shankill Road district and educated at Queen's University, 1957–62 (same class as Deane & Heaney). He left Ireland for Spain in 1965, then emigrated to Canada in 1966. His first book, *Catalan Poems*, shared the Commonwealth Poetry Prize with Chinua Achebe's *Cry, Soul Brother* (1972). He has published five books of poetry, three short story collections, two novels, and one book of translation.

Cage (a novel set in Mexico, Oberon Press 1987) won the 1987 Ethel Wilson Prize for Fiction, B.C. Book Awards; The Selected Poems of Jose Emilio Pacheco (New Directions) was awarded the 1987 F.R. Scott Prize for translation by the League of Canadian Poets & F.R. Scott Foundation. He has two children—Grania & Liam—and is married to Angela Mairead Coid. Currently working in collaboration with Gabriel Zaid, Jose Emilio Pacheco, and Sandro Cohen on an anthology of Mexican poetry covering poets born between 1940 and 1960.

His poetry appears in such collections as the Penguin Book of Canadian Verse; Poets of Canada *(Hurtig, ed. J.R. Colombo);* Contemporary Poetry of British Columbia *(Sono Nis, ed. J. Michael Yates);* Soundings 72 *(Blackstaff, ed. Seamus Heaney);* Antologia de la Poesia Actual Canadiense Inglesa *(U.A. de San Luis Potosi, ed. Manuel Betanzos Santos);* Aproximaciones *(Ediciones Penelope, compiled by Miguel Angel Flores).*
His stories also appear in Best Canadian Short Stories 72 *(Oberon),* Stories of Pacific & Arctic Canada *(Macmillan, ed. A.P. Schroeder & Rudy Wiebe).*
He was associated with Prism International *from 1968 to 1989 as Managing, then Poetry, then Co-, then Advisory Editor.*

Five Points North of Steveston

1

Trees, trees;
Shade, shade.

I have been deep
In counting their many darknesses.

The light steps through on stilts—

Like fishermen in those
Odd lands—

Leaning face-down
To a small Sargasso of salal.

2

Curled and whiskered

The knuckles of the new ferns
Touch the dangled nets of sunshine

With an innocence
That sets the streams

Screaming, like girls,
Out into the open.

3

There, the heat plucks at them,

Drawing their breath
Through the green gills of the willows,

Making them dizzy
With this notion that they might be air.

4

Sometimes I wish our only worry were

To remind our daughters
That they must pin on hats
To Morning Prayer. Glad

They sit leeward of the sermon
And its gusting holiness,

Shaded
From the breathing of the young men.

5

O stilted fishermen,
Wading in their shyness,

You land nothing of note, nothing
Larger than the heart,

Your fingers rubbed, blinking with scales
Athwart the stained denim of the morning.

KIM MALTMAN

I was born in Medicine Hat in 1950 and grew up nearby in a small government residence village associated with the DRB base in Suffield. In the wake of numerous cross-continental shuffles, I currently live with Roo Borson, in Toronto, where I work at York University as an itinerant particle physicist.

The three poems are from a just-completed manuscript entitled Technologies/Installations. *Fourteen years ago, when I was at* UBC, *I think I was trying to write this book, or something like it, in tone or in content—I'm not sure if that represents persistence or stupidity.*

The Technology of the Persistence of Memory

When the first blossoms, which one never seems
quite to remember, have announced the unexpected,
the sudden flurry of spring, one is reminded of
the old exuberance, but, more and more,
it is to the disquieted house on the hill
that one returns, the grass and fresh dug dirt, the small
fire smells of childhood, trophies of the memory
now gradually mummified, wrapped in the opaque
vapors of wood and old glass. In the house again
one wanders the rooms, pursued
now by the worn handhold on the stair railing,
now, for a moment, by some indefinable smell
that tugs an hour at the memory.
Often the mind is like a homing pigeon
and now it is on the old cedar chest that it dwells,
longing for the return of those old ghosts,
ghosts that could repossess the huge bodies
that return to it now as if by remote control . . .
But it is nowhere to be found,
though, to the mind, the smell of cedar, come upon
will always recur there, haunted by the continuity of
age and decay. It is as if
it never existed, as if it were from
a story, a dream, another life.
And there was a time when this brooding was composed of
desires so ordinary one could hardly name them.
Desires not unlike love,
which they sometimes resemble
but are not.

The Technology of Metal, Turning

The snow comes down,
blows or drifts,
inanimate, without intention.
Nonetheless, there are parts of the city
where those without shelter
freeze, or huddle over gratings, or
death comes by degree beginning with this night.
To some it is a comfort to believe
some larger reason moves behind this.
That pleasure is not created, but bestowed.
Heavy snow has come, too,
to the mountains,
and many hunting there are stranded.
It is possible at times like this,
in need of warmth,
to kill and gut a deer,
to see the body, cut, steam violently,
and spend the night inside the freshly opened carcass.
Afterwards this comes to be recounted with such
powerful nostalgia that,
in having been told the story only once,
and with the din of machinery, as well,
around me, so that I had to strain,
and listen with great concentration,
the smell of metal, freshly lathed,
is tinged still with the smell of blood.
It says the soul does not exist,
that there is nothing to diminish pain,
or pleasure,
or to give it permanence.

The Technology of the Metal
at the Heart of Sorrow

The angle of sun—it entered, traversing the worn linoleum
beyond the screen door, effortless, as if moved by some
unaccountable kinship with the present. Just kids we would
wander, letting the breeze of our own motion cool us, the dogs,
uneasy, curled up, panting underneath the steps, sullen looks
that might, without a moment's notice, dissolve into a fitful
sleep. The lilacs would be in full bloom then, sweetly decadent
at midday, overpowering by evening. On such a day grandmother would arrive, on one of those sporadic summer visits that
seemed only to occur when our own changes and enthusiasms,
odd fancies that seemed, of the moment, inexhaustible, were at
their cyclic peak. All afternoon she'd sit, a little apart. Repeat
for us meandering storybook tales of empire and war, empty
country villages, the face glimpsed once across a battlefield, and
later, unbelievably, in Winnipeg—the police and, yes, a Russian
spy!—quaint turn-of-the-century English cousins who filled our
grandmother with livid fantasies of the "Canadian Wilderness."
And then, as if between breaths, lulled to it, the trips to Bath
and Brittany, and Lawrence, whom she'd married in the first
euphoria of the war's end. Now and then the dogs would stir
and one might twitch suddenly, in some grotesque semblance of
a dream. Then grandmother would pause, or drift away, it
seemed, and feeling for her some imitation of a sorrow she did
not herself feel, we would slip on that odd mixture of longing
and unease. It would be late then, always a little later than we
could have guessed—almost evening—and the lilacs would have
taken on that faint metallic edge, which we had not noticed during the day, and which sets them apart from other blossoms.

JILL MANDRAKE

I received an MFA (Creative Writing) from UBC in 1980. I am currently on the editorial board of *Zajets* literary magazine, and my field of interest is local history.

"Marilyn and the Lucky Penny" *was written in Burnaby, BC. It is dedicated to a friend who asked me the whereabouts of Marilyn the usherette after the Henry Theatre closed. I took a wild guess, which resulted in this story.*

Marilyn and the Lucky Penny
For Corinne Rubin

Marilyn was getting Dave to drive her to 1006 Cornwall Street. It was a cedar shake house, dark green in colour, where Marilyn had lived a few years before.

A few years before, when Marilyn got laid off as an usherette at the Henry Theatre, she ran out of money almost instantly and got depressed. Then she was afraid to leave her basement apartment at 1006 Cornwall, suffering from what some people called a nervous breakdown.

She moved in with her sister, eventually got another job and recovered almost completely. She was left with just one handicap: she couldn't go anywhere near Cornwall Street without having an anxiety attack. The situation wouldn't have been so bad had Cornwall not been a main street, with Marilyn having to pass it on her way to almost everywhere in town.

After a long span of Cornwall-anxiety, Marilyn confessed to her family doctor: "I can't go anywhere near Cornwall Street. I flipped out in the house there where I used to live, and now I have bad associations with the whole street. Too many memories." Marilyn didn't lend any more details than that.

Her doctor had been on the edge of retirement for ten years. In his clinical way, he made four statements: "There is only one cure. Make yourself walk past this house where you used to live. Stand there and stare at it. Remember the expression, 'Face your fears and they go away'."

Marilyn couldn't bring herself to walk past her former residence, and she got Dave to drive her. Dave would do just about anything for Marilyn—he just didn't want to have to park on Cornwall very long. He didn't like the street either. Hardly anyone did, especially the residents, as all the buildings were ready to collapse.

On their way across town to 1006 Cornwall, Marilyn and Dave picked up a female hitch-hiker who looked terribly lost. The first thing she said when she got in Dave's Pontiac was, "I'm addicted to expensive drugs, you guys, and I'm going downtown. My name is Sherrie."

"I guess we're going downtown too," said Dave, "but we're making a stop on Cornwall Street, if it's okay with you."

"A quick stop?" Sherrie asked, as she settled near the passenger door. Marilyn noted that Sherrie was both jumpy and shy-looking.

"I hope it's a quick stop," said Marilyn. "I want to go past the place where I used to live. I had a nervous breakdown there, and I just want to have a look at it."

When Dave stopped in front of Marilyn's old house, they all stared sideways out the half-open passenger window. Marilyn had to peer over the top of Sherrie's head.

"I can see why you wigged out," Sherrie said, turning around, "the place has bad vibes."

The place happened to be vacant, and a real estate agent was on the disrepaired porch, pointing things out to two other people.

"Can we go now?" said Sherrie.

Marilyn and Dave headed downtown, and before Sherrie got out of Dave's car, she said "I like you people."

"I thought she was going to want a hand-out," said Marilyn.

"She should like us," said Dave, "we drove her downtown when we weren't really going downtown."

"Well she didn't know that," said Marilyn.

"Are you feeling better?" Dave asked.

"Sure, Dave. I've felt better all year, thanks to you. That anxiety I get is a small problem."

Very shortly after that day, Dave left Marilyn for somebody else. He left her for Karen Lee, who had a hot temper and wasn't as nice to him as Marilyn.

Marilyn didn't see Dave at all after that, although she made the effort. She'd go to places they used to go, just like the songs used to say, and Dave was never there. When Roy Orbison played at the Cave, Dave wasn't even there. "He must be dead," thought Marilyn. She never saw Dave but she did run into Sherrie the hitch-hiker. Sherrie was on Granville Street, and started shouting, "Hey, I know you. Where's your boyfriend?"

"I can't talk about it," said Marilyn, and pretended that she was running to catch a bus. Not one hour earlier, Dave's mother had called Marilyn, inviting her to Dave and Karen Lee's wedding. "Confidentially," said Dave's mother, "I always wanted you for my daughter-in-law. For the daughter I never had. I wanted someone special to leave my possessions to. When you're my age, Marilyn, you're forced to think of things like this. I'm more than sixty years old."

Marilyn was so glad that her Cornwall-anxiety had gone away. That day when Dave had asked her, "Are you feeling better?"—Marilyn didn't quite know now to answer. Her anxiety attacks were a bit like a nervous stomach. All that rumbling unrest would start to surface whenever Marilyn lost someone precious, or lost a job—jobs weren't precious but she needed them anyway.

Indeed, the Cornwall-anxiety was a small problem; part of a bigger uneasiness that Marilyn seldom thought about. She knew she wasn't alone in this uneasiness. Everyone she knew was in the same boat, with fleeting sweethearts, little money and a train of disrepaired porches.

"Keep telling yourself, you're not alone," Marilyn would say. When she was working at the Henry, she'd console people after sad movies: "Keep telling yourself, you're not alone." She was a bit like William Castle, the king of horror, who advertised his scariest film by saying, "Keep telling yourself, it's only a movie." His scariest film was *I Saw What You Did*.

Sometimes after a classic and thought-provoking film at the Henry (for example, the 1968 remake of *Romeo and Juliet* was popular at the time), people would stay in their theatre seats and have great discussions. Marilyn never had the heart to kick them out, and she and the projectionist would join these conversations when they had the after-work energy.

The Henry seldom showed classic and thought-provoking films, though. Maybe one showing per month. Soap operas and horror movies both sold the most tickets.

"God how I hate that rubbish," Marilyn would tell her friends. No one knew whether she meant the movies or the snack bar provisions. "No wonder you have a nervous stomach," people told her, "you eat popcorn, nibs and bridge mix."

The theatre seats had slashes in them, and weren't comfortable to sit in. The tougher patrons slyly cut them with their penknives. Marilyn sometimes caught them in the act and kicked them out. They respected her. One of the tougher patrons was quite nice, and when he wasn't in jail, he'd drop around the Henry to see Marilyn and talk awhile.

This man's name was Vince. When Marilyn split up with Dave, people lost track of her for awhile, but at some point she apparently asked herself, "Where is Vince, after all this time?"

She discovered that he was in the lower mainland regional correctional centre, and went to visit him one rainy day round the new year. No matter what shape she was to find Vince in, Marilyn wanted to say that she cared.

She first had to wait at the gate house, along with the other visitors, in order to sign in, leave picture I.D., get frisked and leave all personal effects in a locker.

The locker assigned to Marilyn was Number 7. Thank God, a lucky number, thought Marilyn. I need one.

There were just a few other women and men visiting, and one of the women forgot her picture I.D. The guards and matrons would not let her in and she said, "I demand to talk to Mrs. Ammo. She'll let me in."

Marilyn couldn't believe a prison matron would really have a name like Ammo, but there it was. Meanwhile, all the guards narrowly eyed the woman without I.D. They said, "Mrs. Ammo is off duty."

"My handbag was stolen and I've lost everything," the nameless woman continued, standing around long after she was asked to leave.

Marilyn felt badly, and like someone who feels badly but cannot do anything, she stared at the concrete floor. It was then that she spied one dull penny near the counter.

I've got to pick it up for good luck, thought Marilyn. Since the other prison visitors were twice as toughened as Marilyn could ever be, she went around and asked them all first if anyone else wanted the lucky penny. Nobody did.

Visiting time was two hours long. When it was over, Marilyn came away with this observation:

When you've never been inside a prison before, and go behind all the locked doors for two hours, as you leave and breathe the fresh air (and the air is genuinely fresh and breezy for it's next to Deer Lake, with its reflected rays of sunlight hurting the eyes until they get accustomed to the outside again), the wispy grasp you have on your freedom makes Cornwall-anxiety look like a Deer Lake picnic, complete with campfires blazing and transistor radios blaring "Land of 1000 Dances."

Everyone enjoys a good joke.

During visiting hours, how can people laugh and joke with each other, and discuss old movies or newly thought-of stories, and frolic in most of the ways people do when they are anywhere but prison?

One Sunday afternoon years ago, Marilyn and Dave were in a rowboat on Deer Lake, laughing over a little thing, laughing over their boat being caught in the lily pads.

At the same time, just out of earshot, inmates of the regional reward and punishment centre were laughing with their visitors over some forgotten joke. The expression everyone uses is, "Didn't we laugh."

DAPHNE MARLATT

Daphne Marlatt has published a number of books of poetry and prose, including *Touch to My Tongue*, *How Hug a Stone*, and *Steveston*. Her most recent are *Ana Historic*, a novel, and *Double Negative*, a poetic collaboration with Betsy Warland. She is a founding editor of the bilingual feminist periodical *Tessera*, and is currently finishing a book of poetic re-visions titled "Salvage."

Thirty years ago (can it be?) i entered UBC as a very shy undergraduate, not at all sure i was a "real" writer, let alone a "real" woman or even a "real" Canadian. I oscillated between autovisionary stories that sounded like poems and poems based on fictional characters i'd never met. Whatever the "real" was, it seemed to be someone else's territory. But then, writing slowly establishes its own territory. Mine seems to be enduringly inhabited by water and women, fish and that "catch" in experience that shifts perception even as it undermines genre categories.

eating

a kiwi at four a.m. among the sheets green slice of cool going down easy on the tongue extended with desire for you and you in me it isn't us we suck those other lips tongue flesh wet wall that gives and gives whole fountains inner mountains moving out resistances you said ladders at the canyon leap desire is its way through walls swerve fingers instinct in you insist further persist in me too wave on wave to that deep pool we find ourselves/it dawning on us we have reached the same place "timeless" you recognize as "yes" giving yourself not up not in we come suddenly round the bend to it descending with the yellow canyon flow the mouth everything drops away from time its sheets two spoons two caved-in shells of kiwi fruit

shrimping

stark against the green bushes green water lucent salmon net, these
steam sprayed with tar caught up at the boom and flowing like a
dirge

dirige Domine who hath dominion dominate in techne lord of the
nets

their boats lined up and wearing shrouds of black for the dark of
bottom waters shrimp who do not pray crawl

                              diminutive and *shrinking*
wrinkled akin to cabbage with crumpled leaves acurl where babies,
baby shrimp she said look at them curled in their cans waiting to be
picked crevette, little shrimp, sitting on his fingers stuck up
playfully there and there my sweet looking good enough to eat she
was wearing her short dress with frilly underwear, so pink this
little crack crevasse(la la) we have taken over this fissure in the
gender of it all

                                  this fiction pink for
little girls that we were the ones plying the net, fore-ply alive in
the reddening of desire from the raw to the cooked dressing her
feminine with just a bit of sauce you don't want to look like a boy do
you?   widening the gap (crevasse) a finger's width just letting her
know what's him (fishing) for her below

and the net goes roaring with the lead weight of it dead weight
down to unseen dark her body crawls feathery legs (undrowned)
feathery head light barely makes out the splurr and creep of net in
the tone of his words my little shrimp

the name of the net the name of the net the name of the net   later
she cannot dredge it up at all

compliments (of the camera)

what she's fishing for, wishing there outside the hairdresser's on
an ordinary street, hair erased by her chiffon scarf old ski jacket
flattened now or faded she faces the camera faces up to being there
and not about to go in or out with this evasive tilt to her head
she's standing not quite square smile reined in at the corners her
eyebrows hope—

trailing a baited line o let me like my look like this is what you
get, the small fish of an idea slipping the hand

this blank where fear settles in she is not quite sure she is not ordinar-
rily traversed by, the street its emblems of desire this man in the
form of a camera does not take the hole where eyes were
                                                    (hers, fishquick

hooked and dressed secure there in the ordinary

years of it, what comes down: the side of his hand slapping her into
a shape she resists—stilled fish. yet the eyes blink

getting used to the taste of fear as that which squirms alive on the
hook o she is sure she exists in the downward slice of his hand
unshutt(er)able up—no, not up, it's a lateral movement fish make,
nothing goes anywhere, but things move . . . that's not where it's
dangerous; it's when you're trying to get out you see

a lot on your plate lifted out of the socalled order of things face
to face with the hole you've been fishing for

Quote from Marguerite Duras, *Woman to Woman*, pp. 4–5

SEYMOUR MAYNE

Born and raised in Montreal, Seymour Mayne completed graduate studies and also taught at UBC. Since the early 1970s he has been teaching at the University of Ottawa. Author of fifteen collections of poetry and prose, he has also edited anthologies and critical texts, and has published four volumes of translation. Recent books include *Essential Words,* editor (1985), *Children of Abel* (1986), *Diversions*(1987), and *Crossing the River: Selected Poems of Moshe Dor,* editor and co-translator (1989).

For the younger writers who were associated with him over the decades, Earle Birney showed the way with his steadfast dedication to the craft of poetry and his restless search for new approaches. What better way to thank him than by writing with the exemplary care and concern he brought to his own work.

Trouble

What is he up to again,
packing up just like that and taking
    my boy with him?
Tight-lipped and stubborn—
I suppose that is what gave him strength
    to leave the casting of idols,
to push us on as we wandered
    south towards new strangers.
But this time there is a glint
    of a deeper darkness in his eyes
and I shudder helping the women flatten
    out the wheat cakes.
The ways of men bring trouble.
I pray, I heed the rules, but I will not laugh
    until he is returned to me.
Isaac, precious one, listen to him
    and be good,
I instructed while biting down sharper
    words for his obstinate father.
Going on a trip at this time of the year
    and at his age?
My little one, why did he pack the animal

with kindling and sticks?
He should have carried you and had you pulled
    from his loins!
Instead he dreams to himself and announces
    he must obey
the commands given only to him in the late
    night silence
when on the hilltop he leans on that crook
and allows no one near him, human or beast.

Another Son

Why does he call me Ishmael now
that I've been kicked out
of the family tent. First they wanted me
and then, got fed up caring. He took
me up the mountain and lucky
the angel and ram appeared
in the nick of time. I was favoured then
and they called me Isaac, and she laughed
the whole Sabbath through and half the week.
But when their spirits fell
and they got tired
and wouldn't let me out with the shepherds
and their girls, they sent me off
to Hagar's tent and told me she would be
    my mother now.
I'm Isaac, I told the woman, Sarah's son.
"For me, you're Ishmael," she replied.

Ishmael, that's what he calls me
and in his aging fits, who knows,
he'll throw us both out into the desert
while he talks to himself about another son,
a perfect Isaac subservient to his dreams.

The Oranges of Sicily

The oranges of Sicily
   yield sanguine red
but does anyone in Bologna
   take notice or mind
as the juice, squeezed
   into glasses
straight as the towers,
mixes with water amnesic
   as the young?

The tongue vows
   it is sweet,
the eyes beg pardon,
arms do not resist
   as fingers
tear away the fragrant
   skin,
and the aroma tells
   no one
the fruit drawing from
   underground sources
punish the flagrant wanderer
   who partakes
of the refreshing flesh
   but can not wholly
forget his brother's blood.

Bologna
May 1988

JENNIFER MITTON

After two years with CUSO in northern Nigeria, Jennifer Mitton came to UBC. She was fiction editor of *Prism International*, and in 1988 received an MFA in Creative Writing. She then spent a year in France, England, and Nigeria, researching and writing her first novel, and is currently at work on a collection of stories. Her stories have appeared in *Fiddlehead*, *Prairie Fire*, *Matrix*, *Room of One's Own*, the anthology *Otherwise Engaged: Stories from Canadians Abroad* (Quarry 1989), and the 1990 *Journey Prize Anthology*.

I have always been interested in illusion and the unexamined life. More recently, when my dog in Nigeria got rabies, CUSO mistakenly sent a brochure documenting violence to women in Victoria, BC, whose apartments were overly near elevators. I resolved to take a course in self-defence as soon as I returned to Vancouver.

The Weepers

In the martial arts it is good to keep half your breath. As you kick, you give a sharp, low yell, using your diaphragm, and you cut the breath off on its way out. The half-breath you've saved will be useful if your opponent gets you in a stranglehold.

But no one needs to take half a breath with them when they die. The first woman in history, Queen Hatshepsut, who gave King Thutmose III a hard time in the 18th Egyptian Dynasty, might have tried to take half a breath along with her when she died. It was probably Thutmose's intention, when he had her face scratched out of the mural in his tomb, to reach into the hereafter and strangle her.

But the days of loading up graves were over, in most parts of the world, when Adrian began to die. The dying were taken to hospitals and given green gowns. These were not burial gowns, and it wouldn't occur to a dying patient to ask to keep one. Rubies and favourite cats are one thing, but no one is going to make much of an effort to hang on to a cotton gown the colour of infection, a colour that makes clean toenails look grey.

Adrian's parents had been dead several years, and he'd lost all his friends through neglect and malice. He rented a basement room in a stucco bungalow with pinkish trim on Springer Avenue.

It was a dull block: there were no plastic flamingos, no portal lions, no woodchip lawns. No one bothered to cross rose strains or to use edgers.

When the chestnut branches grazed the power line, Adrian's neighbour (whose name he didn't know) hauled a coil of thick orange cord over the lawn, propped a chainsaw against his hip, and joylessly felled the whole tree. He then spent the afternoon sawing it into firewood rounds. The sawdust clotted among the fallen leaves until all turned brown and Mrs. Genezi, Adrian's landlady, came out in rubber boots and gardening gloves and her husband's windbreaker to rake the lawn. She raked well onto the neighbour's side and filled three big garbage bags.

Adrian, returning from the 7–11, where he'd gone for milk, thought briefly, as he leaned to keep his balance on the hill up from Hastings Street, about the neighbourhood children. They might miss playing in the chestnut tree. On the other hand, they might prefer playing on the new stump: they could jump from it into the leaves, although certainly, the now soggy leaves would have less appeal. And as Mrs. Genezi looked up from the third twist-tie, Adrian saw the thoroughly raked lawn, and he told himself that after all, there weren't many children in the neighbourhood, and not once had he seen any playing in or around the chestnut tree. He insisted on carrying the bags out to the alley.

A few days later he lay on what had suddenly become his deathbed, with his first weeper, Marsha, in attendance, and as he stared at the ceiling, it came to him that this sappy thinking about the children and their jumping games had been a warning sign that he was very ill. But hardly sappy enough, he felt, to justify the overnight transformations. One day his face had been an indivisible live sculpture, rough skin blemished with ingrown whiskers over the throat, and the next, a clumsy Saran wrap of reptilian hue lumping together flesh and bones as slippery and disconnected as packaged chicken legs. The skin was drawn over the nose bridge and cheekbones, and yet it overlapped, sagging, under the eyes and ears. His lumpy mattress and fifteen-year-old box-spring were now a damp, rancid deathbed. All this before the municipality had collected Mrs. Genezi's three garbage bags.

In the eighteenth century people began to fear death, and it became unfashionable—unthinkable—to keep the dying at home. Hospitals sprang up all over the world. By the second half of the twentieth century, people couldn't even talk about death. They certainly didn't wait for the dying to smell before they put them in the hospital, and there, the beds were on rollers; when a patient's rate of dying accelerated sharply, he was wheeled to another ward.

"But what luck," Mrs. Genezi told her friend Pia over the telephone. "The poor man dying at the beginning of a hospital strike."

"Did you dial 999?" Pia worked at the edges of the sticker on her telephone that read, "IN CASE OF DYING, DIAL 999." Presumably, the caller would reach a volunteer trained to gather people who would help. A trick to enhance privatization, Pia thought; but now, with the strike, a welcome resource for her friend, who had once been so helpful in the Department of Romance Languages, where Pia had come close to taking a degree in Italian.

But Alura Genezi would not have her house full of professionals or volunteers. She waited for Adrian's friends and family to take him home with them. But no one called or came, and this, she said, was when she'd remembered her Italian grandmother and the custom of weepers.

Pia was all for it. Never mind the good weepers would do Adrian, drawing out his memories, helping him through his last door, encouraging him to leave every bit of breath on this side. "It will help you, Alura," Pia said. "And if it works! We'll have a new social model!" Pia was presently concerned with socio-political history, and saw the weepers idea as a sort of division of labour.

"In my grandmother's village, everybody knew everybody else," Mrs. Genezi said. "And the really good weepers were known across the country." But how did one find a good weeper in Adrian's twentieth century Burnaby?

"Get his address book," Pia said. "Call the names with lots of crossed-out numbers."

Mrs. Genezi sat in her sunny kitchen nook with the telephone and the pantihose liner Adrian had propped above his extension. The liner was ruled in red ball-point, rather more evenly at the top. The last spaces were empty. The only doodles were the enlarged dots which followed some of the numbers. Two men's names were listed, and neither was home.

The women were disappointing.

The first one Mrs. Genezi found home said, "Oh, he won't want to see me: he hates me."

"Adrian? Adrian owes me five hundred dollars," said the second. "You tell him that, see if he wants to see me."

"I only arranged his vacation . . . we went out once or twice . . ." said another.

And the last one made a racket—washing the dishes, Mrs. Genezi supposed—so she had to ask everything twice. "I've never heard of him," this one said. "We just moved."

Pia told Mrs. Genezi not to give up. "Call them back; ask if they know anyone else who might know him," she said.

This time Mrs. Genezi got some leads. "Yes . . . some dancer. Nicole," said one. "Oh, yes: Nicole Lapointe. A French girl."

"I can't imagine him *having* a girlfriend," said another. "I mean I practically had to . . . sometimes I wondered if he was gay or what. He talked about a woman called Hannah, but who knows. Hannah Lind."

Then there was the woman washing dishes. "Didn't you just call? I honestly don't know him. There's a name on the wall: 'Marsha,' do you want the number?"

Within the hour, Mrs. Genezi had lined up three old girlfriends for that evening. "You don't think we're rushing things?" she asked.

"Why wait until he's dead?" And Pia, who had no family commitments of her own, offered to come over around eight o'clock.

At eight fifteen she stood by the chair at Adrian's bedside—a funny old chair; it made her think of the ones Van Gogh had first drawn—and was thinking of priests and surgeons, when a woman with dark stockinged legs clicked by the squat window. Adrian, who had not looked anywhere but at the ceiling, seemed to stiffen at the polite knocking.

Mrs. Genezi looked at her husband's watch, which, now that the leather strap had disintegrated, she wore on a chain. "That will be Marsha. She asked could she weep between nine and ten o'clock this evening; she had a party to go to, or perhaps it was mass."

Marsha was thin and breathless. She held her dripping umbrella out as if it were a divining rod, and Mrs. Genezi stood it firmly against the wall, and brought Marsha downstairs to Adrian's bedside. "Pia's here," she said. "But you asked to go first. I haven't forgotten."

Marsha held back as if Adrian were a wounded scavenger.

"Is he . . . how is he?"

Mrs. Genezi ignored this. "Please, just begin—we're here if you need us, but go ahead as if we weren't." She set two more Van Gogh chairs by the window.

Marsha gripped the chair.

"Adrian? I hope you're not feeling too, too . . ."

"Don't worry about how he's feeling, dear, just start remembering the life you shared," Mrs. Genezi said. There was a loud knocking at the basement entrance. Mrs. Genezi waved at Marsha to go ahead, and went silently, briskly, to the door. Never, thought Pia, had she seen her widowed friend so completely at ease.

"I'm Nicole," said the visitor. "The second weeper? I figured he'd live in a basement."

"Good, come in, Nicole. You're so kind to come, and Marsha has started us off—if you wouldn't mind waiting—let me take your coat." Mrs. Genezi took Nicole's fur and led her smoothly to a chair.

"Adrian?" Marsha was saying. "I . . . it's too bad it had to wait until you . . . we've just let our lives go on . . . I suppose I couldn't . . ."

"The memories, dear," Mrs. Genezi said. "Coffee?" she mouthed to Pia and Nicole. She waved Pia to stay sitting down, and the three of them turned back to Marsha and Adrian.

Marsha sighed. "Adrian, we did have some good times. Some very good times. Do you remember?"

Adrian blinked.

"For instance," Marsha began again, raising her fingers, "For instance walking in the leaves, yes—when we lived in Montreal we used to walk on the mountain, do you remember the squirrels, we always stopped to watch the squirrels . . ."

Nicole groaned and moved up to the window alcove. Marshal glanced around. "And on the beach," she continued, "that was here in Vancouver of course, the sound of the waves . . . and the halo the moon got." Marsha sounded panicky. "And then walking down the streets at night, oh, on Robson Street, or St. Catherine's . . . and then there was walking around the seawall in Stanley Park . . ."

"Enough walking, Christ. What about fucking?" Nicole was swinging her high-booted legs.

"Oh, I always enjoyed making love with him. With you, Adrian," Marsha said quickly, nodding. "Sex was very good. There was no problem with sex. No, sex was fine. It was very good." She leaned forward, toyed with the sheet, then dropped it with a movement of self-consciousness. Adrian stared at the ceiling.

"Oh, there were good times . . . some very good times . . . I . . . I hope I've helped in some small way . . ."

"Gag," Nicole said.

Marsha turned to Mrs. Genezi. "Is this what you were looking for?"

"Me? I'm not looking. I'm not dying. But you're finished? Thank you very much, Marsha. No, please stay, I've got cake." She showed Marsha to the chair beside Pia and motioned Nicole to go next. Marsha looked miserable.

Nicole walked stiffly to the bedside. She stared down at the dying man's face.

The doorbell rang, and Mrs. Genezi got up again.

"I don't know, Ade," Nicole said. "Hard to pack it into a few minutes." She called up at Mrs. Genezi, who was showing a red-cheeked woman down the stairs. "How long have I got?"

Mrs. Genezi shrugged. "Take as long as you need. This is Hannah, the third weeper. Pia, Marsha, and Nicole. So you're all here. I'll get the coffee," she said. She motioned Marsha to say put in her chair. "They might need you," she said. When she came back she pulled her chair nearer to the radiator and settled in. Marsha was gripping her chair again; Pia was taking notes.

"Might as well start with money," Nicole said. "No way I was going to ask my uncle in Versailles again, and you said, 'Well, then, chérie, why don't you just jump on a hovercraft?'—and you took that antique chair, well everything in the castle was antique—and threw it into the mirror? But we made up that time, remember? God it was cold in that place, and old Jean-Jacques several hundred rooms away . . . God, we had nothing else to do but fight and fuck . . ."

For a moment Nicole's expression was affectionate.

"Which reminds me of your jealousy," she said. "Remember you used to ask why I wanted to see my friends? You didn't say, 'Don't go,' or 'I want to have you all to myself.' You said, really slimy, 'So, Nicole, why do you think you have to hang around with that Betsy Ringer?' You said she was going to end up in an asylum. Just because you couldn't stand how you'd walk in and there we'd be at the table; we'd be drinking coffee, and Betsy'd have an ashtray full of butts and she wouldn't even look up.

"You said I had tendencies myself. *Me*: neurotic! You just wanted to know what I was thinking. At all times. Where I was going and who with. 'Why dontcha come, Adie?' I'd say. 'Because I don't find those people very interesting,' you'd say. I didn't find *you* very interesting either." Nicole looked around at the others, who were breathing in and out in a sleepy way. "I'm getting to sex," she said. She turned back to Adrian and sat down.

"Sex," she said. She said it again, slowly: "Sex. Making love. Did we have any *idea* what that meant?"

"He's looking!" cried Marsha. The three women jumped up. Marsha was right: Adrian had turned his head, ever so slightly, towards Nicole.

"This is very good," said Mrs. Genezi.

"Sex. Making love. Sex," Nicole said quickly. "That's what you want to hear about, is it?" She laughed. "Well, you know . . . it was all *right*, Ade. Sometimes you let go. Remember we were camping and we nearly started a forest fire, we had to haul water from the lake in jerry cans, and we were running around, coughing, so scared, then when we got that under control, we came together accidentally, and we started fucking on the ashes, everything was wet and steaming, it was like the dawn of time, and we kept going and going, remember?"

Adrian nodded slightly.

"Yeah, well that was the only really good time," Nicole said. She sniffed, looking him right in the eyes. "And all those women where you worked, and then *you* on about the men I saw. Who? Harold? You know, the funny thing is I did try to go out with Harold after. Did you know that? He was even more of a controller than you. Well, Ade. I think I'll give this a rest." Nicole got up. She leaned over and squeezed Adrian's hand, which lay grey over the white sheet. Adrian didn't squeeze back. "Go for it," she said, turning, waving her braceleted hand at Hannah.

But it was Marsha who got up. "I . . . remembered something," she said.

"Of course, dear," Mrs. Genezi said.

"Adrian?" Marsha stood beside the deathbed. She clenched and unclenched her hand. Adrian had gone back to looking at the ceiling.

"Adrian, I . . ."

"What are you afraid of, Marsha? *Losing* him?" Nicole laughed. "He's *dying*."

"I know that." Marsha's voice was lower, stronger, now. "Adrian?

There are some things we both need to remember. I didn't say them before, because I thought . . ."

"Why not cut the intro," Nicole said.

Marshal whirled around. "Why not *shut up*!"

Nicole might have been looking with her tongue for some gum in her mouth. She shrugged, looked down from her alcove spot to Mrs. Genezi and Hannah and Pia.

"Go ahead, dear," Mrs. Genezi said.

"Okay. Okay, Adrian. It's hard to imagine you, sick like this, grey . . . You look very bad. It's hard to imagine you once kicked me around. I think, I try to think, what did I do to deserve that? You didn't drink. And I always knew when it was coming. But I never knew why."

Adrian stared at the ceiling.

"Isn't that something." Nicole said flatly. "He beat you and he doesn't remember. Beat you and *you* don't know *why*! He never beat *me*, I'll tell you."

"Maybe he never loved you, either," Marsha said. She put her hand over her mouth.

"Oh, love! Love and sex and death! That's what sells products. God, it's women like you . . ." Nicole trailed off. She started swinging her leg again.

"You do remember, don't you, Adrian?" Marsha said. But Adrian was looking at the ceiling.

"Help him remember," Mrs. Genezi said gently.

"Okay: we'd been to a movie and you saw a car for sale and you got upset because I didn't like the colour."

"Holy Christ," Nicole said.

"You wanted to walk by it again, but I was in heels, it was freezing . . . I wasn't enthusiastic . . . So when we were at the owner's you were polite to him so I knew you were upset, and I was scared. All the way home I was asking you things, thinking, I won't talk about the car, that will upset him, no, that's not right, I will talk about the car, because that's why he's upset, he thinks I don't like the colour, but then, he'll know I'm just lying if I say I like it now, unless I can convince him I've changed my mind? You know? Remember?"

Adrian was still staring at the ceiling.

"So we got in the door and you just kicked off your shoes and went into the living room and sat down on the couch and turned on the television. I came in and asked what you were watching, and bam! You just smacked me across the face, asked me how I thought I could get off with the way I was acting, and I asked you which way, and you said, 'Oh, Christ, don't play this game with me,' and you hit me again. Remember? Don't you *remember*?"

"This is very good," Mrs. Genezi said. She took Pia's hand and held it on her flowered lap. Nicole stopped swinging her legs. And still Adrian stared at the ceiling.

"Go to hell, then," Marsha said. She took a kleenex from the box Mrs. Genezi handed her, but she didn't use it; she wasn't crying. "You go ahead," she said angrily, not looking at Hannah.

Hannah had the flush of women who are well loved. "It's me, Adrian," she said. "Hannah Lind. I don't think I'm angry with you. It was a long time ago. Our big deal was when I got pregnant. You said you were sorry, but you were too young . . . you just couldn't take the responsibility . . . you had a lot of travelling to do . . . You were even crying. I walked out. I hoped you'd come after me but you didn't. I took the train. I kept thinking, I'm pregnant, and I'm taking a train by myself. I was only scared of the idea. But I had a miscarriage.

"What else. Oh: remember a couple years later you showed up with your camera? That struck me because we never took pictures of each other when we were lovers. And then when we ran into each other in the airport. You were fat, smoking a lot." Hannah laughed. "If it had been ten years earlier and me fat and smoking you would have said, 'Put on a little weight?' But I couldn't say it."

"So say it now." Nicole offered the others sticks of gum. Pia saw that it wasn't sugarless, and mouthed, "No thanks." Nicole flicked the wrapper into the wastebasket and made snapping noises.

Hannah shrugged. "We had about twenty minutes before our planes left, and it was hard to think of things to say. I realized you were never very interesting. You were just blond, sort of good-looking. When you were young.

"And that time you talked me into coming over to that room on, what was it, Burnaby Street? I think you wanted money but I can't remember: the place smelled terrible, and your eyes were so dull . . . That was five years ago? So you were forty? You looked wasted. You look a lot better now even though you're . . . you know what I mean. And you said I looked good and I knew it. I guess I was the ugly duckling." Hannah was forty and looked thirty. "It's hard to believe he's going to die," she said, turning to Mrs. Genezi. "I keep thinking I should look at him in a different way. Are you really going to die, Adrian?" she asked gently. Adrian stared at the ceiling, but made a tentative, reaching gesture with his hand. A purple starfish. "Yes, you are," she said softly. "You must have a lot of regrets."

Pia squeezed Mrs. Genezi's hand. "What a terrible life!" she whispered.

Mrs. Genezi nodded. "You try," she said. "Try going further back."

Then Adrian spoke.

"I'm only one man," he said to the ceiling.

"Of course," Pia said easily, settling into the deathbed chair. "You're Adrian."

"Please . . ." Adrian's eyes closed.

"Don't worry, Adrian," Pia said briskly. "Ade. Adie. Do you remember when we were in kindergarten? We used to hang on the monkeybars, you at your end, and me at my end—in my kilt. You had a funny smile upside down. Sometimes I held my skirt so it wouldn't go over my head, and sometimes I didn't.

"Remember your mother made cake with cinnamon and apples? And on the first day of school you told the teacher you had to go straight home because your mother was waiting with cake? I asked you if I could come to your house after school . . ." Pia gave a happy little sigh.

"Kindergarten! Then you moved away . . . I didn't know you were moving until you had gone, and then I didn't believe it. But then *we* moved! I was sitting at the front of the second row in my new school, and I turned around and there you were in your same spot! We traced leaves and you let me use your jackknife to whittle. In grade three we practiced kissing. 'I know a boy we can kiss,' I told the twins, Cindy and Mayda. Remember them? Remember how I warned you first in a note so you could keep your mouth closed?"

Now Adrian was smiling. Hannah and Marsha raised their eyebrows; Nicole snapped her gum; Mrs. Genezi nodded gently.

"When did we go on that overnight field trip? Were we already in junior high? It was so cold, and someone said we should zip our bags together and roll up in a big line. You and I were swearing; you said it was neat that I was a girl and I could swear . . . We went skiing; we graduated, we couldn't stop making love, and if it wasn't safe or whatever and we couldn't make love, you put your hand just there and I came and came. Oh, Adrian."

Adrian was blinking. He started to sniff, and his chest rose and fell in jerks. He was having trouble getting the air out.

"You went to university back east but the second year we couldn't stand it and I moved east too . . . we lived in a two and a half and there were all these bugs . . . we ate spaghetti all the time with no meat in it at all . . . remember, Adie? Then we got married and we both worked for a few years, and then we had our first baby . . . she was perfect . . . she hasn't had an easy life, but she's doing well, she married a lawyer in Toronto . . . and our son has just started pre-med at McGill . . . You always say to me, 'Pia . . . we are so happy.' Do you remember?"

Adrian nodded. The tears ran down his cheeks.

"I am dying, and we have been happy," he said. And with his eyes still shut, he groped for Pia's hand, and his breathing slowed.

DANIEL DAVID MOSES

Daniel David Moses, a Delaware from the Six Nations lands along the Grand River in southern Ontario, is a founding member of the Committee to Re-Establish the Trickster, a writers' group working to reclaim the Native voice in literature and to facilitate the creation and the promotion of literature by Native writers. Mr. Moses' most recent publication is *Coyote City* (Williams-Wallace 1990).

Part of what that means in practice is an emphasis on story-telling, on presentation, on orality, on writing as both a personal and communal experience. This shift back to the ear and the freedom one finds as a writer there are illustrated by the following poems.

Some Grand River Blues

Look. The land ends up
in stubble every
October. The sky
today may feel as

empty. But just be
like the river —bend
and reflect it. Those
blues already show

through the skin inside
your elbow —and flow
back to the heart. Why
let a few passing

Canada geese up
set you? Just remind
yourself how the land
also renews. Don't

despair just because
they're already too
high to hear. Your heart
started beating with

their wings the moment
you got sight of them
—but that's no reason
to fear it will still

when they disappear.
Look away now. Let
loose. See? The river's
bending like a bruise.

Grandmother of the Glacier

The icefield she had in her head started
sliding the instant she died. *Was murdered*
would be more precise—would also explain
how her corpse became this high and open

ravine. But who's got the wit to split words
when that ice is coming at us? The world
can't ever again be that room we sat
in a circle in—the mainland rain hard

on a window as we listened to her
trying to explain about words. *Winter,*
she grinned. *That's the constant thought behind all
our words. In Canada we never can*

forget the edge on the wind. But the edge
on a knife cut in, cutting off more than
her words. So now it's hard to remember
how that edge and this cold thought grinding down

out of her head ever seemed separate.
Now they're a mouth that bites off and chews and
it's getting so close that breath flakes like snow.
So we go mute too—that mouth edge so red

that words drop from our own lips like stones. None
are as finished as those of hers that fell
into our hands. But the stars now are shards
of ice—they too are cutting in. There's no

time for her method—to split and polish
words against our own skin. Is that how hers
got so coarse she could embrace and contain
not only the stars but the rest of this freeze?

Her body's been swallowed. Ours may be next.
But even though we throw them in, her words
keep surfacing. May ours too be heard from
again—edging some terminal moraine.

The Chain

This poem has come to bring you good luck. It is the
original poem, not a copy. It has gone around the world
nine times. Now the luck is on its way to you. It will reach
you about four days from now, providing you share this poem.

This is no joke. Don't you want to get lucky?

Read this poem to twenty you think need good luck. Don't
give money. Fate has no price. Don't keep this poem to
yourself. It must leave your mouth within ninety nine hours.

A Royal Air Force officer found a hundred thousand pounds
after he read this poem to his men.

Joe Elliot made forty thousand in the markets but lost it
again because he did not share this poem.

Six days after reading this poem in the Phillipines, Gene
Walsh lost his wife. He had failed to heed this poem. And
the cost of sending home her remains— .

Read this poem to twenty friends and see what happens after
four days.

This poem comes from near Ohsweken and was written by Daniel
David Moses, one of the rare Delaware Indians.

This poem must be heard around the world. So read it to
your associates and you will get a surprise. This will
happen even if you're not superstitious.

Did you know that Constantine Dlas heard this poem in
nineteen fifty one? He asked his secretary to spread the
word to his office staff, more than twenty souls. Five
days later on two million from the lottery he retired.

Arla Daddit, a single office worker, read this poem but
forgot about it. On the fifth day he lost his job. Later
he found this poem again and read it around and three days
later got a better job and a girl friend.

Dolan Fairchild read this poem and, not believing, threw it away. Nine days later he was dead.

Remember. You must share this poem. It brings good luck. Send no money. Don't ignore it.

ERIN MOURÉ

Born and raised in Calgary, Erin Mouré lived in Vancouver from 1974 to 1985. She presently lives in Montreal. She attended UBC as an Arts student (Philosophy) in 1974–5, and for six weeks in 1975–6. She dropped out after Pat Lowther's murder and has worked for CN and VIA Rail ever since. Her fourth book, *Furious*, won the Governor General's Award for Poetry in 1988. Her most recent book is *WSW (West South West)* (Véhicule 1989).

In looking through my poetry, these three all seem typical of the time I spent in the mid-seventies, living in a small room on York Avenue, attending UBC, supporting myself by working as a cook. "hazard of the occupation" was workshopped in Pat Lowther's class, which I attended until her murder, at which point I quit school and turned to cooking. What isolation and unease I felt in those days before feminism entered my consciousness and I started to explore my relationship to language itself!

margins

Nights when i am no longer
available, even to myself.
You climb the long blur
of stairs to my door & speak
like a tourist of the day's
work making plywood; i stand
alone in the shrunken coat
of my skin, map future
escape thru ribs & tendons:
when you reach to embrace, your hand
gropes thru my breast, embeds
within the wall. & arching down
bright from the high fluorescent
reach of ceiling, mouth wasted
w/syllables, you thrust
thru my body & enter
rusted coils of mattress, its tufts
& contours catch against your arm;
you cry out shocked for me &
i peer thru cigarette
haze from corners where i lean
writing words in the impossible
margin between us

Finally you sit smeared upon
sheets, untangle your chin
w/fingers, tell the floor
how to win at electric tennis.
In your absence i search
my throat for alibis, mumbling
all the unnecessary
prerequisites to love, mumbling
lies to the walls; even they turn
away from the margin
gaped between my arms

hazard of the occupation

what is said about the earth is
only that it breaks
apart. the child severed
from one arm in a laundromat
is sutured to the limb; it refuses to
belong: does he know where his arm
goes?
this is how easily a man breaks apart.
flesh as thin as words.

in the morning, your muscles ache from
the places they go in the night.
tho you argue, they will not
raise you from the bed.
you cannot forsake your arms.
outside, a hummingbird refuses to
land on the roof.
shingles break apart,
the hummingbird spins its wings above.
there is no word for what happens.

the table breaks when you lay your hands
upon it, splinters thru the floor.
facts, too; they do not remain fact.
on the page, words rearrange,
accuse you, shout about abuse.
the hummingbird lands.

your legs glare from the corner, accusing
you of theft; they want
divorce, requital, an argument over particulars.
pages hum; presses are
bolted into guns.
this time you remember nothing.
your legs dodge down
the road, sick w/explosions:
in your throat, the word
ascends; its wings break
against your tongue

for Rudolf Hess, on his 80th birthday
(1974)

tho spring comes at last
it remains
in closed beaks of birds
tapping the gravel courtyard
warning vines to twist leaves
across stone walls & chimneys
smokeless for 30 years

& you   hess   stand
80 years old in spandau
courtyard   feel walls growing
higher behind your eyes
   this gravel is not a field
   the sparrow at which you stare
   no luftwaffe   it is not
   so broken

you   hess   stand & beg
a sparrow for spring
raincoat humped over your back
fists packed into pockets
racket of artillery dry in your ears
caught once in that river
of power like a shadow

now   hess   stand
in the grained light
six million cries walled
inside your skull
voice of your comrades riddled w/
jackboots   those
men who could not feel guilt
dead   or mad behind stone walls
                stone chimneys
                stone cries

your raincoat a fence
suspended against memory
as the courtyard sparrow
taps holes thru your shadow
thru the walls behind your eyes—
tho you beg
& it answers   it cannot
free the voices

JANE MUNRO

Jane Munro grew up in the Vancouver area, raised three children, completed several degrees, taught, travelled, and wrote when possible. She now lives with her second husband, Bob Amussen, and those children who are in town. Books: *Daughters* (1982) and *The Trees Just Moved into a Season of Other Shapes* (1986).

Roo Borson, Kim Maltman, Erin Mouré, Andrew Wreggitt, and I went over to the Grad Centre for a beer in the fall of 1975. We'd just learned that Pat Lowther's body had been found in Fury Creek. Shaken, we debated whether or not to continue in Pat's poetry workshop under the direction of Robert Bringhurst, the substitute teacher. Roo, Kim, and I decided to carry on; Erin and Andrew withdrew.

Satori

Leonardo's sketches of noses around Florence
are casual representatives
of work in progress. They're akin to
leaving the pencil lines in on Shadbolt's owls.
Or, more elegantly, the drying of a brush
permitting light and speed
to run with a horse across paper.
XuBei Hong in long cuffs and sequined slippers
trusted his first gestures
the way personnel officers rely
on the impression a subject makes, walking in.
I tire of labour and the meticulous
great piece of turf Dürer,
in his deliberation, rendered so magical
that I might shovel his fifteenth century weeds
in with my backyard plantain and dandelions.

Woman Clothed by the Sun

Aubie: sister
         with hair, with tresses
         red as the rising sun:
         pomegranate,
         gelled from night's private skin
         slowly, mid-December.

L'aube: the dawn.

This morning, her face
through the glass
of the back door—
                  have you seen the sky?
                  quick, quick—it's fading.

Last night her baby dreamt of being born.
Aubie dreamt of bearing down, of the head's release,
the child's rush, uncurl.
She dreamt she cried —
                  elle arrive! arrive!
                  vite, vite, vite!
—and in her sleep she feared
he was far gone in his dreams of silent landscapes.
The man beside her could not hear
her dream of his child's dream teeming in her.
                  But that is too much to expect
                  Who could peel away those rinds?

The skyline's comb unbraids the dawn, frays it.

She turns down the mandarin I offer—
                  I've had breakfast
—then changes her mind, grinning, nodding,
taking the orange to eat in front of the window.

I tell her the first winter I nursed a baby
we watched lots of sunrises. He'd yell with hunger
at the ruddy light.
                  It's enough to make my breasts leak,
                  seeing a henna sky like this.

14,600 Carrots

From the bottom of the stairs
your eyes: moon slices in an ebony mask
seen through a telescope trained
up from the street and rolling
to follow the soft-shoe as you sashay
under the porch roof, proscenium
shading this whimsy. Your face

almost cork-black, reminds me
it's not often the darkness of your skin
is visible. Usually, it's the pink
of sunburn, blue smudges of tiredness
I notice. For a while I measured
the contrast of our arms, then
it was like getting night vision

and seeing through the dark of skins.
Seeing through the masks people get issued
coming into the world, onto their own
front porches. Seeing through mahogany irises.

The inner eye bosses twin slaves,
training them on its sets. Perception
may dance without script or critic
across a private stage. I've munched 14,600
carrots and can see, day or night, but
the shock of your theatre reminds me
neither vitamins nor good intentions
direct the tricks of vision.

RONA MURRAY

Rona Murray was born in England in 1924, spent her early years in India, and came to Canada in 1932. She has published six collections of poetry, an anthology using the craft of pottery as a metaphor, and a collection of short stories. Several of her plays have been produced both in Canada and the United States. She has now retired from teaching and is working on a non-fiction book concerned with her childhood and adult experiences in India. She obtained her MA from UBC and her PH.D. from the University of Kent, England.

Earle Birney was my advisor and friend. I was the first student to take an MA in the English Department with a creative writing thesis and as a result, I suppose in order to prove writers were capable of thinking, Earle gave me a reading list that defied belief. Fortunately, the examiners barely referred to it. Those were good days. These poems were written in Metchosin, BC, during a summer in which, having returned to the coast, I experienced a joyous closeness to the physical world about me. Earle wrote, after coming across "Blackberries" in a journal, to tell me how he envied me this environment.

Blackberries

fat on the tongue
burst purple
under an August sun

my nails
stained black
hour after hour pick
wine and winter jam
but these berries are so profligate
I cannot catch
their pulpy fruit
before its weight
pulls vines to earth
and spills in inky
waste

Peaches
—little golden suicides—
fall from the west wall
break
gentleness
on tarmac
Apples
lie in grass
until their pith
is eaten out
and empty balls of tissued skin
tease wasps
too full to sting

It is too much
Cockayne is here
and all day long
I try to force some order on
a universe
so absurdly generous
it stuns
the small and dubious
human mind

When

you pull your pots
from the kiln

warm and smooth
as new eggs
I
cradle them
move my fingers
across their glazes

the almost magenta
the blueness
the little hummocks
awash in transparent seas

Sometimes
an ideogram
or
hieroglyph
moves into
relief

sometimes
the flash a flame leaves
as it licks
about
the molten forms

Kiln day
is punctuated with small sharp sounds
of pleasure
the pinging of pots as they cool
our voices tossing back and forth
together

The foghorn

and the fog
roll in together

No mountains show
out there
this morning
and one by one
the islands disappear

Now even
the great dead maple
where the kingfisher waits
moves
into mist
joins
the white silence stretched
between
long aching calls
and emptiness

MORGAN NYBERG

I grew up in farming country near Cloverdale, BC, and was one of the first graduates of UBC's Creative Writing Department in 1966. At the moment I am writing fiction exclusively, but have written a lot of poetry as well. Winning the Governor General's Award for 1987 for my children's novel, *Galahad Schwartz and the Cockroach Army*, has fuelled me up for the next twenty years of literary travail.

Rubén Darío was an influential Nicaraguan poet writing during the late nineteenth and early twentieth centuries. In a bookshop in Quito, Ecuador, where I lived from 1984 to 1986 I found this poem published as a thin illustrated book. I was struck by its playfulness and grace and perhaps most of all by its innocence, a quality hard to find in today's children's literature.

To Margarita
by *Rubén Darío*
translation by *Morgan Nyberg*

Margarita, how lovely the sea is.
The smell
of lemon blossoms drifts faintly in the breeze,
and I feel
a lark's song in my soul, your voice's sweet
spell.
Margarita, there's a story I'd be pleased
to tell.

There once was a king who reigned
in a palace of diamonds bright,
under a tent made of the day,
on a throne of malachite.
An elephant herd had he.
He wore a gold cape, too,
and had a princess very sweet
and pretty, Margarita,
as pretty and as sweet as you.

One evening this king's daughter
saw a star begin to shine.
The princess was very naughty;
she thought, "I'll make it mine."

She wanted to fasten that star
to a brooch, this little girl—
also a feather and a flower
and a poem and a pearl.

Beautiful princesses
mean so much to you:
they gather lilies, gather roses,
gather stars. All this is true.

So over the sea and under the sky
the princess travelled far
to get what she desired:
that shining silver star.

She followed a heavenly road
beyond the moon, but didn't bother,
before she left her home,
to ask permission of her father.

When from the parks of God she
at last to earth returned,
all around her body
a gentle twinkling burned.

"Where on earth!" said king to princess.
"I've been searching high and low.
And what's that thing on your chest
that is causing you to glow?"

To him the princess said,
because she wouldn't lie,
"To get my star I went
into the blue and boundless sky."

And the angry king replied,
"Such a foolish child! So curious!
I told you not to touch the sky.
Now God is going to be furious."

"I didn't mean to misbehave.
I only know I've flown
in the wind and over the waves
to make this star my own."

"This I can't allow,"
the angry king did scold.
"Return to the sky right now
and put back what you stole."

The princess shed a tear
for that flower of light she loved;
but Jesus then appeared
and smiled down from above.

"In my fields that special rose
I offered her," said he.
"They are my children's flowers—those
who, dreaming, think of me."

In brilliant robes arrayed,
the king gave a command
and four hundred elephants paraded
where the ocean meets the sand.

So pretty is the girl!—
for on her brooch a star
shines with a poem and a pearl
and a feather and a flower.

Margarita, how lovely the sea is,
and your breath is the blossom scent the breeze
sweetly holds.
When you are far away from me, child, keep
this day in your soul
and keep a special thought—for me
and for the story that I told.

MORRIS PANYCH

Morris Panych was raised in Edmonton, received his BFA in Creative Writing from UBC in 1977, and attended East 15 Acting School in England. *Last Call* was produced by Tamahnous Theatre in 1982 and was the artistic hit of the season when it first appeared in Vancouver theatres. Since then it has received a cross-Canada tour, and a CBC TV production, as well as numerous performances across the country. Plays by Morris Panych produced since *Last Call* include *Contagious* (1984), *Cheap Sentiment* (1985), *Simple Folk* (1987), and *7 Stories*(1989). Mr. Panych is also a well-known Vancouver actor and director.

After finishing my Creative Writing program at UBC, I was determined never to write again. I studied acting in England for two years and returned to Vancouver to become a professional actor. It was during one of my periods of unemployment that it occurred to me to write a good acting vehicle for myself.

Last Call! A Post-Nuclear Cabaret
An excerpt from Act II

A retaining wall amid the post-nuclear wreckage of bombed-out buildings. A grand piano. Bartholomew Gross tends to Eddie Morose's gunshot wound. Bartholomew wears institutional prison greens and an over-sized suit jacket. He carries a revolver. On one side of Bartholomew's face is the beginning of what looks like a very odd skin disease. Eddie is still in his pajamas and a housecoat. He is blind and wears dark glasses. They sing:

BOMBS AWAY

BART   *Can you imagine the astonishment*
When the big one went?
All the laughing and the music stopped
In a deadly silence, when it dropped.
What a blasted accident.

EDDIE   *If I could have seen your face,*
I'd have said goodbye.
But the light's so bright you lose your sight.

      In a holocaust, the words are lost.
      And I only heard the cry.
BART   *What an ironically amusing twist*
      For the evolutionist.
      From a protoplasmic nuclei
      We develop and diversify
      Into radiation mist.
EDDIE *Did you see the tragedy?*
      Did you wonder why?
      Why we had to self-annihilate?
      Was it sad regret or was it hate?
      Or did we simply die?
BART   *How disconcerting for the human race*
      To erase mankind.
      Who'd believe that so deserved a fate
      Could be thus achieved by means so great
      They would leave it all behind?
      (Bart is studying the condition of Eddie's wound.)
BART   Well, this looks pretty serious, Morose. It looks to me like we
      won't be going anywhere for a few days. Well, don't get all
      uptight about it. Look at it this way—this place is as good as
      any. I suppose you're wondering right about now why I had to
      go and shoot your foot.
EDDIE I was sort of wondering. Yes.
BART   Well, let me put it this way—there are certain things that are
      beyond the realm of our understanding. One of them is man's
      violent disposition. Why, I recall, not too long ago, in the psy-
      chiatric unit of one of our penal institutions, where I had an
      opportunity to spend several months—meeting a very well-edu-
      cated member of the upper class. Lived in a huge mansion on
      Marine Drive. And why would they go and lock him away, you
      ask. Because it seems that he went and decapitated his next-door
      neighbour with a pair of electric hedging sheers. Later, in consul-
      tation with one of the resident psychiatrists, he revealed that all
      of this had transpired over who the hedge belonged to that sepa-
      rated their properties. The neighbour wanted the hedge cut
      down, and he wanted it left as it was. Needless to say, the psy-
      chiatrist was astounded.

      "You're an intelligent man," he said, "Couldn't you come to
      some kind of agreement? A compromise? Perhaps cut down half
      of the hedge, and leave the other half standing?"

      "We could have," said the man. "But it wasn't a question of
      property. It was a question of honour. I had to be on my guard
      you see . . . just in case he got any funny ideas about wandering

over the property line, and having an affair with my wife."

"Why would you assume that?" asked the psychiatrist.

"Why not," answered the man, "I was having an affair with his."

So you see, my good man, violence often precludes any measure of conciliation . . . even in the best of circles.

EDDIE   Well, I thought we were friends. I thought we'd come to an agreement about that. You wanted a partner for your cabaret.

BART   We are friends, Eddie.

EDDIE   You shot me in the foot!

BART   Yes. But if we were enemies, I would have shot you in the head. But I didn't.

EDDIE   Yes. Thanks.

BART   Mind you, there comes a time in any friendship when things start to fall apart. When you start seeing the other side of a person. Where on the one hand you seem like a perfectly nice guy, on the other hand you just never know. You might turn out to be as bad as me. And we can't have that, can we?

EDDIE   No.

BART   No. I'd have to kill you.

EDDIE   You've been saying that for three weeks

BART   Yes, but . . . there's nothing else left to kill.

EDDIE   What would happen to your cabaret? Your show?

BART   Maybe that's how it ends, Morose. I make a speech to the audience, emphasizing the innate wickedness of mankind. Referring to history to back me up. And then to make my point absolutely crystal clear, I kill you. Yes. I can see it now. The lights fade. The moment is tense. I point the gun. . . .

EDDIE   Wait. Don't you think it's a bit early? Wouldn't you like to describe some of the more entertaining circumstances surrounding the nuclear war?

BART   Haven't we done that?

EDDIE   No. We haven't told them about our travels. Or how we met in the first place. Remember?

(Eddie starts to play Travelogue. Bart doesn't remember.)

BART   Oh, yes! I remember. I remember the day I met Eddie Morose along the road. "Have you reached some sort of philosophical dilemma?" I asked him.

EDDIE   Not really.

BART   Would you care to elaborate on that answer, sir?

EDDIE   Not really.

BART   Are you at a point of personal crisis then?

EDDIE   No. Not really.

BART   Then why are you standing in the middle of the highway in your pajamas?

EDDIE   No particular reason.

BART   Not a friendly chap, I thought. Perhaps there's more to this than meets the eye, I thought. Tell me, are you going East or West?

EDDIE   That depends.

BART   Ah. A politician! Depends on what?

EDDIE   On which way you're going.

BART   Well I was going North.

EDDIE   Then I'm going South.

BART   But no sooner had he said this, than he began heading west. It was at this point that I paused for a moment to consider the two possible reasons for this apparent contradiction. The first being that he was a liar. The second, that when it came to matters of direction, he didn't know where he was going. I decided that he was a liar. "Excuse me, sir," I said, "but I don't like your attitude."

(Bart points the gun at Eddie's head.)

EDDIE   Is that a gun pointed at my head?

BART   Was he being unnecessarily superfluous, I wondered.

EDDIE   I don't have any money, if that's what you want.

BART   Obviously, my good man, you are not aware of the current monetary situation, vis-à-vis the recent collapse of our financial system. Even if you had a million dollars in your back pocket, it wouldn't be any good to me. Even if it was gold bullion, my friend. Everything of former value is now worthless. In fact, I knew a fellow, not unlike myself, who walked away with the entire Emily Carr collection from the Vancouver Art Gallery, and ended up having to trade it off for half a can of questionable-looking pork and beans. A sad comment on the state of the arts, I think. Times have changed. And with nothing of value to steal, criminals are being forced into other occupations. I've gone into the entertainment business. I plan to open a cabaret. As soon as I find one. Entertain the masses, that sort of thing. It's especially true in these times of global annihilation, that people need a little fun in their lives, don't you think?

EDDIE   There's nobody left to entertain.

BART   It just so happens, my friend, that I've heard otherwise. I have it on good authority that some places were spared the inconvenience of nuclear war. And that's where I'm headed.

EDDIE   On whose authority did you hear this?

BART   A radical, I thought. On my authority, you half-dressed half-wit. And I'm sure you'll agree that I'm the one in authority here.

(Using the gun again)
EDDIE I see your point.
BART It was then and there that Eddie Morose and myself came to our understanding. And so together, we headed off into the wilderness. To find our cabaret.
EDDIE With a few diversions along the way. *(They sing.)*

THE TRAVELLING SONG

Oh we've travelled through it all.
Had a laugh. Had a ball.
Saw the worst of the absurd.
If not saw, at least we heard.
Heard of things to appall.
Make your epidermis crawl.
Oh, bombs away. Oh, bombs away,
Travelling everyday.
We saw the nuclear debris.
Heard the tales of tragedy.
BART Where are we going?
EDDIE Spain!
BART *Bombs away!*
they bombed Seville the other day
but that's okay.
I hate the opera anyway.
And what's the fuss?
It didn't drop on us.
Can you figure it? Figure it? Figure it?
In Seville the civilians are in a fit.
Throughout Spain radiation is in the air.
And it's plain all the Spanish will lose their hair.
If it rains.
And rain it will.
So who the hell needs Barbers in Seville?

Bombs away,
Oh, bombs away—
Things are in a fix;
Though they signed a non-aggression pact.
Can you simply pull a magic act
From a bag of tricks?

Picasso,
He could have painted quite the scenes.

> *From what I hear, Iberia*
> *Was blown to smithereens.*
> Guernica. What was Guernica? A few Guernicans?
> *Compared to much more modern means*
> *Of obliterating all the Spanish genes.*
> *(Bart has a rose)*

BART   Fleures! Fleures para los muertos!
> *(He tosses it to the ground. There is an explosion.)*

EDDIE   I'd like to sing a short lament.

EDDIE   *I saw Madrid, when I was just a kid,*
> *But I didn't see Barcelona.*
> *But now Spain's been blitzed*
> *And my eyesight is fritzed anyway—Olé.*
> *(Bart tries to stop Eddie but he continues.)*

BART   Bravo!

EDDIE   *I would have loved to see a bullfight*
> *But there's no bulls and I've no eyesight.*

BART   Bravo!

EDDIE   *I once knew a señorita—*
> *Her name was Lolita*
> *She was a flamenco dancer*
> *But now she's a cancer casualty. Si, si.*

BART   Gratia.
> *(Bart stops Eddie from continuing.)*

BART   Yes, folks. Spain is gone, but not forgotten. Why, who could forget Pisarro? Certainly not the Incas. Cortez? Certainly not the Aztecs. Franco? Certainly not the Spaniards—you can bet. If there were any Spaniards to forget.

EDDIE   And now what about France?

BART   Paree?

EDDIE   Oui, oui!

BART   *With a soupçon of atomic chemistry*
> *You can make sauce Bordelaise out of Paris.*

> *I saw Paris in the springtime,*
> *But it vanished in the Fall.*
> *(EDDIE plays the "Marseillaise")*
> *How gastronomic to cook the French.*
> *It's a modern neutron recipe*
> *Without the mess and without the stench.*

> *Bombs away, oh, bombs away!*
> *Au revoir, Paree.*
> *though they promised not to use the bomb*

Can you stop a war from going on
With a limited arms recipe?

This could use a little salt
This could use a little Salt II.
No matter what you do to change the taste,
It still ends up a sticky paste.

EDDIE   Maintenant, mes amis
La lament du Paris . . .

I saw the Seine
When I was seventeen,
But I didn't see the Champs d'Elysées.
Now I'm blind anyway
And the Champs d'Elysées is finis—
C'est la vie.

BART   Magnifique!

EDDIE   *I would have loved to see the Métro*
now I can only see it retrospectively—
Oui, oui—

I once knew a girl from Paris—
A wealthy young heiress
With long hair of gold.
But now she is old and heirless—
Oui, oui, yes, yes—
(Eddie is again interrupted.)

BART   We won't forget France, Ladies and Gentleman. Even if we
wanted to, we couldn't. Why, who could forget Marie
Antoinette? Not to mention Cardinal Richelieu. Or Maurice
Chevalier. And when we look back fondly on the works of Zola,
Camus, and Sartre, we'll remember with a hushed reverence—
what it meant to be truly—depressed.

EDDIE   And now we must do England.

BART   England?

EDDIE   Oh yes they'd love it.

BART   Really?
(Bart sings.)
Goodbye, goodbye—
remember not to cry
When you see old Britannia flying by.
They were hit—
never realized.
Oh, oh, oh, the English were surprised.

There goes Piccadilly
There goes London Zoo
Say goodbye to Lady Di and Charlie
And Charlie's little Willie, too.
There goes Leicester
And Manchester
And a little bit of Wales.
Is that Hampshire?
That's for damn sure.
Goodness, how Britannia sails!
What's that blimp, sir?
That's Westminster
And behind it Regent's Park.
It's a blitz to end them all.
Look sir, there goes old St. Paul
But this time it's on the mark.

Bombs away, oh, bombs away—
Goodbye Dear Old Sod
You've been blitzed before Londonium
But it wasn't with Plutonium
In a missile from abroad.

So much for England
Bloody pity, too
That the sun has finally
Set on you.

EDDIE   And now we present The English Lament.

I saw Big Ben
When I was only ten
But I didn't see
East Croydon.

Now England's gone to dust
And my eyesight can't be trusted
Anyway—I say.

I would have loved to see the seaside
But I can't see, and there is no tide.

I once knew a Bobbie.
His name was young Robbie.
He was one of London's finest.

But now he is minus his head
And dead, dead, dead, he's dead . . .
(Bart is deteriorating rapidly.)

BART   I think it's time for the finale, Morose.

EDDIE   No! What about Russia?

BART   You know, my friend, a person would assume that you had an aversion to self-sacrifice. Don't think of it as death. Think of it as art.

EDDIE   But we can't talk about the nuclear war without at least mentioning Russia. And the U.S., or Pakistan, or Israel, or South Africa, or Argentina.

BART   But we'll be here all night!

(Eddie sings:)

Heard of things to appall.
Make your epidermis crawl.
Oh, bombs away, oh bombs away,
Travelling everyday.
We saw the nuclear debris.
We heard the tales of tragedy.
(Eddie plays the "Volga Boat Song." Bart sings:)

In Leningrad the scene is just as mad.
Each Bolshevik is either dead or sick.
("Nutcracker")
Moscow had some lovely parts.
The Bolshoi and the Moscow Arts,
The Kremlin and the People's GUM,
And Lenin's tomb.

Tchaikowski could have written
About how Moscow was smitten.
What was 1812 compared to modern doom?

Boom. Boom.
("Kalinka")
Boom. Boom. (Etc. . . .)

BART   *Too bad! Comrade!*
Tak chto! Ho, ho!

EDDIE   Tepyer mei presentski
Po Ruski Lamentski

I saw Kiev

When I was just eleven
But I didn't see
Kirgizskaya.

BART   STOP! I'm getting travel sickness.
         (Bart is starting to lose even more of his light grip on
         reality.)

BART   It's time for the finale. It's getting late. I see the dawn creeping
         up over the hills.

EDDIE   It's not dawn.

BART   How the hell would you know?

EDDIE   Because, I can hear coyotes. Owls. Crickets.

BART   Crickets?

EDDIE   Sssh. Listen.

BART   *(Whispering)* What about the finale?

EDDIE   No, why don't you put down your gun and go to sleep?
         (As Eddie plays a chord, Bart begins to fall asleep.)

EDDIE

DESERT SONG.

Close your eyes.
Daylight is still just a dream.
Don't open your eyes—
Night skies are not what they seem.

Though the fires are burning,
They're still miles from here.
So don't worry, this desert's the best place.
Oh, the air here is cool.
Close your eyes, rest your head—
And the coyotes will sing of the dead.
Singing: Oooooo

Though we're tired and lost
And forgotten it seems,
This is no time to think about crying.
Oh, the morning will find us
So go to your dreams
And the night owl will sing of the dying.
Singing: Oooooo.

Though the angel of Death
Has no mercy tonight,
The Angel of Sleep is forgiving.

So don't worry, don't grieve.
Close your eyes, it's alright—
Now the night wind will weep for the living.
Singing: Ooooooo.

Don't open your eyes—
Night skies are not what they seem.
(Eddie quietly leaves the piano, in search of the gun.)

GEORGE PAYERLE

George Payerle, BA 1968, MA 1970, was born of Hungarian parents in
Vancouver twelve days after Nagasaki. One of the students who attended
during the Creative Writing program's inception as a Department, he
returned to teach short fiction in 1988–9, and now writes full-time on
Tenth Avenue, where he lives with his wife Phyllis and daughter
Bronwen.

*I wrote "Wolfbane Fane" in the summer after I graduated from the
department. It constitutes part of an unfinished book called "Fane"
begun during my final MA year. The piece first appeared in* Event 3:3,
*was published as a chapbook by Robert Bringhurst's Kanchenjunga Press
in 1977, and enjoyed a reprint in the* Pushcart Prize III.

Wolfbane Fane

O mother, drive us out
Of the throat of hell
Where we are eaten and broken.

JON FURBERG, *THE WANDERER*

Across low dull slopes of the sea, Wolfbane Fane peers from the
bow of his longship through mist toward the northernmost isles of Britain.
He knows his eyes are green. Behind him, twoscore savages in furs oar
silently. Only a squeak and a gurgle announce the approach of Fane's
Wolf, long swansneck arching the carved head high into scrolls of mist.
Too bland a wolf, Fane thinks. Religious. A spiritual wolf, carved likely
by some secret Christian. Asger the Oakbeam, woodcarver to the Earl
Furor of Fane—an unlikely Christian. But Christians, broods Fane, are
unlikely entirely. A creeping chill of Christians inches up Fane's considerable back. Cold spider. And down hindwise through the tangled canyon of
his arse.

The lookout mumbles something imcomprehensible from the masthead
and points. Fane growls. The spider reaches for the boulders of his groin.
Fane crushes it and sees a glow in the dim lump of Britain. The kraken's
eye. He motions to Skar, who passes the word: Head for the church and
the mead hall. Don't fuck around. Kill anything that moves unless it's too
much trouble or you want to bring it home.

Wolfbane squeezes the haft of his six-foot steel axe, grunting like a half-wet pump. A pent sea churns in Fane. His eyes glow. As his ship grinds onto the shingle Fane's eyes are green demons leaping for shore. Having grunted himself to a steady snarl, he runs through muddy paths and cart-tracks, the crest of his own wave, and falls upon a low, shapeless building emitting chinks of light. Bellowing "Wolfbane," he smashes through the door into a greasy flicker of spent drinkers who flounder in disbelief. The axe crushes heads and tables, scattering blood, brew and tallow. Trestles and drinking horns bounce from Fane's shoulders. Fane sees everything and nothing. A squat Celtish man in rough wool bashes him from behind with a stump. On his knees Fane already has swept an arc of shattered legs. Knives flash before him but Fane drinks his own blood, spins the steel haft as a staff, butts and flails, catches a screaming wench in the belly and rolls over her. Finding his rhythm, Fane whirls to cleave the broad Celt like a block of wood.

As his men flit past to plunder, Fane attacks the building's beams and earth. The roof caves in upon him. He hacks his way through to clear air. Surrounded by howls and hewing, he works a motley of huts and sheds toward the monastery on the hill, already taken. Fane slows in a tangle of slaughtered monks. After a few tentative whacks at the walls, he ceases. Silence. Only the tinkle of stray stars through thickening mist. Occasional screams from the cove. The odd groan. Soaked in blood, sweat and sperm, Fane shivers. Dry, dull pains wander in his spine.

"Waldo!"

Pale Waldo, Fane's gnome, peers from between the legs of a woman half-buried in bales of cloth under the stern decking.

"Hasn't she bit you to death yet?"

"She's out cold, chief."

"Hm. Find Skar. Church down the coast somewhere. Before morning."

Fane turns on his concupiscent Norsemen, flicking the axebutt at asses and heads. "Stir, you halfling whoremasters! If you can't take it along, break its neck."

Limping from a chance encounter with a panicked boar, Skar approaches.

"Wolfbane! You're wounded."

"By Thor's balls, I'm dead. Get the men moving."

"It's no good. We can't hit again tonight. The word'll spread."

"So we'll spread faster."

Some days later, Fane discovers a place called Lindisfarne, where he leaves a bell cloven that had rung once too many, and sacrifices fifteen monks on their own altar. He broods among lichen-mottled rocks near the sea. Skar approaches, hesitantly fondling his weapon.

"Wolfbane, maybe we should rest for a while. Find some women—"

Fane growls. Pale mutilated bodies stumble before his eyes among the waves and rocks. Drizzling dawn.

"You're shivering. A nice green cove. We've just been going from one place to the next. . . . The men're getting twitchy. Must be a village over there we could sneak into before noon. These women'll fuck anything."

Fane takes a sudden swipe at the boulder in front of him. Sparks and splinters. The steel axe hums. Fane shakes the jolt out of his arm and sucks throbbing teeth.

"Next thing, you'll wanta go home."

"Well why not? Pretty soon we'll have more than we can carry—"

"Fat. Go home and get fat! Sit on the vik and wait for your fat father to break his neck. No. We go back up the coast. Get what we missed."

"Then home?"

"Sheep tit!" Skar glimpses white water in Fane's eyes.

Fane's Wolf prowls up and down the east and west coasts of Scotland. Fane's eyes sink deeper into his skull. His crew see that the fever no longer leaves him after battle, and grow desperate. The haze of deadmen clears for Fane only when there is something to kill.

Standing to his knees in rubble and guts, Fane peers through the early light of one more sacked village. He sways, a failing bull shaking blood from his eyes.

"Skar! Where's the next town?"

"There is no next town. There aren't any more towns. We've had it. Let's go home."

Fane slogs toward Skar, his eyes old fires in their pits.

"No more towns, Skar. Nothing more." Wolfbane Fane wheezes, heaves, and flings up his axe into Skar's face, who falls. Fane's crew bunch like a pack of old and exhausted dogs. Fane blunders through them, felling bewildered men among their booty. Protests and irresolute arms rise against him, as though this must all momently be revealed as a berserker's jest. It is not.

Having laid waste his crew, Fane demolishes the Wolf, shattering planks and timbers. Up to his armpits in brine, he severs the stern with a last blow and stands sagging among debris.

Only Waldo survives, hidden in the stern, floating out to sea.

Fane stands alone. Among the shadowy horrors tumbling about him, he can see nothing to raise his axe against. The currents of his great body falter in confusion; his genitals sink like plumbs to some final uncertainty. He turns to the land. It rises upon his vision, dim but wastable.

Shouting his own name, Wolfbane attacks the landscape. His groans and pain hew forests, fens, sparks and showers of earth. For a day and a night and a day, Fane cleaves a swathe into the uplands, parting crags and lowering valleys, pissing horse-streams and sweat into mud of his own making until at last the sea floods through and in a great cry rolls over him.

Washed out Fane, wrinkled and drained, lies stranded on a fresh shingle shore, steel axe clenched in his senseless fist. Curls of vapour unfurl from his furs and matted hair.

A young woman in white robes inches down the rocks to the water's edge. She looks out the glinting firth toward the sea, and stumbles on the bulk of Fane.

"Poor man. Shipwrecked in the storm."

She bends over him, searching for heartbeat and breath, finding little. Her pale hair falls over his eyes, the lids of which she parts with light fingers. Glassy. She fondles his balls. Nothing.

Seagulls mumble and wail in perplexed circles at this new development.

The woman clambers back over the boulders and up the ridge, sweat beading on her pale-gold skin and trickling between her breasts to the tangled curls of her groin, which no one can see. She has left a troublesome white vision to lie bottomed in Fane's night.

Squat monks and peasants return with her to haul the bulk of Fane, axe and all, into a monastery cell.

Over a period of weeks the Christians refurbish him. They take his steel axe, place a silver bar, and mount it as a crucifix in the lower gallery, perhaps in anticipation of Loyola. Fane recovers strength and colour, but not memory or sense. The young woman comes to him bringing broth and delicacies and sits by him in the garden—a practice which he regards with as little apparent awareness as he regards everything else, and which the monks discourage against the day when he will become sensible. She accepts this as befits her humble nature. Her name is Caea.

As Fane improves, he is set to work in the fields, where he manages and manhandles vegetables. Finding him intelligent though uncommunicative and uninspired, the monks decide to scribe him. Apprenticed to an ancient priest intent only on illumination, Fane is discovered to have considerable scriptive talent and a certain austere taste. On the death of old Scrotus, Fane becomes a fully journeyman scribe. But his eyes remain clouded.

One morning after several years of this, the matin-bell awakens Fane with a momentous erection and longings to recall his dreams. He peers through gluey eyes and italic haze. Spider. Spinning from the roof of his cell. Fane trembles and slaps his crotch to crush the recollected crawler there. Christians.

Wolfbane Fane in skivvies leaps from his plank bed and, bellowing, charges to the lower gallery. He uncrucifixes his axe, cleaves the lay-brother garbage disposer who chances upon him, and proceeds to matins with eyes like a clear morning in winter. Fane's eyes are fangs, starved amimals leaping before him into the sheepyard.

Monks, priests, prie-dieus and lecterns scatter. The sibilant swoop of Fane's axe tumbles pillars and masonry. Among the wreckage, shredded manuscripts flutter like gilt-flecked butterflies.

Caea, in white, wreathed in her flying hair, struggles through the dust and falling stone.

"No, Fane! No! You mustn't—"

Fane halves her from the hairs of her head to the secret curls of her fork. He stumbles on her body, but continues, blundering through heather to sit and brood in a soggy fen.

Drizzled Fane chews grass ends, fearing the nameless dull pains lurking in his spine and the dark cavities of his bowel. In self-defence he envisages a plan. Stray Norsemen enserfed in upland villages, weapons, and boats to carry them to the West, which has since become Ireland. Fane foresees his kingdom. He proceeds, eating roots and moor hens, wiping his ass with heather.

At the side of a certain road, very much like any other Fane has come upon, a road leading down to a wooded and tilled valley, there sits a woman of indeterminate age braiding ox-hide into horsewhips. Fane eyes her suspiciously, hunching his stolen furs closer about his shoulders. It is her presence alone that makes the road remarkable.

She looks up at him with the maddening neutrality of old women. Her face resembles the leather she works. Fane contemplates twenty-foot whips, plaited from the hides of weather-beaten hags, to be employed in the flaying of Christians.

"So you're the demon."

Not knowing how to take this cryptic and familiar greeting, Fane pauses and scowls.

"My name is Wolfbane Fane. I'm a man."

She shrugs. "You slaughtered forty monks and a woman and demolished a monastery. Don't complain if people call you a demon."

Fane growls and hefts his axe. "If you know all that, old woman, you should know to sit by the road and keep your mouth shut."

The woman shrugs again. "Your dreams trouble you. You will die."

"I know that already!"

"You will have disasters. I'll die soon, but before that you will have disasters."

"I make my own prophecies!"

Fane axes her, glowers for a time, then belabours her body with the horsewhips before hacking them to pieces. He goes on, jowls and entrails sagging like lead.

In woodlots and fields, creeping by night into their huts, he finds the men he wants. He enters drinking halls disguised as a goatherd and gathers Danes, Jutes and Norwegians over mead. Fane hears stories of an ancient Roman camp inhabited by ghosts. Marshalling his force there, he discovers a huge mass of iron nails buried in the earth. Impressed by his sagacity and the green lunacy of his eyes, Fane's men energetically prepare to conquer Ireland. They construct a forge. They fashion swords, axes and helmets from the Roman nails, and brew ale to banish whatever ghosts Agricola left to guard them.

On the coast, just before embarking for the West in stolen boats, Fane finds Waldo sitting on a rock at high-water line, eating raw fish. Waldo trembles but continues to chew.

"What're you doing here?"

"Waiting."

Fane grinds his teeth and glares.

"Can I come with you?"

"Waldo, you're a fool."

"I know, chief. Would you like a fish?"

Wolfbane's progress through Ireland outrages druids. The bulky Fane, singing his own name, refusing to lie down under a dozen mortal blows, threatens to become more potent than oak trees in the Westmen's imagination. The druids send their eldest to beguile the viking.

This druid, though blue and wrinkled, breathes with dignity.

"Mighty Wolfbane, has it come to this? Look how the Christians have done you—"

"What do you want, manpoacher?"

"I was about to ask a similar question. We have been sitting by, saddened to see you wasting yourself and your fellows, to say nothing of these," sweeping his arm at large, "your kith in the West—"

"Nearest I've got to kith are these savages that carry swords in my name."

"Surely, noble Fane, we are more your blood, of Yggdrasil, not that bent Christian tree, than the priests who have beguiled you. We share the Rune. Our gods are brothers—"

"My gods are the savages I slaughter."

"What does it gain you? You see what these priests have done to you? Make peace with us, and you shall be King. Where are your great carved chairposts, where are your proud women? You sit here on a stump surrounded by doggish men. What does it gain you?"

"Nothing. If I want to be King I can be King. I can split your skull for an alehorn. It gains me nothing. The Christians are savages, but womanish and crafty. Like you, priest. You want to snare me. You want to get my dogs out of your pigsty. You want me to go murder some Christians for you and come back to hear peasants gripe about the weather until you find some way to get rid of me. I'm sick of murdering Christians. You offer me nothing, priest, and I've got that already. It's what I understand. Now go away; you make me a talking fool."

"Forgive me. I didn't realize you are a reflective man—"

"Reflective my ass! You don't even offer me the relief of knocking your brains out. Get away! I'm a coward. I need something to kill. Do you have any blood?"

Fane seizes the druid by the throat and roars,

"Do you have any blood, you wormeaten rag? How dare you stand here listening as though I were a noddled old woman? Where's my friend Skar, where's the forty poor stinking armpits of barbarians that shipped south with me? Only Waldo, tame pup. . . .

"That's right, that's right, just stay right here where I've got hold of you and maybe I'll forget you're not worth butchering. I don't need flies and drooling old men, I need something with teeth, or something that screams and runs, a mountain, anything but this."

He pauses, panting, wafting the old man absently at arm's length.

"Any man must be a coward who can't get himself killed. Slinking Christ curse your blue bones!" Fane slings him in a blue heap to the floor. "If you've any blood, cut your throat and wet down the dust. A coward, you hear? I can't die!"

Various shaggy figures at the edge of firelight giggle furtively in their beards and ale. Fane glowers round.

"A dog. A good dog to kill. Where are my dogs!" The shadows diminish. In the stillness Fane turns again. "Or a magician. Tempt me, Druid! Make magic, so I can kill you."

A pause.

"Pah! Even a mad boar wouldn't confuse you with something alive."

The druid gathers himself, a bluish shade by the fire. His throat creaking like an old joint, he manages some crotchety resonance.

"Wise Fane, perhaps there is something more than I can say. Perhaps my daughter—"

He beckons. Caea steps from the shadows, tall in white robes and catching firelight in her hair, quite unhewn.

Fane regards her, looks about vaguely for his axe, and swoons face down in the dust, hair singed at the fire's edge.

The druids dose him with monk's hood, known as wolfbane, and bewitch him from his derelict vikings, who mill around like so many coracles in an eddying sea. Waldo pants after his master, but is waylaid by a hired wench and bamboozled in a root cellar.

Cunning, these druids. They fashion of Fane's axe a steel chain and bind him with it to cliffs where sea-eagles tearing at his eyes wake him from the bane.

Fane droops through hazes of poison, blood and spume. He thrashes and bellows into the wind whirling about him like the cries and talons of birds, until, dry crackles issuing from his throat, he droops once more. Wolfbane hangs in his lock and chains with a dull will, as though the determined weight of his bulk might of itself tear loose and plummet into the broken waves. Pale ghosts of nippled linen flicker in miasmad Fane. His spine, his thigh-bones and the marrow of his arms ache like one many-rooted and immensely diseased tooth.

Dimly clacking and chewing a parched tongue, he decides dying might well not be worth its end. Immediately despising himself for this thought, he swears to speak no more of anything to anyone, himself included. Settled there, bottomed in the vast cavern of his own darkness, Fane aches, harassed by ill-humoured phantoms.

As the itinerary of his present disasters wanders in and out over the personal geography of Fane, his genitals weigh on him, sodden lumps jammed into his groin and likely to breed a plague of wormy conclusions there.

Thus firmly wedged between self-abnegation and exposure, Fane seems unaware of Caea, who picks her way toward him across the rocks. She sees him, head slumped, hanging as though all possible gravity gathered in him and pointed to the meandering white centre of water below his feet.

In the windswept, shadowless light something loose and shadowy stumbles behind the hard points of Caea's squinted eyes. She reaches under her blue cloak and withdraws a key, with which she unlocks Fane's prison. A hairy-balled boulder, he plunges into the sea.

Wolfbane slides back to consciousness smothered in bedclothes and down. This puzzles him as a recollection of death. He grunts experimentally, wondering if movement is a possibility still open to him, until he feels something tickle his organ. Caea is lying beside him. Fane decides that after a certain point, amazement profits a man nothing.

"I decided to choose my own regret," she says. "And so, as the Christians say, I committed an act of faith. My father wore the key around his neck; I cut his throat. Then I claimed you by the right of salvage."

It comes over Fane that she has done something on his behalf. That business in Scotland, plucking him from the dregs of his own disaster and feeding him soup—that had been merely Christian and untrustworthy. But this is something new in Fane's experience. Wed to a woman by salvage, handed the chains of his axe and the blood of her father. Fane takes pause.

Her brush is brown and highlighted gold. He chews there reflectively for a time, lunges into her, finds himself surrounded and exploded. Wolfbane Fane has awakened in a strange place, with the sense of a man who steps from a boat and finds his feet neither wet nor on land, but walking over water. In this Fane sees no credibility.

He excuses himself at a reasonable hour and seeks a bog, wherein he sits chewing mudgrass.

He searches out nude Waldo, still nibbling mushrooms from the groin of his root-cellar whore, and drags him forth by one buttock into the yard.

"Nodog! Half-whelped spawn of a sheep! How can you have less sense than your master?" Fane regards inverted Waldo with fierce, lunatic inquisition.

Waldo sensibly remains dumb and is dropped into the mud.

"Looks like we're staying. I will be a Lord and live in a stone house. Get some clothes."

Fane sits in a pigsty, thinking.

He decides that at times further stupidity is inexcusable.

Caea, as a result, becomes pregnant and Fane delighted.

When she tromples unclothed in a vat of grapes he falls upon her joyfully, ignoring the fact that never before in Ireland or elsewhere has he encountered grapes.

Fane encourages agriculture. When, on occasion, confronted by militant groups of Westmen, he goes forth with regret to crush them. He wears his chain for a belt and, axeless, swings it for a weapon.

Throughout, he buries implausibility in unfrequented corridors of his bowel, venturing only now and again, roughly at lunar intervals, to soothe whatever suspicious conscience lurks there—timorous, savage, and seeking blood-certainty to guard its back and defend its front. To accomplish this placation, Fane thrashes his breast with fists and stones, secluded by night in the bog.

The full octave of cries accompanying this exorcism arouses myth and terror among his subjects.

Caea awaits him one winter night wrapped in a wolfhide robe by the fire in his hall.

Enter Fane, solemn, stiff about the joints, and berimed. She smiles, shrugs the robe from her shoulders, and says, "Fane, beat mine too."

His suspension continues until Caea gives birth. Hearing the first cry of his new blood, Fane sweeps aside a herd of women to enter the room. He finds Caea swaddled, sweaty, drained to a fading sheen, and dead. Midwives and greybeards huddle behind him, saying nothing.

Fane lifts her body, meditatively tries the weight, and lays her down. He remembers deadmen and fish, the boiling down of corpses for soap. He takes the chain from his waist.

"The child, you ancient middens. Where is my child?"

Nothing.

Fane bellows like the bog at full moon and flails. Old men and midwives fall broken, sheaves of an abandoned harvest.

"My child, I will have my child and make him no child again!"

Wolfbane blunders through doorways and furniture, a fuddled cry sailing full against a lee shore of his own making. After crashing for some time through whatever he encounters, Fane becomes methodical. He searches house to house, village to village, hut to hut, investigating barns and pigsties, bludgeoning whomever he suspects of hidden knowledge and hence leaving a trail of fractured thieves, druids and old peasants. Again, nothing.

At last, when the carcass of a newborn goat is flung anonymously at his feet, Fane rests. It occurs to him that all this is getting him nowhere.

He summons an artisan.

"We will build a monument." Fane unrolls a diagrammed parchment to all intents and purposes depicting Stonehenge.

"A circle of pillars. Beams across the top. No frills. An altar in the middle, arranged so the sun hits it at dawn on the first day of Spring and sunset the last day of Winter. When it's done, we'll bury the woman under the altar."

"What do you want to make it out of?"

Fane muses, surprised.

"Pine. Or oak maybe? Stone for the altar. What else?"

"Why not make the whole thing out of stone? Big, solid pieces. Lasts. Looks good."

"That would take a hell of a lot of stone! You can't move things that big."

"Get some strong men, some good white oxen, and a lot of time—you can do anything."

"How long?"

"Long."

Fane considers.

"Well, then I wouldn't be around to see it, would I?"

"No, more'n likely you wouldn't. But what difference does that make?"

A pause.

"I guess you're right. Yeah, I guess. . . . But look, by then nobody'd even remember what it was for. There wouldn't be anything much to bury, if anyone did."

"No. But what difference?"

Fane regards the artisan. He looks over the artisan's shoulder at the lowering sun. The phantoms of his eyes stagger.

"I suppose you're right. Why don't you do that. I'm going to build a ship."

In the west of Ireland, while his ship is being built, Fane walks down a road hoping to be set upon by bandits. By the side of the road, an old woman sits plaiting ox-hide into horsewhips.

She says, "You have had disasters. You will die."

Avalanches come loose in Fane. He waits for their dust to settle.

"You said that last time."

"Before you die you will have disasters."

Fane stands looking down at her, fingering his chain, thinking it would do little good for the mountain to fall on her.

Without looking up, she says, "But sometimes all a man can do is go find a new axe."

Fane, of several minds, continues down the road until he sees smoke, whereupon he seeks out and thrashes a shepherd.

Having selected his crew, Fane gathers them, points to the setting sun, and says, "We're going there."

"What do we do when we arrive?"

"Depends what's there, sheep dung. Don't think so much."

Fane's ship arrives in what might as well be Newfoundland. His crew find this congenial and virgin. There are trees, fish, land and no one to fight.

"How soon do we go home and get the women?"

"Idiot. Are you a goat? A cow? What does a dog want with pastures? We'll sail around this and go on."

"We can't sail around it. There's no more water—we're on the other side."

"There's always more water."

"No. We're going back for the women. What kind of chieftain are you anyway?"

Fane lays waste his crew and ship, except for Waldo who hides under a rock with crabs.

Travelling overland in a sense of vacancy sufficiently large to be invincible, solitary Fane realizes at length that he is being followed. His followers unobtrusively, and for the most part invisibly, herd him toward their village. Since their colour seems strange and their manner uninspiringly docile, Fane's curiosity and frustration impel him to suffer direction.

In the village he is surrounded by coppery savages who fall on their knees before him and raise a chant unmistakably religious. Disappointed of his assumption that they intend this as prelude to dismembering him, Fane, in exasperation, speaks.

"You senseless spawn of pigs, get off your knees! I'm just another funny-coloured savage. Can you row a boat?"

This produces no useful result. Wolfbane mimes a vessel, makes paddling motions, and points to the westering sun.

Wolfbane Fane peers through mist from the lean prow of his Wolf. Across long swells, light glows in the dark lump of Britain. Armed with a fresh axe of Damascus steel, hair streaked grey, ageing Fane crouches at the head of furred oarsmen and creeps in on the tide.

He leaves his men with the boat and hunches toward the light-chinked door, where he bursts in and stands watching drinkers, benches and tables swirl in confusion. Eerily, groundmist rising from his lower regions, Fane returns to his crew.

"It's no use," he says.

"What do you mean it's no use?"

"It's no use. Shove off. We're going home."

"What? It's just a village like any other village—"

"Do as I say. There's all these guys drinking in there ... it's just no use."

"Old woman! You should have stayed home by the fire. Out of the way."

"Back in the boat, halflings, and watch your mouth!"

His crew advance on Fane.

"Get out of the way, old fool, no-one's grandfather. Old men should be fed to the wolves."

Fane shrugs, hefts his axe, and lays waste a final crew. He finds Waldo in an empty barrel, and says,

"It's no use, Waldo," and breaks Waldo's neck.

He destroys the ship, impatiently, and flings his axe into the sea. Throwing helmet, shield, belt and furs after it, he turns again toward the drinking hall, wearing only his woollens, carrying a piece of gold.

The place is dark and full of knives. Fane enters. He throws down the gold, asks for mead, and drinks. The darkness full of knives falls upon Fane and overwhelms him.

E.G. PERRAULT

E.G. Perrault was born in Penticton, BC, and now resides in Vancouver. His three novels are *The Kingdom Carver*, *The Twelfth Mile*, and *Spoil!*. He has written numerous poems and short stories, as well as radio and television plays. Several of his documentary films have won international awards. Currently he is working on a feature film. He was a member of Earle Birney's first Creative Writing class.

"The Cure" represents one of those extremely rare occasions where the story virtually writes itself. It was written in one day and never went to second draft. The UBC Raven published it first, and it now appears in several anthologies.

The Cure

It all began with the stamp album though the Lord alone knows when it really began. Years and years, maybe, with him carrying on like that whenever her back was turned.

"I threw your stamp album in the furnace, Richard," she told him out of a clear blue sky after supper one night.

"You shouldn't have done that, Hilda," he said. That was all he said; didn't even raise his voice according to Mrs. Grindley.

"You can't say I haven't warned you time and time again," she told him. "Snippets of paper all over the living room table, people tracking through all the mud holes in town and then across my carpets just to look at your stamps. Didn't I warn you now?"

"Many times, dear," he said and walked out of the room and up the stairs as though the whole thing was over and done with.

She says he hadn't been right since he retired from the post office. Always mooning around, looking for something to do. His friends weren't exactly the kind you'd want in the house; mailmen mostly, all of them pipe smokers or tobacco chewers according to her. It didn't seem fair somehow for him to be visiting away at all hours without her so he stayed around the place most of the time doing nothing. The Devil finds work for that kind.

But the fact is she lay half an hour in bed that very same night, waiting for him to come in and turn the light off. Twice she called out, "Richard, come to bed this minute." Her voice is strong for a woman. No answer. So she climbed out of bed and went down the hallway to see what he was up to.

He was in the bathroom. She saw him through a crack in the door standing in front of the mirror looking at himself, preening like a peacock, making clown faces at himself, carrying on like a monkey in a cage.

"Richard," she said, "what do you think you're doing?"

"Shaving," he said, and started to take his shaving tools out of the cupboard.

"You never shaved at night in your life," she told him, "and you don't need to start now. Yesterday was your shaving day." He didn't argue with her; just followed along to bed not saying a word.

That's the first she remembers. Other things fit into the picture now. He became interested in the brass and silver in the house. I saw him with my own eyes many a time sitting at the kitchen table polishing the teaspoons with a chamois cloth.

Mrs. Grindley swears she didn't have a notion until the day she found a looking-glass in his trousers pocket. That's nothing, you say? Maybe so, but when another one turns up in his vest, and another in his dressing gown and still another one in the hip pocket of his gardening denims you'd be as surprised as she was. Little oblong mirrors they were, the kind you and I would carry in a purse. She waited until supper time to tell him about it.

"I see you have a new hobby, Richard," she said, throwing a mirror on the table in front of him.

"I often wonder what I got for a husband. Carrying on like a drugstore dandy! What have you got to be proud of," she said. "Twenty years ago you were no beauty and time hasn't done you any favours." My, it must have been something to hear her give him his comeuppance. She's got a wonderful tongue, that woman!

He just sat there with his head bent over his teacup and let the words tumble down like brimstone on Sodom and Gomorrah. She thought he was taking it to heart until she noticed that he was smiling into his cup. It was plain enough what he was up to and she didn't waste any time pouring his tea back into the pot.

"You ought to be ashamed," she said, and broke the mirrors like soda crackers in front of his eyes. "Primping like a movie star actor! You try that sort of thing again and I'll do more than just talk."

She's a woman of her word; you know that as well as I do. Have you seen the place since she done it over? Richard was the reason for that. She threw out everything that could make a reflection: that lovely walnut bookcase they used to have, the brass around the fireplace, vases, silverware. It must have broken her heart to do it, but then she had the house redecorated; new drapes and bric-à-brac, wallpaper in every room. When it was all over she gave him the bills and a good talking-to for the trouble he had caused. There was some satisfaction in that.

It seemed she had him beaten. For a week or more she watched his every move. There's no cure like a complete cure, they say. He seemed to come back to normal again and took to sitting in the kitchen in the evenings, staring out into the dark garden, saying never a word. She let him sulk; and then one night coming into the kitchen in a hurry she caught him with his face right up to the window glass, smiling at what he saw there.

I hate to tell it, but she threw the salt cellar across the room and knocked out a pane above his head. He was lucky to get away with a few splinter cuts. You can't blame her altogether. I ask myself what I would have done at a time like that.

She couldn't leave him alone for a minute. It might have looked harmless enough to watch them walking along on a Sunday afternoon, but you should have seen how she steered away from store-fronts and weighing scales, and that sort of thing. Poor woman!

She came to my house one day as close to tears as I've ever seen her.

"He was out in the backyard after the shower today," she said. "I caught him behind the tool house kneeling over a puddle of rain water. What can I do with the man?"

"Get his mind off himself," I told her. "Maybe his friends can help."

"You know how I feel about his friends," she said.

"Hasn't he got any interests—besides stamp collection," I said. "My John spends hours in the basement with his jigsaw."

"Noisy machinery gives me a headache," she said; and I know it's true for a fact; she has a bad time with migraine.

"Take him visiting," I told her. "Let him see how husbands should behave. Bring him over here and we'll have a nice evening together." She agreed to that and they came over one Saturday. I made up sandwiches and things. John and I didn't let on we knew about the trouble.

Richard just sat there saying nothing and Mrs. Grindley had to talk for both of them. I have to hand it to her she carried it off well, until Richard pulled his little surprise.

"Pardon me a moment," he says half-way through the evening; and he was gone before she could open her mouth.

Now what could we say under the circumstances. You can't go following a guest through the house. Mrs. Grindley began to fidget and look over her shoulder in the middle of sentences. John and I suffered along with her; but he was back soon enough smiling and contented.

"I believe I'll have another of your macaroons," he said to me as natural as you please, and from that time on he talked right along with us. You never saw such a change. John thinks he stopped a few minutes in front of the hall mirror. Whatever he did it picked him up like a nip of toddy on a winter's night. Mrs. Grindley didn't take him visiting again. Couldn't run the risk.

Imagine the poor soul with such a responsibility. She couldn't leave the house for more than a few minutes at a time. I phoned her two, three times a day and visited when I could to see how she was making out.

"You can't go on like this," I told her finally. "Someone should be called in, one of those doctor fellows that knows about these things."

"I do believe he's not quite right," she said.

"It's as plain as can be," I said. "What normal healthy man would carry on like that? You talk to a mind doctor about him."

"I believe I will," she said.

That doctor shouldn't be allowed to practise. He started to blame the whole thing on her.

"You don't give him a chance," he told her. "You don't take any interest in what he does or what he wants to do. I really believe you're not in love with the man."

"Nonsense!" she shot right back at him. "I married him, didn't I? He's had the best years of my life."

"Why didn't you have a family?" he asks her, although the question had nothing to do with Richard.

"On a mailman's wages I could have a dozen children, I suppose," she said.

Oh, he told her a good deal more; and the harder she tried to make him see reason the more confused he got. He had it figured that Richard had no friends, or interests, or recognition. All he had left was himself—which is little enough at that. When Mrs. Grindley explained that Richard was probably trying a new way to aggravate her he wouldn't hear of it. "You give that man a little love," he said, "and he'll be well in no time."

He was wrong as can be, she knew it, but she had to clutch at straws. It was terrible the way she tried. I was over there many a time and saw her, fetching his slippers, pouring him a second cup of tea, and smiling at him when there was no need at all to be nice.

The strain showed on her face but she knew her duty and she did it. As for him, I'm sure he didn't understand what was going on. He let her know he was suspicious.

"What do you want from me?" he'd say.

"Nothing, darling, just for you to be happy," she'd say.

"You're working too hard at it," he told her. "I'd rather have you the other way." Oh he said mean, cruel things; flew into rages which was something he'd never done before. But Mrs. Grindley stuck to her guns. The worse he got the nicer she became.

"I'm knitting Richard a pair of socks," she'd say, and smile across at him slumped in the window seat. "Hold your foot up 'til I see how this is going to be."

"You know my size," he'd say.

"Green's his favourite colour," she'd say, letting on she hadn't heard him.

"Green's your favourite colour," he'd snap. "Talk about something else."

I wonder now that she didn't leave him; but then neither of them have any place to go. The house is all they've got and they're not spring chickens. Mrs. Grindley isn't the kind to run away at any rate. She tried everything she knew to win him over; took to wearing bright flouncy dresses instead of the good practical greys and purples that she's partial to; had her hair curled up a new way and wore a touch of colour in her cheeks. She'd walk up to him right in front of me and peck him on his forehead.

"It's Yorkshire pudding for lunch, Richard," she'd say. If she got a growl out of him she was lucky. He just couldn't see what she was up to.

And then overnight everything changed. You've seen them yourself. Remember last week at the bazaar—embracing like newlyweds in front of the fish pond with half the town milling around them? That happened overnight.

"It's a miracle," she said to me over the phone that morning. "He's like a schoolboy with his first lover. Last evening I tried to kiss him good-night—he started to push me away and then such a change came over him I couldn't believe it. He pulled me back and squeezed me 'til I fairly begged for breath."

Oh I'll tell you she was excited. It's been the same ever since with him playing lovey-dovey every hour of the day. I don't see how she puts up with it really—him stepping out of closets when she least expects it to plant kisses on her that would put Rudolph Valentino to shame. He gives no thought to who might be watching.

"Let me look at you," he says, and he gazes at her with such a tender expression that it sends the shivers up my spine. It's not fitting in a man his age.

"It's too good to be true!" she tells me. "I'll put up with any amount of his nonsense so long as he forgets about his looking-glasses."

Too good to be true indeed! I see through his game plain enough, and I haven't the heart to tell her. I wouldn't breathe a word of it to you either except I know you can be trusted to keep it to yourself.

Watch how he gazes at her. Watch how he looks deep into those big, shiny eyes of hers. What will happen in a year or two when old age dulls them? What will he do then? Love! He loves what he sees in her eyes, and he sees himself there, twice over. It's a sin and a shame the way that man has treated her.

KAREN PETERSEN

Me? I used to be a feminist, but now I'm just a fascist. Meddling with other people's writing pays my bills these days. I loathe, hate, abhor, detest, and vilify mashed potatoes at every chance I get. And I was born in Whitehorse. So, you can see why. . . .

UBC memory? Murky due to endless hours in Grad Centre bar. Maybe the time I almost hurtled through Faculty Club skylights into Dean of Arts' lap (me blindly bearing Prism *galleys after more hours in Grad Centre?). Maybe that seduction by the visiting prof (visitation by the seducing prof?). Come on, he got us* ALL *that year. Nope sorry, no memories.*

Cranefly

Some joke.

        Behind-the-hand titters
        of our evolutionary elementals
        drone endless as our ancestral regret
Big mistake
           that historic deal struck
              with our genetic genies
Remember
           our salad days?
           root-eating too fond of ruminating
           eyeless, legless, wingless and worm-like
          locked within the flesh of the fields
         our fangs
furious
           nothing to do but eat
joyous
           in our sensory deprivation
and dream
           of seeing the world, knowing grace
          the deal was sealed
              damn wishes
            made in haste
           mourned at leisure
      after our metamorphic musth and rush

we grubs graduated into an elderly summer
sprouted with hope into regret and protest
our wish still locked in a ridiculous body
  dawn of deceit
      enroute to a single day, if that,
      of living off the fat of our glands
      mouthless we are mute to vent horror
creatures so clumsy, we leave our legs twitching
as we dance with our shadows
in the lonely light of our own slow death.

Some joke.

Satyr's Rat Soup

crippled again by that slut Spring
all sprouts spout their own blood
back into their own spurting faces
it's the Season to spill their need

but my luck has me lack the sap
to spur even a handful of passion
my purple rivers run underground
rapt in the trap of Winter's leaving

the bitch didn't have much to say
having had enough of studs like me
wrapped in the rust of our sot-hood
impotence is all I have in abundance

I squat to gnaw the soup she left
trying to trust in her stupid myth
my lot's enwrapped in these rat guts
steaming heroic in the melting slush

PMS Rules OK

enmired in the slop of estrus
Yin analogy bloody convenient
passive even numbers
plod through valleys
slog through streams
oranges ripen and reek
this tiger's NOT bitchy
she is simply pissed off
broken lines are only a matrix
of dots and dots only periods
after all
so damp mop the old clichés
proof of the first paradise
galled at gagging with grief
this is what makes more
(and less) of maleness
putting up with putrefaction
is a test of skill before
the seeping surfaces, still
we wonder where intuition went
and have pity on even our sweat

MAIDA PRICE

After spending the first half of my life reading, I decided to spend the second half writing and began commuting to UBC for my MFA. I'm now living in Vancouver and studying for an MA in English.

Perhaps all that travelling back and forth to UBC started something— many of the stories I write have to do with travelling. My characters are moving from one place to another or are caught, dislocated, in a different place, where things no longer look the same.

Looking for Mexico

Bandits lived in the countryside, the story went, dark ruthless men often disguised as lawmen who shot travellers and buried them in some desolate spot, then drove off in the tourists' car looking for more wandering tourists. Not to speak Spanish, to go out of the cities and towns, to wear jewellery—especially gold jewellery—or drive a large car, were said to be dangerous activities. Once the *bandidos* had all the cars they wanted, Anna decided, they sold them to their brothers-in-law in Oxaca or Cuernavaca, men who had chosen to farm instead of maraud, and there were presumably no bandits in Oxaca or Cuernavaca with brothers-in-law in Jalisco, since the farmers working the fields beside the road here used donkeys to pull their rickety carts in the fields and on the road. Impervious to the stories, Anna nevertheless wore only her wedding rings.

This stretch of road was straight and empty of even donkeys, although far ahead an object bubbled and fragmented in the heat waves. Closer, it appeared as an arch over the road, and then finally resolved into striped bars blocking the way. Two men in khaki shirts stood by the bars and stared impassively at the car as they stopped. A third man, also in khaki, stared from a guard house set beside the bars.

"What is this?" Anna asked. Despite herself, she felt a prickle of fear. "Are we at the border?—is this the army, do they search for drugs? Maybe this wasn't such a good idea."

"I thought you wanted to see the real Mexico," Michael said. He was still annoyed. "Well, here it is."

Anna murmured, "Do they have guns?" as he rolled down his window.

"¿Donde a?" said the man from the guardhouse. Anna saw now that *Barrera de peaje* was written on the side of the building, and she flipped hastily through her dictionary. Michael handed over a bill and rolled up the window and she understood what the barrier was before she found it: toll gate. The two gatekeepers raised a bar each and Michael eased the car through.

The land past the barricade was exactly the same as the land before it: scrubby, dusty, grey and beige—but Anna felt they had crossed a tangible line. They were now in Mexico. She stretched her arms up behind her head so her breasts lifted out and the rib bones pulled against her skin, and then brought a hand down to rub the back of Michael's head. "You're as dark as a Mexican already," she said. "I'll never get a tan like that in a million years. And your shirt is khaki, too. Any guns hidden under your clothes?"

She did get a response, although it was just a wry grin and raised eyebrows before he turned back to the road. "Okay, okay, I get the message," he said. "I'm just tired, that's all. Year-end gets worse every year."

There was no point in starting an argument now so she just said, "Sure," and rubbed his shoulder.

After a while he said, "Pretty good road for an unspoiled countryside." They came up behind an old truck with wooden sides, the back full of men casually hanging onto the boards or dangling their legs over the end, and passed it. After another few miles a signpost indicated the road to Punta Mita was to the left and they turned onto it. The sea was ahead of them now, the only thing in the landscape sparking and reflecting the bright sunlight until the orchard suddenly appeared. A surprise, a brilliant green gift package tossed onto the flat taupe land, it was row upon orderly row of large trees festooned with fat green globes hanging down on darker green vines. The globes were the size of basketballs or heads, faceless. "Look at that!" Anna said. "It's a piece of living surrealism. Or earlier— Rousseau-ish. A striped face is going to peer out at any moment. What kind of fruit is that? I've never seen it before."

"No idea," Michael said, "but it must be profitable to justify all that water in this desert." It was the kind of answer Michael gave. He saw the world in figures and columns, counting even the elemental things that pulled him so strongly: the number of conquests, of comforts, of meals, of drinks. A balancing went on: jogging against calories, fooling around against Anna's ignorance, time against money. Despite his answer the orchard, even more than the barricade, marked for Anna their entry into a new place and a new time, which was the unspoken but palpable reason for this trip in the first place. She twisted in her seat to stare back. "It's wonderful," she said.

The orchard receded. The road curved to the right again so they were once more heading west with the sea on their left, the road a flat concrete strip running through scrub until even that disappeared and they were surrounded by nothing but grey dust. "Desolate," Michael said.

"It's an alluvial fan." Suddenly the road ended, with nothing to indicate an end or an arrival except a neat straight edge of concrete, and Michael braked hard, then drove slowly over the ruts and into an empty parking area at the edge of the land. He cut the engine and there was a moment of absolute silence before the susurrant murmur of the sea reached their ears. Anna opened her door and stepped out; little puffs of dust rose about her feet as she walked in the chalky silt. Michael came to stand beside her at the edge, which they saw was a bank above the beach. The fishing village of Punta Mita, an untidy cluster of palm-roofed huts on the sand, had nothing behind it but the dusty fan and nothing before it but blue water. It was protected from the open sea by a semicircle of broken rocky islets that shaped a pond of calm water in front of the village. The only sign of the times was a squat cement building with two propane tanks leaning casually against the back wall, and even that had a palm roof which extended out over a patch of sand. There were no roads, no cars, no telephone poles, and no people.

"It's a paradise, or Eden, the beginning of the world," Anna said. "We must have all come from someplace like this."

"More like the end of the road," Michael said. "And no water. How can they live with no water at all?"

"There's got to be water—a spring or a well. Look, there's a tree."

"Let's walk around," he said.

"Do you think we should?"

"Why not?"

Nothing moved but the sea outside the islets. The village, so silent and simple, had in its very silence and the complete lack of people a lurking watchfulness, so it seemed dangerous to enter it, to intrude, to disturb. Let sleeping dogs lie, she thought. This was a feeling Michael would not understand, so she said instead, "It's not set up like towns at home, with public roads and sidewalks. It's private."

Michael had already dropped over the bank. "You wanted to see Mexico, don't chicken out now."

She followed. He had already moved far ahead in his haste to make himself count as one. The path, wide enough for only a single person, snaked among the huts, touching each one at some point and sometimes actually passing under the rickety supports of a living room, between boxes or tables. It gathered the village together, always remaining just a single person wide; neighbours could reach across it to touch hands as they sat in their legless chairs or dozed on a cot. Occasionally there were enclosed rooms but most of the living must have taken place in full sight of all. And yet there were no people. Anna, catching up, said, "We're in their homes without being invited. And where is everybody?" He raised both shoulders in a shrug that pulled his shirt tight against his back, allowing the sharper lines of his shoulder blades to jut through, and walked on. He had already pulled ahead and was past the spot where suddenly, between the moment Anna looked down at her feet and looked up again, an old man appeared. Thin, weathered, stooped under his palm roof, he stared hard at Anna.

"Buenos dias," she said. He remained as impassive as the lizards on the wall outside their hotel room. He was so powerful, yet so solitary a figure in the sprawling village, that Anna hurried to pair up with Michael. She tucked her hand into the back of the waistband of his shorts.

"Don't do that," he said, "you're pulling them down."

"I'm not."

A long ditch filled with garbage marked the end of the path and the village limits. Faced with crossing it and then returning along the edge of the water, or returning through the village, Anna plunged through. Dozens of oil cans sprawled around more primitive garbage, bleached bones and frayed rags. She skirted a dark swampy patch. All was so hot and dry there was no smell, no decay; an unidentifiable black shape may have been merely a stick.

Through, victorious, she was comfortable walking back along the water's edge. No longer deserted, it swarmed with young men busy among the boats, and although they carefully watched this strange couple, the blond woman and the very dark man, they seemed not at all disconcerted and exchanged easy calls of *buenos dias* with Michael. Anna leapt happily over the faded nylon ropes holding the boats to the shore and did not speak.

The protected pond in front of the village was only waist-deep where they stood, halfway out, and even shallower in some places. A single boat, leaving much later than the others, glided alongside, the men silent now although one raised a hand in acknowledgement, and headed for the channel between the islets.

"I didn't think they'd fish on Sundays."

"No holidays in paradise. They can't afford them."

"I didn't mean as a holiday," she said, "but as a day of rest—they must need those. They don't need holidays, they have it all here, every day, all day." She waved her mask and snorkel in a circle. "Let's stay in a village next time we come."

"Where? In a tent?" He hummed *La Cucharacha*.

"All right, I'm a romantic. But let's stay in *Mexico*, not Touristland, not just drinks around the pool all day."

"Don't start on that again. I came here to relax, not drag all over the countryside."

"Why come then? We might as well stay home."

He reached for her hand. "Come on, let's go through the channel and around the islets, where there's some depth."

"The surge through the channel looks pretty strong."

"We'll stay together and you'll be fine."

She kept him in sight underwater until a powerful rush of sea at the channel mouth threw her back and thickened the water with sand. Fighting to stay in place, she raised her head to look for Michael across the surface and a breaker hit her square on, filling her snorkel, forcing her back, until she managed to clear the tube and get safely under the water which was no longer safe, but dark and churning, full of rocks that scraped and grabbed like unwanted hands that would not offer an anchoring grip. She inhaled water and choked. *Up* lost its meaning.

At the last moment her head cleared; she let the current carry her towards shore. It spit her suddenly into the calm shallow pond.

Trembling, she stood and ripped off the mask, releasing a fall of water. Her stomach hurt; she looked down to see thin lines seeping watery red blood cross-hatching her stomach and thighs and arms. "You bastard," she said, "I trusted you when you said we'd go together." Raising her head, determined, she looked for another way to reach the open sea but the surf blocked the flanking beaches as securely as it did the channel. To climb across one of the rocky islets and enter on the other side was also impossible. Bathing her cuts, she bent closer to inspect underneath the surface of the water and found it teeming with crab and anemone; a creature moving quickly out of sight suggested octopus. Small translucent egg clusters hung suspended in the warm water, buffeted by the passing schools of tiny fish. Michael, finally returning, unconcerned, reported so much sand in the outside water nothing was visible.

"We were going to go together," she said.

"Well, there was nothing to see anyhow."

Later, she asked, "How would I call the boy?"

"Just drink it from the bottle."

Anna held her local *refresco* between her hands and gazed toward the water, now looking innocent and blue even at the channel. The vista was framed by the ruffled points of the dried palm-frond umbrella over their beach table, for the concrete building had turned out to be a restaurant which had, as well as seating under the extending roof, a small cluster of beach tables. "Isn't it gorgeous?" she asked no one in particular. Michael, inscrutable behind his sunglasses, might have been watching the two small children who drank *refresco* at the next table under the watchful eye of their bikini-clad mother.

"Mikey would like it here," Anna said. "We should bring him next time."

"Uh-huh," he said.

After a while she put on her sandals and walked across the hot sand to the restaurant, for the boy had totally disappeared. No one sat under the pavilion. On a small table beside the old-fashioned water-filled pop cooler, Anna found forks and napkins but no straws or glasses. She went to the dark square of the kitchen door and peered in. It was not just dark inside but black, and the even blacker figure of a thick woman bent over a propane campstove set on a box. Other boxes were scattered about; there seemed to be nothing but boxes. Sensing Anna, the woman straightened and angrily gestured *get out*! The power of the outflung arm drove Anna back as surely as the surf had driven her back. Ten feet from the door she collected herself and called, "¿La paja?"

The woman appeared in the doorway. "No!" she said harshly.

Anna reported to Michael: "You wouldn't believe the kitchen."

"You wouldn't believe this dog."

Anna peered under the table. It was simply a yellow mongrel sleeping beside Michael's chair.

"You can't see it from there, but the thing is covered with open sores, I guess from the fleas. About every two minutes it scratches. Doesn't even wake up. You should see it."

As if on cue, the dog scratched without waking.

"Can't we chase it away?" She scratched her own leg in anticipation.

"Shoo," Michael said. "Git! Go home!"

"Probably only understands Spanish."

"Casa! Casa!" Michael said. They laughed and the tension between them broke.

The boy reappeared and Michael waved. "Trigame, por favor, una cervesa y un refresco," he said, and then, carefully, "¿Que es esta?" pointing to the dog. The boy stared, slid his eyes sideways at Anna, and shrugged. He was only eight or nine. Michael tried again: "¿Que es la palabra por esta?"

"Perro."

"Yo no deseo perro."

After a minute the boy understood. "Ahhh!" He ran around the table, yelled at the dog, and gave it a mighty kick that raised the animal a foot in the air and sent it scurrying around to lie in the shade beside Anna.

"¿Si?" said the boy, triumphant. Anna could see the dog's ulcerated sores.

"Senora no deseo perro." Michael was enjoying this.

The boy stared again, first at Michael, then at Anna, but he obeyed. As he circled around behind Anna, the dog saw him coming and leapt to scurry out a few feet, then waited, poised, for an opportunity to get back into the shade. Yelling, the boy picked up a rock and pitched it at the dog, which had started running as the boy stooped. The boy compensated exactly for the speed of the running dog and the rock struck it squarely on the hindquarters. Perro yelped and disappeared into the dark hole of the kitchen.

"¿Si?"

"Okay, okay, si," Michael nodded.

"Okay!" the boy said. "Okay!"

"Some improvement; that kitchen is already so awful I'm not sure I can eat lunch," Anna said tartly. But they both grinned down into their empty bottles, and when the boy too disappeared into the kitchen they howled with laughter. Anna wiped tears from her eyes with the corner of her beach towel. "Poor perro," she said. "We should have let him stay."

Michael started laughing again. He couldn't stop. "Imagine if I'd said, 'Yo no deseo Senora?' He'd be throwing rocks at you before I could stop him. Yo no deseo Senora." This struck him as funnier than the banishment of the dog.

Anna, caught up in the joking, pouted flirtatiously and said, "*Oh*. You don't love me anymore," and was then horrified: she had spoken the unspeakable. She laughed too, to keep it a joke, but it was all out on the table now, and when lunch came she couldn't eat; the crisp limey skin of the fish stuck in her throat and the salsa, which raised exclamations of joy from Michael, only brought tears to her eyes. To keep her mind empty she watched a group of little boys playing just offshore, apparently the only children in the village aside from their little waiter. The silence added to her sense of being stunned. Even the cries of the playing boys were swallowed up; there was only the rustle of the palm leaves over the table, Michael's fork against his plate, her *refresco* tapped down on the table. Then one of the boys gave a yell that was audible over the silence and raced past their table holding a silver hook stabbed into a tiny octopus. He ran into the kitchen.

"My God," Michael said. Anna was unperturbed.

"Well, I could tell it was fresh," he said. "This lunch is the first real Mexican cooking I've had." Anna could have said I told you so but didn't.

Michael hummed *La Cucharacha* in snatches, and happily drove on the wrong side of the road on the corners. Anna pictured him, with his wet hair slicked back and the unbuttoned khaki shirt flipping in the breeze, hanging from the back of an open truck. She examined the red scratches etched across her red flesh, for the palm umbrella had not protected her from the subversive attack of the sun reflecting off the sand. In the heat her thighs stuck to the plastic seat covers; they released with a faint ripping sound. Tucking the towel under her legs solved the problem of sticking, but her burned flesh throbbed and took on a life of its own. At the orchard, its green promising coolness and shade, she commanded, "Stop here for a minute." Michael stayed in the car; Anna walked across the hot pavement and onto the access road, built over the open roadside ditch, that led to the orchard. "Avocados." She turned back to face the car and called with delight: "Avocados!" Michael raised his arm a languid inch in acknowledgement. At the same moment the smell of the open ditch rose to hit her. She gagged.

The ditch was deep and wide, and its surface heaved with the alarmed movements of the thick dusty white lizards coating its sides and bottom. The ground crackled as if alive and breaking; it moved and tilted and Anna felt that she was the one moving, clutching and reeling like a drunk, while the land stayed still. And the smell. It was a presence calling out not only of lizards but of rag and bone, drought and hunger; rotting avocados, rotting flesh. She looked at the ditch, and then at the orchard, in disbelief.

When she stopped moving, the ditch stopped moving. She moved again, the ditch moved again; she was still and the ditch became still, and looked simply like a ditch full of sticks and rocks. She moved again and ditch began its sickening rise and fall. When it was still and silent, it was one kind of thing; when it moved, another; and when Anna, wondering which was the real ditch, picked up a rock and thumped it down into the ditch, yelling "Yo no deseo Senor!" it became something else again.

LINDA ROGERS

I grew up in the University Endowment Lands and crossed the golf course twice a day on the way to school. I don't remember ever being hit by a ball, but it is possible. I do remember when Earl Birney came to read and that might have been the real reason I decided to grow up and write poetry, a rather ridiculous profession. Birney read the poem about pissing on a little tree and killing it. I was impressed.

Now I live at Mile 0 in Victoria where the seagulls are a greater danger than golfballs. Everything is aimed at your head. Even though I consider myself smart in a ditzy way, I am trying to write with my body. At the centre of my sometimes baroque poems is my uterus, where the music and the children come from.

Mile Zero

Mile Zero is a pile of rocks
marking the place
where this world ends
and the next begins.
The soft intelligence inside
is a woman,
moving her lips in time.

She lies down and listens,
believing in magic,
believing that stones
carry the tune
and the power of absolution.

These stones are rubies,
blood in microfiche,
blood of her stillborn
crying for milk,
blood of her mother
going out to sea with stones
sewn in her skirt,
blood of trees with chainsaws
singing in their hearts,

blood of her living
children poisoned and sick,
their hair falling out.

The stone in my shoe
is a poem
that brought me to this place.
Sometimes, love,
do you think of me lying here
taking dictation.

Something Brilliant for One Hand

Jacqueline Dupré played her cello in bare feet
and died of a nervous disease.
I would like to say
her hands continued to play,
her feet to listen.
I would like to think she auditioned for heaven,
her body twisted by pain,
and someone high up in the hierarchy of angels
cut her open and found
some singing birds, or maybe
mechanical lips, or even
a tiny porcelain doll
bowing in time with an old recording.

Love is a sickness too.
I shouldn't have taken off my shoes.
I got so tired of hearing your voice on the phone
and never touching,
I cut off my hand and put it in an envelope.
When it came in the mail, you must have noticed
it smelled of sex.
It played your piano, something
brilliant for one hand.
Touched you everywhere,
didn't I?

Converso

My grandmother didn't know
the collects by heart.
She had to take off her gloves and follow
the words with her finger.
To tell the truth,
I followed her home from church
and watched her undress through a crack in the door,
as if that door was a wound
that would let me into the family

Bible, the broken glass
some covered
mirrors and circumcisions.

But women reveal only gender,
their scars all female,
another layer of silk.

When my grandmother died,
ash on her forehead,
the sign of the cross,
I ran from the house,
her Chanel perfume,
her satin shoes.

I stood on the roof—
wild as a banshee, my mother said
my shapeless Sunday dress   exploding.

LAKE SAGARIS

Lake Sagaris, born in Canada in 1956, now lives in Santiago, Chile, where she works as a writer, translator, and correspondent for the London *Times*, *CTV News*, and others. Her books include *Exile Home/Exilio en la Patria* (Cormorant 1986), *Circus Love* (Coteau 1991), *Four Seasons in a Day* (forthcoming) and two anthologies of Canadian writing translated into Spanish. Her poems and short stories have appeared in many periodicals and anthologies.

How to choose three poems from a book designed to function as one organic whole—how to separate roots from blossoms, leaves from branches, buds. From Circus Love, *fragments of politics, people, flesh, and flight. Borrowed from the threadbare circus, trundling from town to town in battered trucks, harbinger of misery and mirth.*

from the title poem *Circus Love*

I'm no acrobat floating
forever over faces   Vibrant
in the loon's cry   I've not
been flung nor do I hang
suspended between hands   Refuse to swing
from my feet   Head dangling
over nets   I want
ah— there the poem
begins to end
Inside the tent
we all live through our rituals
rigid as dolls or flexible as
whores   We try to balance
toes on balls like globes
The world whirls we
cling or fly

The elephants who preceded us have left
their mark in the sawdust, huge
grey clouds crowd into
storms around the ring
bring back sensation, earth

hugging toes, before
ascent began

Let me remind you
before I slip from
this swing to your
arms   The net below
is of my making
has a purpose
you are only
my circus
love

Let our children

for Carmen Gloria Quintana and Rodrigo Rojas, burned alive
July 1986; and for Pablo Vergara, who died in the explosion of a
hydro tower

Let our children be
open doors and guardless
borders   May the rocks they hurl
hatch and teach them flight

       (in the mirror our skin is
       slack from so much stretching
       on life's bow   We fire them
       over the horizon   They could land
       in feathers or in flames)

No child was born to burn
alive but soldiers have done this
more than once   Learning to write
our children trace the victims' names
on tissue hearts

and they ask why
and act
with words, dynamite

after they're gone
footsteps, laughter
run lightly through our veins

El trauco

Oh my dark
oh my black
love

The *treiles* screech at all hours
and seasons, you told me, as the
mist flowed around us
and the slashed moon
sank under the ocean
singed by the fire
about to ignite the horizon

You lectured me on
underground displacement
guerilla methods for subverting
barbed wires & enemy lines

but I am clumsy
and a barb drilled my palm

You muttered about tetanus
while I spun with the sky
turning around us
dew wet and pulsing
a star ready to fall
from grace to where
your skin mothsoft in my mouth
murmured like the night
pouring from my fingertips

The *trauco* is a deformed man no more than a metre high, who haunts the
forests of Chiloe, enchanting and seducing young maidens. *Treiles* are birds.

ANDREAS SCHROEDER

Andreas Schroeder has, as he puts it, "committed literature for the past twenty-five years." His eleven books include works of poetry, fiction, translation and non-fiction (e.g., *The Late Man*, *Shaking It Rough*, *Dustship Glory*). He has published approximately 250 articles for a wide variety of national magazines (*Maclean's*, *Canadian*, *Saturday Night*) as well as many radio plays and documentaries, literary criticism, and commentary. He lives in Mission, BC.

During the Creative Writing Department's early heydays (1966–70), a number of its students made annual mid-term treks to the west coast of Vancouver Island (Long Beach) to write, drink, and surf. We'd construct tarp and driftwood shelters right out on the beach, set up our type-writers, and write our brains out. (I wrote a major story each year for five years that way.) "One Tide Over" was written on such a junket.

One Tide Over

And they said unto him,
This saith Hezekia, This day
is a day of trouble,
and of rebuke, and blasphemy:
for the children are come
to the birth, and there is
not strength to bring forth.

2 Kings 19.3

At first he was just a curiously hooded figure, a solitary, meaning-less monk. I asked him if he was leaving and he said no.

I asked him that because his sleeping bag lay almost directly on the road flanking a convenient campsite ten feet away. I assumed he had packed and was just leaving the place. Or unpacking in preparation to occupy it. It didn't occur to me that he was camping right *next* to it, almost on the road. He just said "no," which became, the more I thought about it, increasingly ambiguous.

When we passed along the road later that afternoon the site was still empty. It was an ideal location and it was being wasted. We decided to move in.

That evening the hooded figure suddenly loomed in the firelight, causing instant mayhem. The dogs exploded, Marilyn shrieked and dropped her paper dish onto the sand, and even I found myself half-rising apprehensively out of my chair. "You're a little close, aren't you?" the voice surled, the arms demonstrating short distance between them accusingly. "A little too close!"

Greg bridled immediately. "You got a deed to this beach or something?"

The figure dropped its arms with an angry shrug and turned to go, leaving a somehow ominous scent in its wake. It couldn't be ignored; we'd had little enough holiday during the past two weeks, and I for one had in mind a three or four day stretch of totally relaxed, unguarded existence.

I got up from the fire and followed him into the dark.

"Just exactly what's the problem?" I spoke into the night in the direction he'd gone. I couldn't see him for his dark clothes and my unadjusted pupils. There was only silence, the far-off wash of the surf.

"Are you objecting to our camping here?" I was beginning to make out his faint outline unmoving on a rock. "Are we camping on your site or are we interfering with anything? Are we in your way?" I just wanted him to talk it out.

"The police would agree you're too close."

The voice was somehow pitted, like parched rock; obscurely alien in the damp tidal world of smooth stone and glistening kelp around us. I suppressed my irritation with difficulty.

"You mean you've gone to the cops about this?"

"The police would agree you're too close," he persisted.

"And I'm asking you, have you actually gone and called the cops?" I was a bit incredulous. "On a beach this wide and this long? You've got to be joking, my friend!"

There was a pause, while the hooded figure bent over a dark lump on the ground and I heard the rustle of plastic, the snap of burning driftwood from our campfire behind me. The wind fluttered my collar briefly against my neck and faded; isolated gull cries drifted up from the receding line of surf to the west. For a moment I almost forgot what I was standing there for.

"The air!" The voice suddenly rose and spilled through the dark like a shower of sand, making me duck instinctively. "It's the air, the air!" He had broken away from the plastic bags and now stood between me and the beach, faintly silhouetted against blue-black sky. He seemed almost dancing with rage. "Why is it?" he exclaimed, waving his arms with extravagant vehemence. "Why can't you? Why should I keep shielding you all the time?" He flapped his arms repeatedly, enlarging suddenly toward me in the dark. I stepped back, startled.

"Don't you people ever think about what you're doing? Don't you ever stop to look where you're going? Don't you ever listen to yourself breathing anymore?!"

I was at a loss for an answer. I wasn't sure I understood the question.

"What do you . . . what in hell are you babbling about?"

There was another long pause. Then, his voice sounding suddenly low and petulant: "A million feet. A billion feet. Why not. Bust the electrolytic barrier. Smack up the DNA. Biological gridlock. Whoopee. You're not you anymore, you're something else. So why should I breathe your air?"

He turned away abruptly and busied himself once more with his plastic bags. I stood there in the dark trying to figure it out. Eventually I decided I'd take a pass. As far as I could make out, he was being either preposterous or impossible, whichever came first.

"Maybe you should go screw yourself," I suggested kindly, and returned to the fire. But I told Marilyn to move her little puptent to the other side of our trailer, away from his camp. There seemed little point in taking chances.

Back at the bar Greg handed me a beer. "Here, cool down with this," he offered, laughing under his breath. "Shuttle diplomacy doesn't seem to be your bag, as my daughters would say." I took the bottle and resettled in my lawn chair, suddenly realizing I'd been muttering curses into my beard. He was right, I was furious about the last five minutes and I couldn't put my finger on exactly why.

Donna lit the Hawaiian kerosene torches and sprayed lighter fluid over the briquettes in the barbecue. Cherie was fooling with the Sony, trying to tune in some rock. Greg dropped into the chair beside mine and pointed his index finger back over his shoulder.

"Now there," he established, "you have your typical washout hiding behind crackpot ideas to justify his failure in the real world. If you can't make it these days you just pick up one of those fancy-pants reasons why you're an innocent victim of your surroundings and you're immediately excused. Hell, you're even praised for being so perceptive. That's how it is these days. We reward failure and tax the bejesus out of success, and then we wonder how we've managed to run up a multi-billion dollar welfare bill." He dropped his empty beer into the fire and pulled out another, digging around in his pockets for his opener. Donna had begun to hum the opening bars of a certain baptist hymn rather too pointedly I thought, but Greg just looked briefly disconcerted, then chose to ignore the dig. "Well we don't really *know* he's a failure," Cherie pointed out, momentarily abandoning the radio. "He's just acting like one." Cherie and Marilyn were Greg's kids, not mine. Donna was his second wife.

"Hang on just a minute." I got up from the chair and moved closer to the fire; it was beginning to drizzle again. "I mean, something about the guy's attitude certainly pisses me off, but acting like a failure and acting like an idiot doesn't amount to the same thing. I know plenty of success stories who act a lot more perversely than this fruit-loop, in my opinion."

"Aw just listen to him," Greg insisted. "You can't mistake that kind of bitchy whining voice. In my experience that always signals a self-proclaimed victim. And they're invariably bad credit risks." Greg was in the rental and real estate business, and the past decade had been difficult.

We stopped to set the awning—an acrylic imitation of some Persian Shah's desert tent pavilion—to keep out at least some of the encroaching weather. Then we resumed our seats and for awhile I just watched the rain glistening off the awning border into the firelight, ignoring the surrounding conversation and brooding about this and that. For one thing, I was still trying to plumb my own annoyance over what had just happened. The crazy biologist—if he was a biologist—had struck a sore point somewhere, but I just couldn't put my finger on it. I had half a mind to go back and pursue the question in greater earnest, but something held me back. Instead, I found myself remembering a conversation I'd had a long time ago with a drunk boxer at the Alcazar Hotel. I'd asked him where the urge to keep fighting with people came from. He'd continued sucking morosely at his beer, preparing, I was sure, some appropriately colorful reply, and then had surprised me with an extraordinary admission.

"You just a squarejohn so this won't probably make much sense to you," he said. "But I do it because I wanna eventually lose. Everybody fights so's to eventually lose. But you've gotta lose magnificently, see, and that's the problem. There's no point to it otherwise." He wouldn't explain it any more than that.

". . . hasn't even got a tent," Cherie was saying, ducking back under the awning and looking astonished and a bit concerned. "It's really starting to pour out there. He'll get soaked right through, won't he?"

"Unless he's just come here today, which doesn't seem to be the case," Greg reasoned, "he probably knows all about the weather around here. This is the wettest part of the coast; it rains practically every day. He must have figured some way of keeping dry. Maybe he's got a tarp of some sort to cover himself."

"Wow." Cherie subsided with a small, somewhat uncertain laugh. "Sure a weird guy."

"Okay all you wild and woolly Indians: time for bed." Donna pointed imperiously to the tent and then proceeded to open tins of Alpo for the dogs' last meal of the day. The toy poodles were so small I sometimes wondered how such bodies could provide enough room for all the necessary organs. Pooper and Snooper they were called. Both were shivering violently, even though it wasn't particularly cold.

Nobody protested for a change; we'd driven almost five hundred miles that day and were all exhausted. Donna and Greg disappeared into the trailer while the kids tumbled into the tent with the dogs. I climbed into the van and spread out my sleeping bag in the back, over the foldout cot. Then I reached up and snapped off the light.

Above me the rain drummed steadily on the van roof, pearling down the windows in many-stranded streams. I lay quietly for a few moments, listening to the rain and the constant rush of the surf outside. Out beyond Frank Island the foghorn had begun its monotonous drone through the mist, and now and then I could make out the upswell of thin voices sounding as if they were coming out of a padded tin can. Greg and Donna in the trailer, arguing again. So much for a cheerful breakfast.

I peered through the window in the biologist's direction, but all I could make out was a dark shape on the ground like a rolled-up carpet. He must be in there somewhere, I thought; somewhere in that cocoon. Probably soaked and cold.

The next morning Donna refused to make breakfast so we unhitched the van to drive into town to a restaurant. The biologist lay unmoving in his plastic-wrapped sleeping bag, ignoring the yapping dogs and quarrelling kids as we prepared to leave. A corner of his plastic sheet had come undone and I could see the large dark splotch where the rain had soaked through to the bottom of the bag. Aside from a number of plastic garbage bags lying wedged between the rocks a few feet from his head, there were no indications of a campsite at all. We piled into the van, kids dogs and all, and headed off up the beach, each of us throwing surreptitious glances at the motionless bedroll as we chattered busily at each other trying to ignore the tension in the air. Greg and Donna didn't look like they'd had much sleep at all.

When we returned ("D'you think maybe he'll have wrecked our camp while we were away?" Marilyn kept pestering Greg on the way back. "D'you think he might have set fire to it or something??") nothing had changed. He was still lying there; the camp was untouched. A thin but steady drizzle had set in over the beach again and the fog was bunching up just north of Frank Island, swirling slowly above the outlying rocks like an army milling about preparing for an assault.

Greg busied himself on the trailer roof setting up the TV antenna, since fog always guaranteed first-class reception. I messed about with the propane bottles and spent the next four hours repairing the intake nozzle on the fridge. Donna stayed inside, listening to the radio and reading pulp novels at the same time. The kids complained about mosquitos and sprayed out two bottles of Raid all around the camp. I couldn't convince them that mosquitos don't come out in the rain.

As I was washing my hands I noticed that the trailer's large side window had been scrubbed and the curtains pulled aside; I could see the biologist's cocoon still lying where it had lain for the past thirty-six hours. "He hasn't moved an inch all day," Donna admitted, following my gaze through the glass. "It's starting to give me the creeps." I said nothing, but she was wrong. Several times over the past five hours I had seen a hand extend cautiously out of the bag to lift the plastic flap at the head end, waving it back and forth as if for air. He was in there all right, alive and inexplicable, like some strange creature moulting or hibernating, or slipping its husk. Several times I had fought an overpowering urge to walk over to that perplexing chrysalis, rip off the wrapping and gaze at whatever would twist and untangle in the unexpected light. But I restrained myself; I was letting myself get carried away.

"Doesn't he ever have to pee?" Marilyn demanded from the sink.

I cracked up and Donna snickered over her dime novel. Greg just muttered "oh for fuck's sake!" and kept watching the Expos beat hell out of the Dodgers. I helped Marilyn with the TV dinners.

After supper when we'd ditched the plates and adjudicated the kids' argument over whose turn it was to slosh the cutlery clean, Greg and I chanced into talking about boat motors and that carried us for about an hour until Greg began to sound like a broken record again and I drifted off. The problem with Greg was that although he was a fairly intelligent man he had exactly two viewpoints to his name, and he eventually brought every imaginable subject in the world around to one or the other of these postulates. The first involved his theory about losers and winners in our society, and the second involved his first wife's alleged sexual problems as a demonstration of the dangers of dedicated feminism. You could begin talking about nothing more meaningful than a pair of shoes yet within five minutes those shoes would have become the quintessential example of his first wife's sexual obsessions or of the woes of our current welfare state. As a result our conversations had become shorter and shorter during the past few years, as I became less and less inclined to have my every new topic of conversation reduced to two increasingly tedious molds.

"He's getting up, he's getting up!" Cherie yelled from the window, banging a fork on the countertop. "His head's coming out of the plastic."

We all scrambled indecorously to the window and squinted into the gloom; it was already well after sundown and even the light above the ocean was almost gone. He was sitting up half out of his bag, still hooded and facing the ocean, his arms levering him slowly to a crouching, then standing position. Without looking back or around, he headed stiffly toward the water and vanished around the dark side of one of the great rock clusters at the surf's low-tide edge. We all stood around the window staring at the spot where he'd disappeared.

"There he is!" Cherie squealed again, and we saw the shape of his head and upper torso rise above the top of the rocks, now completely black in silhouette. He stood motionless on the rock facing the sea, and that's where we left him when we finally tired of staring at the unchanging tableau. He just stood there unmoving, fading in the oncoming night.

"He's *still* there," Marilyn noted two hours later as we prepared for bed. "You can just see him when the lighthouse beam swings around this way."

That night I watched him for a long time through the van's windows, standing until just before dawn in the steady drizzle on the rock. Every seventh second the searchlight lit him up like a ghoulish apparition; during the intervening six seconds he did not exist. At four-thirty in the morning he finally climbed off the rock and returned to his sleeping bag, wrapped himself up with inordinate care and finally subsided into the by now familiar cocoon.

The next morning I didn't join the expedition into town ("Goddamn bitch!" Greg growled to me under his breath. "You can have them!"). When the van left I set off across the sand toward Frank Island instead, feeling mostly jumpy, tired and irritable all at the same time. There was an old eagle's nest on the island I'd discovered years before, and I felt I ought to go sit there for a while to settle out. It was just a plan for the sake of a plan; I had no particular idea in mind. I simply felt pressured by too many vague and contrary impulses. The last two weeks had begun to make me feel increasingly like a restless crowd.

I ambled along the glossy wet sand just ahead of the waves, idly watching the sandpipers scurrying about like little bright mice at their feeding, bemused by the way they seemed to share their every emotion in perfect unison, like an entire aerobatic team wired into the same nervous system. The fog and mist had disappeared clear back to the horizon and I could see the tiny gillnetters and trawlers dipping and yawing out there, their stabilizers extended and their silver net-drums flashing like Morse code signals in the intermittent sun. I sat down on a rock and watched them, feeling an odd mixture of pleasure and annoyance. From a distance most things almost made sense, almost always seemed explicable. Up close it was always another story. "Wrong question," the boxer had told me at the Alcazar pub, before he'd gotten drunk and changed his story. "I don't know who I am any more than you do, and anyway, who gives a shit. They just keep comin' and I just keep knockin' em down." He'd taken a long swallow, shrugged. "Oh well, one of these days I guess I'll run into some lanky sonofabitch who won't go down. Around about then I'll probably find out a few things I don't know now. Maybe a few things I always wanted to know. But right now I just figure I'm the best there is, and that's enough for me." He grinned at me a bit conspiratorially and winked. "I'm not," he acknowledged, and there was a trace of something like pride in the admission. "But I'm sure as hell convinced I am."

At Frank Island the eagle's nest wasn't there anymore. Somebody had torn it from the cliff and left it scattered among the salal. I sat on the cliff top for a while anyway, watching the surf. On my way back I picked up four sand dollars for the kids, and an odd bit of root driftwood that looked like a Chinese character for something.

As I rounded the rocks just ahead of our camp I suddenly saw the biologist out of his wrappings, rummaging about in his plastic bags.

I ducked immediately and pulled back, circling rapidly to the other side of the trailer, easing quickly through the door and pulling it shut behind me. The curtains were drawn and I pulled them apart slightly, just enough to get a good view of what was going on. He was crouched there in profile, still digging around in the bag, and when he finally found what he was looking for it was a large nailbrush with which he proceeded to scrub his hands. He scrubbed vehemently, without water, drawing the stiff brushes slowly but harshly along the lengths of his very long fingers, continuing this for almost an hour, stopping every now and then to inspect the result. Finally he stood up abruptly, threw the brush back into the bag and flapped his hands briskly as if flicking off sprays of water. The gesture was not triumphant or contented but rather adamant or even angry. He continued to flap and flap like some stiff malfunctioning bird, hopping forward and back on one foot, then the other. Then he stopped, slipped back into his sleeping bag and wrapped himself up very carefully, as before.

That night all hell broke loose on the beach. It began with the balky propane valve which plugged or jammed, effectively knocking out the trailer's entire support system. At one blow we lost our light, heat and cooking facilities, and the water pump's manual override drew only the thinnest trickle of water from the tanks. After a supper of cold pork and beans we tried to salvage the evening by pulling our lawnchairs close to the campfire and breaking out several cases of beer, but within a short time Greg and I were arguing drunkenly and Donna was chiming in wherever she could. An hour later we had reached the shouting stage and not long after, Greg managed to throw out some remark that scored a direct hit on some unshielded part of my circuitry and I blew up.

"You narrow-minded fatuous goddamn hypocrite!" I remember bellowing at him, summing up two years of accumulated petty irritations. "If you've got to spend your life acting like a mindless robot, you can damn well clank around by yourself; I've got some more flesh-and-blood living to do!" I flung my beer furiously into the fire and stormed off into the night, so livid I could hardly see my own feet for the first five minutes and kept stumbling over driftwood and rocks. I couldn't remember ever having been so outraged in my life; I kept feeling as if I were watching me from some numbed, out-of-bounds corner of myself, utterly astonished at my capacity for wrath and insult.

I stomped down and then back up the entire length of the beach several times, until I'd cooled down enough to take my bearings—finding myself at that point not far from the cluster of rocks the biologist had climbed and stood on for so many hours the night before. Leaning against the barnacle-encrusted slope of stone and kicking distractedly at tangles of kelp at its base, I caught myself wondering just what the strange bastard might be thinking right about now—he must have heard everything; he'd been lying only twenty feet away.

I looked around me at the night and the surf; the beach black and exhausted like an empty battlefield. Far in the distance to the south of Frank Island a beach party was underway with bonfires and cars; to the west at a lesser distance, partly shielded by the van and trailer, the campfire and gesticulating couple flickered faintly through the telescoped dark. I pushed myself off the rock and trudged slowly closer to the van, having no plan in particular, even feeling somewhat displeased at the direction I was taking. I had no intention of returning to the camp at this stage.

As I neared the fire the voices began to rise. I could see Donna jumping up from her chair occasionally, hammering her beer on the armrest in protest or emphasis, and Greg leaning closer and closer, stabbing his forefinger at her face. The kids were nowhere to be seen. I tried to catch some of the argument but was still too far away and now disinclined to come closer; I wanted no further conversation with any of them that night. Suddenly Donna lunged out of her seat, cried out something with a vehemence that registered sharply even at the distance I was from them both, and stumbled blindly from the fire, heading straight toward me in the dark.

The move caught me completely off guard. For a moment I froze in an irresolute panic. Then I began to back quickly into deeper darkness, but had moved only half a dozen steps when it abruptly paled all around me. A set of headlights swept down from the south end of the island, illuminating the shore with a rapidly brightening aurora, an upsurge of brilliance, blazing, until, for a few seconds, the entire beach was lit with an almost neon intensity. And in that paralyzing light we were all helplessly exposed, transfixed like the startled hunted and the fleeing, the perfidious nightstalker in us all pitilessly revealed, our shadows grotesquely stretched into long guilty giants, hugely surreptitious and furtive—

Then the light abruptly narrowed and fell, plunging the beach back into darkness, as the car veered off the shore and aligned with the road, now dipping and lunging drunkenly along its length. And suddenly I thought good Christ! it's heading straight for that damned biologist, he's lying right on the road, they'll run right over his head, he's a goner for sure! And an instant later I saw him rear up in the twin beams like some crazed prophet overwhelmed by the impossible radiance of God, and the car spun, fishtailed, spun and fishtailed again and leaped straight toward the sea, roaring, plunging, and then it hit the rock. I watched the headlights dive into the sand, the bright tail-lights lift and loop crazily through the dark and then the heavy whomp! of bursting metal and glass, a second whomp!! of exploding gas and then the brilliant bouquet of flame engulfing all. For a few seconds the blaze had me totally fascinated, mesmerized.

Then we poured out of the darkness toward the flames: Donna, Greg, I, Marilyn, Cherie, people we'd never seen before, other campers, participants of the party at Frank Island. By the time I got there someone was already clawing at the left front door, the only one not bent out of shape by the impact. Inside I could see a dim scrabbling, a frantic twisting of arms and legs and torsos that spilled out onto the sand as the door broke free, disentangling into two young men, whitefaced and laughing and strange. They paid no attention to their rescuers at all, simply stood by the burning hulk without seeming to see it, babbling something about the face, the face, every few moments convulsing with a frantic hilarity that was at first unnerving and then quite frightening. Most of the onlookers quickly drifted back into deeper shadows, some disappearing altogether; during the occasional upleap of flames I could see their pale floating faces or the flash of spectacles among the rocks just beyond the circle of light.

When someone finally led the youths away, some of the onlookers crept back for a short time, staring at the wreck in silence or commenting on it in low voices. The flames were already beginning to shorten, the shape of the hulk regaining its outline, looking for all its mechanical accoutrements like an enormous upended insect exhausted by the struggle to regain its feet. When the flames flared slightly now and then you could almost see it twitching. Later when the flames had disappeared completely, the entire skeleton glowed a deep, almost translucent red, with tiny brightly starred sparks sputtering along the shell. It was then that I noticed the headlights still glaring; somehow the battery had escaped the flames and was still feeding current to the bulbs.

I turned to point this out to someone and found everyone gone. The twin beams pointed directly at our camp and lit both trailer and van quite brightly. Through the window I could see blankets and pillows being moved around, the occasional flash of an arm or leg and now and then a white face, eyes shielded against the light, staring irritably through the glass. Finally a dark blanket dropped against the window and the movement stopped.

I returned to the van and climbed into my sleeping bag. The headlights from the wreck shone in through the windows and reflected from glass to glass. It was impossible to sleep.

Annoyed, I got up again and unpacked a blanket to cover the windshield. As I walked to the front of the van I saw the biologist in his usual place, rolled up inside his piece of plastic. The cocoon gleamed in the headlights, a soft, iridescent green.

On abrupt impulse, without really thinking, I straddled the prone body, reached for the plastic flap and yanked. The face shot from between the folds of the sleeping bag, blinked once in the glare of the headlights and froze.

I stared. Before me was a face. What I was staring at was certainly a face. But what I was staring *into* were its eyes, as big as portholes and aghast as gulls. Seething inside those eyes, from horizon to horizon as far back as sight could reach, so densely packed it was painful to watch, were billions upon billions of microbial people, as tiny and shimmering and frantic as bacilli, a limitless, tossing sea of miniscule heads and shoulders and fists. They were all facing away from me, clamouring urgently, waving toward some distant point.

In my head I heard the confusion of my responses like brief overflows of sound through doors along a corridor. A short spill of astonishment abruptly caught and mopped up. A half-roar of laughter snapped on and quickly off. A low growl of fear unlocked, then promptly slammed and barred. More sounds and their echoes, from doors in me not yet opened or tried. Then towels and blankets hurriedly stuffed into cracks and hung over windows. Finally only silence, the corridor empty, nothing. I just kept staring, not moving a thought, just waiting for the sound of my breath to return. And then one of the tiny people, happening to turn around, caught sight of me.

Or maybe it was the suddenly open eyes that attracted him. Or her. (It was impossible to tell.) In any case, it yelled and waved, and then some others turned to look, and then I could see into their eyes as well, as more and more of them turned and stared, and I saw the sudden glints, the early tremors of idea, the abrupt widening of irises, deepening and filling with relentless intention and possibility, like the first atoms loosening their grip on the beginnings of a landslide. Abruptly, in a flash I realized what was about to happen, but in that burst of realization, I lost my nerve as well.

Flinging the plastic back over the face I lunged up and into the headlight glare, stumbling along the beam until I had reached the overturned wreck. With two wild blows of a piece of rock I smashed the sealed bulbs, glass bursting from their casings and spilling over my boots. Immediately, our camp, the biologist and the beach disappeared. I stood immersed in total darkness. So dark, I couldn't even see myself.

And while I stood there, waiting for my eyes to adjust to the surrounding night, I began to realize the extent to which it was possible that nobody was saying what everyone had been seeing; the extent to which we were all committed to the same conspiracy; the extent to which we had all become hopelessly indebted to our own extortionate fraud—a swindle that had insinuated its million tentacles among us so quietly, we could no longer afford to admit we were thoroughly compromised. It was as if it had somehow managed to become part of the air, that we inhaled with every breath and against which we no longer had any defenses. If you listened very carefully you could almost hear it, a faint presence like a far-off humming, like the distant murmur of a turning world, grating implacably on its axis.

I dropped the piece of rock and walked slowly back to the van. In the continuing dark I felt around under the seats for a carpet bag I remembered putting there, and when I found it, filled it with whichever of my possessions I could find. Then I closed the van doors, zipped up my jacket and headed off down the beach, toward the road.

It was probably pointless, there was probably no defense against it, but on the other hand you could never be sure. With any kind of luck and a little traffic, I could conceivably be elsewhere by noon.

ROBERT SHERRIN

I've published one novel, and my short fiction and non-fiction have appeared in magazines in Canada, Switzerland, and Scotland. I am also an exhibiting visual artist.

"North by North by North" is the second of a trilogy of stories set on a BC coastal steamer and is based on my experiences while working on such a vessel to earn money to pay for my studies at UBC. The trilogy was published originally in The Capilano Review *in 1980.*

North By North By North

Vukovich threatened me last night
    I'd been in the hold he'd been in the can showering terrified again by the great distance between his birth place and where he is now I don't think he was used to being constantly in motion scared of water scared of lifeboats scared of men living in close quarters His bunk was like a berth on an old European train all dark shrouded with tattered blue bedsheets canopied like the beds of kings shut tight like the dwelling places of peasants
    Vukovich has a bread knife sharp when he stole it from the pantry sharper now that he went ashore yesterday and bought a stone oil and a big bottle of vodka He liked me to walk with him through the old parts of Ketchikan on the elevated boardwalks past the shacks that we told him are the gathering places of whores at night
    We don't really know We tie up at 1600 and cast off at 1800 We've never seen darkness there but Vukovich would touch my shoulder when we walked keeping watch He was taller than I You wouldn't like him
    He had a hairy chest tufts on his back and after a shower smelled of damp mutton He used to talk about priests then he talked about fucking and killing
    He kept his knife in his bunk slept on his back one hand on his thigh the other above his head draped over a cord always near the knife that lay like a hard short snake on the roof of his bunk
    Vukovich sleeps
when he sleeps at all
right below me

He knows you He talks about you asks about you wants to hear what

you smell like feel like taste like His is the curiosity of a child   coming
out in quiet bursts in the Cook's Mess when we huddle over our plates
before the last sitting   or in the room after breakfast when I lie on the
deck and slip my feet under a barbell and begin my situps
  two hundred and fifty
  That's when Vukovich talks
  I go   one   two   three
  He goes   She must have soft feet   she must taste salty between her
breasts   she must smell like parfait   He laughs   that softslow softslow
soft thudding of breath
  I count as I go up and down   saying yes to everything he says as my
sweat comes out   my hot back hitting the cool deck   my hot back hitting
the cool
  where it sounds like fire but the white is like snow giving way as we fall
into a drift   All our little senses are tuned to distant transmitters where
our skins are maps of little river valleys cooling   Our skins are suddenly
inside us   no more talk   no more motion   just the cradle of our rocking   and no more thought   just the echo of it slipping into the small lakes
above Skagway   so hot so cold   pulling you in and cooling you off and
taking you away   We talk no more   We lie in our cool crackling like
stilled engines
  Now   again   my wet back on the cool deck
  Vukovich's feet dangle over his bed   a peach in his mouth fingers wiping his lips   chest dark with hair   and his slippers busted open at the
sides   hanging off his toes like a gaffed fish coming over the side
  Vukovich sits with his knife beside him
  saying you must be a good one
  saying you must practise a lot
  Vukovich who waits for me on sailing nights so he can watch me change
and see the marks on my back   and if we're alone
  like we always are
  you and I in your satin sheets   or on your father's leather couch   or
your mile wide wall to wall   All our limbs are interlocked because we
have only a few hours   then it's another 8 days and I never know if you'll
be there   Sometimes after I return to the ship and you return to your
father's house I tremble   and for a huge stalled moment dream of Jayne
Mansfield   blonde hair bobbing   breasts still desperately jiggling   the
wreck slewing away and her eyes unfocused   her head so softly bouncing   I see you in the Healey rounding the curves   missing a shift   hitting
a wall   or being with someone else who wants you to drive him afterwards
  then we're back on the floor
  then I'm back on the ship and Vukovich watches me change waiting
until my shirt comes off so he can look at my back and trace the red with

his slow finger   I know he is thinking of knives
I know this as my wet back hits the cool deck
one last time
and I say 250
while Vukovich's leg dangles from his bunk

Last night I was in the hold   Vukovich was in the shower standing with
his back to the curtain   feet in his old leather slippers going mushy in the
water   He is suspicious of places where men gather in groups   so scared
of disease he doesn't sit on the toilet seats   but on his hands and shits
between them   He always covers himself but he looks at others   watches
for it   wants to know
what?
if they look the same   work the same   want the same
Some of us want release
Some of us want satisfaction
Vukovich wants out   so he stays away from most of us   leery of men in
naked groups   afraid of men who touch themselves with their towels   show themselves to each other and talk about it   joke about it and
want it all the time and would probably put it in one another just to find
that release
that sad satisfaction
that getting out of oneself   that all of us want
But Vukovich won't talk about it   He speculates as he showers alone
with his back to the curtain   and yes   we all shower alone but sometimes
there are others in the room or in another stall while the water beats us up
and makes us hot and some of us
who are like me
cover our ears as we lean into the sound of aircraft   pretending we're not
in a shower stall on a passenger steamer always going north   Some of us
who are like me
weave back and forth in the water that pounds down   We listen for that
total silence which means we are truly alone in the company of others   Our backs are to the curtain as we move into and out of   into and
out of the beating water
And we know who we are
and why we want no one to know
we are just like those who are like me
So last night Vukovich was in the shower with his knife   he was moving
behind the curtain and I was below him in the hold   way way down in the
V of the ship where I'd stretched myself on a slanted board in my shorts   I
took three deep breaths and began to sit up and lie down   sit up and lie
down   while Udo worked the weights   grunting   his pecs puffing out
and falling back until he couldn't lift the weight anymore   He was wet

and his shorts stuck to him   So he lay on the deck and counted for me as I went up and down and thought of

how you put your thumb into the waistband of your Cigarette jeans or your Fiorucci jeans or your C Kleins   how you sometimes slide your hands into the front of them with just your thumbs showing   move back and forth on your heels and accuse me of being suspicious   accuse me of being possessive   of being intolerable

Udo counted and rolled to his side and his gut went in and out as he closed his eyes and spoke numbers   His breath was soft and rocked

back and forth on your heels until I start to imitate you and you start to smile and we both get into the Healey and drive to your father's house

He has money   so you have money and you do what people are supposed to do with money   buying things   using them then throwing them away   People with money buy things and people without money sell things and people with nothing get bought and sold

We went to your father's place because he has all these things: the lean steak in the walk-in cooler and the Jamaican woman who minces it for us   the heavy plates she puts it on   the silver forks we use to lift it to our mouths   and the crystal to hold the wine   the speakers that release Steve Reich   and the big rooms that are always empty because luxury means having a lot of waste   Your father has a great deal of waste and we used it   rolling in his empty rooms until we went to your room and danced in the mirrors   then played over and under your satin sheets   They look like water in the sunlight   They sound like fire when we move

Last night my back was wet and the slanted board was coarse   soaking me up as Udo counted to 180 where I stopped   too weak to talk but he reached up and pulled me down   We lay on the cool deck saying nothing   he dry now   me wet   water moving all around us   After a time I got up   Udo said he needed a shower   and I did too   so we marked our numbers on the chart and climbed the ladder out of the hold

I was making for the can   towel around my waist   Udo was in his cabin looking at a skin mag with Moon and they nodded to me and called me in and showed me a blonde woman with big breasts on a couch   with a pig   She looked like she was having an enema   but she wasn't   She looked bored and the pig looked bored and the men in the room who looked at Moon's books were very quiet   No one said a word   No one was excited   They all looked disappointed   I closed the mag   It was called BIZARRE and I gave it back   I wanted a shower   I wanted to be clean

Udo spoke to Moon

He said it was sick

Moon nodded   It was   He'd been aboard eleven years   almost half a million miles   always going north

I was in the can   It was quiet   I took off my towel and looked at my

body   It was stained with sweat   I pulled my skin   It was tight   I
tapped it and it responded like a drum   then I stretched and felt dizzy for
a moment but looked down at my feet in their plastic thongs and I felt
better   I moved forward and yanked at the curtain and was going to step
into the shower when I saw Vukovich   He wheeled   The water wasn't
running   There was no sound   just the light and the darkness of Vukovich turning   and he was still turning   body twisted   stiff with himself   His one hand moved to cover it or to pull it down while the other
snaked out and whipped back and I stood there seeing but not knowing
seeing but not seeing
then the knife was coming and it flashed loudly   screamed silver
and   there it was   moving at my face   and I was seeing it but not knowing it and I was hearing Vukovich's voice cut at me   hearing the can door
being pushed open   then I was pulling back and smelling the fever of the
knife as it went near to my face   Then it went away from me   but its
voice and its smell stayed behind   Udo was yanking me away   reaching
at the same time for Vukovich but Vukovich was yelling and spelling
things with his knife
I kill you
He was spelling it out for me   I KILL YOU
He was talking to me   I KILL ALL OF YOU
He'll always be talking to me

Then he was in his towel and he was gone   I was sitting on the floor and I
was sick to my stomach   Udo removed his towel and cleaned me
off   stood me in the shower   talked to me from the other side of the
curtain while the water beat me and I saw you in your father's bathroom
under the silver water as it hits you and hits you and hits you till you step
out   and someone hands you a towel
because someone will always hand you a towel   part of the difference
between us
I felt the water hit me and I leaned into it as I felt you lean into yours
alone in your father's house except for the one who hands you a towel
wipes you off   powders your skin   and touches you more than I do
serves you better than I do
loves you like nobody else
because she really belongs to you since your father told her so
My father told me to bend my knees when I lift and not always do what
others tell me to
Your father tells others to do exactly what you ask of them
So I lean into my father's wishes
and you lean into yours
Now I'm under the water knowing Vukovich wants to kill me because I
saw him stiff

I'm under the water that beats me while you're having the water tow-
elled from your body   thinking only of yourself while I'm thinking that
I'm always heading north with Vukovich in the bunk under mine

And now   today   Last night still threatens me after I showered and after
Udo told me he'd look out for me   I dressed and went to the galley to eat
eggs and talk to Vukovich but he wasn't there
   So I ate eggs   did them for 3 minutes in boiling water
   and lopped their tops off with a spoon
   and dipped toast into them
   left 3 empty shells on the table in the Cook's Mess
   I went to the fantail but Vukovich wasn't there   went to the hotbox
but Vukovich wasn't there   went to the wops' room but no Vukovich   went back to Moon   nothing   Udo told me to sleep in a different
bunk   Moon told me to drink 151 overproof   A saloonsman gave me 4
lines of coke
   I went back to my room   No Vukovich
   I breathed it in and out all night
   no Vukovich   no Vukovich   no Vukovich   no Vukovich

I dreamed of you while the night saloonsman Silvoed the tableware and
placed fresh linen on the deuces   I dreamed of you in your father's house
telling Marianne that I was not staying for dinner but that I was staying
for lunch and that she could have the afternoon off or else she'd have to
stay on the main floor
   Whichever you prefer Marianne
   I dreamed you loved me as the night saloonsman grilled steaks for
himself and his two juniors   I dreamed you waited for me   read books
for me   and wrote letters to me while the night saloonsman talked religion with the night baker   eating his steak rare with lots of onion and HP
and a piece of pie right from the baker's oven   I dreamed you shorter than
you are with hair longer than it is   I dreamed you in your Healey waiting
to drive me south at season's end   I dreamed you dreaming me back to
you   I dreamed you showered while the night saloonsman took the call
from Moon and donned his white tunic   buttoned up the brass buttons   and went to the galley to prepare 2 tea   toast and marmalade for
the bridge   I dreamed you drove too fast while the saloonsman vacuumed
and I felt the Healey going over me looking at myself on the roadway
looking up at a cop   my hand reaching over   swaying like a bullrush but
half my face is in blood and the cop can't answer   wouldn't answer
because I won't ask him   I feel the wet and I lie back on the cool
pavement under the flashing lights after midnight at the corner of Broad-
way and Macdonald   I dreamed the answer to my question but you
didn't   just the cops and the lights and the wet and the cool as the night

saloonsman finished up and rang the engineers to go on watch   I dreamed you over and over until the night saloonsman came in and rocked me on the shoulder

0600   he said to me in his soft voice

I pushed you away and rolled over   got up   donned my stripes   and saw that Vukovich wasn't there

I felt tired   as if I'd dreamed my sleep away   I pulled on my shoes and headed straight for the can   the night saloonsman ahead of me

He was already in the can   turning to me   eyes wide   His eyes were wide as mouths   His hands were pulling at the collar of his tunic and his ankles were awash with water   He was moving his feet up and down like a bewildered child trapped in a puddle of mud

The water sounded like eggs frying

And the water was the colour of the roses on your satin sheets   For a moment I saw you in bed then I saw the night saloonsman turn to look again and turn to look again

and turn to look at me

He was gagging into his hands

His voice was like air pulling on an edge of steel   It said nothing but it told all one has to know

So I stepped into the rosewater and saw you stepping from your shower   your footprint on the brown carpet as I heard my feet hit the water and someone pushing on the can door behind me

So I touched the night saloonsman and nudged him to one side and looked

There was Vukovich   his back to the curtain and the water beating him   his buttocks plugging the drain   and the water lapping over his legs to carry the rose colour out of the stall

There was Vukovich with the curtain pinned by his shoulders and his face turned up to take the hits of water and the rose colour all over him

There he was with his mouth open   teeth showing

There he was with his throat cut   open   like a mouth under his mouth   like the distended gills of a fish coming over the side   still in water but no longer something that swims

So they put him on ice in the hold and no one lifted weights for the rest of the cruise   They took the knife out of his hand   gave it to the cops who came for him when we docked again in Vancouver

The cops looked down at him and said nothing

You waited a long time for me while I talked to the cops who asked me things I couldn't answer   who made me hot   who made me sweat through my shirt   made me sit there on the cold steel chair

And I thought of you   and the marks you'd leave on me that no one saw when I returned to the ship tonight.

HEATHER SPEARS

Heather Spears was born in Vancouver in 1934 and has lived in Denmark since 1962. She was educated at UBC, where she was a poetry editor for *Prism International* in its beginnings, and attended the Vancouver School of Art. She has published six collections of poetry, the last two being winners of the Pat Lowther Memorial Award. She is also an artist, and has concentrated on drawing newborn and premature infants, and recently on children of the Palestinian Intifada. She travels and exhibits and lectures extensively with her work both in Europe and America. She received the Governor General's Award for Poetry in 1990.

The two poems included here were written in Vancouver during visits from Denmark. Living in Europe, in a "permissive" welfare state, I am struck by the bizarre aspects of Canadian society, in these instances, the appeals for donations to the sick and the extreme fascination with sexual deviation (I was making courtroom drawings here in 1986).

Powell Street Bus, Vancouver

Every second bus ad
between the ones for Skytrain, stockings and sun lotion
is a demand for money
by Associations of the Sick.
The smiling mother
flanked by (and embracing) her smiling children—
a boy and a girl—
is quoted as hoping there will soon be a cure
for cystic fibrosis:
"this genetic killer
of children and young adults."
Which goes without saying.

Why is she smiling?
Her children are doomed.
But then we all are,
not even more or less.
The beautiful smiles of the children
who after all did not ask to be born
are sincere if posed,

and nobody's coughing.
There are pockets of joy in the worst of lives—
even the ones
that get worse

Robert Noyes
B.C. Supreme Court, 12–13 February 1986

Having drawn you for two days
over and over (the same drawing,
because I sit in the same seat
and because I am accurate)
and now, standing at the bus stop
with the last light
changing the inner contours of the North Shore mountains
the way, at 2 PM, from some high window
it found its way to your cheek and defined
the quivering masseter, muscle of pain,

I realize that I am standing in your body, that my eyes
and hand have taken in more than I intended,
the sullen slope
of your shoulders in the beige corduroy
jacket becomes me, the lifted
narrow chin and eyes
slightly lowered to compensate—
looking straight ahead—
guarded and candid
blurred and intolerably vulnerable

but it was tolerable: I drew,
the glass wall between you and free people
contained you like an isolette (I am used to this)
there are actually 2 drawings
because sometimes you'd lean forward
and all I saw
was the corduroy pulled across your back
and the crown of your head
and the fingers of one hand
that supported your face.

You have listened to your life
as a series of letters and assessments
by bewildered headmasters
and discomfited psychiatrists

behind which the romping bodies of small boys
the colour of my "skin-colour" pastel
were allowed to hover
within reach of the memory
that persists in your hands
hanging empty from your wrists

an "excellent dedicated teacher"
who touched inappropriate people
very inappropriately

angry citizens in badges
are sitting upright behind me
repulsed and fascinated—
in the breaks, their seething for justice
brims into words

the voice of the lawyer
continues, the judge slumps
and fingers his chin,
you are judged, are here to be judged
"dangerous"—
still in your body my mind speaks:
"By good fortune
I did not hate but
by bad fortune I loved
and fell from grace
like an angel
leaving a red gouge in the sky
irreparable"

RICHARD STEVENSON

Richard Stevenson (b. 1952) graduated with an MFA in Creative Writing from UBC in 1984 and was editor-in-chief of *Prism International* in 1983/4. His books include *Driving Offensively*, *Suiting Up*, *Horizontal Hotel*, *Wiser Pills*, and *Whatever It Is Plants Dream* (all poetry titles).

I thought it best to choose three poems from my three most recent books (all appearing in 1990). Since I work in a variety of styles and tend to write both personal and political poems, I thought showing the poet as father, social observer, and metaphysician might give an idea of my writing concerns and aesthetics.

New Black Shoes
for Marika

Gangway grannies! Heads up grandpas!
Single Moms with sullen broods in tow,
Christmas shoppers with coin slots for mouths
unstitch your brows, open Al Jolson eyes.

Marika's got new black patent leather shoes!
Is a bowling ball rolling clickety clack
down the mall. Nothing short of a potted palm
will stop her. She smiles in each shiney toe.

She doesn't need to click her heels thrice
and repeat "There's no place like home"
to get from Oz to wherever she's going,
and this sure as hell ain't Kansas!

Planets, whole galaxies of Christmas lights
gleam back from those toes. "I'm Dorfy, Mom.
I'm Dorfy!" she exclaims.   Look at me go!
The wizard, whatsisname's got nothing on me.

So who cares if he's off on a coffee break
and none of his photo-taking elves are on seat.
This ain't Oz or the North Pole, Mom, but I've got
black patent leather shoes. I'm Dorfy. I'm me.

Why Does It Cry So

Why does it cry so? Mohammed asks,
our electric iron sputtering, spewing
water in his hand. Why does ours cry
when his doesn't? I think: electricity,
heating coil, boiling water, steam.

How marvelous that he should be
so ignorant of this thing we take for granted;
how exciting to be able to see
God's mysterious ways working
the creases into my pants.

How sad that Mohammed
should feel the compunction to be
so god-damned polite in asking us
if he could use ours to iron his.
We feel embarrassed and humbled too

that ours should have such a forked tail
and depend on such transfusions
as the god of electricity will allow.
How far the cord has really stretched
that we should find our shirts
floating like kites with so many keys attached.

Split-Leaf Philodendron
monstero deliciosa

"Monstera deliciosa, Monstera deliciosa . . ."
the split leaves mutter to themselves.
You'd swear they were just coming to
or were amnesiac—were dreaming
whatever it is plants dream when
under sedation. You ply their lips
with a little water. Buff the leaves
to a high gloss with a soft cloth
and mineral oil. The stems sweat

"Where am I? What am I doing here?
Who are you?" echoes the blue pseudo-
pod of the TV screen. The mad scientist
leans over his new busty creation.
She props herself up on her elbows,
her eyes growing white with fear
as she discovers for the first time
the nature of her growing predicament.

Were all this coming to the plant in Latin
it might empathize with the poor woman.
As things are it is difficult enough
to bifurcate into another couple of leaves—
what with the interrogation of the Gro-lamp,
the shock of cold water you give the roots.
This could be Eden. You, the good doctor,
bent on resplendent naugahyde, suddenly see
your own reflection. Are buffing apples again.

DONA STURMANIS

After obtaining my MFA in Creative Writing, my first job was working as a waitress. Money was not forthcoming from my poems and short stories, but I was determined to make a living as a writer. I became a freelance journalist and writing teacher, which is what I do now. The creative writing, happily, has persevered in spare time. I have had poems published steadily in little magazines, and hope to issue a collection soon. For the last four years I have also been working on a biography of the late Pat Lowther.

The two poems here are recently written. "When Two Funny Ladies Died in One Month" signifies two of the very few current events serious enough to personally upset me. "Bag Lady" is reflective of my ongoing attempts to master relationships with the opposite sex. My son Leif, who's seven, takes after me by talking too much and reading until he gets a headache at night.

When Two Funny Women Died in One Month

When I-Love-Lucy died
there was a federal budget leak
and I constructed progress charts
for the annual report
of a stock exchange about to fall

When Saturday-Night-Live-Gilda expired
Chinese students staged a hunger strike
and with my son I watched Japanese
drum dancers at a children's festival
while the sun leapt in the sky

When I realized something funny was missing
the evening news was boring
the rain pelted ferocious
and I was doing nothing

Comics to the end,

these gals of the guffaw.
After the unsuccessful heart operation,
Lucy sat up and asked
if the dog had been fed.
In her last interview, before she was dead,
Gilda told husband Gene,
When I'm gone those ladies are going to beat down your door,
you could really make it fun and obscene.

Lucy was my titter lady
when I was a little kid,
and lay with the measles in bed. .
Gilda made me lighten up
when I was a teenager
and thought everyone
was sick in the head.

If Lucy could chuckle
through hiroshimas, macarthyisms,
bays of pigs, luthermurders,

If Gilda could giggle
through mylais and watergates
ayatollahs and oil spills,

What woman will come forward to laugh
when the greenhouse effect
has blocked out the sun?

To make jokes and throw pies
when the nuclear stores
of the world go off all at once?

Will it be God as a woman
amused for a moment in the darkness
as she spies the tiny exploding light
called Earth and whispers
to some universal companion,
"I told you so?"

Bag Lady

When you came to me
you thought all of it
was neatly packaged
carefully labelled & stored
to be opened as you came to
or needed it:
family in cupboard
kids in fridge
needs of the spirit
in a box
love special clothing
to be worn
until it wore out
& you an efficient journeyer
til you met me the bag lady
who wore all her clothes at once
carried all her packs
in a big shopping cart
how does a streamlined traveller
deal with a walking household
items always moving
but always a mess
you can roll the shopping cart
down the hill
you can grab away
the suitcases and paperbags
and leave them in the bushes
but undressing me
is a different matter
it takes forever
to reach the orderly heart

FRED WAH

Fred Wah is from the Kootenays. He attended UBC, the University of New Mexico, and State University of New York at Buffalo. He has taught at Selkirk College, David Thompson University Centre, and the University of Calgary. He won the Governor General's Award for Poetry in 1986. His most recent book is *Limestone Lakes Utaniki* (Red College Press) and his present project is a biotext, *Season's Greetings from the Diamond Grill*.

The writing I'm interested in working on at the moment includes a kind of verse-novel biotext, a series of critical poems, Music at the Heart of Thinking, *and the usual address to spiritual geography. These pieces should indicate that range.*

Artknot 13

Marian Dennis Running Arms
Susan Penner Curly Hair
Bald-like Sleigh Machine
Pyramid Wheeler Outstretched Seattle

                                 Moon
flight crayon pink plywood backing
for christmas une guerre civile 1971
memory embraces on the lawn chair
her legs (Susan's?) disappear 1977 1987
whistling

(Biotext fragment #57)

What anima got through the family ghosts? Immediate meditation taken to each chakra as this hand holds out a stubble of language, body alone and a little pissed off.

Avalanche of news: something synaptic renumbered days and places as a gambled problem posed plot.

What about Sweden and Scotland and Ireland and Ontario? Or even Pender and Main some spring Sunday morning, quiet, on the way to the train station? Bottomed.

How about having her just talk her life or offer anything more than inherited impossible structures made up from no scratch?

She turns, over Saskatchewan, a large mother of place and love but bitter.

He, his eyes sparkle, brown finger with long, slim nail points to the green spot 8-spot and he smiles gold teeth as he takes his lottery book out of an overcoat pocket and slaps the worn pages on the cafe counter. His laugh.

Any more imprint shadowed on the rose? Pea inside the brain?

I'd get into Ruth's death business but

with those salmon over the lichen those lines over the lake
or up Arnica Hill (that's workable. that's work)
unlike rock of ages
her life's fountain words a full song of messages painting
the watercolour washes blue and then green and then red
rock herm along the road to her house
remember's where you are before you're there

                                                     Ursula

container drifts
out to painless sky
plantain rockbed possibly, possibility
between the creek and Shingley Beach
necessary love, Oh necessary, love
forget about it for meaning
her lake forages cats and donkeys all us family
and our little star fishes our deathing life
born for example not working but not to worry
dif fits into this slot
but that's the depth of this bridge
unlike

TOM WAYMAN

After working at many trades and occupations, most recently college teaching, Tom Wayman now lives on an estate near Nelson, BC. Squire Wayman's newest collection of poems is *In a Small House on the Outskirts of Heaven* (Harbour 1989).

I was a student of Earle Birney's in 1964–5, and his life then and after seems to me to approach mythic proportions. Hence my poem, "My Old Master." I've learned since that time that teaching involves both love and hate of your students, as I try to demonstrate in "Did I Miss Anything?"

Did I Miss Anything?
Question frequently asked by students after missing a class

Nothing.   When we realized you weren't here
we sat with our hands folded on our desks
in silence, for the full two hours

      Everything.   I gave an exam worth
      40 percent of the grade for this term
      and assigned some reading due today
      on which I'm about to hand out a quiz
      worth 50 per cent

Nothing.   None of the content of this course
has value or meaning
Take as many days off as you like:
any activities we undertake as a class
I assure you will not matter either to you or me
and are without purpose

      Everything.   A few minutes after we began last time
      a shaft of light descended and an angel
      or other heavenly being appeared
      and revealed to us what each woman or man must do
      to attain divine wisdom in this life and
      the hereafter
      This is the last time the class will meet

before we disperse to bring this good news to all people
    on earth

Nothing.   When you are not present
how could something significant occur?

      Everything.   Contained in this classroom
      is a microcosm of human existence
      assembled for you to query and examine and ponder
      this is not the only place such an opportunity has been
          gathered

      but it was one place

      And you weren't here

My Old Master

When my old master grew even more ancient
he climbed a tree.
"What are you doing up there?"
people on the ground yelled at him.
"I'm going to pick an apple
for my love," my master called over his shoulder,
not pausing in his ascent.
"I want to reenact the story in the Bible
the way it actually happened:
the man
gave Eve her apple."
"Nonsense," people shouted at his back.
"But even if it was true,
there is plenty of fruit
you can reach safely from the ground."
"I've seen those," my master said
as he clambered higher.
"They won't do for her.
I have to find her something faultless."
"You are far too elderly
to be fooling around in trees,"
the people screeched at him.
"Come down this instant."
"Love is never old," my master replied,
his voice only faintly audible.
His lanky, bony legs
were nearly out of sight.

Then he was gone.
Those standing under the tree
looked at each other and shook their heads.
"No fool like . . . ," one said,
not needing to finish the sentence
since the others already were nodding agreement.
"If a terrible accident happens to him
it will just serve him right," another said.
A pattering of applause
endorsed this statement.

As if on cue
from high above

they heard a crash
and the tearing of foliage.
"Now he's done it," somebody on the ground said
with great satisfaction.
Indeed, after a minute or two
they could begin to make out in the topmost part of the tree
the body of my old master
bouncing and
spinning and rebounding
apparently out of control
as he fell through the branches.

But to my old master, the sensations he was experiencing
were not as awful as those below him
hoped and feared.
"For some reason, this tree
has taken off like a rocket
leaving me suspended in midair,"
my master observed to himself as he travelled
now upright, now head over heels.
"This is more than a little thrilling
except I'm being beaten black and blue
by the limbs flying past.
Lucky I got as far as I did
before this extraordinary event occurred."
And sure enough, in a few more minutes
the watchers on the ground could see
that whatever position his body assumed
in its tumbling, painful descent
my old master continued to grin triumphantly
as he clutched in his outstretched hand
a perfect apple.

IAN WEIR

Ian Weir is a Vancouver-based playwright and novelist. His stage plays, which include *The Idler* and *The Delphic Orioles*, have been professionally produced in Canada, the United States, and England. In addition, he has written nine radio dramas (six produced by the CBC, and three by the BBC), and numerous episodes for television. His juvenile novel, *The Video Kid*, was recently published by Scholastic-TAB.

C'est la Guerre was commissioned in 1989 by Alberta Theatre Projects in Calgary, as part of their annual festival of new Canadian plays. It's actually the first "short" play I've written since I was a student in Doug Bankson's UBC playwriting class a decade ago—the class which must bear part of the blame for the fact that I am now a full-time playwright.

"C'est la Guerre"

CHARACTERS
Dinsdale, *a condemned man*
Laroche, *a Captain of the Legionnaires*
Thierry, *a Legionnaire*

SETTING
The desert. Shortly after dawn. The present.

LIGHTS UP ON . . .
An empty stage. A wall. Dinsdale stands against it, hands bound behind his back, awaiting execution. He faces the audience, but gazes steadily past them. Toward the horizon. Unflinching. A man among men.

DINSDALE The moment of our death is fixed in time. It cannot be altered, only faced. And our facing of that moment will define us.

Here. Now. Alone, under a merciless desert sky. In the brown desolation of endless sand. Eyes fixed upon a single green oasis in this wasteland of the soul. A solitary tree, and a pale blue pond of fish. A frail reminder of frailer life in this place of dusty death.

But alone. Alone, while the desert wind keens the passing of a man, and the black-flies moan his Requiem.

LAROCHE *(Off; barking)* Positions!
DINSDALE *(Heroically)* And so farewell. For it is a good place to die. A good time to die. I am ready.
LAROCHE *(Off)* Aim . . . !
THIERRY *(Off; suddenly)* Hang on. Where's Beauchamp?
Dinsdale looks off, startled.
LAROCHE *(Off)* Beauchamp?
THIERRY *(Off)* You said he could help with the execution.
LAROCHE *(Off)* Then where is he? *(Shouting)* Beauchamp?
Dinsdale looks around, momentarily unnerved.
LAROCHE *(Off)* Well, then someone go find him.
A murmur of off-stage voices from the firing squad. Laroche enters, carrying a sabre, and takes a couple of steps toward Dinsdale.
LAROCHE *(Apologetically)* Sorry. Slight delay. One of the lads . . .
DINSDALE *(Steeling himself again)* Captain. Pass on the message. I spit in his eye.
LAROCHE Beauchamp's?
DINSDALE Death's.
LAROCHE Ah. *(Nods approvingly)* Brave fellow.
Laroche exits. Dinsdale turns back to the audience.
DINSDALE C'est la guerre. This has always been an expression of mine.
Slight pause.
A pale blue pond with fish. I stood beside it last evening. A pale blue pond, and in it the reflection of a man.

It waits, you see. The moment of our death. Waits through all the nights and days and years. Hidden, just out of sight, with an icicle smile and a dagger beneath the cloak. It waits for us to come. And in that moment—this must be understood—in that moment lies the truth of each one of us. For a good death, a brave death, cancels out what came before. In that moment alone, we stand revealed. As we truly are. As we truly have been. All along. Even when this was not . . . well-understood.

I have not always been well-understood. C'est la guerre. But now my moment is come. And I am ready. *(Slight pause: shouting)* Ready!
Laroche pokes his head into view
LAROCHE *(Apologetically)* Yes, of course.

He disappears again.

LAROCHE *(Off)* So where is he?

THIERRY *(Off)* Yes, well that's the question.

LAROCHE *(Off)* But look—do we really *need* Beauchamp?

DINSDALE *(Beginning to lose his composure again)* No!

THIERRY *(Off)* We promised him, sir. And you know how disappointed he was to miss the last one.

DINSDALE We do not need bloody Beauchamp!

A moment, then Laroche enters

LAROCHE I'm terribly sorry about this . . .

DINSDALE Look! You've already got six men lined up. Six bullets, Captain—and I only have one heart.

LAROCHE *(Trying to ingratiate)* Still, an unusually large one . . .

DINSDALE Irrelevant!

LAROCHE But I promised him, you see. He's been looking forward for days. They don't have much of a life, poor lads—stuck in a desert, getting sand in their shorts and swatting at flies. This sort of thing is a treat.

DINSDALE But it's my death.

LAROCHE Yes, and it's shaping up as such a good one. We've taken note of this, and we're impressed. And if we could just impose on your time for a few more moments . . .

Laroche fishes a cigarette from his pocket, puts it between Dinsdale's lips, and hurries off (without lighting the cigarette). Dinsdale stares after him. Then he turns back to the audience.

DINSDALE *(Cigarette in mouth)* I used to smoke. It was something I did well. But Madeleine objected. My wife.

Spits out the cigarette.

Silly bitch. Not a bad silly bitch, in her way. Though there were many things she did not well-understand. She'd never understand this, for instance. Me, standing alone in this desert, awaiting the fatal volley in which all will be revealed . . .

The male spirit was a mystery to my wife. That primal need to dream, to dare, to sail tall ships and trek across burning sands. I tried to explain, once. She said, "why don't you go duck-hunting with your brother Bert?" I speak to her of endless oceans and perilous lands, and she speaks to me of ducks.

C'est la guerre. *(Pause, shouting)* Ready!

LAROCHE *(Off)* In a minute.

Pause.

DINSDALE There's the problem, you see. To be a man among men . . .

who lives among women. It saps the spirit. It becomes impractical to sail tall ships when your wife awaits you, and Beth needs braces, and little blue-eyed Lucy needs a ride home from Brownies. So instead, you . . . well, you— . . .

There is no shame—I want this clearly understood—there is no shame in being an accountant. I was a good accountant. A brave accountant. I *would* have been a brave accountant had the opportunity presented itself. It is not my fault that accountancy does not call upon the deepest reserves of the male spirit. I was ready and willing if summoned. I want this understood.

(Shouting) Ready, damn it!

Slight pause

It is not easy to be a man among men among accountants.

C'est la guerre.

But I would have coped. Coped with Madeleine's inane observation that I was perfectly free to quit my job, that the family could live on her investment income. I would have coped with the braces and the Brownies, and the desert of the soul, and the endless calculations, and the alarm-clock at 6:30 every morning and the dinner at 6:30 every evening, and with Bert and his bloody ducks and with the eternity of sameness and with all the tall ships that had sailed without me. Oh, yes. I would have coped. It was Madeleine's affair that drove me to my present extremity.

(Shouting) Ready!

LAROCHE *(Off)* Yes, almost, I think.

Dinsdale struggles again to compose himself, then essays a mirthless, man-of-the-world laugh.

DINSDALE You'd already guessed, I suspect. When a man faces a firing squad in the desert, you can bet that there's a woman at the root of it all. A betrayal, a broken heart. A manly spirit, battered and bowed and driven past all endurance. Oh, yes.

I speak of the affair which Madeleine failed to have with her tennis pro. She broke down one evening, and confessed. How she had been tempted by his limber thighs, and his pencil-thin moustache, and his rippling strokes. And how she had refused, because she felt sorry for me.

Madeleine. Sorry. For me. I laughed, of course. A hollow, mirthless laugh. But then I began to think. I looked around at the wasteland of my life, and saw clearly that it lacked—utterly lacked—the very things which make existence tolerable for the manly spirit. I pondered. Long and hard, I pondered. And as I pondered, I drifted into the back yard and began to build my fishpond.

I cannot explain this to you fully. In moments of extremity, the mind makes leaps. It was perhaps a subsconcious response to an archetypal image. An image of life in a desert. I don't know. I didn't pause to analyze. I acted.

THIERRY *(Off)* Look, sir—here he comes!

LAROCHE *(Off)* Beauchamp—hurry up, man!

DINSDALE A good fishpond, a deep fishpond, beneath the solitary willow tree. I terraced it, and landscaped it, and put fish in it. And when I had finished, I would stand beside it in the evenings, and look down.

Laroche pokes his head into view

LAROCHE Good news. We're almost set.

DINSDALE *(Voice rising)* Hour upon hour I stood. Alone, under the merciless summer sky. Alone in the desolation of brown grass, left parched and withered by the sprinkling regulations. And standing there, I realized . . . that a man can be defined only in the moment of his death. So I resolved to wait. Bravely, unflinchingly, to wait. And I am ready.

LAROCHE *(Off; barking)* Ready!

DINSDALE For that moment.

LAROCHE *(Off)* Aim . . . !

THIERRY *(Off)* No, sir! Don't say it! Not in a crowded theatre!

LAROCHE *(Off)* What?

DINSDALE What?

Fractional pause. Then the firing squad bursts into laughter

LAROCHE *(Off; laughing)* Thierry, you little cauliflower. Now look what you've done.

THIERRY *(Off)* Sorry, Captain. Couldn't resist.

DINSDALE Shoot, damn it!

LAROCHE *(Off)* Come on, lads—pull yourselves together.

DINSDALE Shoot!

Laroche enters, still giggling. Dinsdale glares at him furiously.

LAROCHE I'm awfully sorry, Monsieur Lamord.

DINSDALE Dinsdale!

LAROCHE Just one more moment, and then we'll—

He stops short

Did you say "Dinsdale"?

DINSDALE Dinsdale!

LAROCHE You're not Lamord? The legend of two continents? Lover of a thousand women, and killer of fourteen men in sabre-duels?

DINSDALE I am Dinsdale. The accountant.

Laroche stares at him.

LAROCHE Uh . . . wait here.

Laroche exits. Dinsdale makes one last effort to pull himself together.

DINSDALE The moment. When all will be transcended, all revealed. Standing tall beneath the merciless sky.

LAROCHE *(Off)* That isn't Lamord.

THIERRY *(Off; disappointed)* Oh, for Pete's sake.

DINSDALE Facing the moment that cannot be altered. A good death, a brave death.

LAROCHE *(Off)* Come on, then. Off we go.

THIERRY *(Off)* What rotten luck.

Off-stage, a disgruntled murmur of voices, moving away.

DINSDALE And I am ready. Ready!

He draws himself to his full height. Pause.

Ready?

He looks off-stage—and is startled and dismayed to discover that the squad is gone.

DINSDALE Captain! Where did you—? Captain?

For a long moment, he stares after the departed legionnaires. Then he turns back to the audience

DINSDALE *(Plaintively)* Someone?

Lights down.

JIM WONG-CHU

Jim Wong-Chu was born in Hong Kong and came to Canada in 1953.
He is a founding member of the Asian Canadian Writers Workshop. In
1986, his collection of poems, *Chinatown Ghosts*, was published by
Pulp Press. Currently he is co-editing an anthology of Chinese-Canadian
writing.

*Behold, the Chinese-Canadian Landscape, arriving at your doorstep with
roses, barking for you like a hawker bargaining pennies. Now, come ride
this carriage with a broken parasol . . . and be ready again tomorrow.*

equal opportunity

in early canada
when railways were highways

each stop brought new opportunities

there was a rule

    the chinese could only ride
    the last two cars
    of the trains

that is

until a train derailed
killing all those
in front

(the chinese erected an altar and thanked buddha)

a new rule was made

    the chinese must ride
    the front two cars
    of the trains

that is

until another accident
claimed everyone
in the back

(the chinese erected an altar and thanked buddha)

after much debate
common sense prevailed

the chinese are now allowed
to sit anywhere
on any train

hippo luck

carmen smiles
hand in hand
we glide the flamenco air

the dance floor whirled a common dish
we danced a pair of common fish

stewing in the back room heat
where men grow thinner
than gambler's chips

I am a miner of the mountain of gambler's gold
between the bowls of borrowed rice
I toss the dice of low life

numb to the feel of each burning tile
its clatter a swirling tatter of dancing steps

stay with me . . . carmen . . .
as surely as lord buddha sits on my right
make it all or nothing

tonight

of christmas

it isn't the scene for the most appropriate ghost
although the thought of recent dying thoughts swirls
amid the ritual unravelling christmas morning

the darkest regions of chinatown awaken
homeless thoughts shed their scabs
the martyrs have burned the heroes returned
and the witches and soothsayers rule

lord kwan shares his table with the christmas pagan god
repartee on mercy and love turns
to ice skating on the sun yat sen garden pond
and whether number ninety-nine has chinese blood

the ice surface is but an infinite lake
in celestial canada

we bring together our loved ones
collect the bone of dead birds
simmer slowly with fresh rice and lotus water
into a gruel of turkey jook

to sate the hunger of our laundryman past

I wish to straddle the eastern dragon
and cruise vancouver harbour
count the buoys and leave markers
along the shoreline

visit the camp of the long dead railway workers
and enquire from the buddha priest hui shen
who sailed this early coast and rode its roller coaster mountains
down to fusang to live among the aztec

I want to ask him if it's true
if it has to be the way it is

and I am where I am

and the surface of the sun yat sen pond
is truly an infinite lake

in celestial canada

ANDREW WREGGITT

Andrew Wreggitt is a poet and screenwriter who lives in Calgary, Alberta. He is the author of four books of poetry, the most recent being *Making Movies* (Thistledown Press 1989). Wreggitt has won major awards for both poetry and screenwriting. He makes his living writing drama for television and film.

I graduated from UBC *with a Master's degree in 1982. My thesis became my second book of poetry,* Man at Stellaco River. *Even though I have lived in a lot of different cities since then, the people I met in the Creative Writing Department continue to be my closest friends. Thank you for that. (I still think we should have had* CRWR *team jackets.)*

Burning My Father's Clothes

Burning my father's clothes
in a metal drum behind the house,
my mother afraid to give them away,
afraid to see them walking by on a stranger
The oily black smoke coils
up through the trees
and out across the snow-covered hills

Here is the coat I remember
from the trip we took
to somewhere
I am lying in the back seat,
my mother asleep in the passenger side
Headlights flashing in his face,
he drives all night like this
in the silence of our sleeping
The world was safe and dark and intimate
His solitude with the white lines,
the flat prairie, the eyes of deer
sparkling in the ditches
and the dull glow of some city
still an hour's drive away
Waking up to see him there and I remember
even the smell of this coat, tobacco,

these deep closets of memory

Burning my father's clothes
The only child
standing in the snow and smoke and silence
I pile the shirts and jackets on
and the orange flames strike at them
over and over
The smoke billows up
and everything is given to the sky,
unwilling and stubborn,
ashes settling on the shoulders
of my own coat

The smoke sweeps through the trees
and up into the hills we worked together,
across the fence we built
And there is not a bird in this thicket,
no rabbits, or mice pushing through the new snow
Nothing moves or grows or mourns
for anything lost here
Only the smoke of my father's clothes,
spiralling up,
then falling in the cold air . . .

the face of my mother
anxious
hovering in the window

Tools

Start with a saw,
broad-toothed, cross-cut
Cold groan of snow and mitts
blackened with grease, creased
palms, cigarette,
damp and bitten
on its yellowed end
Start anywhere
The 1930s in northern Saskatchewan,
monkey-wrenching the Model A
with scraped knuckles,
the hay-wagon axle
Work and sleep
turning each day over,
a piston rod, in the slow
cold, oil of winter
Cattle press their blunt noses
to the trough,
roll their eyes and bawl,
complaining as they crowd against spruce poles
Start with a stove that needs to be filled,
snow swirling up from the south,
the broken water pump,
the swollen porch door

Or start here instead
An old man in his garage,
laying out tools, socket set
in descending order
Half-inch, three-eighths
Screwdrivers, flat, Phillips,
biggest to smallest
An old man, fiddling
a stubborn jig-saw,
not coming in for lunch
when he's called
"too busy just now,"
though nothing here needs fixing

A young man stands against
the bright doorway,

a shadow fallen out of the future,
sunlight drifted like snow
into the dark toolshed
"Your tea is getting cold"
The engine lugs, pulling itself
over, one piston
thumping slowly
after the other

This descending order of sockets, wrenches, saws

> Somewhere, cattle bawling in the night,
> hungry, pressing forward
> Or the spew of a storm blowing
> through thin, sagging fences,
> snow swirling on the horizon,
> on the edges of sunlight
> Pliers and hammer,
> cigarette clamped in stained teeth
> or balanced here on the work table,
> ash ready to

fall

Start anywhere

DERK WYNAND

Born in Germany in 1944, Derk Wynand came to Canada in 1952, studied at UBC in the sixties, and is the author of six collections of poetry,
most recently *Heat Waves* (1988), one of fiction, *One Cook, Once
Dreaming* (1980), and *Under the Cover of a Hat / Green-Sealed Message*
(1985), translated from the German of H.C. Artmann. He has just completed a term as Chair of the Department of Creative Writing at the
University of Victoria.

*Credit (or blame?) to the teachers: Doug Bankson, with his patience
when burdened with the essential non-literary baggage; Michael Bullock,
with his finer sense of my mother tongue; J. Michael Yates and the aes-
thetic jackboots with which he kicked lots of us closer to literature.*

from *Snowscapes*

skating down a dutch canal what do you think of snow
on ice over water or brimstone and fire do you hunger

for edam cheese gouda and bittersweet chocolate or the
red cheeks of that young woman behind you much sweeter

can you hear a rhythmic breathing the hiss of her skate
and does it remind you of calvin does that disturb you

would it if you were not skating down a dutch canal can
you concentrate on red lips and blondness or merely on

snow-covered windmills on whitewashed houses now do you
imagine her inside and you the would-be lover her pious

father staying up late reading hebrew never a man to
put up with bundling do you picture him at work cutting

diamonds for african merchants does it trouble you to
think about jewels cut for swiss watches would it be

easier to recall his love for all germans his daughter
skating behind you singing of claus and of marsman their

worship of cheese as you skate in a straight line to
rotterdam sister city of zurich where you loved her

Stall

The discovery of mangoes
and the eating of mangoes.

The long decision, the perfect
choice, at a Chinese Lo Cost store,
of two or three mangoes.

The exact shade of a hand,
probing, probing a rind
and pulp of mangoes.

The absolute solitude
of making such choices.

The encounter, at the Lo Cost store,
with a woman who has almost
Eurasian features.

The sudden bluish-black
tinge of your daydreams.

How you ripen then and fall
for her at the Lo Cost store,
and how she lingers. How you
linger at the mango stall.

Queluz Palace

In the great hall of mirrors,
among the cut crystal and the gold
and the angels painted on the ceiling,
you flung out your arms all at once
and began to spin in circles,
in wider and wider circles
across a marble floor where Dom Pedro
had danced with Doña Maria, his future queen,
and I could hardly believe my eyes,
though you danced in every mirror
and on every facet of glass and on each
of the marble tiles on the floor
and in the gold, and the best angel
slowly peeled away from the ceiling
to fly, after long years of waiting
just for that moment (it was before noon
on August 3, 1986) and no matter
how I pinched myself or rubbed my eye,
he did not stop swinging you round
in wider and wider circles,
as I stood by, stupefied, stupid,
only watching helpless, and your feet
slowly rose from the polished marble
and you floated, in a straight line now,
out of the hall with the angel,
toward one of the smaller chambers,
which not even the king's own servants
had ever been allowed to enter,
toward a room without glass or gold
where, mercifully, I could not watch you.